... AND
MARRIES
ANOTHER

...AND MARRIES ANOTHER

Divorce and Remarriage in the Teaching of the New Testament

CRAIG S. KEENER

Copyright © 1991 by Hendrickson Publishers, Inc.
P. O. Box 3473
Peabody, Massachusetts, 01961–3473
All rights reserved
Printed in the United States of America
ISBN 0–943575–46–X
Fourth Printing — June 1996

Library of Congress Cataloging-in-Publication Data

Keener, Craig
    And marries another: divorce and remarriage in the teaching
of the New Testament / Craig Keener.
    Includes bibliographical references and index.
    ISBN 0–943575–46–X (pbk.)
    1. Divorce—Biblical teaching. 2. Divorce—Religious
aspects—Christianity. 3. Remarriage—Biblical teaching.
4. Remarriage—Religious aspects—Christianity. 5. Bible.
N.T.—Criticism, interpretation, etc. I. Title
BS2545.D58K44   1991
241'.63—dc20   91-47185
                                                        CIP

Table of Contents

Preface

This book reflects several concerns. One is a concern standing behind any book that I write: a concern that people grow in their understanding of the scriptures and that they better interpret and apply them to their world today. This concern draws on many years of study of the Bible and its world, and it is reflected in the documentation in the endnotes for those who wish to examine them.

The principal aim of this particular book, however, is not scholarly but pastoral. Many loving and compassionate people have been wounded by spouses they trusted, only to be wounded again by fellow-Christians who did not know what to do with them. Many who have sinned against their spouses by divorcing them without scriptural grounds have never been called to repentance by the body of Christ. Divorce is a tragedy, and often the church's confused response to it has only compounded the tragedy.

In the community where I minister, there is a shortage of single young men; some men, therefore, feel they can afford to be casual about their relationships with women. Wives often work hard to keep a stable home, while the husbands run around on them or get high on drugs; men's girlfriends often may get nothing more out of them than a baby. The Christian community fortunately is not as promiscuous as the culture around it; but because new believers who have already experienced shattered relationships are coming to Christ daily, broken relationships are an issue we must confront all the time.

In other communities, it is often the wife who leaves her husband, sometimes under the pressures of ministry or perhaps because of the husband's commitment to live out the gospel. Sometimes one of them was not careful about choosing a marriage partner, or they married before either one was converted; sometimes one has chosen to turn his or her back on the Christian lifestyle, despite the other party's faithfulness to God and the marriage. Whatever the reason, there are many broken lives which cannot be simply ignored.

In this book, then, I will blend pastoral concern with research into the culture of the New Testament period in an effort to address the issues of divorce and remarriage in the church today.

WHY THE EMPHASIS ON CULTURE?

Evangelicals have traditionally given attention to the "grammatical-historical" method, or, in more recent times, to the "historical-critical" method. We have always recognized that understanding the cultural background is vital for comprehending the Bible more fully. Yet, despite the abundance of translations and study helps, most Christians know very little about the first-century world. All too little is done in the average church and Christian Education department to help Christians understand what the text meant to its first readers and how to move from what the text "meant" in that culture to what it "means" for our lives today. This lack is fostered by the limited attention these issues receive in many schools where many ministers receive training.

This book will not summarize the cultural context of the New Testament—that awaits another book. This book focuses only on the issues of divorce and remarriage in the New Testament, and it seeks to place the relevant New Testament passages in their historical context.

Why is it necessary to place biblical texts in their proper cultural context to understand them? Because the context in which we read something affects the way we understand it. The word "Lord" does not mean the same thing in a church service as it does in a Hare Krishna chant. A protest against child labor meant something different in the England of the Industrial Revolution from what it does in the lamentations of an elementary school student explaining why he should not do his homework.

In the same way, many of Jesus' teachings addressed particular issues and were spoken in culturally relevant ways. Understanding those issues and those ways of speaking can enrich our grasp of what Jesus really meant and how his teachings must impact our lives today.

All of us recognize that some texts are specific to the situation they originally addressed. As Gordon Fee has pointed out, none of us takes Paul's admonition to Timothy to bring his cloak from Troas (2 Tim. 4:13) personally. Can you imagine all of us descending on excavations at Troas, furiously trying to find a first-century cloak, then trying to identify it as Paul's, and finally, worst of all, whichever one of us was successful, taking it to Paul? This is indeed a difficult commandment for us to fulfill today.

Yet whole books of the Bible claim to address specific situations. Didn't Paul say, under the inspiration of the Spirit, that he was writing the epistle to the Romans to the saints in Rome (Rom. 1:7)? Doesn't that mean that he was addressing situations in Rome? Didn't he use the Greek language, with Greek figures of speech and illustrations? In the same way, doesn't 1 Corinthians answer questions the Corinthians had (7:1), often point by point? In the same way, Matthew and Paul make different points on the subject of this book because they are addressing different readers in different situations.

Ultimately, *everything* in the Bible has a cultural context. No matter how much it may bother some of us, God did not choose to give us a book of statements that automatically apply in every language and culture without translation and explanation; he made things more complex—and more interesting—than that. He gave us a book full of historical stories and full of letters and prophecies that God addressed to specific peoples acting in specific ways—the kind of book that most cultures in the world can actually relate to. By reading these stories and letters and prophecies as case studies of how God spoke to people acting in certain ways, we can see what he also says to us today.

We do not know everything about how people thought or talked in the first century. But even if we do not know all the background, it is important to read the biblical texts as God speaking first of all to the needs of the original readers. Reading the Bible the way it was written—God addressing specific situations through his inspired servants—is much healthier than just citing verses to back up our arguments without considering the intended point of those texts. I could "prove" my case in this book the way some advocates of the other side have "proven" theirs, by simply quoting verses. But I have preferred to write a book that deals with the biblical passages in question by giving attention to the cultural-historical context in which the inspired authors wrote, so we can better understand what they actually meant. In this I believe I am following the best tradition in evangelical scholarship.

HOW THIS BOOK IS WRITTEN

There are different ways to write a book. Scholarly books meant to argue at a scholarly level are written quite differently from popular books designed to make a point on a popular level. And there is a great variety of degrees between these two extremes. It is hoped that this book will fill one of the niches between biblical scholars and those who are faithful to the Bible but who have little formal theological training. The scholarly literature itself is far less informative (and inspired!) than the Bible, but where scholars provide cultural or historical insights that help us better grasp how the first readers would have heard the New Testament texts, we are indebted to them, and I have drawn upon their insights.

On the one hand, this book has thus kept most of the technical notes and explicit references to books or articles in the endnotes. Greek—the language of the New Testament—has been avoided wherever possible. Where I have written of Jewish, Greek, and Roman sources, I have not assumed that the reader is already familiar with the technical language employed by historians of the ancient world. I have sometimes sacrificed precision of language[1] in favor of clarity of expression for the intended readers. I have also avoided most discussions of authorship, date, and other introductory questions that would sidetrack the basic issues with which this book is dealing.

On the other hand, by explaining the cultural contexts behind the New Testament documents and the issues the writers seem to have been addressing, I have sought to provide information to which most readers would not otherwise have access. The endnotes are necessary to substantiate the case and to provide sources for those who wish to investigate the data further, but the reader is not obligated to consult the endnotes to follow the argument of the book.

The contents of this book are the results of my own research; all references to ancient texts are taken from my study of those texts themselves (in the original language or in translation), unless otherwise stated. Except for the 1967 work by Pat Harrell, some of whose research paralleled my own, I purposely avoided surveying the secondary literature on the subject until after this book was nearly complete.[2] As is usually the case when one pursues one's own research first, I have found that some of my work covers familiar ground already covered by others, whereas some of my proposals are essentially new.

A number of conservative evangelicals have written books advocating a position similar to my own—divorce is to be avoided, but there are certain circumstances under which divorce and remarriage are acceptable[3]—so much so that an opponent of this position characterizes it as the "evangelical consensus."[4] Indeed, most Christians I know who have no Bible training outside their local churches, who have never heard any views officially articulated from the pulpit, read the New Testament as allowing remarriage in some circumstances. They are devout Christians not simply responding to the decadence of the culture; they can cite specific biblical texts which they are sure allow remarriage.[5]

This book differs from most of its popular predecessors in that it includes a much heavier emphasis on cultural background. It differs from some of its scholarly predecessors in its relative brevity, its explicitly evangelical audience, and its preference for cultural-historical context to grammatical details or involved interaction with secondary sources. It also differs by means of the new and broader market which Hendrickson Publishers has graciously provided.

This book could have been approached from one of two angles, depending on which major segment of the church was being addressed. In some large parts of the church today, the innocent party in a divorce is forbidden remarriage. I will refrain from naming denominations, but the readers most familiar with the issue can no doubt think of at least several on their own. I know all too many Christians who have been wounded by several of these denominations and by their unrealistic and unbiblical stand on divorce and remarriage. I know of one church in which almost half the members were divorced, either due to lifestyles before their conversion or because their spouses had left them. But none of these members were eligible for leadership roles in that congregation if they had remarried, no matter how godly their present lives were.

In other large parts of the church, divorce is viewed as a tragic but often inevitable consequence of living in modern society. Discipline and correction are not given to the guilty party. Scripture warns against the unjust judge who pardons the guilty as much as it warns against the judge who condemns the innocent; either sin is wrong, and neither should be tolerated as the attitude of our churches. Unscriptural divorces are grounds for church discipline, but the innocent parties in divorces need to be compassionately encouraged, not penalized for a sin that was not theirs to commit.

This book particularly addresses those who would judge or penalize the innocent party. Obviously many divorces (such as where both parties agree to a divorce on grounds of incompatibility) have no "innocent" party; but it is equally plain that many divorces do have an innocent party, according to Scripture. That I write this book primarily to address the injustice of condemning innocent spouses should not be taken to mean that I think Scripture treats divorce lightly. Scripture is quite straightforward in prohibiting divorce under all normal circumstances, and I take this as a given. The issue under dispute is what should be done with the innocent party, or with the other party after genuine repentance and restitution have taken place.

The bulk of this book will concentrate on analyzing the major passages in question, Matthew 5:32 and its context; Matthew 19:9; 1 Corinthians 7; and 1 Timothy 3:2. Most of our personal observations for how to apply this data will be reserved for chapter conclusions and especially for the conclusion of the book. This book is offered with a prayer that its message will bring healing to many who have been wounded in the body of Christ our Lord.

I must express appreciation to Patrick Alexander, my editor, for his helpful suggestions and corrections; the errors that remain are, of course, my own responsibility. I want to dedicate this book to Ben Aker, my former professor, who first taught me that biblical scholarship could be a valid tool for ardent lovers of the Word.

1 The Introductory Question: The Relevance of this Book

Why still another book on divorce and remarriage for the Christian market? Because the issue is a pressing one that much of the church of Jesus Christ has failed to address responsibly. On the one hand, it has become all too easy to cite several proof-texts and so pass judgment on other people's lives or ministry. On the other hand, it is convenient to ignore certain texts and to pass over the horribly tragic character of divorce, thus blending into the false values of modern North American society.

When I began my Bible college training, I met brothers and sisters who had been divorced before their conversion but had felt called to ministry after their conversion. Although most of the students I knew seemed to sympathize with them, these prospective ministers were told by certain professors that they may as well give up on their calling altogether, because this very conservative denomination would not license them. They were caught in a fix: most districts did not want single ministers, but the denomination forbade divorced ministers to remarry under any circumstances.

It did not seem to me that the Scriptures were being handled in their entirety. What about Christ's forgiveness for sins of the past? How did we treat former drug addicts, atheists (such as I had once been), or even persecutors, yea, murderers of our own brothers and sisters in Christ, like the apostle Paul? How did we deal with those who had slept around with anyone and everyone, but since they had never made a formal commitment, were not now being excluded from marriage and ministry? The response from the most biblically centered teachers was agreement with my concern; the response from those who liked to settle complex matters by quoting Scripture out of context was a few proof-texts, proof-texts by which they dismissed the life and ministry of others equally as called by God as themselves. Never mind that proof-texts can be marshalled for other positions contrary to their own; never mind that various groups, on the basis of baptismal formulas or other details, would use proof-texts to argue that these teachers themselves were not saved! Proof-texts they offered, and proof-texts were enough for them.

One brother from my home church had begun to feel called to ministry and came to Bible college. He was an ardent witness for Christ, a strong student of Scripture, faithful to what he believed the Scriptures taught. He had the courage to study them for what they said, rather than what other people told him they said, and I respected him for that. But before his conversion his wife had been having affairs and had finally divorced him. He was consequently told that he could not be a minister. Wisely, he switched denominations, as many before him had done.

Some divorced believers, however, devastated by rejection from churches where they otherwise felt most at home, have been lost to ministry altogether. My guess would be that some, unable to feel welcome in many of our churches, have even left church altogether. We can glibly say, "Anyone who cannot stand under trials is not a worthy Christian anyway." But Jesus minced no words when he threatened eternal punishment for those who cause his little ones to stumble, who turn people away from the Kingdom instead of going after them to serve them and nurture them.

As I studied the Bible in detail, I eventually came to a conclusion that I had long resisted, namely, that we must read the Bible in light of its own cultural background. The more I yearned for God's truth and threw myself passionately into finding it, the more appalled I became at the church's ignorance of Scripture and the wanton use of proof-texts to judge people without sensitivity to either the text or the pastoral issues involved in these people's lives. The more I faced the text for what it said, the more I became convinced that it was time for us to recognize how far we have really strayed from what it teaches. On the basis of a handful of texts, some of our churches will, on the one hand, exclude divorced people from ministry, regardless of the grounds; while on the other hand, though the New Testament repeatedly condemns materialism, our congregations, and often our clergy, are shot through with it. The Scripture mandates that elders must be "able to teach," and yet I have heard many sophomore Bible study leaders in InterVarsity, teenage students on secular university campuses, who can teach the Bible much better than many trained pastors, simply because they have the courage to exercise enough faith in the text to expound and apply it rather than giving a religious speech decorated with Bible memory verses.

I saw too much hurt when I pastored. There were so many broken lives to deal with, and most of the brokenness was confidential: no one else in the congregation knew that half the members were going through serious crises at any given time. The Bible is a very relevant book if we allow it to speak to us as a story of how God related to people in the past. In this way the Bible thus relates to our needs today as well. But it is nothing more than a reflection of our own theology if we treat it as a series of proof-texts, and most of the proof-texting theology I have seen is irrelevant to the wounded lives we as ministers must confront daily. Examples of the urgent need for ministering to those hurting from divorce are legion.

One brother in the congregation was separated from his wife, because she had run off with another *woman*. Although he seemed to me to be one of the most passionate-for-God people I knew, he was blaming himself for the situation. It did not sound to me like he had been responsible for what had happened to him, but only after seeing other, similar cases did I understand the kind of agonizing introspection such a tragedy creates, an introspection increased by the false guilt imputed by the false standards of many of our churches. After he moved away he became a youth minister in an urban church, and the next summer, while I was out street-witnessing in his city, I ran into him. He was out street-witnessing, too, and he shared with me the enormous growth that God had brought into his life. Nevertheless, there was a conflict with denominational officials, and when his wife finally filed for divorce, he had to switch denominations. He has remained faithful to God, and God has opened new doors of ministry for him.

I knew a sister who was married in her late teens. Her new husband ran off the next day and she never saw him again; she was so shaken that her father had to file the divorce papers for her. But because of that incident, when, years later, she married a minister, he was unable to get credentials in a particular denomination. Both of them are now ministering together in another denomination in a different part of the country.

One of the brothers I most respected in Bible college, who served others with all his heart, seemed to me to have a solid marriage. I learned only later that his wife had been committing adultery during much of their marriage and had refused to sleep with him during that time. She had attended the Bible college, too, and while no one would have thought to blame the Bible college or denomination for not teaching her better, the denomination's policies treated the husband as if he had failed in his marriage. I would not advocate blaming either the Bible college or the denomination for her behavior, but I do not see why her husband should be faulted for it any more than her denomination should be. The brother had tried everything to get her back, but finally he filed for divorce and quietly left town in shame, believing that his denomination condemned him. Those who knew him felt hurt for him, and those who knew the situation communicated their sympathy; but the unrelenting standards of the denomination punished him rather than disciplining his wife, who was no longer within range of its discipline. He has since happily remarried and is serving God with all his heart. He is also barred from ministry in the denomination in which he chose to remain.

I was told of a woman whose husband ran off with another woman in their congregation and then divorced his wife. The adulterous couple—I call them adulterous because their new marriage was certainly not valid in God's sight—simply began attending another church of the same conservative denomination in the same city, while the deserted wife languished unconsoled, bearing the stigma of a divorce, wondering whether judgmental eyes preyed upon her. She probably questioned what she might have done to deserve this; finally she left town.

It seems that many of our congregations see divorce as a matter of uncleanness rather than a matter of sin: we neither call the guilty to account for sin nor defend the oppressed, but we lump them together into a category called "unclean" that we do not wish to touch, lest it contaminate us. In so doing, we show compassion on neither party. And by judging all divorced people as if they had chosen their situation, we do not reflect the justice of the God who defends the oppressed, the God who stands up for the widows bereaved by their spouses' death—and those of the divorced who have been bereaved by their spouses' betrayal.

Rigid interpretations of verses ripped out of context have long been used to formulate "Christian" doctrines; and rigid "Christian" doctrines have long been used to oppress others. One example is how white North Americans enslaved Africans, and, when they finally got around to letting the enslaved hear about Christianity, they told them to submit to their masters because they were under the curse of Ham and could not be saved if they failed to obey. Texts where Paul, who had to deal with the culture he was in before he could bring changes to it, calls slaves to submit to their masters, were used to say that Paul thought slavery itself was good. Texts which said that masters and slaves were equal before God (e.g., Eph. 6:9) were naturally less well attended to by the slave-owners.[1] And of course, once slavery was abolished, texts about restitution for economic injustices were ignored.[2]

It is, of course, true that the abolitionists who opposed slavery were in the main evangelical Christians; my point is that others who claimed to be Christians (and some of them probably were Christians) were using Scripture to justify their oppressive position. It is also true that the oppression of innocent divorced people in some of our churches is nothing like the oppression the slaves experienced. But both instances reflect how glibly other people's situations can be judged by proof-texts and how far we as the church often are from loving our neighbor as ourselves.

In the same way, some women have been told that Christian submission means absolute obedience, sometimes including submitting to beatings and other abuse, or they are told that the Bible teaches their social and/or intellectual inferiority. The women's movement in the 1800s was fueled especially by the same holiness and revivalist elements that backed the abolitionist movement. Women leaders of that time saw a parallel between their own oppression and that of the slaves.[3] It is easy for us to forget today that women could not vote in the U.S. or Canada until 1920, and the first nation to allow them to vote was New Zealand in 1893.[4] Unfortunately, many who have argued for the complete subjugation of women have argued their case from Paul's letters without regard for their historical context or, for that matter, without regard for Paul's writings as a whole.

Is it any wonder that the strong Christian tradition of the black church in America has been challenged by some black activists who consider Christianity racist?[5] And should we be surprised that the evangelical roots of women's liberation in nineteenth-century America have now given way to many feminists who consider Christianity repressive? A significant part of the church has been making the same response to divorce—a few glib proof-texts without regard to the ancient or modern situations and apparently with little concern for what they are doing to the credibility of the gospel. No matter how loudly some of us may insist that Scripture does not say what these people interpret it to mean, it is others' rigid interpretation that will be cited by opponents of Christianity who wish to show it as a tool of oppressive traditionalism.

I have seen the reaction to this abuse of Scripture in the universities, and I have seen the lives of students shattered by this false caricature of Christianity. Some of these students will never hear the gospel again; others we can still reach, one by one. But seeing their alienation from what Christianity really is, due to its misrepresentation by Christians, breaks my heart. To make a long-range difference, we must address the way the church is living and treating its members, to give the world less grounds for rightful criticism. In other words, we must learn to be genuinely "above reproach" for our culture—and before God.

I had plans to write many books with the research I was collecting on the ancient world, and one of them was going to be a book on divorce and remarriage in the New Testament. I wanted to make my contribution to the defense of those I had seen doubly wounded, wounded first by the very persons in the world they had most trusted, and second by impersonal ecclesiastical policies that kicked them when they were down. Although many in the church have always stood for truth, many have not done so, and this is all the more tragic because the church of all groups of people should have always been the first to condemn oppression. Nevertheless, this book was, admittedly, not highest on my list, but one I hoped to write later in my career. (Who wants to start off his or her career with a controversial book?)

What moved me to make it one of my first books was a deep tragedy that happened to a minister to whom I was very close, whom I will call Stephen. I will tell Stephen's story in slightly more detail than the others as my closing sample of why this book needed to be written.

No one had suspected that Stephen and his wife Jennifer[6] would ever divorce, least of all Stephen himself. He was happily married, he loved his wife, and it was his firm conviction and that of others who knew them well that she loved him. Because she came from a broken home, she still had some struggles with her past; but God has healed many who have come from such backgrounds, and Jennifer seemed to all of us to be strong in her faith. Before they were married, most of their time was spent talking, praying, studying the Bible, and witnessing together; they did everything honorably, and Stephen had every reason to believe, from her lifestyle as well as through prayer, that this was the woman for him.

But after several years of marriage, some plans they had felt to be in God's will fell through. There were a number of different factors in what followed, but from that point observers in their local church could notice that his wife's attendance slowly began to decline, and she eventually began to gravitate toward a lifestyle similar to the one she had lived before her conversion. Stephen felt helpless, angry, confused, and hurt; he watched and pleaded with dismay, trying to get help but unable to find any on which both of them could agree.

Stephen could not believe what was happening, because his wife had been a godly woman ever since he had known her. But shortly after this, he learned that she and the husband of one of her closest friends had begun an affair. His wife and the man she had joined got an apartment together; she announced that she was leaving Stephen and would file for divorce. Even today he would still protest that she did it in the kindest manner possible, given the circumstances, and he would not even privately mention any of this as an indictment of her; her behavior was, in his eyes, simply taking to its logical conclusion the life of compromise in which we find most North American Christians involved every day.

Stephen never harbored any bitterness against her, only sorrow for what he perceived as her turning away from Christ's call and grief over the loss of their marriage. He was bitter against the man who had taken his wife's affections, but in time the love of Christ in his heart flushed that hatred out and taught Stephen to love him, so that he says he could embrace him as a friend today if the opportunity to do so were to arise. It was harder, however, to deal with the Christians who felt it their place to condemn him for his now ambiguous marital status. He fought the divorce for roughly two years, until, at the end, he was weary enough with waiting that he too was more than ready to be free.

During those two years of waiting it was only God that held his heart together. For most of the first six months he dug up everything he could ever have done wrong and wondered why God had brought this judgment against him, even though God was supplying his every need and blessing him in leading people to Christ through his own pain. He went over every argument he could remember having had with his wife and repented in great detail; but he had reaffirmed his love for her daily and genuinely felt that he had been a good husband, perhaps more than most husbands he knew whose wives had been faithful.

It was the most horrible time he had ever lived through, much more horrible than the times he had been beaten or had his life threatened for sharing Christ on the streets. The physical pain of such beatings lasted only momentarily, and the few scars they left were scars in which he could boast of God's grace; but the wounds initiated by the rending of one flesh seemed like they would never go away, until the divorce went through. In the end, God reminded him of the book of Hosea, and reminded him that God himself experienced deep rejection from his own people. That rejection did not bring into question God's love for his people, and in the same way, Stephen's divorce was not an indictment of his love for his wife.

But what eventually stung more than the separation itself was the attitude of certain parts of the body of Christ. One couple wrote from far away saying that they were breaking fellowship with him until he reconciled with his wife. They concluded their letter by claiming that this pain he was experiencing was God judging him for sin in his life. Although he recognized the letter as strangely reminiscent of the encouragement of Job's comforters, it shattered his soul. His wife had already told him repeatedly that she was not interested in reconciliation, and she had responded to any attempts to pursue it by filing for divorce; but still he was to be held responsible for reconciliation! It further came to his attention that, since he had moved (partly at her urging, since the other man lived in the same city as she did), false rumors had begun circulating about the reason for the separation. He wondered why brothers and sisters would circulate rumors about him without even bothering to come to him with their accusations or to ask him if they were true.

Some believers refused to "take sides," i.e., to offer any encouragement; they could only say, "Well, it always take two to break up a marriage." He wondered where in the Bible it said that. Under Old Testament law, after the adulterous partner was stoned to death, what words were spoken against the surviving partner? Did Hosea chase Gomer away? (One Christian couple did indeed suggest to him that Hosea and God lost their spouses precisely because they came across as unapproachably holy, which drove poor Gomer and Israel away. But such a position does not even require a response.)

Stephen was wrongly treated by parts of the body of Christ. Since when does the Bible allow us to judge one another without confirming matters by two or three witnesses and without confronting the person and hearing her or his side? And since when does the Bible mandate searching for sins the person "might" have committed that led to the divorce? Some spouses leave faithful partners for no reason having to do with the faithful partner. In other cases, I have seen husbands and wives faithfully remaining with partners that do horrible things, yet the misbehaving partners would never be indicted by the church because their spouses are faithful. What disturbs me even more is that some of these faithful spouses, by remaining with misbehaving partners, may be exposing themselves to AIDS and other sexually transmitted diseases, and the faithful ones will in many churches come under the shame those same churches place on everyone infected with AIDS. Those churches are no longer acting like the church.

Some people who hold strongly to their preconceived positions of what Scripture says will at this point accuse me of an unethical emotional appeal. My response is that yes, I am purposely appealing to the feelings of my readers; but no, it is not unethical. Our Lord Jesus saw the multitudes and was moved with compassion. He not only had compassion on the oppressed who suffered as objects of others' exploitation; he even prayed for the forgiveness of those oppressors who nailed him to the Cross and had compassion on those who grievously wronged him. That those who have experienced a tragedy nearly as traumatic as the death of a spouse should bear a continued shame from parts of the church is unconscionable. And for those who have never experienced the rejection of the church (a church that sometimes would not accept your repentance as sufficient even if you felt you needed to repent for what happened to you), Stephen says that it feels like being hit with a brick by the person you would have most hoped would offer strength.

To stop with this depiction of some people's insensitivity, however, would give a very one-sided portrayal of what Stephen experienced; because it was only the many Christians who did indeed act like Christians that brought him healing and strength to face each new day of pain. It was the moral support of brothers and sisters in a local interdenominational church, who found out about his situation mainly by second-hand means, that brought him through the first months. It was brothers and sisters in some black churches that carried his spirit after he moved to another part of the country. Most of these black Christians were poor, and in their community Christians regularly faced the sort of struggles he was facing. To this day he normally feels more comfortable in a predominantly black church than in a white one, although Stephen is white.

Even many officials in the conservative denomination he was in tried to help him, although ultimately its written policies could not be sidestepped. By this time another way to fulfill his call had already been provided by a fellow-minister who invited him to join his denomination. But even with regard to the first denomination, he claims that despite its official stand, most of the people in it who knew him personally were compassionate and supportive, and he maintains his sincere appreciation of that movement. (As he puts it, "Nobody's perfect.")

He worked through the grief over the next two years and when the divorce finally went through he felt free. The divorce is now a matter of the past, something that rarely crosses his mind, except when he faces discrimination and stigma from certain sectors of the Christian community on its account. He is finally just "single," and he will have not the slightest reticence about marrying again when he finds the right person who shares his call and convictions. Despite the pain inflicted by some parts of the body of Christ, he attests that his overwhelming experience was one of healing from the church; only the love of his brothers and sisters brought him through the pain he had experienced.

But it appears to me that not everyone who has been divorced against her or his will has had such positive support from the body as Stephen did. Stephen was blessed by God to have had so many friends; he was also blessed in that he had a firm grasp of the Scriptures and of personal evangelism and so could become useful again in serving others with or without an official position of ministry.[7]

I confess sadly that I know brothers and sisters who, unlike Stephen, have experienced more rejection from the body of Christ[8] than encouragement. In some cases, they were not the best mates they could have been; but this was something to be worked out between them and their spouses, not something for which Scripture allows their spouses to divorce them. In other cases, they were divorced not only in spite of being good Christian spouses but *because* of it: they had refused to participate in what they considered a sinful lifestyle, and they had not been "worldly" or "exciting" enough to tickle their spouses' fancy.

Stephen would like the freedom to move in all evangelical circles as a brother in Christ, ministering according to the gifts his Lord has given him. He knows many charismatic and evangelical circles where he will face no prejudice because of his experience, and he has already found many wounded people, both believers and nonbelievers, who open up to him because he too was wounded. But I could not use Stephen's real name, because the sad fact is that there are also segments of the body of Christ where his brothers and sisters in Christ would not treat him as a brother once they heard of his experience.

Yet an undeserved stigma is in truth not a stigma at all. And those who have been broken and shattered by whatever pains this world has brought against them can feel all the more deeply the cries of a world God so deeply loves, a world drowning in pain, a world alienated and without hope except for the Cross of our Lord. If all of us who follow Jesus can become sharers in his pain—feel the pain of his body torn by racism, divided by unshared wealth and unalleviated poverty, rent by secondary doctrines which may be worth believing but not worth breaking fellowship over—if we can feel his pain, the pain of a love so great that it drove him to the Cross to reconcile an alienated world to himself—then we will have felt the pain of the ultimate rejection. Because as Hosea so eloquently witnessed, the pain of a broken marriage is but a shadow of God's pain, the testimony that no one has wounded any of us as much as all of us have wounded God, that he pleads day and night for our hearts, our lives—and so many of his people give him so little, absorbed by all their other loves. If *whatever* pain we experience helps us feel the pain of others, if his comfort to us enables us to comfort others, then it will have been enough.

This is the pain that Stephen and many like him have experienced, and we as the body of Christ would do well to learn from their pain, rather than to cast them aside.

2 | Anger and Lust—A Model for Reading Divorce Law in the Sermon on the Mount

As Christians, we acknowledge that Jesus is our Lord and that he has the right to tell us what to do. That means that his teachings are binding for our lives, and this includes his teaching on divorce. But before we can obey his teachings, we must understand them. In this chapter, we will begin to investigate the nature of Jesus' teaching and what that means for his followers today. By comparing how we read several other sayings of Jesus, we may gain insight into how to read Jesus' saying about divorce.

Jesus' call is radical and demands nothing short of total commitment. But *knowing* this is not enough; we must read his teachings like we believe that they have authority over us. Our real goal in studying his teachings must be to find out what Jesus meant by what he said, rather than just what we would like to think he meant. Reaching this goal involves more than simply translating his sayings from Greek to English; it also involves understanding the figures of speech, the literary and cultural allusions, and the issues which Jesus was originally addressing. If we really respect our Lord's authority, we must be willing to expend the effort to find out what he was really saying to his original hearers, rather than just what it sounds to us like he was saying, in a culture far removed from Jesus' first hearers.

One matter we will pursue in some detail is how the words of Jesus as recorded in the Gospels would have been understood by ancient readers, especially by ancient Jewish readers. To do this, we will need to look at similar sayings by other ancient Jewish teachers and compare how they were understood by their contemporaries. This method will be employed in the three chapters of this book dealing with Jesus' teaching.

Before we explore Jesus' saying on divorce in Matthew 5:31–32 (in the next chapter), it is helpful to examine what Jesus says in the immediately preceding paragraphs (Matt. 5:21–30). This will set the divorce saying in its context the way Matthew wanted us to understand it. Whatever principles help us understand Jesus' other sayings in this chapter should also be able to guide us in understanding 5:31–32 in the following chapter.

JESUS' OTHER SAYINGS IN MATTHEW 5

Matthew summarizes Jesus' teaching as a summons to repentance in light of the coming kingdom of God (4:17). He then gives us an example of radical discipleship—disciples forsaking their livelihoods and families to follow Jesus (4:18–22). Finally, he brings us to samples of Jesus' teaching about the lifestyle of the kingdom in more expanded form.

Some people in Jesus' day wanted to bring in the kingdom by force, but Jesus warns that the kingdom belongs to the meek, the merciful, the peacemakers, the oppressed who continue to love (5:3–12). This is the truly repentant, unselfish lifestyle he demands of his followers, and professed followers of Jesus who do not live this way are about as useful to him as tasteless salt or invisible light (5:13–16).

The paragraph which follows tells us how to read the rest of Matthew 5: Jesus is going to interpret, not refute, the law of God (5:17–20). Although Matthew makes it clear that Jesus clashed with many religious teachers of his day on a number of points, he does not want his readers to miss the point that follows: Jesus was not opposed to the Bible itself. He had come not to weaken God's authority expressed in the law, but to make God's claims all the more relevant to his hearers' lives. The particular way Jesus' words are phrased in this section illustrates how skillfully Jesus used the teaching techniques and figures of speech of his day.[1]

In the section which follows, Jesus six times quotes the Old Testament and then interprets its meaning. One of his sayings in this section involves divorce; others involve such topics as anger and lust. It becomes clear in these sayings that Jesus is demanding something much more serious than ordinary human religiosity; he demands a pure heart. It also becomes clear in these sayings that he employs graphic images and figures of speech to get his point across, rather than qualifying every possible way his words could be taken. Examining two examples of Jesus' teaching in this chapter will help provide a model for how we can analyze his teaching on divorce which follows them, because, for some reason, many readers today apply Jesus' saying on divorce more strictly than they apply his sayings on anger and lust in the same context.

EXAMPLE 1: ANGER AS MURDER

The first of Jesus' six "antitheses," or more properly, expositions of Scripture, is this:

> You've heard that it was said to the ancients,[2] "Thou shalt not murder"; whoever murders, will be liable to judgment.[3] But I tell you that whoever is angry with his fellow[4] will be liable to the judgment; and whoever says to his fellow, "Empty-head!"[5] will be liable to the supreme court;[6] and whoever says to him, "You fool!"[7] will be liable to the fiery Gehenna.[8]

In this case, no one would suggest that Jesus is opposing the Old Testament law against murder; we recognize that he is instead agreeing with it and applying it to the heart. Even the sort of anger or hostility that *generates* murder is really illegal under *God's* legislation.

No offense is minor under this legislation, whether anger or an insulting word. Some writers have suggested a progressive heightening of the "minor" sins in this verse, from anger to a lesser insult ("Empty-head!") to a greater insult ("Fool!"). But "Fool" is *not* a stronger insult than "Empty-head"; the two insults are equivalent in force.[9] The equality of the sins mentioned here has posed a problem for most interpreters, who see the punishments as listed in increasing order,[10] from judgment in a court, to judgment before the supreme court, to hell.[11] But even if "Fool" were much more severe than "Empty-head," would it merit punishment in hell instead of judgment by the Sanhedrin, the Jewish supreme court, the punishment listed for calling someone an "Empty-head"? And is there any reader who could suppose that the supreme court would have tried people for the offense of calling someone a name,[12] or that a lower court would have even *known* when someone felt angry?

Jesus cannot mean that the punishment here is effected by anyone but by God. The one who is angry may not even be known to be angry by a human court; but the "judgment" probably refers to God's judgment,[13] before his tribunal, rather than that of any earthly court. (God's judgment is the most common New Testament meaning of the term "judgment.")

In the same way, the "supreme court" here does not mean the earthly Sanhedrin; the phrase was often used by later rabbis to mean God's *heavenly* court (as they saw it, an academy of either angels or deceased scholars of the law).[14] Nor was this image of a divine assembly limited to the rabbis; it has its roots in the court of Yahweh in the Old Testament,[15] appears in the Dead Sea Scrolls,[16] and is probably implied in Matthew 18:18.[17]

That all three terms of punishment refer to God's judgment cannot be doubted, since in the following parable Matthew shows that reconciliation with one's fellow-disciple is an urgent matter in light of the imminent approach of God's justice.[18] In this parable, God's justice is represented by an earthly tribunal, or court, fitting the image that Jesus has already presented in v. 22.[19] In other words, Jesus takes anger and angry words quite seriously.

Jesus' rule against insults is much stricter than the usual later rabbinic teaching on the subject, as may be demonstrated by an example:

> If he spit and the spit did not reach the person—what then is the law? Said R. Yosé, "It is in line with the following rule: he who humiliates his person with mere words is exempt from paying any sort of compensation."[20]

How could anyone but God enforce sanctions against what someone did in his heart, or against calculated insults in a private setting?

The rabbis did, however, feel that reconciliation with one's neighbor was a crucial part of reconciliation to God and could not be ignored.[21] In their teaching, a person who offended his fellow should go to whatever lengths necessary to secure his forgiveness,[22] something Matthew seems to imply in the parable (vv. 23–24).

But neither Jesus (Matt. 23:13–33) nor the rabbis[23] were averse to addressing someone with an insulting title if they thought they deserved it (i.e., if they opposed God). This suggests that it is the falseness and injustice of the accusation, blurted out in anger, that makes it sinful. It is, in a sense, bearing a false witness against one's neighbor before the heavenly tribunal.[24] And false witnesses always received the penalty that the person they accused would have suffered if convicted—in this case, eternal death.[25]

The point of all this is, that if one does not get matters right with his brother or sister on earth, he will be condemned before the heavenly court, for one who shows no mercy now receives no mercy then (18:34–35). Indeed, to the extent that the earthly community, the church, is able to ratify the heavenly court's judgment in the present, it is to do so (18:15–20), and it should discipline the angry member.[26] Angry words bring into question the legitimacy of one's membership in the true community of Jesus. As Jesus says, they reflect the same inner attitude that murder does, even if the outward act is restrained by society's laws and penalties.

Attention to how Jesus' hearers and Matthew's readers would have read this text has been important. The central thrust of this text could be gathered simply from attention to the context of the passage; but attention to Jesus' and Matthew's own style of communicating, and how that would have addressed ancient hearers and readers, has helped us to understand better what the text means. This will also be the case with the other requirements in the Sermon on the Mount, including its warning against divorce.

EXAMPLE 2: LUST AS ADULTERY

In the second of the six "antitheses," Jesus shows that lust is adultery in the heart:

> You've heard it said, "Thou shalt not commit adultery." But I am telling you that everyone who keeps looking[27] on a woman[28] to desire her has already committed adultery with her—in his heart. If your right eye causes you to trip, rip it out and throw it away from you; for it is better for you that one piece of your body perish than that your whole body be thrown into hell.[29]

Jesus' words in this case agree fully with the views of many other Jewish teachers of his day;[30] but we may suppose that then, as today, many religious people did not behave in their heart exactly the way their doctrine said to behave.[31]

Some pagan writers also stressed that virtue was a matter of what was in the heart.[32] Some writers even specifically disavowed engaging in sexual fantasies[33] and called on others to do so.[34] But philosophers normally argued this only as a sign of their freedom and self-sufficiency, not because they shared Jewish convictions about fidelity to one's spouse or spouse-to-be. Some, affirming their freedom from the constraints of marriage, nevertheless sought other means to relieve their passions, without even scrupling about doing it in public.[35] And to many people in the Greco-Roman world, it was normal or even good to gaze on an unmarried woman to desire her.[36]

Judaism saw coveting another man's spouse or future spouse in far worse terms than the strictest of Greek philosophers;[37] merely gazing on her beauty was asking for trouble.[38] Sexual immorality could occur in the mind or heart as well as between two bodies,[39] and some rabbis condemned it in no uncertain terms:

> The School of R. Ishmael taught: Why were the Israelites of that generation in need of atonement? Because they gratified their eyes with lewdness. R. Shesheth said . . . [on a different matter. This is to] teach you: Whoever looks upon a woman's little finger is as though he gazed upon the pudenda.[40]

The second-century school of Rabbi Ishmael further taught that, "Thou shalt not commit adultery" also disallows stimulating oneself sexually,[41] and a prominent early third-century rabbi charged that one who commits adultery with his eyes or his mind is an adulterer.[42]

Once when a rabbi I know was pointing out in the most gracious manner the differences between Judaism and Christianity, he noted that Judaism did not condemn lust as Christianity did. That was an unfortunate example on his part, since ancient Judaism condemned lust quite often, as we can observe from examples like these. But it cannot be denied that Jesus' threat of hell is more severe than is usually found among even the most hyperbolic statements by rabbis on this matter.[43]

But when Jesus says that desiring another person's spouse is bad, he has far older precedent for his position than Jewish thinkers of his own period. The seventh of the ten commandments declares, "You shall not commit adultery." But the tenth of the ten commandments declares, "You shall not covet anything of your neighbor's, including his wife." Furthermore, in the Greek translation of Exodus that circulated widely in Jesus' day, the tenth commandment *begins*, "You shall not covet your neighbor's wife." The word this Greek translation uses for "coveting" a neighbor's wife is precisely the word that Jesus uses in this passage. Perhaps not every

Jewish listener would have agreed that this act was equivalent to adultery; but they certainly could not have denied that it was against the law of Moses to do it.

In Palestinian Judaism, the woman was virtually always blamed for a man's lust. As some of the traditions put it, how could a man protect himself if she went into public with an exposed face or (especially) hair?[44] Jesus, however, places the responsibility for lust on the person doing the lusting.[45] He would not have gone along with the court defenses of some rapists today who protest, "She asked for it!"

The Gospel of Matthew often illustrates its own moral teachings with concrete examples, and the issue of lust is no exception. Herod Antipas, though master of Galilee, was mastered by his own lust (14:6);[46] this sin led him on to judicial murder (14:10). Matthew provides his readers with a stark contrast in Joseph, who, though betrothed and thus almost married to Mary, was willing to withdraw completely from the relationship if that were the right thing for him to do (1:19). One may thus follow either the evil example of Herod or the righteous example of Joseph with regard to desire. The only cures implied in Matthew for susceptibility to desire appear to be the same cures suggested by Paul and the rabbis: self-control or marriage (cf. 19:4–6).[47]

Jesus goes on to suggest that if one is mastered by such desire, one should cut off whatever appendages lead to the sin (5:29–30).[48] This is no doubt part of Jesus' teaching technique of radical hyperbole, though if cutting off the eye or hand would stop lust, this would indeed be far better than going to hell. But Jesus is ultimately saying that whatever sins would keep us out of the kingdom of God, however dear they may be to us, must be cut off.[49] Matthew, in contrast to Mark's parallel saying, mentions the eye first, no doubt because it is the physical organ most directly involved in the particular sin just described. The loss of eye or hand would not stop sin in the mind;[50] but the point is that whatever the cost, sin must be stopped.

In our culture, where the media typically dehumanizes women and exploits human sexuality to sell its products, and where young men and women find most worldly role models advocating sexual promiscuity, invitations to mental prostitution are intense. This passage does not imply that such sins are unforgivable (cf. Matt. 18:21–35); rather, it summons all who think that they are already religious enough for God (5:20) to think again. The kingdom of God is entered by repentance (4:17), and once we have submitted to the yoke of his kingdom, we are freely transformed and enabled by grace to live in a new way. The gift of forgiveness does not precede the decision to follow Jesus, but neither is it dependent on the perfection of our obedience, as Jesus' first disciples in the Gospels (especially in Mark) demonstrate. That is all another story and another book, but it may be important for readers to keep in mind when this passage seems unbearable for young people who have succumbed to mental temptation.

It is interesting, however, that many Christians have struggled with anger and lust, but have regarded these past sins as light acts once they have repented and put them behind them. Many of these same Christians interpret the saying about divorce and remarriage which follows in a very different way, although the implied punishment and strength of the saying are *exactly the same* as they were for the sayings about anger and lust. Could it be that we excuse our own failings as violations only of hyperbole ("Jesus could not have meant *that!*"), while consigning others more readily to hell for sins of which they may have long since repented? It is a question at least worth considering when we turn to our discussion of the divorce and remarriage saying of Matthew 5:31–32 in the next chapter.

CONCLUSION

The thesis of this chapter is that Jesus' examples of the repentant lifestyle are graphic and demanding; he does not settle for less than total commitment. He demands everything we own (Luke 14:33). Is this all hyperbole, rhetorical exaggeration? In one sense, yes; the earliest followers of Jesus, who recorded his sayings, did not rip out their eyes or, having given away all their possessions, live homeless on the street. But in another sense Jesus' demands are not exaggeration at all: the earliest followers of Jesus did claim victory over sin's power in their lives and did divest themselves of whatever they did not need to live on to care for one another's needs. Jesus' demands are far more radical and life-changing than most of his followers in North America like to admit, and we do precisely what his hyperbole forbids us to do: tone down his meaning to fit the way we are already living.

What we have seen in these first two examples are two vital characteristics of Jesus' teaching: First, his demands are radical and total. Nothing short of absolute devotion will suffice, if we are to be true disciples of the Kingdom rather than disciples as worthless as tasteless salt or invisible light (5:13-16).

Second, Jesus couches his words in the rhetorical style of his day. In a day before television and other visual images dominated the way people thought, graphic illustrations and succinct, uncompromising assertions would best grab hearers' attention and make them consider their ways. But most assertions in such a succinct form require qualification before they are to be taken as law. For instance, while it is always wrong to look on another person with dehumanizing desire, is sexual passion always wrong, even in a role subservient to love in marriage?[51] If we answer, "Of course not, but that was not the point of Jesus' statement," we will, I think, not be far from the mark. And is anger over injustice against others wrong, if properly expressed? Did not Jesus, Paul, and James all freely express such anger against false teachers or those who oppress the poor?

In the same way, Jesus, who forbids oaths and says that one's word should be good enough by itself (5:33-37), nevertheless takes an oath of abstinence in 26:29. What Jesus meant in 5:33-37 does not include what he did in 26:29, although oaths and vows were related practices. And that is again my point: some of his general rules are examples that must be qualified in new situations. It is not enough to simply affirm that Jesus said something; we must also put what he said in its context of how people, and especially Jesus, were understood, before we impose his teaching on others.

While Jesus has some strong words about those who tone down his teachings (5:19), he also has strong words about those who mercilessly cause his little ones to stumble (18:6) or who lay on these little ones burdens they themselves would not so much as touch if they were in the same situation (23:4). Paul regards as in spiritual danger both those who subtract from the implications of the Gospel, such as those in Corinth who thought they could be immoral and still be joined to Christ, and those who add to it, like his opponents in Galatia who held the view that Christians had to do it *their* way to be proper Christians. If we are going to train other people in Jesus' teachings (28:19), we had better make sure we get them right (James 3:1).

As I hope to show in the next chapter, those who read Matthew 5 as excluding all remarriage for all divorced people and those who ignore it and so take divorce lightly, are both missing Jesus' point by quite a considerable distance.

3 Jesus on Divorce: Matthew 5:32 ("No Divorce, but . . .")

In the preceding chapter we examined Matthew's context for one of Jesus' sayings about divorce and observed that it has to do with God's radical requirements for the people of the Kingdom. We noted two features of special significance for our discussion: first, Jesus' teachings demand total commitment; second, they are given in forms that were more easily understood in their own cultural setting than they are today. This latter circumstance requires that some of them be qualified when applied to daily living in our culture.

This chapter examines Jesus' saying on divorce that follows the sayings on murder and adultery. Its context after the saying on adultery indicates something of its meaning in Matthew 5. It essentially provides a second example of adultery, another example like lust. Why this statement is taken more seriously than the statements about lust or anger is difficult to fathom, unless it is because this statement is easier for the church to enforce, or because it does not affect its enforcers as directly. But *all* Jesus' statements in this chapter are meant to be taken quite seriously (5:19).

The issue should not be whether these statements are to be taken seriously, but precisely what effect Jesus wished to have on his original audience. Unquestionably Jesus wished to oppose divorce; what must be addressed is whether he also intended to oppose divorce under all circumstances or to forbid remarriage to a party in the marriage who had wanted to keep the marriage together. In other words, is it Jesus' intention to discourage divorce by his saying or to forbid remarriage for an innocent victim of divorce? As we have already seen in chapter 2, taking Jesus' words out of context may ignore the subtleties of his style of teaching.

If there are circumstances under which it is appropriate to call someone an offensive name (as Jesus does in ch. 23), there may also be circumstances under which divorce and remarriage are not adulterous (i.e., when the other party has already broken the union). There are plenty of other general prohibitions in the Bible that do not appear to apply to all situations: children's obedience (Eph. 6:1) may be qualified by a higher loyalty to what is right (1 Sam. 20:34); more controversially, the obligation to speak truth (Eph. 4:25) may be qualified by the need to protect someone's life (Exod. 1:19; Josh. 2:4–6; 1 Sam. 16:2–3; 2 Sam. 17:14, 20; Jer. 38:27; cf. 1 Kings 20:38, 22:22; 2 Kings 8:10, 10:19; 2 Chr. 18:22). The narrative portions of the Bible often show us how the principles we read in other parts of the Bible are to be applied in practice. Indeed, the other parts of the Bible usually have "narrative contexts" too, since they are normally addressing situations or issues relevant to their readers, which we should keep in mind when we read them.

We must then examine Jesus' saying on divorce in Matthew 5:32 from several angles. First, what kind of saying is this? Did Jewish teachers often state general principles that were understood to be qualified by specific situations? If so, then Matthew's and Paul's exceptions may simply explain the more general statements found in Mark and Luke.[1] Second, what is the meaning of the exception clause, "except for 'immorality' "? We will answer this by reviewing present proposals and then by examining the relation between adulterous behavior and divorce in antiquity. Finally, we will ask whether the grounds for divorce allowed in this passage can be separated from grounds for remarriage.

WHAT KIND OF SAYING IS THIS?

You've heard it said: "Whoever divorces his wife, let him give her a certificate of divorce." But I tell you that whoever divorces his wife— except for the issue of immorality—makes her adulterous, and whoever married a divorced woman commits adultery (Matt. 5:31–32, author's translation).

Jesus' saying on divorce, like the other sayings in this chapter, is in one sense a statement of divine law and in another a statement of principle that any wise teacher might give. To understand the import of the saying, we must grasp both features of its meaning. We must understand in which sense it is divine law and in which sense a wisdom saying.

A Wisdom Saying

Jewish teachers in Jesus' day filled a number of different roles. Many scribes may have functioned just as scribes functioned elsewhere in the Greek-speaking world: professionals employed to read and write legal documents.[2] In Palestine there were also other teachers involved in communicating traditional wisdom and in teaching children how to read, especially how to read the Bible.[3] Some of these teachers were legal experts, interpreting the laws for priests or people.[4] Of these legal experts, some, mainly Pharisaic teachers, came not only to be addressed respectfully as "rabbi," but to be regularly designated by others as rabbis.[5] After AD 70[6] this became the official title for the Jewish leaders who sought to guide Judaism in the right direction.

Although some of Jesus' followers tried to draw him into legal disputes (e.g., Luke 12:13), few of Jesus' sayings in the Gospels are explicit legal interpretations. More of his sayings fit into other categories of teaching traditions, especially wisdom sayings (like proverbs)[7] and prophecy.

Many of the sayings in Jesus' sermon on divine law in Matthew 5:21–48 may have originally been spoken in non-legal contexts, but if *any* of the "antitheses" has an originally legal force, it must be this prohibition of divorce.[8] Most of the other prohibitions— anger, lust, swearing, and hatred of enemies—are difficult for a court to detect, much less to enforce.[9] But divorce, like the prohibition against legal retaliation, *could* (though need not) involve a Jewish court in its action, if only to issue a certificate of divorce.[10] The prohibition against swearing would involve a court official only if someone needed a rabbi to dissolve an invalid vow.

But the context of the divorce saying suggests that we take it more in line with the other sayings here: a combination of a wisdom saying and a prophetic summons, whose sanctions were guaranteed by the apocalyptic judgment of the heavenly court. To the extent that Matthew presents it as law, it is "apodictic law," more like the ten commandments than detailed case law. Further, all ancient legal scholars knew that broad principles of law had to be qualified for specific cases. Although, as we shall argue below, the assembly of believers would be called upon to do its best to enforce such rules, even in Matthew these teachings are not primarily rules to be enforced by the church. They function especially as an end-time summons to repentance and as a call to live a lifestyle that opposes anger, lust, divorce, falsehood, and so on.

Jewish teachers often used vivid imagery and dramatic presentations to communicate their points. Some rabbis had their own characteristic ways of saying things,[11] and Jesus is no exception.[12] In his book *The Sword of His Mouth*, Robert Tannehill catalogues some of the forms of Jesus' sayings and the impact these would have been calculated to produce on their hearers. Tannehill documents the imagery in Jesus' sayings and shows capably that the force of Jesus' sayings is often other than what a culturally insensitive modern interpreter might assume.

As we noted briefly in the last chapter, many sayings of Jewish teachers grabbed their hearers' attention with "hyperbole" or rhetorical exaggeration.[13] This was also a standard part of Greco-Roman rhetoric and would be understood as exaggeration for rhetorical effect, not to be taken literally.[14] Modern readers, who are accustomed to think of exaggeration as a form of deception rather than as a colorful, interesting portrayal or metaphor, are apt to miss the impact of ancient hyperboles.[15]

Jesus uses hyperbole, for instance, when he tells his disciples that it is easier for a camel to get through the eye of a needle than for a rich man to enter the Kingdom. His astonished disciples question then whether anyone can be saved. Jesus reminds them that even though it would be humanly impossible, it is possible with God for people to be saved. His point in the context refers to the rich young ruler, who had just chosen maintaining his wealth over following Jesus. That is, a rich person who has more to lose by following a Lord who demands everything is less likely to submit to the radical demands of the Kingdom, because he values his wealth too much.

Calling something a hyperbole, of course, is not an excuse to ignore what it says; the exaggeration is used precisely to force us to grapple with the radicalness of what it says, to shake us into changing the way we think and live. But it does warn us not to read everything as literally as if we were reading a report by some scholar or journalist today.

Wisdom sayings, as one gathers quickly from the book of Proverbs, are general principles stated in a succinct manner[16] designed to grab the reader's attention and to make a point. But wisdom sayings do not exhaust all that is to be said on a subject, nor did anyone suppose that they did. For instance, Proverbs often speaks of wealth as God's blessing; just as often, however, it condemns wealth acquired by evil means. It is not that some wisdom sayings in Proverbs contradict other wisdom sayings; rather, each states a general principle, and most principles would need to be qualified if we were to try to enforce them in every situation. This includes many of the sayings of Jesus reported in Matthew 5, such as the saying about divorce.[17]

The Legal Application of the Saying

To affirm the "general" nature of wisdom sayings is not to claim that they, and particularly the wisdom sayings of Jesus, never influenced the formulation of regulations. Moral wisdom would be applied to the formulation of civil law, and the Jewish sages were known for grappling with both practical wisdom and legal issues. Further, the early Christians would need to draw on Jesus' moral teaching to determine exactly how Christians should live. This would have implications for the "laws" of church discipline.

Matthew's readers would thus have needed to *apply* the principles of Matthew 5 as law to some extent. Because the church, like the ancient synagogue, functions as a judicial assembly, we must do our best to ratify the judgments of the heavenly court.[18] This means that we must follow Jesus' legal teachings[19] recorded in Matthew 18:15–20: if there is sin in the church, we must seek to privately reprove[20] the sinner.[21] If this attempt to restore the person fails, then we must take one or two other believers who can function as witnesses.[22] If that attempt fails, the two or three who witnessed that the person is continuing in unrepentant sin must bring the matter before the gathered assembly, and one final plea for the person to repent must be given. This gathered assembly then functions as a judicial assembly;[23] but whereas the two or three witnesses under Old Testament law were to be the first to execute judgment against the sinner (Deut. 17:7),[24] here the two or three witnesses[25] are to be the first to pray (Matt. 18:16, 19–20),[26] and their prayers will be efficacious.[27]

If the church is to enforce, as best as possible, the will of God on earth as it is in heaven, within the church itself, then sin must be dealt with in a serious way. This instruction on church discipline is, of course, conditioned by the context of forgiveness (18:21–35); just as the earthly court executes judgment on the authority of the heavenly court in both Jewish and Christian tradition, we are to forgive the repentant person freely, just as God does. But unrepentant sin must be judged, until repentance is forthcoming. Sins such as murder and adultery, which merited the death penalty under Old Testament law, could no longer be punished by death when Rome withdrew the right to enforce capital punishment from Jewish courts; but it came to be believed that whatever punishments could not be executed by the earthly court, would be executed by the divine court.[28]

Jesus' interpretations of the law, even if they were not meant to be placed in a code of law per se, would thus come to be used as an authoritative rabbi's exposition of the law by a church concerned to maintain the right understanding of God's Word.[29] Yet a general statement of principle must be qualified when it is used to address specific situations, and this is what we find when this saying occurs in various specific contexts. For instance, in Luke 16:14–18, where Jesus begins by challenging the Pharisees on the issue of inward righteousness, he goes on to say:

> But it is easier for heaven and earth to pass away than for one mark[30] to drop from the law. Everyone who divorces his wife and marries another one commits adultery in doing so, and the one who marries a woman who has been divorced from her husband commits adultery in doing so.[31]

Luke includes only this one example of Jesus' radicalizing of the law, but the way the rule is stated, it admits no exceptions. The context in Luke is actually a challenge to use one's money rightly, but the function of these words of Jesus sandwiched between two money parables suggests a summons to radical commitment, both in money and in the rest of one's life. It functions as one of Jesus' many vivid statements designed to shake his hearers into recognizing moral truth.[32]

But in Matthew, where the rule appears in the context of the exposition of Scripture and where there is an emphasis on the church disciplining its erring members, the rule is more likely to be *applied* in a legal way. That is why it is significant that in Matthew the saying is qualified: "except in the case of immorality."

The same principle of interpreting this saying appears in Paul, who seems to have heard it in its unqualified form (1 Cor. 7:10). Paul cites that unqualified form, but then immediately qualifies it—explicitly mentioning that he is doing so—when he applies it to a specific situation. As we shall observe more closely in following chapters, Paul permits divorce and remarriage under certain circumstances (7:12–16), even though Jesus' general principle does not mention exceptions. In other words, both Matthew and Paul understand that Jesus' rule is a general statement and does not apply to every case, and that the exceptions should be stated before the rule is *applied* as a rule.

The "exception clause," which allows divorce in the case of "immorality," is not found in Mark, Luke, or Paul as part of Jesus' saying.[33] Since this clause makes good sense in the context of first-century Judaism, as we shall argue in the next chapter, it is possible, on the one hand, that it is original with Jesus and that Mark, Luke, and Paul simply omitted it.[34] On the other hand, evidence suggests that Matthew added it as an explanatory note to the original form of Jesus' saying.[35] Our contention is, however, that if the exception clause is not original with Jesus, its meaning is implied in his teaching, and Matthew is entirely correct to report it.

Why would Matthew insist on such an exception? Precisely because Jesus' teaching on divorce, like most of his other teachings, is not detailed legal formulation like those of some other teachers of his day. He emphasized finding *principles* in the law, viewing God's Word as prophetic demand rather than merely case law demanding legal extrapolation. If Jesus' words were to become legal formulation in any sense, they would have to be qualified as legal formulations are. And if Jesus' words were not to become a *mere* legal formulation, the real principle inherent in those words must be preserved *against* a legalistic interpretation of those words— a legalistic interpretation much of today's church has unfortunately chosen to follow.

It was perfectly natural in Matthew's day to suppose that any law would need to be qualified; that there were exceptions to general rules which would need to be articulated was simply assumed. For instance, Quintilian, a famous Roman rhetorician of the first century, cites a Roman law but proceeds to show that exceptions are implicit within it:

> "Children shall support their parents under penalty of imprisonment."
> It is clear, in the first place, that this cannot apply to an infant. At this point we turn to other possible exceptions and distinguish as follows.[36]

Quintilian's book is about rhetoric and he was thus making the sort of argument that lawyers would have used when they approached legal texts.

It was also perfectly natural for ancient writers to rephrase famous teachers' sayings in their own words; this was a standard rhetorical exercise practiced by all those who received a normal Greek education. It seems far safer to accept Matthew's interpretation of Jesus' saying—as requiring qualification before it can be applied in a legal way—than to accept the interpretation of some modern readers who understand neither the culture nor the forms of speech employed in the first century. In other words, before we can consider remarriage sinful, we must ask whether or not Jesus would have regarded the particular divorce that preceded it as "valid."

WHAT IS THE MEANING OF THE EXCEPTION CLAUSE?

"Except in the case of immorality" probably reflects the language of Deuteronomy 24:1, which apparently permits divorce "for the matter of uncleanness."[37] The Hebrew word here translated "matter" comes over into Greek quite naturally in the term here translated "case."[38] In other words, Matthew sees Jesus as explaining the meaning of the law in Deuteronomy. He interprets "uncleanness" as "immorality."[39]

The question is, What does he mean by "immorality"? The term itself is straightforward enough and refers to any kind of sexual immorality, from intercourse between two unmarried people to adultery and homosexual activity; the New Testament and Jewish writers could speak of it in quite broad terms, since the only form of morally acceptable sexual activity in the Bible is between a husband and wife. In the context of grounds for a married couple to divorce, the term might seem to imply that one member of the couple has been engaging in an extramarital affair. But while this may seem straightforward, the enormous array of proposals about what "immorality" means in this passage appears to challenge any such simple answer.

Interpretations of the Exception Clause

What we will do in this section is summarize examples of the vast diversity of views that have been proposed to explain Matthew's statement. It must be frankly admitted that many of those who have proposed the most restrictive interpretation of "immorality" for this passage are conservative Protestant or Catholic scholars who have the most stake in traditions that veto divorce under all circumstances. Although this fact does not impugn the judgment of the scholars whose views follow, one may notice that they evidence a consistent urge to remove any exceptions from Jesus' ruling, even though most of these scholars come up with very different ways to remove the exception.

Some interpretations of the passage argue that this "exception" is not actually an exception at all. One writer proposes that the clause just means that a woman is not being caused[40] to commit adultery by being remarried in the case of immorality, because she has already committed adultery![41] The problem with this proposal is that it is simply too ingenious: were it correct, there would be little reason to state the exception clause to begin with, since it would not add anything to the statement. And if one wished to make such a point, it is peculiar that the point would be stated in such a manner that so few other interpreters throughout history could have caught it.

A related suggestion argues that the one case in which a man may put away a woman is if he is committing fornication with her, i.e., if they are not authentically married.[42] Against this is the plain statement that the woman is said to be "his wife" in exactly the same terms as in the Mosaic text cited in 5:31, and "divorce" is the same term as used in the preceding verse. Had Matthew intended us to understand this exception as something other than divorcing a wife under certain conditions, he failed to make this clear. Further, the term translated "immorality" can refer to any kind of sexual misconduct, not only to premarital intercourse. There is thus no natural reason to specify that the clause should mean, "except with a partner to whom he is not really married." Finally, given the "hot topics" of Jesus' day (discussed below), a far more natural interpretation presents itself (also discussed below).

Others would argue that while the exception is an actual exception, it is a rare exception, one that applies only to illegitimate unions.[43] This view argues that it refers only to marriages that should not have been contracted to begin with, marriages that have essentially been null and void all along.

This view is usually applied to the degrees of forbidden kinship, i.e., the incest prohibitions of Leviticus 18. Scholars who hold this view typically say that Matthew merely permitted divorce if one were married to a relative forbidden by Leviticus. Although such a view has become popular,[44] it has a fatal weakness: there is nothing in the semantic range of "immorality" to limit the term particularly to incestuous unions, and there is nothing whatsoever in the context to suggest that Matthew implied such a limitation. A reading of Matthew simply on the basis of context, general usage of the term, and Jewish conceptions of grounds for divorce, leaves no grounds for the inference that "immorality" here is limited to incest.

Some advocates of the incest or forbidden marriage interpretation cite later rabbis who discussed divorce with regard to Leviticus' prohibitions.[45] But saying that some rabbis discussed the issue is a far cry from saying that these same rabbis would have read a statement about "immorality" as narrowly referring to incest. Other particular examples of immorality could have come to their minds just as easily, and the rabbis indeed discussed broader sorts of immorality[46] in the context of divorce.[47]

Other scholars who think "immorality" in Matthew 5:32 means "incest" compare Acts 15:20, 29; 21:25, which, they argue, proves that the early Jewish Christians had to deal with the incest issue among Gentile converts.[48] This reading of Acts 15 is sometimes proposed on the basis of the Jewish assumption that Gentiles committed incest.[49] This proposal is, however, quite problematic; the Jewish view that Gentiles were incestuous was only a subset of the broader Jewish idea that Gentiles were *generally* immoral.[50] Nor, if it were the Jewish view that incestuous *marriages* were a major issue among Gentiles (enough so that this, rather than general Gentile immorality, would come to mind when reading "immorality"), would Luke have written this into his history. Luke, quite familiar with Greco-Roman society, would have been as aware as Paul that this view of Gentiles favoring incest was a misconception (1 Cor. 5:1).[51] There is not the slightest evidence that Acts 15 refers specifically to incest, rather than to immorality in general, any more than there is evidence for that assertion in Matthew 5:32. To read Acts 15 in this way, and then to read that misinterpretation into Matthew, is a curious method of interpretation indeed.

Another narrow—and in this case also wide of the mark—suggestion is that "immorality" here is *spiritual* adultery, constituted by rejecting Christ. In this case scholars might find a precedent for the church's right to annul genuine marriages.[52] But Paul in 1 Corinthians 7 explicitly disallows divorce on the grounds of spiritual incompatibility, and while there is plenty of precedent for "immorality" referring to spiritual adultery in biblical tradition, there is no precedent for this meaning in Matthew, who elsewhere refers to it only as a physical, sexual sin (1:19; 15:19; cf. 21:31–32). Matthew thus gives no hint that he means something other than what he normally means by the term.

The problem with all these interpretations is that they impose too *specific* an interpretation on the word "immorality." This term implies *any* sort of sexual sin, except when the context designates a particular kind; and the context here fails to narrow the meaning of "immorality" down in any way.[53] "Immorality" here is not just premarital sex, nor is it just incest; it is any kind of sexual unfaithfulness to one's current spouse. Since the kind of unfaithfulness normally perpetrated by people already married is adultery, the kind of immorality that would most often be implied here is adultery.

"Immorality" as Adultery

Despite the frequency with which it apparently occurred in prominent[54] Greco-Roman society,[55] adultery had always been seen as a shamefully immoral act,[56] a breach of covenant[57] that constituted the theft of another person's most precious possession[58]—the sole affection of his wife.[59] Suspicion of improper activity with upper class men's wives could lead to severe penalties, such as banishment to an island.[60] Adulterers also could face death at the hands of husbands or fathers under certain circumstances.[61] Adulteresses were forbidden remarriage to freeborn Romans.[62]

Adultery had long been grounds for divorce in Greco-Roman[63] and Jewish law. In fact, Roman[64] and Jewish[65] law *compelled* the husband to divorce his wife if she were found to be in adultery;[66] Roman law since Augustus had included penalties for the husband who failed to do so,[67] since he was considered to be "pimping" his wife.[68] In both Roman[69] and Jewish[70] law, an adulterous spouse forfeited her dowry.

The view that Jesus here refers to adultery is sometimes attacked by proponents of other views who note that the specific term for "adultery" is not used here.[71] This is a curious argument on the part of those who wish to limit the expression even more narrowly to incest—which most of those who criticize the adultery view do—but the objection should nonetheless be entertained. Why would Matthew employ a term normally signifying something broader than adultery, if adultery were all that he meant?

My suspicion is that Matthew used a broader term because he did indeed mean more than what is narrowly signified by "adultery." Most sexual infidelity committed by a married person can come under the heading of "adultery," but Matthew probably wishes his exception to permit more than the word itself specifies.

While it is probably going too far to read "immorality" in light of 5:28 and to use a spouse's lust as an excuse for divorce,[72] Matthew's point seems to be that sexual sin within marriage need not be limited to a wife's having intercourse with another man;[73] what if she habitually pursues the other man, but he refuses to return her affections? She may not be technically guilty of adultery, but it is certainly sexual immorality in the broad sense.

Such an interpretation of "except for the case of immorality" may actually be how the earliest Jewish Christians would have read the phrase. Those rabbis who argued that a man could divorce his wife only for the cause of unchastity meant by this any sort of indiscretion or unfaithfulness, including a woman going outside with her hair uncovered (which in that culture meant that she was looking for another husband):[74]

> The School of Shammai thus takes the Hebrew terms *erwat dabar* in Deut. xxiv.1, translated "some unseemly thing," in their literal sense to mean "some uncovered thing. . . ." In other words, according to the Shammaites, not only actual adultery may be the cause of divorce, but anything that shows immodesty and that indirectly leads to a suspicion of adultery.[75]

This interpretation is not limited to one school of rabbis; it was also held by Philo, a Diaspora Jew quite in touch with Greek thought. He maintained that whatever pretext one found for divorcing one's wife, it must relate to the fact that she has somehow violated her marriage ties.[76]

Matthew need not have been quite so generous in his interpretation of "immorality" as these rabbis, but his allowance does seem to be broader than one's spouse actually engaging in physical intercourse with someone else. If she is seeking an affair, it is grounds for divorce whether or not she actually finds someone willing to accommodate her desire. It seems that Matthew wishes to make his qualification of Jesus' teaching broad enough to allow divorce in various concrete legal situations.

It is also possible that persistent misconduct, rather than a single act of adultery, is in view.[77] This possibility would accord with both the broad nature of the term "immorality" and the Matthean emphasis on continual forgiveness—for the *repentant* anyway (Matt. 18:21–35). The meaning in this case would be that this exception really is barely an exception after all—divorcing a perpetually unfaithful spouse does not dissolve a marriage, but simply makes official that the unfaithful spouse has already dissolved it by repeatedly denying it in practice. This would not have been the most natural interpretation for ancient Jewish readers, but in the context of Jesus' teaching on forgiving the repentant it may be assumed: past sins, even if they are recent past sins, are not held against someone who has repented and stopped doing them.

In any case, this passage clearly permits the innocent party in a divorce to remarry. In the Old Testament, of course, the adulterous spouse was executed, so the remaining partner would have been permitted to remarry as a widower, even if Moses had not allowed circumstances for divorce in Deuteronomy 24:1. Our contention is that Jesus' teaching does not impose a greater hardship on the innocent party whose spouse has continued in adultery. (Indeed, given the view that the heavenly court carried out capital sentences which could not be executed by the earthly Jewish courts, the adulterous spouse's legal, spiritual status is already death.)[78]

Not everyone takes such a lenient view toward the innocent party who is cheated on or abandoned, however. One scholar argues that the divorce allowance is only for Jews, not Gentiles, which is why only Matthew mentions it. This means that Gentile Christians are not permitted to divorce for any reason. This is based on a rabbinic opinion that divorce was a right given only to Israelite men.[79] But if Matthew agreed with such a view, it is odd that he does not make it explicit, since all these teachings in his Gospel are intended to be passed on to the Gentiles (28:19).[80] And are we to suppose that Mark, Luke, and Paul had no Jewish readers in their audience, for whom they might wish to suggest this Jewish tradition which would have let some of their readers off the hook? Finally, early Judaism was diverse, and most Jewish people in the Greek world seem to have followed Greek divorce customs. Are we to suppose that Matthew expects his Greek-reading Jewish readers to know which line of Jewish tradition he is here citing and then to read this into his text, particularly when our evidence for that tradition is sparse and late?

Others say that Jesus made this more lenient exception in public, but that privately he told his disciples what he really demands of disciples: they were not permitted divorce even in the case of adultery.[81] While one could argue this on the basis of Mark 10:1–12, it is simply not what the parallel passage in Matthew says, and it is impossible to argue in the case of 5:31–32, which the reader will naturally hear as Jesus' radical demands to those who would be disciples of Jesus. And if the argument does not work for 5:31–32, it is presumably not what is meant by the later passage, either.

Divorce But Not Remarriage?

Some scholars argue that this passage indeed permits divorce in the case of adultery—but does not permit remarriage.[82] It must permit divorce in this case because one is simply formalizing "the break between husband and wife that has already occurred through the wife's immorality" according to Jewish law. But, especially in light of 19:10–12, advocates of this position argue that it does not permit remarriage.[83] These scholars further argue that Matthew includes the exception clause because in Jewish Palestine, the law *mandated* divorce for adultery. Matthew's readers, in contrast to Mark's and Luke's, would be compelled to comply.[84]

Although this is a grammatically defensible position, it does not reckon adequately with a number of factors. First, if the exception does not permit remarriage, there is little point in stating it. No one would have disputed that wives could be divorced against their will in Palestinian Jewish law or that either spouse could be unilaterally divorced by the other in Roman law. What if one spouse began an affair and wished to move out? How would the remaining spouse prevent this from happening? The "exception" does not clarify much about Jesus' saying if it applies only to divorce.

Second, if the exception permits divorce, the average first-century Jewish reader would *assume* that it permitted remarriage, unless explicitly informed otherwise;[85] part of the very nature of the divorce document was to free the wife to remarry. (The husband's right to remarry was assumed.) While Jesus may here forbid the guilty party to remarry, he does allow for a valid type of divorce which in turn allows for a valid remarriage for the innocent party.

Third, these scholars' appeal to a grammatical ambiguity in chapter 19 is a curious procedure for interpreting 5:32. It would be unreasonable to expect the reader to wait fourteen chapters to have his or her original mistaken impressions corrected. Indeed, it would be much more likely for the reader to approach 19:9 in light of what had already been taught in 5:32.

Fourth, it is not accurate to say that only Matthew's readers and not Mark's or Luke's would be compelled to divorce adulterous spouses; as noted above, contemporary Roman law, followed by Mark's divorce saying in other respects, also required divorce. And as William Luck observes, *biblical* law approved of divorce as a discipline (Jer. 3:1; Isa. 50:1; Hos. 1–2), and Jesus denied that he was abrogating biblical teachings (Matt. 5:17–20). Further, Luck notes, Matthew is not elsewhere averse to calling readers to stand against culture (including Jewish courts) where that culture would actually contravene Jesus' teachings.[86]

Fifth, Matthew 19:10–12 is directed toward "those who are able," not "those who are divorced," an argument that seems to resemble Paul's case for singleness (1 Cor. 7, below). We will address this argument in considerably more detail in the following chapter, in our treatment of Matthew 19:1–12.

Finally, forever disallowing the remarriage of the innocent party seems to annul Jesus' law of mercy (9:13; 12:7): if Jesus' emphasis in this passage is the sanctity of marriage, then penalizing rather than defending an innocent partner appears more like the sort of interpretation the "hard of heart" foes of Jesus (19:8) would offer than the kind that Jesus would offer.[87]

But, protest such scholars, Matthew 5:32 does not allow the innocent divorced *wife* to remarry; if she does, it is claimed, this text accuses her of adultery. Why should the innocent husband be treated any differently than the innocent wife? But to understand this text one must consider the implications of Palestinian Jewish law. Palestinian Jewish customs would have been familiar to Jesus and to most of Matthew's readers, whereas they would have been mostly irrelevant to the readers of Mark and Luke. (Earlier we criticized scholars for making a Palestinian Jewish custom peculiar to Matthew as opposed to Mark or Luke, but that was because it was also a Roman custom.)

Since Jewish law permitted the husband to marry more than one wife at a time and did not envisage sleeping with a virgin or a prostitute as adultery (though he was obligated to marry the former), the husband could not legally commit adultery against his own wife; he could only commit it with another man's wife. This is a widely recognized feature of Old Testament and Jewish law,[88] and Matthew neither commends it nor critiques it; it is simply the custom that existed in his day.

Matthew 5:32, then, claims that the marriage is valid in God's sight until one party dissolves the marriage through unfaithfulness. In the Palestinian Jewish society described above, one who marries a divorced woman would always commit adultery in these terms, because the former marriage either would not have been dissolved in God's sight, as Jesus says, or would have been de facto dissolved by her adultery. That unfaithfulness could dissolve the marriage bonds and call for divorce could have been assumed by Mark and Luke without needing to be stated; that the innocent husband in such a divorce was free to remarry would also have been the normal assumption, because divorce on such grounds would be a valid divorce. Because Mark applies the rule to the husband as well as the wife, we may assume that in a monogamous society where the wife also had the right of divorce, the innocent wife would also be permitted to remarry. Matthew's wording assumes Palestinian Jewish customs and makes them part of the hyperbole.

We are arguing on the premise that Matthew assumes his readers' familiarity with Palestinian Jewish regulations. It is, however, possible that Matthew here challenges rather than assumes Jewish law. The phrase usually translated, "he (the divorcing husband) makes her (his wife) commit adultery," may actually mean something quite different than such a translation implies. Luck has pointed out that the verb is passive, and there are very few examples where the passive form of this verb has an active meaning. In other words, Matthew could be claiming that the divorcing husband is the one guilty of adultery, against Jewish custom: he "adulterizes" her, treats her unfaithfully, by divorcing her without adequate cause.[89] This would fit the context: the innocent wife of 5:32 is no more guilty than the lusted-after woman of 5:28 or the brother hated without cause in 5:23.[90] If Luck is correct on this point, there is no indication that she is being called an adulteress by remarrying. But given that the text goes on to say, "Whoever marries a divorced woman commits adultery," the interpretation I have given in the above paragraph may fit the evidence somewhat better.[91]

Whichever of these two alternatives one adopts, the most natural interpretation is that divorce (and consequently remarriage) is permissible under certain grounds: when one partner, in this case the wife, has dissolved the union by her infidelity. Once the marriage is functionally dissolved, the legal ratification of that dissolution is a necessary step unless the party that has sinned repents and makes restitution. Even in this form, Jesus' saying retains some of its hyperbolic force: other exceptions may be elicited by other circumstances, as we shall see from Paul in 1 Corinthians 7. But the principal point is unmistakable: divorce is an evil to be avoided at all costs, and only when the salvation of the marriage is truly impossible is it valid. And the salvation of the marriage is impossible only if one party in the marriage has unilaterally decided to end it by seeking to leave or by acting adulterously. In such a case, divorce is the formal declaration of what is already true in fact: the marriage is broken, and the guilty party is responsible for it.

As we noted before, the one narrative example Matthew gives us to decide the proper procedure for the "exception clause" occurs in the opening narrative of his Gospel. It is the case of Joseph, who, when believing that Mary had been unfaithful to him during their betrothal, was ready to divorce her (1:19). The text says that he was "righteous": he was willing to divorce her, but wished to do it privately to avoid shame for her. But the reader, acquainted only with Jewish (or even Greco-Roman) law would have every reason to assume that Joseph assumed the freedom to remarry, unless Matthew had informed us otherwise.

This starkly contrasts the negative example of Herod, whose relationship with his brother's wife is an explicitly adulterous and incestuous (by Old Testament standards) liaison. Herod's problem is not that he is engaging in a second marriage on valid grounds, but rather that his relationship with Herodias began in sin and can never be ratified before God (14:3–4). There is all the difference in the world between a guilty Herod and an innocent Joseph; and the Jewish-Christian reader of Matthew, approaching the opening of Matthew's Gospel for the first time, would most naturally assume Joseph's right to remarry and would maintain this assumption through the rest of the Gospel unless it were explicitly contradicted by what followed. Is this impression in the first chapter of Matthew explicitly contradicted later in the Gospel? Some of the strongest claims that Jesus disallowed remarriage after divorce of any sort appear in discussions of 19:1–12, to which we turn in the following chapter.

CONCLUSION

Jesus articulated the principle that divorce was wrong, but his earliest followers understood that there could be innocent parties in the breakup of a marriage. Matthew shows that the partner's unfaithfulness is a valid grounds for divorce, and that a valid divorce cancels the marriage bond, allowing the innocent party to remarry in exactly the same way any single person can marry. The radical demands of the Kingdom prohibit sin; they do not condemn the innocent.

4 | Jesus vs. the Pharisees: When Is Divorce Sinful?

Matthew and Mark both tell us that Jesus addressed the issue of divorce in a legal discussion with some very strict Jewish pietists.[1] With this in mind, the narrative in Matthew actually seems closer to the way the discussion would have gone in Jewish Palestine. Mark has apparently omitted or left unexplained some details as irrelevant to his own readers' needs, and Matthew has drawn out the sense the legal discussion would have had in its original Palestinian setting. For that reason, our analysis will focus on Matthew, making comments about differences of detail in Mark only where necessary.

In Mark 10, the Pharisees ask Jesus whether divorce is lawful or not. Although this sets up the narrative nicely, the fuller question of the Pharisees in Matthew 19—whether it is lawful to divorce "for any cause"—is more in line with what first-century Jewish teachers discussed among themselves and with what they might have asked Jesus had they wished to engage him in a debate, the contours of which were already familiar to them. They ask, "Is it lawful for a man to divorce his wife for any reason?" (Matt. 19:3). Had Jesus said *yes*, he would have sided with one school of rabbis; had he said *no*, he would have sided with another school of rabbis, which was more particular in its grounds for divorce. The issue in the text thus becomes, not whether or not divorce is ever permissible, but on what grounds it is permissible. This would have been a more natural question for the Pharisees to ask.[2]

THE SCHOOLS OF HILLEL AND SHAMMAI

Scholars have long recognized the relevance of first-century Jewish teaching on divorce to this passage.[3] The teaching is most succinctly summarized in the Mishnah and another of the earlier rabbinic works:

> The School of Shammai say: A man may not divorce his wife unless he has found unchastity in her, for it is written, Because he hath found in her *indecency* in anything [Deut. 24:1]. And the School of Hillel say: [He may divorce her] even if she spoiled a dish for him, as it is written, Because he hath found in her indecency in *anything*. R. Akiba says: Even if he found another fairer than she, for it is written, And it shall be if she find no favour in his eyes. . . . "[4]

> In this connection did the House of Shammai say, "A man should divorce his wife only on grounds of adultery, as it is said, 'because he finds something obnoxious about her.' " And the House of Hillel say, "Even if she burned his soup, as it is said, ' . . . something. . . . ' " Said the House of Hillel to the House of Shammai, "If the word 'something' is stated, then why is the word 'obnoxious' added . . . ?"[5]

The school of Shammai was more predominant in Jesus' day;[6] the school of Hillel became more prominent by the end of the first century.[7] Since Josephus and Philo appear to hold a position more lenient than the Shammaites, it could be argued that on this issue the Hillelite side prevailed in the time of Jesus,[8] but this view is open to question. Josephus was writing toward the end of the first century; Philo's view may be closer to the Shammaite position after all, and both are at any rate writing in Greek for Greek audiences for whom a more lenient position would give a better impression of Judaism. That a husband could divorce his wife without the stricter grounds of the Shammaites, however, is unquestionable;[9] the Pharisees did not control how other first-century Jews practiced divorce, and even if they had, the Shammaites could not have regarded Hillelite divorces as invalid. Otherwise they would have had to go as far as Jesus had in calling subsequent marriages adulterous!

Some scholars have objected to any reference to the dispute between the schools of Hillel and Shammai here. Such scholars point out that this text complains that the Pharisees were testing Jesus, as they later did in chapter 22, and that testing involves something more serious than asking with which group of Jewish sages Jesus wished to side.[10] Our answer to this is threefold: first, the challenges given to Jesus were not always of a directly threatening nature. One of Jesus' disputes in chapter 22 (22:23–32) was a standard matter of dispute that would not have involved him in any political or legal "hot water";[11] in another case, Jesus' answer short-circuited Pharisaic opposition precisely because it was a standard Jewish answer to the question they had posed (22:37–40).[12] Second, the Pharisees may have heard him teach on the issue in terms like those recorded in Matthew 5:32, and their teachers of the law may have wished to use their arguments sharpened on each other to challenge Jesus' possible ignorance of or challenge to their law.

And finally, Jesus' language is much stronger than that of the school of Shammai in calling the wrongful divorce so invalid that the consequent union would be adulterous.[13] Although Jesus may have meant this hyperbolically, he clearly meant it more authoritatively than did the Shammaites, who did not enforce their opinions so rigorously as to invalidate divorces on other grounds. This does not mean that Jesus is not arguing within the confines of the rabbinic debate; it does mean that he claims a greater authority than the other rabbis did.

GOD'S ULTIMATE PURPOSE: THE TWO SHALL BECOME ONE

Jesus' answer pits a literal reading of one part of the law against a literal reading of another part of the law, as Jewish teachers often did to make their points.[14] In this case Jesus underscores their ignorance of Scripture with the charge, "Have you not read?" (19:4; cf. 12:3; 21:16, 42; 22:31),[15] and then appeals to the creation story.[16] Although subsequent laws may show what God permitted in his dealings with fallen humanity, it is the creation story that shows his ideal and the way that life will be in the coming kingdom of God.

The texts Jesus cites from Genesis[17] declare that God made humanity both male and female and that husband and wife became one flesh when they were united sexually.[18] In many Jewish comments on this text, it was understood that the first person had been a mixture of male and female until God removed the female part from Adam, making it into Eve.[19] Jesus' citation of the second text may have argued that in marriage this unity of male and female was restored.[20] Whether Jesus intended to evoke all the Jewish ideas clustered around the creation of man and woman or not, it is clear that he appeals to God's original purposes as the standard for life in the Kingdom.[21] God meant for two to become one, and that original purpose could be violated only by divorce or by the prior intrusion of another party which would disrupt the union.[22]

At least some Jewish pietists, the sect who lived in the wilderness of Qumran, had already decided that Genesis 2:24 forbade second marriages,[23] although their view does not seem to have influenced the rest of Judaism.[24] It is disputed, however, to what degree their teaching against second marriages applied to divorce and to what extent it was merely a prohibition of polygamy in that community.[25] One of their texts literally forbids having two living wives simultaneously,[26] but it is not clear that a divorced woman would still be considered a wife;[27] what is in view is apparently "Belial's trick" by polygamy,[28] since the text is at pains to explain that King David simply had not known any better.[29]

The other Qumran text that addresses the issue is similar to this one and plainly allows remarriage in the case of a spouse's death.[30] But again it seems directed especially against royal polygamy, which led Solomon astray (1 Kings 11:1) and was already condemned in the law (Deut. 17:17). Since the prohibition here is from the Deuteronomy passage prohibiting royal polygamy, and since the context is instruction to a king, this passage has even less to say about prohibiting marrying another wife after divorce than the first passage did.[31] Taking this as a prohibition against taking a second "wife" or as a proscription forbidding remarriage after divorce would occur only to those already familiar with Jesus' saying. No one who considered the divorce as valid would consider the man who remarried after the divorce as married to "two living wives." This is important, since some have appealed to the Dead Sea Scrolls' alleged opposition to remarriage after divorce to argue that this is what Jesus would have been understood to mean.

It is noteworthy that Jesus uses this image of spiritual unity to argue that marriage should not be dissolved by people, not to argue that it *can* not be:[32]

Thus they are no longer two, but instead "one flesh."
So let no one separate what God has joined together (Matt. 19:7).

Jesus does not forbid ratifying a separation that has already taken place through the other partner's acts which have already broken the unity of the "one flesh." This is a valid divorce, rendering the innocent person free to remarry, because that person is no longer married to a previous spouse.

WHY DID MOSES ALLOW DIVORCE?

Jesus' appeal to God's original purpose showed the way the Kingdom should be, but the Pharisees were ready with a response:

did not the law of Moses include divorce? (And would not the law be intensified, rather than abrogated, in the world to come?)[33]

Their way of putting the question, however, stacks the deck unfairly: "Then why did Moses command to give her a putting-away document and to divorce her?" (19:7). While Moses commanded providing a document for the woman if she were being divorced,[34] no doubt to protect her,[35] no one really thought Moses commanded everyone to divorce.[36] Perhaps they thought that divorce was mandatory under certain circumstances, such as adultery. But Akiba, who allowed divorce if a husband found someone more beautiful, would surely not have said Moses commanded the husband to divorce her for this. The Pharisees use these words in Matthew because they are trying to portray Jesus as going against Moses' commandments.[37]

But Jesus rightly responds that Moses nowhere commanded the divorce of a wife; God permitted it.[38] His opponents should have caught his point immediately. The rabbis, like other ancient legal scholars, recognized "concession" as an established legal category—something that was not quite right to begin with, but had to be allowed because people would not be able to do what was fully right.[39] Jesus is saying that God permitted divorce as a concession to human weakness, but that, with the coming of the Kingdom, God's original demands were being restored and the concession revoked. Far from being against the law of Moses, he tells the Pharisees, he really upholds it more strictly than they do:

He said to them, "Moses permitted you to divorce your wives to accommodate the hardness of your hearts; but from the beginning it did not happen like this" (Matt. 19:8).

The principle cited against them is similar to the law of mercy Jesus uses in 9:13 and 12:7; compassion is the right way to interpret the law, not "hardness of heart." His point is that Moses put up with their divorcing because the best he could get out of hard-hearted people was legal protection for the one divorced against her will. But if they had been compassionate and open to his ways, God could have held them to his original and ideal standard all along: they were not to initiate divorce.

We may illustrate this with one of the rare stories in rabbinic literature where the rabbis are actually forced by their rules to side with a man against a wife who was pleading for the divorce not to happen.[40] Hinena the son of Rabbi Assi "threw a writ of divorce to his wife, saying to her, 'Here is your writ of divorce.' She sobbed in a loud voice, and her neighbors came in." The neighbors tried to help her, but the rabbis ruled in favor of Hinena.[41] The rabbis felt that divorce was a tragic matter, but they nevertheless upheld the scriptural "right" of the husband to a divorce if that was what he wished.

THE IMMORALITY EXCEPTION: TO ALLOW DIVORCE OR REMARRIAGE?

Some scholars have argued that the exception clause in 19:9, "except for immorality," allows only for divorce but does not permit remarriage.

In other words, on this view one can divorce for a spouse's infidelity, but this does not make the person who divorces on these grounds eligible for remarriage. This argument is based on the word order in 19:9:

But I tell you[42] that whoever divorces his wife—except on the grounds of her immorality—and marries another woman, commits adultery.

This is not the most common word order, and opponents of remarriage have made much of it, reading it as supporting two conditional statements: one cannot divorce his wife except on the grounds of adultery; whoever remarries (regardless of the grounds for the divorce) commits adultery.[43] Although some of these writers will admit that word order in Greek is less significant than it would be in English[44] and that the construction under consideration is extremely rare[45] (which might make its character difficult to judge) and somewhat ambiguous,[46] they nevertheless affirm that the word order here sustains their case that the exception clause applies only to divorce, not to remarriage as well.[47]

To this, several replies could be offered. First, the reader comes to 19:9 in light of 5:32 and finds the exception clause in precisely the same place as before. Because Matthew has not moved the clause does not mean that it does not modify both parts of the sentence; as Murray points out, this would yield a saying of quite uncertain sense, since the principal verb "commits adultery" depends on both "divorces" and "remarries."[48]

But while this is true, this awkward construction is not best explained either by accident or by following the order of 5:32; after all, Matthew does vary the Greek words in the clause, and he could have varied the order of the words as well.[49] So we move to our second and more cogent challenge to the view that only divorce, and not remarriage, is permitted in this text: the simple fact that only divorce should have been directly qualified in this case. Those who point to the curious syntax are right to regard the clause as qualifying the nature of divorce rather than directly addressing remarriage; they are mistaken only in the conclusion which they draw from this grammatical peculiarity.

The clause follows the verb "divorces" not because the subsequent marriage is at issue but because the divorce is, as 5:32 has already shown. *If the divorce is valid, so is the remarriage*; Jesus calls remarriage after an invalid divorce adulterous only because the divorce was invalid, due to insufficient grounds. Early Jewish law also judged the validity of the remarriage entirely on the validity of the divorce.[50] The issue is entirely whether or not the divorce was legitimate, and it is thus to the issue of divorce that the exception clause must be appended.

To argue that remarriage is forbidden after a valid divorce is to argue entirely on the basis of an inference not stated in the text. The text, indeed, militates against such an interpretation; a valid divorce by standard ancient definition implied the right to remarry (the phrases used for it relate to "releasing" someone from an attachment to allow them to engage in another such attachment).[51] No ancient Jewish reader would have read Matthew otherwise. Again, the exception clause would have little practical value if the divorced person could not remarry. If Matthew meant something other than what his first Jewish-Christian readers would have understood him as saying, the ambiguous positioning of his exceptive clause does not make that clear, nor does he provide any other indications that he wishes his readers to understand his phrase in a manner different than the way they would have naturally read it.

The argument made by proponents of the "divorce but no remarriage" view that many church fathers forbid remarriage and that they were closer to the New Testament culture than we are does not help the case against remarriage in Matthew: these same church fathers often read their own culture's growing asceticism into these texts and preferred a literalistic harmonizing of texts to a consideration of what the authors meant in their own historical situation. We must sometimes choose between what the inspired authors were communicating in their own situation and how later Christian interpreters have understood them. The choice should not be too difficult here. The church fathers themselves preferred the earliest Christian traditions to those of their own contemporaries, and Jesus clearly favors the authority of inspired Scripture above that of human tradition (Matt. 15:3–9; Mark 7:5–9).

"EUNUCHS FOR THE KINGDOM'S SAKE"

Some critics of remarriage after divorce have also argued that the paragraph following the divorce saying, which advocates some people becoming "eunuchs for the Kingdom's sake," applies specifically to those who are divorced. Although the text itself says that this injunction applies "only to those to whom it has been given," these writers argue that this parallels 13:11 (despite the different wording) and that it therefore applies to anyone who will really be Jesus' disciple.[52]

This argument should be evaluated from several directions. First, Jesus' other teachings, such as forsaking possessions or family to follow him, never include such a qualification: "This is only for those who can accept it." On the face of it, it would seem that he means that this particular teaching is only for some disciples and not for all.[53] This indeed is how Paul must have taken the saying if he knew it, since he recommends singleness for those with the "gift" of self-control and marriage for all others, including those formerly married (as we shall argue below concerning 1 Cor. 7).

Against this objection, opponents of remarriage have complained that Matthew nowhere singles out one group of disciples as higher than another group.[54] This complaint is somewhat wide of the mark; Jesus may call different disciples to different tasks without some being "superior." For example, he sets apart the Twelve (10:1) from other disciples. Promises to a special group are rare, but do occur (cf. 13:52; 16:17–19, 28; 24:45–51).[55] Statements that grace to meet a requirement to enter the Kingdom is given only to a limited group are also rare; elsewhere in Matthew other discipleship commands are addressed to whomever will submit to them.

Matthew 13:11 (cf. 11:27) is not analogous to the saying in 19:11–12, because it is a statement about what already has taken place, rather than a call to a way of life. If it were analogous to 19:11–12, then 19:11–12 would imply that all believers already have the grace to avoid marriage; but the "let him accept" calls for action, whereas 13:11 does not.[56]

The context also refutes the idea that Jesus' statement is directed only toward the divorced. The disciples, learning that one cannot flee a bad marriage (normally arranged by well-meaning parents), propose that it would be better not to marry to begin with.[57] They are not concerned so much with what Jesus said about remarriage; their solution of not marrying to begin with would surely be counterproductive if that were the basis of their complaint. Rather, they were uncomfortable about his prohibition of divorce except on the narrowest grounds, absolving their right to get out of an intolerable marriage and removing the threat that could keep the wife subordinate.

Jesus' teaching in 19:11–12 is therefore a reply to their remark about *first* marriages, not *remarriages*. Some who are called to live the sort of life the disciples were living with him would, like him, be better unmarried and be able to live this way for the Kingdom.[58] Paul is an example of such a radical lifestyle, although he recognizes that most of the first apostles were married and took their wives with them in their traveling ministries (1 Cor. 9:5).

The language of becoming "eunuchs," quite offensive to Jewish sensitivities, would have grabbed the disciples' attention.[59] A eunuch could not enter into the congregation of Israel (Deut. 23:1); how then could one become a eunuch for the sake of the Kingdom? Further, literal eunuchs were not thought to be devoid of lust, but only of procreative capacity.[60] But Jesus' graphic language here, like his imagery of cutting off hands or feet elsewhere, is designed to communicate a solemn point: the Kingdom is more important than anything else, including marriage, and it will cost some of Jesus' followers the right to marry.[61]

But as in Paul, those who cannot marry refrain not because previously cancelled marital bonds demand it; they abstain from marriage because the nature of their *call* demands it, perhaps because they have no one likeminded who will share their call (a not unusual situation, cf. Phil. 2:20–21). Although Moses and many other prophets were married, some even to prophetesses (Isa. 7:3), others had to bear hardship with regard to their marriages (Ezek. 24:16–18; Hosea 1–3) or were forbidden to marry altogether (Jer. 16:2–4). Such demands had to do with God's specific call, not with previous marital arrangements. All who will heed God's call today must be prepared to accept a celibate lifestyle if this is his calling. Matthew 19:10–12, like 1 Corinthians 7, denies that all disciples are actually able to pursue the lifestyle, but it does require us to accept it if God gives us the call and ability to pursue it.

Of course, finding people today willing to renounce North American materialism and self-centeredness to proclaim Christ and serve human need is difficult enough. Thus many disciples who want to live out the lifestyle of the Kingdom may have trouble finding any spouse, much less a second one, unless revival and repentance come to the church. All believers, whether previously married or not, must be ready to serve Christ radically and wait for a spouse who shares those convictions.

CAN EITHER PARTY DIVORCE?

In Matthew's statements, only the husband has the right of divorce (5:32; 19:9). This follows the Palestinian Jewish law that Matthew addresses. Mark 10:12, however, also warns against the wife divorcing her husband. Which way did Jesus say it?

It is entirely possible that Jesus warned against the wife divorcing her husband with reference to what Herodias and other high-level Jews had done in line with Greek culture.[62] Matthew could have omitted this as irrelevant to his hearers. But it is just as likely that Mark has expanded Jesus' original saying, just as Matthew expanded it in a different way. In the Greco-Roman world as a whole, women also held the right of divorce, and Mark may have wanted to make sure that no one could twist Jesus' particular words to get around his meaning: it applied to both husbands and wives, to whomever had the power of divorce.[63] That Mark has brought out the meaning of Jesus' saying for a different audience by adding the clause is all the more likely if Matthew is correct in placing Jesus' debate here in the context of the discussions of Jewish schools on this issue.

Jesus may thus have been defending the rights of women, who, according to Jewish legal interpretation, could be divorced by a whim of their husbands.[64] The fact that wives were rarely divorced on frivolous grounds—the monetary aspects of the marriage contract would see to that—did not protect in theory those wives who could be.[65]

But Jesus is evidently doing more than just this. He is arguing for the sanctity of the marital union, and arguing that it must not dissolved under any circumstances. If it is dissolved, only the sinned-against partner, who did not dissolve it through adultery or an invalid divorce, is free. This is the real point of Jesus' saying: do not break your marriage. Nurture it, preserve it, live as one with your spouse as it was intended in the beginning. He does not lay extra burdens on those already wounded against their will; indeed, were he to see his words so abused, he would have charged the guilty with the same hardness of heart with which the Pharisees were charged. Just as Moses' words cannot be wrenched from their context, or their original purpose distorted for personal reasons, neither can Jesus' words be removed from the context of Jesus' intention. And if we do not have mercy on others, he has promised that he will not show mercy to us.

CONCLUSION

If we adopt the reading of Matthew 19:9 suggested by those who oppose *all* remarriage following divorce as adultery, we must advocate breaking up all marriages subsequent to the first. Although the present-tense verb in 19:9 need not imply that an invalid remarriage involves continuous adultery during the entire period of cohabitation,[66] this is the only way to take it if we rely on an extremely literal interpretation of the grammar, as those who disallow marriage in this passage otherwise do.

If the first marriage was never dissolved in God's sight, and if adultery cannot dissolve the marriage bonds, then any subsequent sexual activity is by definition adulterous. The only solution to such an adulterous union is to dissolve it, which would mean that all second marriages can be dealt with only by repentance and separation.

Most opponents of remarriage are content to regard remarriage as a past sin and to keep the new marriage intact, but this demonstrates that in practice they are not willing to follow their own strict, culturally uninformed reading of Jesus' words.

If Jesus is not speaking hyperbolically, if any marriage after an invalid divorce is therefore adulterous, it is only because the divorce was invalid and the original partners are still actually married in God's sight. This means that those who intend to hold this strict rendering of the text must be consistent: they must initiate church discipline against all remarried persons as adulterers until they break up the new "marriages." Does this position seem extreme? It is the only consistent conclusion to the no-remarriage interpretation of these texts.

The only example of an invalid union in Matthew is that of Herod and his brother's wife; and John the Baptist, God's spokesperson, gives the only possible solution for such a union: Herod must put her away (Matt. 14:3–4). A union conceived in adultery, a union conceived in reckless disregard for a standing, valid marriage, can only be rectified through dissolving the new union.

But if what we have argued above is true, then a valid divorce—that is, a divorce on valid grounds—permits an innocent party to remarry. If Jesus' language is hyperbolic, of course, we may suppose that God's forgiveness also covers past divorces even for guilty parties, if they have repented and the marriage can no longer be recovered. (I refer here particularly to those who were divorced before their conversions.) But what is at least plain in this text is that remarriage is not forbidden to those divorced with valid grounds.

5 | Paul and Divorce: 1 Corinthians 7:10–16

In this chapter we will find that Paul, like Jesus, permitted divorce and remarriage under specific circumstances but not under others. In the next chapter we will investigate more closely the rest of Paul's argument in 1 Corinthians 7, where we will find that Paul's only words discouraging divorced people's remarriage are no different from his words discouraging marriage in general.

Although Paul seems to have known Jesus' prohibition of divorce in the absolute form in which it appears in Mark, he does not apply Jesus' prohibition to all circumstances. In his view, divorce and remarriage are permissible on appropriate grounds. He permits remarriage of divorced people (1 Cor. 7:27–28) with only the same reticence that he shows for the marriage of virgins (7:36). Although Paul, like the Stoic philosophers, urges contentment with one's present circumstances, he has no objection to improving one's circumstances should the opportunity arise (7:21b).

Before we can read Paul's divorce passage the way the Corinthians themselves would have read it, we must understand something of divorce in the Greco-Roman world. Corinth is located in Greece, but because Corinth was a Roman colony in Paul's day, its culture was both Greek and Roman, as its inscriptions show. An understanding of first-century divorce in both Greek and Roman societies will thus help us better grasp what Paul was saying to his first readers.

DIVORCE IN ANTIQUITY

Divorce had become notoriously common in the fashionable upper classes, so much so that some women were said to divorce in order to remarry and to remarry in order to divorce.[1] Our sources cannot, of course, tell us anything about the percentage of marriages that ended in divorce, and we know even less about how the lower classes, who made up most of the empire, really felt or acted toward it.[2] But divorce was undeniably common enough to dominate upper class gossip preserved for us in the writings of ancient satirists, and it is likely that the scandalous behavior of certain aristocrats attracted the sort of attention the analogous behavior of many movie stars attracts today. In other words, divorce, even scandalous divorce, was a well-known phenomenon in the first-century Roman world.

Although divorce may have been granted only under the most extreme circumstances in earlier Rome,[3] it had long since become quite easy for a Roman man to acquire one.[4] Plutarch, a writer nearly contemporary with the New Testament, implies that any man who fails to seek a divorce when he has a "bad" wife is cowardly:

> Yet it is not difficult for a man to get rid of a bad wife if he be a real man and not a slave . . .

If only vice were so easily eliminated, he laments![5] And by this period,[6] a Roman woman could obtain a divorce as easily as her husband.[7]

Thus a Roman marriage could be terminated by mutual agreement or by either party declaring the marriage ended.[8] Because private consent was what was thought to hold a marriage together, lack of mutual consent in favor of continuing the marriage was held to dissolve the marital bonds.[9] This kind of "no-fault" divorce involved no stigma, and a dying or divorcing husband might even be concerned enough about his ex-wife to arrange a new marriage for her.[10]

This is quite different, of course, from the Jewish custom followed in Roman Palestine, as we observed when we briefly noted Jesus' saying in Mark.[11] In ancient Judaism, only the husband could initiate the divorce, except under the most extreme circumstances in which a court would require him to terminate the marriage at his wife's demand.[12] Since a divorced woman would face definite social stigmas in Palestinian Jewish society,[13] such women probably did not seek divorce often. It thus makes sense that, although Paul seems to use "divorce" and "depart" interchangeably in the rest of 1 Corinthians 7,[14] he tells the wife not to leave and the husband not to divorce her in the passage where he refers back to Jesus' teaching (vv. 10–11),[15] in line with the Palestinian custom.

Although mutual consent was sufficient grounds for divorce in Roman society, particular occasions *demanded* divorce. Under Roman law, adultery required divorce, as we pointed out earlier. Other issues could provide "grounds" for divorce without requiring it. The category of "fault" (Latin *culpa*) became important in disputes about money; the wife might not get her full dowry back if her behavior had led to the divorce.[16] But the idea of a "guilty party" was not commonly brought up in divorces,[17] and "grounds" for divorce were sometimes as light as the desire to improve one's financial status by contracting a more profitable marriage.[18] Plutarch warns that a wife cannot trust in her nobility, wealth, or beauty to protect her, and ought therefore to work all the harder to be a good wife.[19] In other words, Roman law provided little security against a person being divorced on weak or spurious grounds.

What we know of Jewish practice outside of Palestine suggests that Jewish people in the Greco-Roman world generally adopted Greco-Roman customs with regard to divorce;[20] this probably means that they, too, permitted it in most cases. Of course, with regard to the *man's* prerogatives, many of the Jewish teachers even in Palestine were quite liberal with divorce, as we noted above;[21] divorcing a wife who was hard to get along with was not at all impious. As a pre-Christian Jewish wisdom teacher points out:

> If she (your wife) does not go as your hand directs, then cut her off from your flesh.[22]

It is said that when the early second-century Rabbi Jose the Galilean could not come up with sufficient funds to divorce his wife (because he would have to pay her dowry), the other sages took up a collection for him.[23] The thought that divorce in general could be immoral apparently never crossed their minds. Philo, a Jewish philosopher living in culturally Greek Alexandria, also agreed with these lenient rabbis.[24] Divorces were not hard for Jewish men to obtain.

This is not to say that most people in the ancient world thought that divorce was a pleasant matter. The Roman philosopher Seneca, a contemporary of Paul, observed that

> Anger brings to a father grief, to a husband divorce, to a magistrate hatred, to a candidate defeat.[25]

Rabbi Eliezer, an early second-century Jewish teacher, complained,

For him who divorces the first wife, the very altar sheds tears.[26]

Whether viewed as tragic or normal, however, divorce occurred often enough in the ancient world for it to be an issue in Paul's churches. It was certainly an issue in Corinth, and this is why Paul must take time to address it in his letter to the Corinthian Christians.

THE SOURCE OF PAUL'S WISDOM

There appear to be two kinds of authoritative material in this passage. Although much of Paul's wisdom in this chapter is said to be "his opinion" (7:12), some of it is directly attributed to Jesus: "the Lord, not I, gives instructions" (7:10). Since Paul thinks that even "his opinion" here is inspired by the Spirit (7:40)—and we who today read this letter in our Bible would agree—what he, and "not the Lord," says, still claims inspiration, and he must mean something by "the Lord says, not I," other than just, "This particular point is inspired by God."

The prevailing scholarly opinion on these verses is that Paul is citing a saying spoken by Jesus while he was on earth, the same saying, in fact, that we have in our Gospels.[27] This saying may have existed in two different forms, as we intimated previously; but regardless of whether Paul knew the form from Jesus' debate with the Pharisees or from his teaching on the law, what is more significant is that Paul, like Matthew, feels the need to qualify the saying. Yes, the Lord rules out divorce; but no, this is not a universal ruling. In Paul's view, it is instead a general principle which admits some exceptions.[28]

What this means is, that Matthew's limitation of Jesus' point was not just Matthew's unique way of handling the saying. Paul, like Matthew and presumably any first-century Jewish expositor, recognized that scriptural laws had to be interpreted. For example, anyone who wished to avoid "working" on the Sabbath would need to define the meaning of "work." Scripture forbade the work involved in cooking on the Sabbath, but not the work involved in chewing one's food; what sort of activities lying somewhere between these two examples should be considered "work"? In the same way, Jesus' prohibition against divorce is a general statement, and even if it is taken as law rather than as proverb, law must be interpreted and qualified when it is applied to a variety of new situations that it did not originally address.

If Paul is inspired by the same Spirit who was in Jesus, it is noteworthy that he is willing to give only his *opinion* that those divorced not remarry;[29] he states their *freedom* to remarry as fact. Therefore all who respect his teaching in 1 Corinthians as inspired and authoritative, even if they reject the part which Paul says is his opinion, must recognize that remarriage after a divorce is permitted under some circumstances. The issue in this passage is, under what circumstances of divorce was remarriage to be permitted?

THE CIRCUMSTANCES OF DIVORCE

Paul makes it clear, on the basis of Jesus' teaching, that neither the husband nor the wife is permitted to leave the other. If the wife does leave, her options are to remain single or to return to her husband. This is the general principle, and it expressly opposes divorce and summons Christians to work for reconciliation in their marriage.

But now Paul must address a situation that Jesus, addressing Jewish hearers in Palestine, had not addressed. What if a Christian man has a pagan wife, or if a Christian woman has a pagan husband? To be sure, not everyone in Jewish Palestine had a godly spouse, either; but outside of Jewish Palestine, Jews ran into more non-Jews, and most non-Jews sacrificed to idols. Could there be any sort of spiritual union with people who worshiped idols (2 Cor. 6:15)? Paul's own words written on an earlier occasion (1 Cor. 5:9–10) might have been taken to mean that there could not be. Some Christians may have taken this as a cue to divorce non-Christian spouses. But as Paul points out (1 Cor. 5:10–11), breaking all relations with non-Christians was not what he had meant. Christians could have non-Christian friends, but they were to avoid those who claimed to be Christians but did not live like Christians.

To acknowledge that Paul did not want Christians to divorce non-Christian spouses is not to suggest that Paul would have thought it acceptable to marry pagans in the first place.[30] But it must be kept in mind that most first marriages were arranged by parents,[31] who, if they were not Christians, might want to marry their son or daughter to a good idolater. Children probably had a large measure of say in the marriage arrangements,[32] but parental scruples had no small effect on the outcome.[33] Further—and this is presumably the main reason for religiously mixed marriages in Corinth—many of the Christians were first-generation converts out of paganism and were married before they became Christians.[34] Now that they found themselves in a marriage with a spiritually incompatible husband or wife, what were they to do?[35]

Paul's answer is that the believer should stay with the unbeliever unless the unbeliever is the one who dissolves the marriage covenant by leaving (7:10–13). In other words, Paul grants an exception to Jesus' general principle against divorce and remarriage, and the exception allows that a believer might be divorced or deserted by a spouse against his or her will.[36] These circumstances are not the believer's choice, and the believer is therefore "not under bondage" (v. 15). An innocent party unable to preserve the marriage against the spouse's will is not to be held responsible for the divorce or forbidden to remarry. For our churches to hold the innocent party responsible and forbid remarriage is to deny Paul's teaching and to oppress the broken. But incompatibility, even spiritual incompatibility, is not grounds for divorce.

Perhaps those Corinthians appealing to spiritual incompatibility as grounds for divorce could have responded to Paul by citing some of Jesus' other teachings; perhaps they had even picked up some of their ideas on divorcing their spouses from what Paul had told them that Jesus taught. Was not a disciple supposed to be willing to leave family for the sake of the Kingdom and expect to find recompense for that loss in the fellowship of the body of Christ (Mark 10:29–30)?[37]

If these Corinthians had this idea, however, they were missing the point of what Jesus had said: a disciple must indeed be ready to suffer the loss of family for the gospel, but this permanent leaving of family is instigated by the family's opposition (Matt. 10:34–38) or their reaction to what they would perceive as the unreasonable demands of the Kingdom (Matt. 8:22).[38] The disciple, then, does not willfully institute the break, for Jesus undeniably did not advocate breaking family bonds (Mark 7:9–13; Matt. 15:3–9).

Jesus' call for a disciple to proclaim the Kingdom might mean a temporary suspension of the disciple's contact with his or her family, and a disciple must obey that call no matter what the cost (e.g., Mark 1:16–20; 10:28); but under normal circumstances, any long-term preaching ministry would allow the preachers to take their spouses with them (1 Cor. 9:5). This could well lead to divorce if the spouse were intolerant of the disciple's new vocation, but Jesus' principle in the divorce passage shows that the disciple should seek to preserve the marriage at all costs short of disobedience to Jesus' call. Only the unbeliever is permitted to walk out of the marriage, because only the unbeliever is not following Jesus.

THE SITUATION IN CORINTH: RELIGIOUSLY MIXED MARRIAGES

First Corinthians 7:10–16 shows that the main reason Paul must address the divorce issue is that some of the married Christians in Corinth wanted to get out of marriages with non-Christians. This is self-evident, but a more detailed understanding of this specific situation is still a matter of dispute among scholars.

Some scholars have argued that 1 Corinthians 7:12–16 alludes to Paul's own experience: at his conversion, his wife left him. This view is problematic, however: if his wife were devout in the law, she would not have left him merely on account of his conversion to faith in Jesus; Jewish laws did not permit wives to divorce their husbands on such grounds.[39] Presumably, then, Paul before his conversion was just one of those rare young Jewish scholars who had not yet married, and this passage does not allude to his own experience.

One scholar has suggested that what is at issue in this passage is that a marriage was being broken up over the issue of conjugal rights (7:3–4) and that Paul found these grounds inadequate for divorce. Paul thus goes on to give the real grounds on which a divorce could be based in 7:15.[40] Although this theory is plausible, we should note that the subject of divorce comes up only as a second category in Paul's treatment of marriage, not in relation to the conjugal rights issue of 1 Corinthians 7:1–6; had he had the specific instance of divorce for celibacy in mind, he probably would have mentioned it at the beginning of the chapter. Paul in 1 Corinthians 7 addresses marriage and celibacy in general, and only in 7:10–16, where he focuses on whether divorce on the grounds of spiritual incompatibility is acceptable, does he directly address divorce.

It is thus probable that Paul addresses the issue of divorce on grounds of spiritual incompatibility simply because this was a live issue in the Corinthian church. Because Paul had information from the members of this church about their disputes (7:1), he would have access to discussion about conflicts in Corinth where the validity of religiously mixed marriages was disputed. Such marriages would have been especially difficult for Roman women of some social standing (cf. 1 Pet. 3:1–6),[41] but Christian husbands may also have wished to divorce their wives if they refused to follow their husbands' religious preferences as society expected them to do.[42]

The Corinthians who looked to spiritual incompatibility as an excuse for divorce may have built their case on arguments already available in their culture. In the Greek translation of the Jewish Bible, Ezra's holy decree compelled Israelites who had married pagan wives to divorce them. The passage uses the same word Paul uses for breaking the marital union here and describes this breaking of the union as "God's will."[43]

Further, according to much later rabbinic laws, the wife of an apostate to paganism could secure a divorce from her husband.[44] This is not the same thing, of course, as a convert from paganism securing a divorce from someone who was already a pagan when the marriage took place, but it shows the terms in which some people viewed religiously mixed marriages. A husband could naturally divorce his wife for behavior that he might consider religiously inappropriate or sinful,[45] such as serving him untithed food or having intercourse with him during the unlawful part of her month;[46] to dwell with such a wife was said to be like dwelling with a serpent.[47] Divorce on moral or spiritual grounds was thus a concept already available in Palestinian Judaism, and related ideas could have influenced some of the Christians in Corinth.

In a later period, rabbis could annul marriages that had been initiated in a manner contrary to rabbinic teaching.[48] If such a practice were known in Corinth in Paul's day, it is possible that preconversion marriages to pagans may have been viewed retroactively as flawed (i.e., what God had not joined together), and some Corinthian Christians may have wished to be free of such flawed marriages.

Similarly, many Jewish people believed that all a Gentile's previous relationships were severed upon conversion to Judaism, because a convert to Judaism was "like a new-born child." It was, in fact, a commonplace that a proselyte's status was that of a newborn child.[49] The convert was no longer the person he had been as a Gentile; his legal standing was that of an Israelite.[50] The line of demarcation, of course, was the ritual cleansing in proselyte baptism.[51] Thus a marriage between two pagans might be seen as invalidated by the conversion of one of the two partners to Judaism.[52]

It is true, of course, that we have no evidence that Jewish propagandists in the Greco-Roman world sought to break up existing marriages; indeed, they wanted to avoid any impression that this was their intention.[53] But if the Christians in Corinth were familiar with some Palestinian Jewish rules, such rules could have supplied the sort of thinking on which they based their argument that as new people in Christ, they no longer needed to fulfill old obligations incurred before their conversion.

Whatever the specific basis on which they argued their case, there were certain social patterns that would have led these Corinthian Christians to think as they did. Marriage tensions were often generated by social disparity between marriage partners. Philosophers commonly warned against marrying a woman of superior social status, because she would consider herself superior to her husband.[54] Not all social classes could legally intermarry under Roman law, although they sometimes did so in violation of that law.[55] This had implications for the social status of the children, as we shall observe below. It is therefore clear that there was already a strong taboo against social intermarriage in antiquity,[56] and when this concept was applied to religious intermarriage, it naturally could bring the spiritual validity of such marriages into question.

But Paul argues that the marriage contracted under any honest grounds is a valid marriage and cannot be dissolved simply because the couple is religiously mixed. While such a marriage is not the ideal, and Paul would presumably oppose initiating a religiously mixed marriage,[57] once initiated it is valid and must be honored.

Paul also addresses what should be done if one spouse has already defected from the marriage. If one person walks out of the marriage without adequate grounds, that person must then remain single rather than remarry, just as Jewish women were not allowed to remarry without a valid certificate of divorce.[58] The ideal is for the differences to be resolved and the couple to get back together; this is what Paul means by, "let her be reconciled to her husband."[59] Jewish law permitted husbands to take their divorced wives back, as long as they had not already remarried, and this seems to have been a common practice.[60]

"FOR THE CHILDREN'S SAKE"

Paul's argument against divorce in 1 Corinthians 7:14 sounds obscure to most modern readers. Although many parents today avoid divorcing "for the sake of the children,"[61] what Paul meant is quite obviously different than what we normally mean by that phrase today:

> For the husband who is not a Christian is nevertheless set apart for God by his wife, and the wife who is not a Christian is set apart for God by one of our Christian brothers in the same way. This must be the case, because otherwise, your children would be counted unclean; but as it is, they are counted as holy.[62]

But his argument would have been easier for a first-century reader to follow than it is today, because it addresses an issue that was a concern in antiquity but is no longer discussed today. The status of the children of socially and religiously mixed marriages was a matter of much discussion among legislators back then.

Roman laws addressed the status of children whose parents belonged to different social classes. While official Roman marriages were only for Roman citizens and not for citizens marrying non-citizens, such marriages were sometimes granted to "Latins" and "foreigners" marrying Romans out of concern for the status of the children.[63] In non-mixed marriages, too, the children's status depended on that of one of the parents; in a purely Roman marriage, the child would take the father's status, and in a purely non-Roman marriage, the child would take the mother's status.[64] Marriages between free Romans and slaves that had not yet been freed were not allowed.[65]

Similarly, one of the issues commonly discussed among Jewish experts in the law was the suitability of different classes of people for intermarriage.

> And they examine [his scroll] in the court of the priests, in the court of the Levites, and in the court of the Israelites who are of suitable genealogical character to marry into the priesthood.[66]

An Israelite girl who married a priest was raised to priestly status; similarly, a priest's daughter who married an Israelite "descends from the priesthood."[67] Although Hillelites and Shammaites, two schools of Jewish teachers in the first century, were permitted to intermarry, their views were divergent enough to raise the question of the propriety of such marriages.[68]

Much of this issue revolved around how intermarriage between different social groups would affect the status of the offspring. Later rabbis, for instance, appealed to what they believed was a very early law to argue that the offspring of an Israelite girl to a Gentile or a slave was illegitimate.[69] Of course, in the case of children of a pagan couple, there was much less to be resolved: some early rabbis, uncomfortable with either saving or damning the children of pagans in the day of judgment, simply decided that they would neither live nor be judged in the world to come.[70]

The status of the offspring was especially an issue with regard to the children of proselytes, and it became an issue of intricate discussion among later Jewish legal scholars. A child conceived in the womb of a proselyte was a full Israelite; but if the mother converted between the child's conception and birth, the child had the status of an Israelite from the mother's side but not the father's.[71] The status of the child of a man who had performed only part of the ceremony of conversion when his Jewish wife conceived was also debated.[72] After conversion, a proselyte was "holy,"[73] i.e., set apart as part of God's people, and so would be any children conceived after his or her conversion.[74] Thus in a later Jewish commentary, a rabbi could argue that the son of the Jewess Esther and the pagan Ahasuerus was "pure" on his mother's side but not on his father's.[75]

Most modern discussions of this passage thus fall wide of the mark. The passage does not mean that children are automatically saved by virtue of one of the parents being Christian;[76] nor does it mean that the infants of Christians baptized in infancy are saved.[77] (One scholar has argued, in fact, that this passage means that Christian children, just like girls in Jewish homes, were part of God's people without receiving a seal of the covenant, and thus that it *excludes* infant baptism.[78])

But the "holiness" at issue here is an issue of status and not of salvation at all. The unbelieving partner may be "set apart," or made holy (7:14), but he or she is clearly not saved (7:16).[79] There is thus no reason to think that the salvation of the children is implied by their "holiness," either. Paul elsewhere argues too forcefully that faith in Christ rather than natural descent is the basis of salvation (Rom. 9–11; Gal. 3–4) to abandon that position here.

Paul seems to be arguing that the children are still in the sphere of gospel influence even if only one parent is saved;[80] and even if the other partner is pagan and might influence the children wrongly, it is not an excuse to withdraw from the marriage.[81] Of course, Paul, like Jesus, is making something of a general statement based on the situation he is addressing. In a culture like our own, where one parent can take the children, would Paul advise the one parent to stay if the other were urging the kids to take drugs or sell their bodies, or if they were being abused?[82] My guess is that in such a specific case he would advise the one parent to take the children and leave, at least temporarily. But Paul's statement works as a general principle: the children cannot be used as an excuse to divorce an unbelieving spouse.

THE BELIEVER IS "NOT UNDER BONDAGE"

Although Paul's point in this passage is unquestionably that divorce should be avoided in all normal circumstances, he also distinctly frees the *innocent* party to remarry in v. 15:

> If the marriage partner who does not believe in Christ walks out or terminates the union, let him go. The Christi..n brother or sister is not "under bondage" (bound[83] to the marriage) in such cases; but God has called us to peace (with everyone).

Some writers here assert that while separation or divorce is permitted here, remarriage is not,[84] but their position is mistaken. As Harrell points out, remarriage was the normal course sought after a divorce; as in Deuteronomy 24,

> Rabbinical law also assumes that remarriage would be the normal course. Thus the essential phrase of the bill of divorcement was, "Thou art free to any man."[85]

The Jewish legal passage in question is Mishnah Gittin 9:3, which reads:

> The essential formula in the bill of divorce is, "Lo, thou art free to marry any man." R. Judah says: "Let this be from me thy writ of divorce and letter of dismissal and deed of liberation, that thou mayest marry whatsoever man thou wilt." The essential formula in a writ of emancipation is, "Lo, thou art a freedwoman: lo, thou belongest to thyself."[86]

The ancient Jewish marriage contracts we have found agree: in the context of divorce, "free" meant precisely that the woman was free to remarry, and meant nothing else than this.[87]

If Paul meant that remarriage was not permitted, he said precisely the opposite of what he meant. No first-century reader would have derived the meaning that some modern scholars have read into Paul's words, perhaps because no first-century Christian reader felt that Jesus' general teaching was meant to apply to every specific case. Those modern scholars who have argued against remarriage under all circumstances have not only read their thinking into

Paul's words because they do not understand him; they have also read their thinking into Jesus' words because they have not understood him, and they read their misunderstanding of Jesus into Paul. We may suspect that Paul understood Jesus considerably better than these scholars do.

BEING CONTENT WITH ONE'S SITUATION

This does not, of course, constitute a *requirement* that the believer remarry. The believer is, in fact, to be content in the situation in which she or he finds herself or himself. Paul shares this ethic with many of the Stoic philosophers of his day,[88] who could also speak of marriage as less than crucial. What should a man seek, Epictetus asks?

> To marry? No; but if marriage be given to him, to maintain himself as one who in these circumstances is in harmony with nature.[89]

The principle, Paul says, applies not only to marriage, but to other "givens" in our lives as well. It is said that many Jews in wishing to appear respectable to the Greeks surgically disguised their circumcision;[90] but Paul admonishes that neither should Gentiles seek to be circumcised nor should Jews seek to efface their circumcision—one state was not better than the other (7:18–19).[91] In the same way, slaves are truly free in Christ,[92] and those who are free are Christ's slaves (7:21–22);[93] one should thus be content with one's situation (7:24). Paul's point in this context is that those who are single should not seek to be married, and (especially) those who are married should not seek a divorce.

But contentment does not mean idleness. It means accepting situations one cannot change, not ignoring opportunities to change one's status if such opportunities are available. As the classical Greek rhetorician Isocrates put it:

> Be content with your present lot, but seek a better one.[94]

Paul is unequivocal that a slave should achieve freedom if this becomes possible (7:21, 23). His argument is therefore not a case against changing one's condition under any circumstances;[95] it is only an argument that one must be content in one's current situation. Just as the Stoics taught contentment in all things, but at least the theoretical equality and hope for emancipation for slaves,[96] Paul could teach contentment that nevertheless permitted

believers to improve their situation. He thus does not use contentment to rule out the possibility of remarriage, but to rule out
improper divorce and to invite those meant for singleness to pursue
that course, as we shall see in the next chapter.

REMARRIAGE AND SIN

In 1 Corinthians 7:27–28, Paul says that remarriage—like the
marriage of a virgin—has problems, but also that it is not sinful:

> Are you bound (in marriage) to a wife? Do not seek to be free (from
> the marriage). Have you been freed (from a marriage)? Do not seek to
> be bound (again in marriage). But even should you marry, you have not
> sinned; and similarly, if a woman who has not been married before gets
> married, she has not sinned.

Paul does not say "free," but "freed." The person who is "freed"
can therefore only be a person who was previously bound, and in
the context this can only mean that the person was previously
married.[97] Given the fact that "freed" in the first line refers to
divorce, we must take it as referring to divorce in the second line
as well; if Paul did not mean us to take the word the same way in
the same set of instructions, he could have indicated this easily
enough by using a different word.

Paul in v. 27 discourages remarriage with an absolute statement,
"Do not seek to be married again"; but immediately qualifies that
admonition by showing that he means it only as advice (7:28). The
references to virgins in 7:28 and, indeed, in 7:36–38, show that
Paul's discouragement of remarriage for those once married is only
on the same level as his discouragement of marriage for virgins.
Those who disallow remarriage for divorcees under all circumstances must also prohibit marriage for virgins. Although the word
Paul uses for those previously unmarried ("virgins") was normally
used in antiquity only for chaste women,[98] Paul would presumably
have applied the same argument to "male virgins."[99]

Paul's reticence about marriage is partly in view of the suffer-
ings Christians were experiencing and could expect in this age
(7:26);[100] in this he agrees with Jesus (Mark 13:17), Jeremiah (Jer.
16:2–4), and some later Jewish writers expecting the end of the
age to happen quickly.[101] But he certainly does not forbid marriage; he merely warns that it will have its difficulties.

Given the stress of life in this world, one who was single had an advantage in devoting undistracted attention to God's work.[102] Marital love naturally involves a degree of obsession with its object.[103] The Jewish marriage contract itself bound both husband and wife to duties which they had to perform for one another[104] and from which they would only be freed by the other's consent. The freedom from any attachment other than the call of God is indeed a great blessing to anyone who is emotionally suited for it (7:7; Matt. 19:11–12).[105]

We may understand Paul's argument on the analogy of some other thinkers in antiquity who had made similar points. It was presumably to be free from worldly concern that Cynic philosophers, while providing for themselves sexual release, normally did not marry. But despite the general rule, there were exceptions; if a woman were truly willing to share the philosopher's lifestyle, he might be willing to marry her.

One ancient writer tells us the story of Crates, the successor to the famous Cynic Diogenes, and his wife Hipparchia. She pursued Crates diligently, ignoring his rebuffs, until finally he stripped before her and said,

> This is the bridegroom, here are his possessions; make your choice accordingly; for you will be no helpmeet [lit., partaker] of mine, unless you share my pursuits.[106]

As the writer goes on to note,

> The girl chose and, adopting the same dress, went about with her husband and lived with him in public and went to dinners with him.[107]

She adopted the crude Cynic way of life and became famous for doing so. This is true even though a later Cynic writer, skeptical that a woman could actually adapt to such a lifestyle, penned a letter in Crates' name criticizing her for faltering a bit in it.[108]

Paul's discussion of this subject employs standard Stoic terms for being free from distraction, and like them he probably believed that marriage was profitable for some but distracting to others.[109] But he differed from them in making the appropriate object of undivided attention our Lord Jesus Christ.

All followers of Jesus would agree that we who call Jesus Lord must follow him wholeheartedly and without compromise. The question that arises is whether Paul thinks that all believers could do that better single or whether singleness is more like fasting: fasting is a profitable way to seek God, but not everyone is physically capable of fasting for the same length of time. If the former is true, then maintaining singleness is the proper goal for all single Christians; if the latter is true, then while singleness provides a great spiritual advantage, it is not meant for all believers.

To decide whether Paul wants all or only some Christians to remain single, we must examine the first part of 1 Corinthians 7 in light of the situation it is addressing. This is important because Paul gives the same instructions to divorced people and to virgins; he either recommends continued singleness for those among both groups who are fitted for it, or he recommends it across the board for all believers among both groups and thinks being "fitted for it" is just an excuse by those less committed to God than he is. This we will examine in the next chapter.

CONCLUSION

Our conclusions here agree essentially with those of Harrell:

From the foregoing discussion, it seems possible to draw the following conclusions: (1) Paul permits Christians who are partners in a mixed marriage to be divorced if the non-believer so desires; (2) the Christian is therefore not under bondage and is free to remarry; (3) Paul is stating on his apostolic authority a reason for divorce not previously mentioned in the New Testament.[110]

Paul does not permit divorce on the grounds of incompatibility; the believer is to do everything in his or her power to make the marriage work. But if the other spouse ends the marriage, and the believer in good conscience knows that he or she has worked hard to keep that marriage together, he or she is free to remarry.

The church, which cannot see human hearts or private situations the way God does, will not always know if one party was actually innocent in the matter of the divorce. (Obviously, we believe that *both* parties cannot be innocent, because a marriage cannot be ended without at least *one* person's desire to end it.) I know of people who purposely acted in such a way as to drive their spouses to divorce them, and then blamed the divorce on the spouse (who must nevertheless share the blame for seeking the divorce if it was not necessary). But I also know of innocent people who were slandered by their spouses when the spouses left them, who were deeply hurt when the body of Christ believed the slander.

The Bible holds the partner who engages in unrepentant adultery or seeks divorce responsible for the end of the marriage, for that partner is closing the door to healing in the marriage; and if the wronged partner is seeking reconciliation, the wronged partner is not to be interrogated concerning where on the range between a "perfect" and a "mediocre" spouse he or she might have fallen. God who knows the hearts of us all will ultimately vindicate or condemn; but his church, if it errs, must err on the side of mercy rather than of judgment. Paul allows for the existence and remarriage of an innocent party, and it is time that many Christians today learn to do the same.

6   1 Corinthians 7 and Marriage

Although Paul in 1 Corinthians 7 allows some divorced people to remarry, parts of the chapter look as if he discourages them from doing so. In fact, the same passages appear as if Paul discourages *all* single people from marrying to begin with. Is singleness the highest call for all believers? The answer to this question is at least as relevant to the divorced believer as it is to the believer who has never married. The advantages of singleness may be the same both for divorced people and for never-married people; likewise, the same human needs may lead both to seek marriage. The questions this passage raises for our study of remarriage thus cannot be ignored.

In this chapter, then, we will examine Paul's praises of the single lifestyle, asking what situations prompted Paul to write these words, and whether he advocates this lifestyle for all, or only for some, devoted believers.

1 CORINTHIANS 7 IN ITS CONTEXT

One problem Paul addressed in Corinth and in much of ancient society is a problem with which most readers will be familiar in our culture today: sex outside of marriage. The themes of sex and marriage tie together most of 1 Corinthians 5–7. In 1 Corinthians 5, Paul addresses a specific sexual offense committed by a member of the congregation in Corinth and prescribes church discipline for the offender. In 1 Corinthians 6:1–11, he continues to recommend church discipline, criticizing members of the congregation for dragging the church's dirty laundry before secular courts.[1] In

6:12–20, Paul addresses a much broader base of sexual immorality in the church; some of the members are patronizing prostitutes! When we reach 1 Corinthians 7, however, we find that not everyone is so keen on having sexual relations. Some members of the congregation, in fact, are against the one kind of sexual relationship that Paul permits, namely, marriage. These same members appear to be even abstaining from sex within marriage. Paul begins the chapter by stating and perhaps qualifying their own premise: a man should not touch a woman sexually (7:1). He then challenges the practice that has resulted from this premise, arguing that it is a little late to espouse this view now that they are married (7:2–5). He goes on in the rest of the chapter to concede part of their position, listing the advantages of the single life, but always diplomatically pointing out that they should not impose their preference for singleness on others who wish to be married.

Paul's reproof in 1 Corinthians 6 is much stronger than his case in 1 Corinthians 7, because the issues are different. He absolutely prohibits sex before or outside of marriage; but individuals may choose whether to seek marriage or remain single, based on the particular gifts God has given them and the situation in which he has placed them.

It is possible that chapters 6 and 7 deal with two sides of the same coin. Some Greek ideals of devotion to God ruled out marriage because it would tie a person down, but nevertheless approved of sex with prostitutes. Some of the Corinthians may have followed this model of devotion and even used it as an excuse to abstain from sex within marriage. In the sections of this chapter which immediately follow, we shall examine how people looked at singleness and marriage in the ancient world as the background for the issues Paul must address in 1 Corinthians 7. Against the backdrop of these issues, it should become clear that the basis for choosing singleness or marriage is not whether or not one has been married before, but the nature of one's gifting and whether or not one is able to change one's situation.

SINGLENESS AND CELIBACY IN GRECO-ROMAN THOUGHT

Many Greco-Roman writers who opposed marriage nevertheless thought that sex apart from marriage was fine, and this distinction between sex and marriage will recur at various points in the following discussion. Many Greek philosophers, for instance, thought that marriage was an unnecessary encumbrance, but nevertheless assumed that sexual release with prostitutes was a normal male activity. Of course, for anyone who held such philosophical views about marriage and yet morally opposed sex outside of marriage, as some Jewish groups did, the only alternative would be true celibacy. As we shall see, this was not a popular position in antiquity, but it did gain some adherents.

Most people in antiquity felt that marriage and active sexuality were the norm. Certain philosophers, like the Stoics, were concerned to perpetuate themselves[2] and society[3] through procreation. The Stoic thinker Musonius Rufus believed that marriage was ordained by Nature itself:

> For, to what other purpose did the creator of mankind first divide our human race into two sexes, male and female, then implant in each a strong desire for association and union with the other? . . . Is it not then plain that he wished the two to be united and live together, and by their joint efforts to devise a way of life in common?[4]

Philosophers were not alone in this sort of thinking; propagandists for the policies of the Roman State also advocated marriage. In the late Republic and early empire, marriage and childbearing were emphasized for the sake of maintaining the number of aristocrats in the Roman world,[5] and Augustus, concerned about the decline of the aristocracy, instituted strict laws ensuring that upper class women marry and bear children.[6] Augustus' legislation did not discourage divorce per se, but it did insist on rapid remarriage and the bearing of more children.[7]

Marriage was also the normal desire of most young women we read about in ancient literature. In the beginning of the story of Cupid and Psyche, everyone marveled at Psyche's beauty, but it meant nothing to her, because while her less beautiful sisters were already married, she was not, and she lamented her singleness.[8] In other romances, as well, the longing for marriage is obvious; it was considered a great honor for a man to gain a widely coveted, beautiful wife.[9] Tomb inscriptions had long attested the tragedy of dying unmarried, for instance, in a sixth century BC Athenian inscription:

> The tomb of Phrasicleia: I shall be called a maiden always. This is the name the gods gave me in place of "wife."[10]

Similarly, a sixth century BC satirical poet jibed:

The two best days in a woman's life are when someone marries her and when he carries her dead body to the grave.[11]

But while marriage had long been the goal of most young men and women, this goal was not shared by everyone. Some refused to marry for fear of broken trust;[12] others argued that homosexual practices were superior to heterosexual activity and regarded women as dangerous;[13] others had religious or philosophical reasons to avoid marriage or sex.

One of the religious contexts in which celibacy was praised was the order of Vestal Virgins. The Vestal Virgins constituted a revered order of Roman women who maintained perpetual virginity.[14] If they were voluntarily defiled, they would be buried alive;[15] the trouble their defilement brought from the gods against Rome had once been appeased only through human sacrifice.[16] Their virginity somehow suggested some sort of spiritual power on behalf of Rome, perhaps because it represented such a remarkable sacrifice in that culture.[17] Nowhere, however, was it suggested that all Roman women should follow the ideal of the Vestals; it was enough that normal women be chaste matrons faithful to their husbands.

Cults far less popular with the Roman aristocracy may have also advocated celibacy. Contrary to some scholars' suggestions, this probably does not include the priests of Isis except for temporary abstinence. They had to be very chaste,[18] but this probably only meant abstention from extramarital sex and temporary abstinence in marriage for purity reasons,[19] such as was also found in other cults.[20]

The priests of Cybele, the Galli, were certainly pledged to celibacy; the initiation rite included their castration.[21] But this was not a popular religious ideal in Roman society; the general response to this mutilation, aside from ridicule, was one of revulsion;[22] those who were thus emasculated were said by the Stoics to no longer be men.[23] Although the supposed allusion to the practice of the Galli in Galatians 5:12 is dubious,[24] Paul was presumably aware of their practice; but it is doubtful that the status-conscious Corinthian Christians would have appealed to such a socially unappealing model for their own celibacy.

But what such religions may have advocated for the few, some philosophers saw as an ideal for the many. The classical Greek philosopher Antisthenes had some reservations about marriage,[25] and Plato's view of the body as a hindrance[26] could naturally lead to further such reservations. A mediating position is assigned to the ideal wise man Socrates:

> Some one asked him whether he should marry or not, and received the reply, "Whichever you do you will repent it."[27]

But Cynics like Diogenes went considerably farther:

> Being asked what was the right time to marry, Diogenes replied, "For a young man not yet; for an old man never at all."[28]

And a later writer, in Diogenes' name, protests that

> One should not wed nor raise children, since our race is weak and marriage and children burden human weakness with troubles. Therefore, those who move toward wedlock and the rearing of children on account of the support these promise, later experience a change of heart when they come to know that they are characterized by even greater hardships. But it is possible to escape right from the start.[29]

As noted in the preceding chapter, of course, the Cynics opposed marriage not out of opposition to a sexual relationship per se, but because it involved distraction. Cynics had other ways of relieving their sexual appetites,[30] so this does not exactly represent a pledge to celibacy. But it does indicate that not everyone shared the prevailing Greco-Roman emphasis on marriage.

Pythagoras is alleged to have discouraged intercourse, at least during much of the year;[31] Epicurus felt that the wise man would not marry or raise a family, with rare exceptions.[32] Many Stoic philosophers challenged these other philosophers' mistrust of marriage or intercourse. Epictetus, a Stoic, takes the Epicurean position to task:

> In the name of God, I ask you, can you imagine an Epicurean State? One man says, "I do not marry." "Neither do I," says another, "for people ought not to marry." No, nor have children; no, nor perform the duties of a citizen. And what, do you suppose, will happen then? Where are the citizens to come from?[33]

While Epictetus did not discourage marriage, he did discourage premarital sex; but even here he insisted that abstainers not require it of others.[34] This is the *closest* we get to Epictetus advocating any sort of celibacy, although he himself did not marry until his old age. Other Stoics also opposed philosophical schools that advocated celibacy.[35]

The fact that some philosophers had to argue against the celibacy position only confirms our view that a case for celibacy was known and defended in their time. The philosophical arguments against celibacy thus provide further evidence that some people in the ancient world opposed either marriage, sex, or both.

MARRIAGE AS NECESSITY IN EARLY JUDAISM

Greek and Roman writers usually urged marriage and rarely urged celibacy. Many of those who urged singleness still advocated sexual release by other means, whether through prostitutes or self-stimulation. As we shall see, most of Judaism condemned celibacy at least as strongly as Greek and Roman writers did; but those who did oppose marriage in some or all cases would have been closer to Paul than most non-Jewish writers, because they agreed with him that godly people should abstain from sexual activity outside of marriage.

Marriage was vital in Judaism. In Genesis 2:18 God had already said that it was not good for man to be alone, and no one thought that he had changed his mind since then.[36] The bulk of early Jewish literature which has survived to our day thus portrays marriage in a very positive light, but celibacy in a very negative one.

It was thought arrogant for noble young men to not get married; meanwhile, young women grieved, waiting for good husbands.[37] A second-century rabbi tells of the sorry fate of a young man who spoke contemptuously of women, thinking that none of those available were good enough for him: when he grew older and wished to marry, no young woman wanted to marry such an old man.[38]

There were of course other reasons for marrying early, like propagating one's family name and the human race. Ps-Phocylides admonishes:

Do not remain unmarried, lest you die nameless.
Give nature her due, you also, beget in your turn as you were begotten.[39]

Many teachers also thought that marriage was the only way young men could be protected from the wrong response to sexual desires. One later rabbi is said to have brought presents for his wife continually, although she was always harassing him, because, as he put it, "It is sufficient for us . . . that they rear up our children and deliver us from sin."[40] Another said, "As soon as a man takes a wife his sins are buried."[41] Some rabbis encouraged a young marriage for Torah scholars, to prevent distraction by temptation.[42] This was at least to some degree a physical matter; a later story is told of disciples who had to sit through a rabbi's lectures so long that they became impotent, probably implying that restraining their semen for too long damaged their bodies.[43]

They were also convinced that God shared their convictions about marrying and bearing children. Some later rabbis listed at the head of seven things banned by heaven, "A Jew who has no wife; [and] he who has a wife but no children. . . ."[44] Some Jewish teachers thought that one who had no wife "dwells without good, without help, without joy, without blessing, and without atonement."[45] This indicates that one was not only missing a great blessing,[46] but that one was sinning against God by not marrying.

Jewish teachers felt that it was best to marry as young as possible, but this practice was not at all unique to Jewish Palestine.[47] Girls in the Greco-Roman world were usually married in adolescence, often in their early teens. In classical Greece, Spartan girls probably married later,[48] but Athenian girls often married before the age of fifteen.[49] Plato suggests that women should marry between the ages of 16 and 20, while men should marry between 30 and 35.[50]

By Paul's day, a high percentage of Roman girls were married in or by their late teens.[51] One writer notes that "Immediately after they are fourteen, women are called 'ladies' by men."[52] The Roman writer Quintilian mourns that his wife bore him two sons before finishing her nineteenth year of life, and then she died.[53] Augustus' laws permitted girls to be betrothed as young as the age of ten, and married as young as twelve,[54] and many girls were married by the age of fifteen:[55]

> Out of 171 inscriptions in Harkness (1896), 67 recorded women married before the age of 15 and 127 before the age of 19. Some were apparently "married" even before the age of twelve; in the sample in Hopkins (1965b), eight per cent were married at ten or eleven.[56]

Probably most upper class women were married by the age of seventeen, although Augustus' legislation did not penalize them for singleness until the age of twenty.[57]

Jewish teachers usually felt it appropriate to marry daughters off as soon as they reached marriageable age,[58] i.e., around the age of twelve or fourteen.[59] This was an act of kindness toward the daughter[60] and toward the man who would be her husband, since men were also urged to marry as young as possible, and so be protected from temptation.[61] It could also have been considered an act of mercy toward other young men, that they might not stumble in sin on her account.[62]

Many rabbis complained that men who were twenty or older, and still not married, were sinning against God.[63] Eighteen was considered the normal age for a man's marriage.[64] We know, of course, that men were sometimes married later than the age of twenty,[65] but this may not have been as common as it was in the rest of the Roman world. The minimum legal age for boys' marriage in Roman law was fourteen or whenever the boy showed physical signs of male adulthood.[66] Roman males were, however, usually older when they married, quite often twenty-five or older.[67]

One reason that marriage was seen as so vital was that procreation was vital; the human race in general and God's people in particular had to continue by this means. This idea, too, was not limited to Judaism. Earlier Greek culture may not have always stressed childbearing,[68] but by the Augustan period it was heavily stressed as the ideal[69] in Greco-Roman literature.[70] Plutarch, for instance, calls the act of marriage a "sacred sowing"[71] and says not to engage in it if unwilling to produce offspring.[72] He could say this in spite of the fact that he also believed marriage for love to be a higher ideal than marriage to get children.[73] Augustus' propaganda advocating much childbearing was no doubt praised whether or not everyone acted on it.

Public appeals to fulfill one's duty to bear and raise children were no doubt necessitated by the fact that many people failed to do just that. Not everyone kept children once they had them,[74] even though raising the children would have followed the popular idea of propagating one's race and line.[75] Judaism condemned both prenatal and what would have been understood as postnatal abortions[76] (the latter being exposing born children to die).[77] Aborting the fetus after its conception was often disapproved by philosophers,[78] physicians,[79] jurists,[80] and people in general;[81] debates as to whether the embryo was a person, and therefore whether or not abortion should be legal, existed in antiquity as well as today.[82] But the frequent discussion of the issue in antiquity only underlines the fact that abortions were common outside of Jewish circles, reinforcing the need for Judaism's polemic against it.

Judaism stressed the bearing of children even more than imperial propaganda did.[83] Rabbi Joshua admonishes that one should marry again and also keep having children, in old age as well as in youth.[84] Harrell cites one Jewish source as saying that procreation was more meritorious than building the temple had been.[85] Another later rabbi said that God nearly let Hezekiah die young to punish him for not trying to have children sooner.[86] It was likewise a horrible sin for a man to waste his semen.[87]

Begetting children was a sacred duty,[88] linked with God's command to be fruitful and multiply, because humans are made in God's image;[89] one who refrained from seeking children was "as though he had diminished the image of God."[90] Failing to beget children was seen as in some sense equivalent to killing them.[91]

Thus husbands were required by the rabbis to divorce their wives if they could not bear children,[92] although they were allowed a trial period of ten years.[93] Josephus complains that he divorced his wife, "being displeased at her behavior"; but the specific offense that he lists is that two of the three children she had born him had died.[94] In another Jewish text, Manoah, who became father of Samson, nearly divorced his wife for barrenness before God miraculously granted her a son by him.[95] Philo writes that

> those who sue for marriage with women whose sterility has already been proved with other husbands, do but copulate like pigs or goats, and their names should be inscribed in the lists of the impious as adversaries of God. For while God in His love both for mankind and all that lives spares no care to effect the preservation and permanence of every race, those persons who make an art of quenching the life of the seed as it drops, stand confessed as the enemies of nature.[96]

But a divorce on these grounds was thought a duty rather than a pleasant matter; one story is told of a wife who so wanted her husband back that God finally intervened to give her a child by him.[97]

SINGLENESS AND ABSTINENCE IN EARLY JUDAISM

But while the bulk of our evidence, especially from the teachings of later rabbis, indicates that Jews in the Roman period valued marriage very highly, there is also evidence that there were exceptions.

Many rabbis permitted prolonged abstinence under certain circumstances. Married disciples would sometimes go away from their homes to study with a famous rabbi, although only with the permission of their wives.[98] The story of Rabbi Akiba staying away twenty-four years but returning with 12,000 pairs of disciples to greet his patient wife[99] is fictitious but illustrates that rabbis considered such extended separation possible for the sake of Torah.[100]

It is said that Rabbi Simeon ben Yohai and another rabbi both left their families for thirteen years to study under Akiba.[101] These examples all portray rabbis in the second century, but we know of one Jewish teacher whose disciples temporarily left their families in the first century: Jesus.[102]

Some rabbis appear to have been so enamored of Torah study that they had no time for marriage, even though this violated rabbinic tradition. Thus an early second-century teacher, Simeon ben 'Azzai, joined the other teachers in expounding on Genesis: Whoever does not beget children is like a murderer, decreasing the divine image by preventing the conception of humans made in God's image. But the other scholars confronted him:

> "Ben 'Azzai, words are nice when they come from someone who does what they say. Some people expound nicely but do not nicely do what they say, or do what they say but do not expound nicely. Ben 'Azzai expounds nicely but does not nicely do what he says." He said to him, "What shall I do? My soul thirsts after Torah. Let other people keep the world going."[103]

The rabbis also sometimes permitted temporary celibacy under extreme circumstances. Rabbi Simeon ben Yohai did not trust his wife enough to let her know where he and his son hid from the Romans for several years;[104] Noah was forbidden sexual relations while in the holy ark;[105] there also seems to be some evidence for prophets keeping apart from their wives so they could hear God speaking.[106] For the rabbis, however, celibacy was definitely the exception rather than the rule.

Of course, the picture we would get of early Judaism if we looked only at the rabbis would be very distorted. The reports of rabbinic teaching are usually later than the first century and are not always representative of the diversity within Judaism even in their own period. It is thus important for us to examine other kinds of Judaism that existed in the first century, before many rabbinic traditions even began to take shape.[107]

There are various strands of evidence for the practice of celibacy in early Judaism. Temporary celibacy to get revelations seems to have been practiced in some Jewish circles.[108] Similarly, according to one Jewish tradition, the Israelite men at the time of Moses' birth decided to practice abstinence until God delivered them, because Pharaoh was killing the sons born to them.[109] According to the second century BC work Jubilees, Jacob waited until he was over sixty years old to marry, to avoid marrying a foreign wife.[110]

Rachel's choice of patient continence[111] was said to be the virtue that won her the right to bear Jacob two children.[112]

But probably none of these traditions influenced the celibates in the Corinthian church. The evidence of abstinence to receive revelations is not widespread, although it is likely that some Jewish visionaries seeking revelations would abstain from sex, perhaps to avoid ritual impurity.[113] The abstinence of the Israelite men cited above was to protect their sons from being killed and does not reflect a normal practice.[114] The point of the passage about Jacob is that one should not marry pagan wives, not that one should abstain from or needlessly delay marriage.[115] The passage about Rachel does indeed praise temporary abstinence, but nevertheless presents childbearing as a divine reward, thus putting it in a positive light.[116]

Perhaps nearer the Corinthian position on abstinence would be the view presented in 2 Baruch that "the conception of children" and "the passion of the parents" were results of the Fall.[117] But even this would at most mirror certain Greek views about passion, calling readers to perpetuate the human race but to keep their desires under control.

But a more practical parallel to the Corinthian belief may exist. The most relevant and widely cited Jewish material on celibacy has to do with the Essenes. If any Jewish group practiced long-term abstinence or celibacy, it was they. It is not completely clear that the Essenes were celibate, of course;[118] it is likely that some of the Essenes, perhaps those who dwelt in the wilderness,[119] were celibate, while others, perhaps those in the cities, were married.[120] Josephus, whose portrayal of Essene celibacy may have been meant to appeal to those of his Greek readers who respected ascetics or were misogynists, allows for two kinds of Essenes: one group is celibate and propagates itself by adopting children; the other group marries and begets children of its own.[121] But even at Qumran, some women's skeletons indicate that, during some period of its history,[122] at least a few women lived there, though they were clearly the minority.[123]

Despite the possibility that Essene celibacy may have been overemphasized by modern scholars, the convergence of the evidence of Josephus and the Dead Sea Scrolls that some Essenes were celibate is significant. This suggests that some pious Jews considered it especially holy to withdraw from public and family life to pursue the claims of God and his community in an undefiled way. They would have abstained from sex altogether, not just from marital bonds; indeed, as Jews devoted to the law, even emissions in one's sleep would be counted unclean. Whether this reflects certain Greek influences (as I think possible), or whether the Essenes derived their views wholly from earlier Jewish ideas,[124] it demonstrates that celibacy did appeal to some circles even within the strictest elements of Palestinian Judaism. Those in the Corinthian church advocating total abstinence from intercourse for the worship of the one true God may have been influenced by some models of celibacy already available in the ancient world.

PAUL'S ARGUMENT IN 1 CORINTHIANS 7:1–7

Paul's opening verse in 1 Corinthians 7:1, explicitly formulated in response to what the Corinthians had written him (7:1a),[125] has troubled many readers:

It is good[126] for a man not to touch[127] a woman.

Most commentators recognize that Paul has formulated this statement in response to the views of some of the Corinthians[128] or to the specific situation at hand.[129] F. F. Bruce is representative of this position:

However congenial he might find the ascetic slogan, "It is well for a man not to touch a woman" (1 Cor. 7:1), he will not countenance any move to impose it as a general rule, or even as a counsel of perfection. For the majority of Christians . . . marriage is recognized as the normal way of life. The only unconditional ruling which he makes is not his own, but the Lord's. . . . [130]

While we agree that Paul is clearly responding to the Corinthians, we must note with some scholars that it is not clear that he is simply citing their slogan before he refutes it. Several possible reasons exist for Paul's statement of the matter in v. 1:

(1) He is citing a Corinthian slogan (as above).

(2) He is giving the argument of an imaginary opponent, as was often done by him and other moral writers.[131]

(3) He is only in partial agreement with the statement and must thus proceed to qualify it.

(4) A combination of the above (e.g., rephrasing a slogan to the point of absurdity or else to the point of common ground with what Paul wishes to say).

Given that Paul has just been refuting those who promote intercourse between the unmarried (1 Cor. 6:12–20), it is not at all
unlikely that Paul wishes to forbid men "touching" women sexually, i.e., in intercourse—outside of marriage. If he is citing a
Corinthian slogan, he may be using it to say the opposite of how
some people in Corinth have taken it; some of them oppose marriage or married sexuality, but he opposes sexuality outside of
marriage, as he has just argued in the preceding context.

It is even possible that what Paul opposes here is a Greek idea
that we discussed earlier, which permitted sexual activity with
prostitutes but felt that marriage would tie one down too much
from seeking philosophy. If so, Paul need not be fighting two
distinct groups, as many scholars have thought (the fornicators of
1 Cor. 6 and the celibates of 1 Cor. 7), but one false teaching that
has taken two turns: marriage is a distraction, but (according to
some of the Corinthians) sexual release is a physical necessity.

In favor of this possibility is 7:2. Married people should act
married (7:2–5), because sexual immorality would still be a temptation if they failed to do so (7:2: "because of immorality").[132]
Slave girls provided a commonly noted temptation for the men in
well-to-do homes,[133] and we know how widely available prostitution was for anyone who could afford it.[134] But many rabbis felt
that marriage enabled men to avoid immorality;[135] some, indeed,
thought of this as marriage's primary purpose.

Paul wants husbands and wives to act married, so protecting one
another from temptation. For a man and woman to "have" each
other presumably means that they have intercourse with each other
(7:2);[136] this is what Paul means by "fulfilling one's duty" (7:3)
and having authority over the other's "body" (7:4).[137]

That Paul means intercourse when he speaks of the husband's
duty to his wife, and the reverse, should have been clear to ancient
readers. Of course, the phrase "the spouse's duty" by itself need
not have connoted sex: to many readers it could have meant money
just as easily. It is true that the idea of money would not occur to
everyone; it would less likely occur to Roman readers than to
Greek or Jewish ones: Roman husbands and wives were not allowed to receive gifts from one another,[138] the husband owned all
the property even if the wife contributed the greater share,[139] the
husband could remove her luxury[140] and she had no legally enforced right to maintenance; theoretically, her dowry might have
to support her.[141] But hellenistic Greek marriage contracts[142]

normally included an enumeration of the marital obligations of both husband and wife. The sanctions for failure to live up to these obligations usually included divorce and forfeiture of the dowry, and perhaps an additional financial penalty.[143]

Some of these texts list the husband's duties as maintaining her as a free woman, not abusing her, and not bringing another woman into the house, although his liberty to engage in extramarital affairs was assumed in the early period.[144] The wife's duties were stipulated as being:

(1) Submissive to her husband
(2) Not leaving the marital residence without permission
(3) No social contact with other men
(4) Not bringing financial ruin to the family
(5) Not doing anything to shame her husband[145]

Jewish marriage contracts seem to have resembled the Greek contracts in many ways.[146] Like the dowry of Greco-Roman law, the ketubah belonged to the wife,[147] providing her with some measure of financial stability. But in contrast to Roman law, the wife had a right to maintenance of food, clothing, and other physical needs,[148] according to the standard to which she had been accustomed growing up,[149] as well as a weekly allowance.[150] If her husband failed to fulfill his duties, she could at least in principle demand a divorce.[151]

The wife similarly owed her husband certain duties, such as cleaning and cooking, unless she had brought a servant into the marriage with her to do the work.[152] These reciprocal though distinct obligations indicated the concern of Jewish law for the rights of women in marriage, weak as their rights were in some other areas.[153]

But the only duty listed in the ketubah that would make sense in the context of Paul's statement in 7:3 is the duty of the husband to provide his wife with intercourse.[154] It was acknowledged in the Mediterranean world that women did not always enjoy intercourse,[155] but men usually assumed that they desired it.[156] First-century Jewish teachers required the husband to permit his wife a divorce if he abstained from intercourse for more than two weeks, even to fulfill a vow.[157] Paul permits times of abstinence only by mutual consent (7:5). He also makes intercourse a reciprocal obligation which both husband and wife owe one another,[158] presumably implying that he expects both to enjoy it.

Paul permits husband and wife temporary periods of abstinence, following some forms of religious devotion mentioned earlier

(7:5),[159] but he insists that it must be only temporary and by mutual consent. Paul goes on to say that this rule is a matter of concession, not of command;[160] apparently he does not think it is profitable for married people to take times of abstinence at all.[161] His concern is again "lest they be tempted by Satan,"[162] reminding us again of 7:2: husbands and wives should sleep together to avoid temptations to immorality.

It is not that Paul does not value his singleness and strength to abstain; but he acknowledges that not everyone has the same gift of self-control,[163] the same ability to remain single indefinitely (7:7; Matt. 19:11).[164] He wishes this also for the "unmarried"[165] and widows (7:8),[166] but recognizes that it is better for those without this kind of self-control to marry (7:9). This is not a call to celibacy as a mark of spirituality; it is a recognition that there are different gifts (7:8), and not everyone has all those gifts (cf. 1 Cor. 12:28–30). This does not mean that someone cannot seek certain gifts from God (12:31, 14:1); but while Paul gives advice that singleness is the best way for those who are made for it, he plainly says that it is not the best way for everyone.

The reason Paul gives for prescribing marriage to unmarried people unsuited for the single life is that it is better to marry than to "burn" (7:9). While singleness might be preferable to marriage for those who have the gift of self-control in this area, marriage is far better than giving way to sinful passion, because marriage is not sinful, for either a divorcee or a virgin (7:28).[167] Paul's advice to singles to remain single is conditional on their having this gift (7:8–9); his only absolute command is prohibition of divorce for those already married (7:10–11), and even this prohibition has exceptions (7:12–16).

The alternative of "burning" in v. 9 reminds the reader of the earlier warnings against the dangers of temptation for those abstaining from sexual activity within marriage in vv. 2 and 5. Not everyone is built for celibacy.[168] Some have taken "burn" here to refer to burning in hell, due to immoral behavior;[169] but the phrase is used continually throughout ancient literature, especially the romances,[170] to designate burning with passion.[171] Additional texts similarly describe other violent, "uncontrollable" responses to passion.[172] Greco-Roman writers do not suppose that burning passion is wrongful, if directed toward an unmarried woman; but Paul does not agree.[173] Lack of a partner does not excuse lust; but Paul does present marriage as a practical solution to the danger of such desire.

But if this is the case, should we suppose that those made single by divorce would be any less in danger of passion than those who had never tasted the joy of married love? Is it not better also for the divorced to marry than to burn? And those who impose their strict reading of the Bible on those who have been divorced against their will, so forbidding them remarriage, perhaps impose a load on other people's shoulders that they would not carry themselves (Matt. 23:4). The legalists who oppress divorced believers in this way, believers who may have already been crushed by their spouses' abandonment, may be among those who cause Jesus' little ones to stumble (Matt. 18:6–7)—placing their own position before God in serious question.

CONCLUSION

Paul's argument in 1 Corinthians 7 does indicate a preference for the single life, for those who have the character to adapt to it. But he also unequivocally permits marriage, and he permits it for the abandoned divorced person as clearly as he permits it for the man or woman who has never been married. He presents a healthy, sexually active marriage as the best defense against sexual immorality, just as most Jewish writers of his day did; and we cannot suppose that this would apply any less to the person who has already tasted the joys of married love, only to be deprived of them through no fault of his or her own.

7 Can Ministers Be Remarried?— 1 Timothy 3:2

Some readers would agree with everything in this book so far. They would agree that those divorced because their spouses were engaging in unrepentant affairs or deserted them are free to remarry. But they would nevertheless bar those who have been remarried from filling certain positions in the church, namely, those of pastor and deacon.[1]

The case for this is largely based on the phrase "husband of one wife" that occurs in two New Testament letters and is interpreted, "husband of only one wife *during his lifetime*," sometimes with an appended qualification, "*unless she dies*." Most churches that follow this interpretation have written their doctrine as if the phrase were entirely clear, meaning exactly what they have already assumed it to mean. But the "during his lifetime," and the common qualification, "unless she dies," are not stated in the text. And given that, as we have noted earlier, the *validly* remarried person was considered to be married to only one person even under Jesus' strict teaching against divorce, this is a curious addition to the text indeed. One would hope, therefore, that the churches espousing such a position would produce evidence that in ancient times the phrase "husband of one wife" would have been taken to mean just what their position implies; but, again regrettably, these churches have been slow to provide this evidence.

This chapter will examine the literary and cultural context of the list of qualifications for church office. We will also examine some grammatically possible (though culturally improbable) meanings of "husband of one wife" and the connection of "wife of one husband" in 1 Timothy 5:9 with its occurrence elsewhere in antiquity. It will also be helpful to evaluate the other qualifications for office; and most of all, we need to inquire into the specific situation presupposed in 1 Timothy. Finally, we should assess how these findings will direct our interpretation of the passage.

THE CONTEXT OF 1 TIMOTHY 3:2

This is a reliable point: If anyone wants to be an overseer, it is a good thing he desires to do. It is thus necessary for the overseer to be above reproach, the husband of one wife, sober, self-controlled, respectable, hospitable to travelers, able to teach, not given to strong drink, not hot-tempered, but instead gentle, hard to pick a fight with, not materialistic. He should run his own household well, which means that his children should do as he says, behaving with dignity. But if someone cannot run his own household, how can he take care of God's church? Nor should he be a new believer, lest he become stuck up and so fall into the devil's condemnation. And it is also necessary for him to have a good reputation in the secular community, lest he fall into reproach and the devil's trap.

Deacons must likewise be respectable, not two-faced, not addicted to much wine, not materialistic, keeping the mystery of the faith with a pure conscience. And let these also be tested first; then if they prove to be beyond reproach, let them serve as deacons. The women must also be respectable, not gossipers, sober, dependable in everything. Let deacons each be husbands of one wife, ruling their children and their own household well. For those who serve as deacons acquire for themselves a good standing and much confidence by the faith which is in Christ Jesus (1 Tim. 3:1–13).

I left you in Crete so you would finish setting things in order and appoint elders in every city, just like I told you: if anyone is above reproach, the husband of one wife, his children are believers and cannot be accused of a reckless lifestyle or disobedience. For it is necessary for an overseer to be above reproach as a supervisor for God's household, not self-willed, not hot-tempered, not given to strong drink, not violent, not materialistic, but instead hospitable to travelers, lovers of good, self-controlled, righteous, holy, self-disciplined. Also he must hold to the reliable message the way it has been taught, so that he is able to exhort by sound teaching and to reprove those who oppose the word (Tit. 1:5–9).

The passages in question are 1 Timothy 3:1–13 and its parallel in Titus 1:5–9.[2] Here Paul addresses the status of "overseers" or church elders (1 Tim. 3:2; Tit. 1:5–7),[3] those we would today call pastors (which literally means "shepherds"; see Acts 20:17, 28; cf. Eph. 4:11; 1 Pet. 5:1–2). Since most churches in the first few centuries met in homes of well-to-do patrons or sponsors, and since a variety of gifts including prophecy seem to have been normally active in the assembly (1 Cor. 12–14, etc.), early pastors probably played a role considerably different from what they do today.[4] The same may be said of "deacons," who are also addressed in 1 Timothy 3:8–13; the term "deacon" is rarely explained in the New Testament,[5] and when it is, it often refers to some sort of ministry of the Word. It is difficult to model our ministries after New Testament models when the exact nature of those models is sometimes hard to figure out!

This is not to say, of course, that modern pastors or deacons must do things exactly as pastors or deacons did in antiquity. The role of elder[6] or overseer[7] was partly derived from cultural models of leadership that already existed in the Greco-Roman world, especially in the synagogues. The early Christians were practical enough to adopt models that worked in their culture and to adapt them according to the demands of the gospel. But while most of us take this into account when we acknowledge the differences between ancient church roles and modern ones, we are much more hesitant to do this with the list of qualifications for these church offices.

A LIST OF QUALIFICATIONS

In this study we will continue our earlier method of analyzing one of the texts in detail rather than several of them, since much of the cultural-historical background overlaps. In this case we will examine 1 Timothy 3:2 in the greatest detail.

Paul recommends the office of "overseer" to whomever would be interested in it (3:1),[8] provided that the prospective overseer meets the qualifications of 3:2–7. The reason for these qualifications is repeatedly hinted at in this text: representatives of the church were to be "above reproach" (3:2), which included having an honorable reputation outside the church (3:7). Pressed on all sides by a hostile environment, early Christians, like their Jewish counterparts in the Greco-Roman world, sought to put their best face forward to the world. I have elsewhere argued that some of these requirements—such as that the teacher of Scripture be male (2:11–15)—address specific cultural situations and are not binding in different situations,[9] and I will not repeat that argument here.

But one issue we must keep in mind in the following discussion is whether 1 Timothy 3:2–3 is meant to be a universal list. There are several indications that it is not. That Paul gives a different (although overlapping) list in Titus 1:6–9 suggests that the list was not uniform and could be varied. Further, had the list already been standard, leaders like Titus—and certainly Timothy— would have already known its content, because they had been with Paul and had seen him appoint church leaders before. Although Paul often appeals to what his readers know, he usually says this when he does so. The very presence of the list may suggest that Paul is establishing some new rules for some new situations.

Still, many of the other requirements in the list strike us as standard New Testament moral teaching. We might consequently be inclined to feel that while the particular elements on the list are emphasized because of the specific culture in which he wrote, Paul would have regarded at least most of these requirements as valid in all cultures, whether they needed to "make the list" everywhere or not. Whether some of these phrases might refer to traits unique to Paul's own culture will need to be investigated below. What is clear for the moment is that all of them fit into the description of being "above reproach" which frames them (3:2, 7).

Lists of qualifications were used for other kinds of offices in the ancient world.[10] Praise of prominent patrons' virtues are scattered throughout the inscriptions of antiquity, and it would not be a great step from praising someone for conforming to standards of honor[11] to listing the standards to which someone who would be irreproachable must conform.[12] It was a philosophical common-place that those with political power ought to be morally superior, for the sake of example,[13] so those seeking offices might be tested by lists of moral qualifications.

The Jewish Letter of Aristeas, intended to give Alexandrian Greeks a favorable impression of Alexandrian Judaism, describes the trans-lators of the Septuagint as "elders who have led exemplary lives and are expert in their own law, six from each tribe."[14] The Dead Sea Scrolls also give some qualifications for leaders, particularly concerning their age (1QM 2.4; 7.1–3; CD 10.6–7; 14.7, 9).[15] The rabbis contemplated the qualifications for judges, who, once tested on a local level, could be promoted from local courts ulti-mately to the Sanhedrin:

> Whoever was a sage, modest, humble, sin-fearing, sufficiently mature, and from whom people gain pleasure do they appoint as a judge in his

own town. Once he is made a judge in his home town, they promote him. . . . [16]

The standard of being "above reproach" was widely held up in antiquity.[17] In Chariton's novel, Mithridates, involved in a scandal, pleads his case: "I have lived all my life until now without reproach";[18] and it happens that this past innocence stands him in good stead when confronted with political and legal trouble in the present. Jewish funerary inscriptions in the Mediterranean Diaspora often boast that the synagogue officials and others they describe were "above reproach."[19] Paul, recognizing the challenges Christianity faced right at the outset from the world's prejudice, was determined to outdo the world's standards of morality and not to let scandal stain the church's reputation.

"HUSBAND OF ONE WIFE"

Some denominations have assumed that "husband of one wife" means "one wife in a lifetime" and do not permit elders or pastors to remarry after the death of a spouse or a divorce. Other denominations assume that the phrase refers only to divorced persons, since the death of a spouse has no moral implications (as if it had moral implications for the innocent party in a divorce!).

Some translations seem to assume and propagate these positions, for example, the NRSV reads, "married only once"; the NIV, "husband of but one wife" (assuming that Paul cannot mean "neither more *nor less* than one").

But this view of the matter cannot be simply assumed. What were the options for interpreting "husband of one wife" in antiquity? Two options that may at least be considered are polygamy and having a concubine besides one's wife.

Polygamy

Polygamy was against Roman law[20] and bore as its minimum legal penalty *infamia*[21]—that is, someone guilty of it would unquestionably not be considered "above reproach." Not everyone in antiquity favored monogamy, of course. Plato advocated that the guardians should hold wives in common in the ideal society;[22] but his view did not gain much ground in popular thought.[23] Lucian in one of his critiques of philosophers satirizes him by making this his "most important view."[24]

But polygamy was still officially legal in Palestinian Judaism.[25] Like divorce, it had some precedent in Old Testament law. Although the practice was not common, it could be taken for granted;[26] the Mishnah allows a man to have up to eighteen wives, and later rabbinic tradition allows even more.[27] One later rabbi is said to have advised men not to marry two women; but if one does so, he should also marry a third.[28] A story—no doubt fictitious—is told of an early second-century rabbi, Tarfon, who "in a year of famine betrothed himself to three hundred women" so they could share the priestly food available to him.[29] Unquestionably Herod the Great entertained an abundance of spouses, having nine wives living at once;[30] but then, not everyone in Palestine was a king like Herod, who had sufficient funds to support a harem.

Polygamy was, of course, criticized, even if not for the reasons we might wish to offer today. Hillel is said to have complained,

The more flesh, the more worms;
the more riches, the more worry;
the more wives, the more witchcraft.[31]

But this seems to mean that one wife could be dangerous enough, rather than that there was anything immoral about polygamy per se! There was some disagreement among later rabbis on the propriety of polygamy,[32] though the opposition was not sufficient to declare it illegal in the Talmudic era.

Nevertheless, monogamy was the norm,[33] and the Dead Sea Scrolls, in contrast to the Pharisaic sages and later rabbis, explicitly reject polygamy.[34] What is more significant, however, is that Jewish people outside Palestine followed the regular Greek practice of avoiding polygamous unions.[35] The fact that polygamy was practiced neither by the Jewish people in Asia nor by the Greeks there suggests that Paul would have had little reason to address this in his letter as a rule for church leaders there.[36] Accordingly, we can rule out the possibility that "husband of one wife" is a proscription against polygamy.

Concubinage

If official, legal polygamy was not practiced in the Greco-Roman world, this should not lead us to assume that men did not engage in other multiple sexual relationships. The evidence is not so great as to suggest that it was the usual practice, but it is sufficient to establish that it was not altogether unusual.

Some of the possible evidence is ambiguous. A first-century BC religious inscription from Asia Minor prohibits taking another woman in addition to one's own wife; but in context, this could well be a reference to adultery with another man's wife.[37]

Some of the evidence would seem to argue against the custom. In Greek tradition, concubinage was not favored, but the Greeks were aware of the practice among other peoples.[38] Roman law also forbade holding a concubine in addition to a wife.[39] Jewish law refers to it in commenting on the institution in biblical times, but the closest equivalent to concubinage in the rabbis' day that shows up in their literature concerns sexual relations with slave-girls, which is roundly condemned.[40]

Yet other evidence suggests that in this period multiple concubinage was indeed practiced in the Mediterranean world. The laws against it themselves attest to the practice by the need to discourage it, and some early marriage contracts promise to avoid it;[41] but there is more direct evidence. The practice of acquiring concubines had become more common during this period,[42] especially among those with lower social status.[43] Such a relationship was more readily dissolved than a formal, official marriage.[44] Concubinage was quite common in the military,[45] since official wives were not legal until the term of military service had been fulfilled, a period lasting over twenty years.[46] Some military discharge documents from the first century favor the soldiers with the legalization of their prior unions as marriages, but add a single stipulation:

> whose names have been written below, to them, their children, and their descendants he has given citizenship and legal marriage with the wives which they had at the time when citizenship was given to them, or, if any were unmarried, with those women whom afterwards they married, provided *only one to each.*[47]

In other words, it was known that some men had more than one concubine. Similarly, Ps-Phocylides warns against having intercourse with the concubines—plural—of one's father.[48]

First Timothy 3:2 could thus prohibit having a concubine,[49] especially having several concubines or a concubine in addition to a wife. But while this practice would have been more common than polygamy, it was probably not common enough in Ephesus to merit its own prohibition. Issues like adultery, divorce, and widowhood were certainly far more frequent.

Since Paul actually uses the term, "wife of one husband" (5:9) as well as "husband of one wife," our investigation of the single-wife husband may be aided by a brief look at the meaning of the single-husband wife. It is not impossible that something different is meant by the two terms, but this cannot be decided until we have examined the function of each in its own context. What can be noted in advance, however, is that women could not practice polygamy or concubinage; the phrase "wife of one husband" must therefore mean something more related to adultery, divorce, or widowhood than to either of those options.

THE ONE-HUSBAND WIFE IN 1 TIMOTHY 5

It may be helpful to review the structure of Paul's argument in 1 Timothy 5 before attending to v. 9 in particular. Our case does not hinge on the following structure, but to set Paul's instructions to widows in a context will make more sense of why he gives requirements for widows. This is especially the case if these requirements parallel those for male church leaders. Paul has been talking about elders, church leaders, in 4:14; his references to "elders" in chapter 5 may thus have to do with church leadership (5:17) as well as with age (5:1–2). Leadership and age may be somehow related, although younger church leaders were also accepted (4:12).

It may similarly be the case that the older women filled a special role in this church, particularly if they were widows; instead of brushing its senior citizens off to the side, the Ephesian church had given them a place of ministry and honor,[50] a paid office of prayer (v. 5).[51] This view has been proposed by a variety of commentators,[52] with whom I disagreed (their external evidence seemed too late) until I looked at the structure of the passage itself. The structure of the passage may suggest a correlation between elders (church leaders) and widows.

> 5:1–2: older men/elders, younger men, older women, younger women
> 5:3–16: the office (?) of older widows
>   v. 3: Honor them (=support,[53] cf. v. 17)
>   vv. 4–6: Widows defined (in sense of office)
>   vv. 3–4: destitute[54]
>   vv. 5–6: godly (spiritual service to the community)
>   v. 7: Admonition to enforce this
>   vv. 8–16: Basis: widows as godly and destitute
>   vv. 8, 16: Destitute—not if others can support them
>   vv. 9–15: Godly
>   vv. 9–10: Moral qualifications for list

vv. 11–15: Younger widows not on list; remarry instead
    v. 11: Sensual desires (cf. v. 6—turning from life of prayer)
    v. 12: Turning from commitment to do this=denying faith, perhaps=wasting community support resources (v. 8 and v. 15)
    v. 13: Moral flaws of those on public support without work to do
    vv. 14–15: Solution vs. danger
5:17–25: Honoring male elders
    vv. 17–18: Job of elders: ruling; extra support for those who work hard at it
    vv. 19–25: Dealing with sinning elders (cf. 5:13)
    vv. 19–21: Procedure
    v. 22: Avoid wrong ordinations
    v. 23: Avoid former abstinence (false teachers could seize on it, 4:3)
    vv. 24–25: Cannot screen them perfectly, but do your best on the basis of these external criteria
6:1–2: Behavior of slaves (third component of traditional household codes)[55]
6:3–19: Those who disagree and teach otherwise (perhaps false teachers who want pay without fulfilling the appropriate service to the community) are greedy.

The structure itself does not necessarily indicate that the widows hold a church office, but the likelihood they do is increased by similar terms of respect applied to persons of honor in the Diaspora synagogues. These were "elders" in the sense that they were normally older members (perhaps patrons) of their congregations: "fathers"[56] and "mothers"[57] of synagogues. The leaders in chapter 5 seem to be different from those in many synagogues, although they may be related. Whereas the officers in the synagogues probably contributed monetarily to the synagogue, in 1 Timothy 5 the elders (who, like fathers and mothers [5:1–2], should be helped by children [5:4, 16])[58] are to receive some support from the church in return for their services, if they have no other means of support.

Although this is the way of reading the chapter that to me seems to explain its elements best, it is also possible that Paul simply means "widows" as a subcategory of the older women, referring to anyone bereaved of a husband who was also truly destitute and godly. Whichever way one reads the chapter, the special widows to be enrolled on the church support list must have a good reputation (v. 10) and be above reproach (v. 7), because, like overseers and deacons, they appear to outsiders as official representatives of what Christianity is about.

The text itself does not explain the nature of the "one-husband" requirement any more than 3:2 spelled out the nature of the "one-wife" requirement, but the context may speak against the term needing to mean that she had been married only once. Paul commands the younger widows to remarry (v. 14) and thus avoid the trouble that was apparently occurring among idle women in the congregation who were spreading something other than sound teaching (5:13–15).[59] Given the most plain report of what the false teachers are saying—which includes forbidding marriage (4:3), perhaps developing the sort of teaching Paul had faced at Corinth—it may well be that encouraging these younger widows to marry is an attempt to combat the false teaching forbidding marriage. Rather than giving them a position of honor and perhaps a role of teaching in the church while they are still susceptible to false teaching (2:11–15), Paul instructs them to get married and accordingly remove themselves from the sphere of the false teachers by negating their basic premise.

If this is why Paul urges the younger widows to remarry, it is also possible that this is why he urges that any widows put on the list must have been "one-husband" wives. It may be that those in positions of honor in this church needed to have been married before in order to stand as an example against the rhetoric of false teachers who rejected marriage. This would, of course, have been implied anyway in the term "widows," but Paul might wish to emphasize the married state of the woman in an emphatic way. Granted that she had been married—no one disputes this anyway—why does Paul use the term, "wife of *one* husband"? For the answer to this question, we must turn to the closest parallels to this phrase which we have in antiquity. Only after we have examined these parallels can we decide whether or not they are relevant to Paul's instructions here.

THE ONE-HUSBAND IDEAL IN ANTIQUITY

Paul is not the first to appeal to an ideal of one-spouse faithfulness. There had been a long tradition of praises to the woman who married only one man, called *univira* in Latin inscriptions and *monandros* in Greek.[60] By examining what this phrase means, some scholars suggest that it is possible to gain insight into what is meant in 1 Timothy 5:9 by "wife of one husband," a phrase which may be related to the enigmatic phrase "husband of one wife" in our passage.

In the early Roman Empire the *flamines* of Jupiter, who were among the most prominent religious officials of antiquity, could

only have wives who were *univirae*;[61] such women, who had been
neither orphaned nor widowed, were thought to bring good fortune to others by their participation in the cult.[62] Vestal Virgins,
the most revered office filled by women in Rome, had to have both
parents living and still-married, so that their line could be considered unblemished.[63] Plutarch tells us that according to an old
Roman custom, the *Flamen Dialis*, the priest of Jupiter, would
"resign his office if his wife died,"[64] which may again suggest that
the idea of good fortune was prominent in the concept of *univira*.

The motivation behind the "one-spouse-for-life" ideal seems to
have developed beyond this bearing of good fortune, however.
Faithful wives are sometimes portrayed as unwilling to remarry
after their husbands' death out of love for their husbands[65] or their
children.[66] Some extreme descriptions of such ideal wives portray
them as loyally mourning and starving themselves at the graves of
their husbands, so that

> There was but one opinion throughout the city, every class of person
> admitting this was the one true and brilliant example of chastity and
> love.[67]

More rarely, men sometimes also abstained from a second marriage. But they might take a concubine though avoiding marriage
per se,[68] since their real concern was generally to protect their
children's inheritance and perhaps to avoid uncomfortable relations between the children and a stepmother.[69] The ideal of not
remarrying after a spouse's death to show loyal love was more often
applied to wives than to husbands.

But while showing loyalty to one's husband by remaining single
had been fostered as an ideal, the Emperor Augustus' laws had
introduced a conflicting ideal: to remarry as quickly as possible to
produce more children for the Roman state, if one were still in her
child-bearing years.[70] The shortage of available women suggests
that most young widows in this period probably did remarry.[71]

The ideal of a "one-husband wife" seems to have also been held
by some parts of the Jewish community, as is evident from the term
monandros in Jewish funerary inscriptions.[72] The language is, of
course, essentially limited to women; there are very few references
to Jewish men abstaining from a second marriage. Ps-Phocylides
205 could perhaps be taken in this regard: "Do not add marriage
to marriage, calamity to calamity."[73] But the context (lines 199–
204) refers to getting a bad wife, so this line probably refers to
serial polygamy, as in the Roman satirists: don't keep going from

one marriage to another trying to find a good wife; get the right one to begin with. And the rabbis were concerned to provide for the widow's remarriage as quickly as possible.[74]

But even the motif of the loyal wife pining away and refusing to marry after her first husband's death is probably not closely related to the specific phrase, "wife of one husband," found in funerary inscriptions. As will be shown below, in the vast majority of cases, it appears on the tomb inscriptions of *wives being honored by surviving husbands*.[75] Surviving husbands could not honor wives who had been married only once but who had also been widows before predeceasing their husbands. The term is not clearly applied to widows until the second century, by Christian writers praising widowhood,[76] and thus reflects a growing climate of sexual asceticism. Thus, in Paul's day, it may have more likely connoted marital fidelity and being a good spouse, as exemplified in a *strong current marriage*.

But despite this lack of express connection between the single widow ideal and the praise of "single-husband wives" in inscriptions, and despite the fact that the ideal of remaining a widow was in competition with the ideal of younger widow's continuing procreative productivity, many commentators think that this usage informs Paul's language of "husband of one wife."[77] If this is true, Paul excludes from these ministry positions all those who are remarried, whether as widowers or divorcees.[78]

Yet there are severe problems with this position: in a church where Paul wished to combat especially false teachers who forbade marriage (1 Tim. 4:3), would he have said something that would have contributed to certain ascetic tendencies in the culture that later became dominant in the church? Further, would he have instructed the younger widows to remarry (5:14), even though that would later disqualify them for church support (5:9, on this interpretation of "one husband")? Widows were *not* to remarry once they were on the list (5:11–12), but those not on the list *were* to remarry, which may imply that remarriage in younger days was not an issue.

Rather than forbidding remarriage to those whose marriages had ended, Paul may be emphasizing that they should have been faithful spouses during the marriage. As we have mentioned, in this period the term "wife of one husband" was not normally used for widows in the inscriptions; most of these inscriptions were dedicated by surviving husbands. This could mean that the wives are praised as not having married another man before their surviving husband, but a more natural explanation lies at hand: the *functional* stress of the term is on the wife's faithfulness as a good wife through the duration of the marriage. The implication may be that had she not been, she would have needed to find another husband, because her current husband would have needed to divorce her.[79] Or it may be that she was faithful to her husband, never taking interest in another man during their marriage. Either way, it is meant as a positive moral judgment about her; it does not simply reflect that she was never so unfortunate as to have had a husband trigger-happy about divorce.

To this it has been objected that "spouse of one partner" is not the most natural way to express marital fidelity; "not an adulterer" would make better sense.[80] But "not an adulterer" would have been too obvious a statement to include in Paul's list of moral qualifications, somewhat akin to "not a murderer." "A faithful and loyal spouse who is a good current marital partner," however, would fit the list quite well, matching the emphasis on ruling the children properly (3:4–5, 12; Tit. 1:6) and the concern about false teachers who were ruining whole "households" (Tit. 1:11) and forbidding marriage (1 Tim. 4:1–3). That it would bar from church support an otherwise godly and destitute widow or preclude from ministry a capable prophet or teacher because of a bad marriage years ago, often before his or her conversion,[81] is an assumption that has to be read into the text.[82] Indeed, this assumption mirrors more closely the sexual asceticism urged by the false teachers than Paul's own position.

Further, marriage to one partner in a lifetime is never applied as a qualification for leaders in the ancient world; it is not even a frequent praise of men (who in that culture filled most of the leadership roles), being reserved most often for women. The ideal of marital fidelity, however, is often required of leaders.[83] And as we shall point out on 1 Timothy 3:4, below, having one's current household in order was a frequent ancient standard for leadership.

THE OTHER REQUIREMENTS FOR LEADERSHIP

For some reason, other requirements in the list are quickly glossed over while attention is focused on "husband of one wife." Although I have known of ministers being removed from office because their children were not under their authority or were not believers (1 Tim. 3:4; Tit. 1:6), in most cases this qualification is simply ignored. "The children have free will and will go their own way," we explain, noting perhaps that it is much harder to keep children under control today than it was back then. (We might ask whether spouses do not also have free will, but such a question could take us afield from our main subject of enquiry here.)

What about the requirement that overseers be forbearing or gentle, not given to quarreling, a requirement which occurs in all three Pastoral Epistles in some form (1 Tim. 3:3; 2 Tim. 2:24–25; Tit. 1:7)? Plenty of ministers thrive on tearing apart other people's theological positions,[84] often more for their own intellectual satisfaction than for pastoral concerns. Many others prefer being in the limelight to being a humble servant building up the body of Christ. Should such leaders be disqualified from ministry until their lives are in order? Perhaps they should be. But such qualifications dealing with present lifestyle and attitudes are much more difficult to ascertain than whether or not someone has been married before. Consequently, these qualifications are more easily ignored, and the alleged marriage requirement is more easily enforced.

What about being "able to teach," a phrase which again recurs in all three letters (1 Tim. 3:2; 2 Tim. 2:24–25; Tit. 1:9)?[85] At the very least, this must include a firm grasp of the foundation of our faith, the Scriptures, and an ability to communicate their message faithfully. In the Pastoral Epistles, it must also include the ability to refute error,[86] something which must be done in gentleness (as we have already noted). Teaching style and educational requirements vary from denomination to denomination, but some well-educated ministers expound their own mental drivel instead of Scripture, while some ministers who have no college education faithfully expound the Word. My guess is that Paul's requirement that ministers be able to teach sound doctrine has to do especially with where they get their material (hopefully the Scriptures) and how faithfully they proclaim its message (1 Tim. 4:13), rather than with their popularity or the letters following their name. We shall refrain from guessing how well many ministers today measure up to *that* standard.

But our improper leniency in some areas is no reason to loosen scriptural standards where we have them right. If "husband of one wife" is a transcultural requirement, not related to specific situations in Ephesus, then whatever it turns out to mean, we ought to apply that meaning across the board.

The question we must then ask is whether every requirement here would have been applied to all cultures, or whether Paul gives this specific list to address the situations that would most naturally arise in the culture. We may all agree that specific styles of teaching (and thus the way "able to teach" would be evaluated) and the characteristics of respectability or self-control[87] would vary from culture to culture; but these requirements themselves could be maintained in lists in any culture. But what about some of the other qualifications?

Hospitality is a fitting example. The term does not just mean entertaining dinner guests once a week; it has more to do with opening up our homes to people who need a place to stay,[88] especially to strangers.[89] This was a Greek virtue,[90] but it was particularly praised in early Judaism,[91] which cited especially the example of Abraham.[92]

When someone traveled in antiquity,[93] it was most natural to find someone of the traveler's own country or trade, who would gladly provide accommodations for the night.[94] Inns charged unfairly high prices and usually doubled as brothels,[95] so travelers often carried letters of recommendation so they would be received by friends of their patrons in other cities.[96]

This would be especially true of Jewish travelers, loath to stay in a brothel if other alternatives were available. Synagogues and schoolhouses could be used for this purpose,[97] but it was best to stay in a host's home.[98] It appears that it was proper for the host to insist that the guest stay, allowing the guest to leave only if the guest insisted.[99] Paul had often profited from this custom in his own travels.[100]

Although the virtue of this kind of hospitality should be practiced in all cultures, it probably appears in *Paul's list* because it was a sign of great respectability in that culture. In our culture, this true hospitality—putting up those in need in our own home—would sometimes be considered *unrespectable.* I have a friend, for instance, who has often taken teenage prostitutes off the street by housing them in his own home; most of them have been young mothers who believed they had no way to feed their children except by engaging in prostitution. He and his wife act virtuously in taking the prostitutes in and sharing Christ's love with them, and they would welcome more help from other Christians willing to do the same.

But many of our churches today would not consider such behavior "above reproach," since it might lay us open to false accusations from non-Christians eager to charge us with scandal. Although the secular community praises Christians for community service, non-

Christians may seek to justify their own sin by making false accusations that ministers find difficult to deflect.[101] (Indeed, such accusations were made against Jesus, who was nonetheless undeterred from his mission to reach everyone with God's message while refraining from sin.) I give this example only to highlight that what is perceived as "above reproach" may vary from culture to culture, community to community, and sometimes (making our work most difficult) among different members of the same community.

The most detailed requirement in this list concerns the overseer ruling his children. This was a virtue frequently extolled in antiquity,[102] and it was often a prerequisite for ruling others.[103] Usually the husband was considered responsible for the behavior of his family, including that of his wife,[104] although there were exceptions to this view.[105] Given the household-based character of early Christian house churches' leadership, division within the family could also pose serious problems for the maintenance of strong congregations.[106]

Because this was a standard view of respectable leadership, this was a necessary characteristic for the early Christians to be "above reproach." But control over the household was also more easily implemented in that period than it is today. One could not be honorable in Greco-Roman society who did not honor[107] and obey[108] one's parents; this held true in Judaism as well.[109] The father also held a traditional role of authority in Roman society;[110] even though the power of life and death[111] was rarely exercised over adult children,[112] the continuing right of the father to decide whether infant children should be raised or discarded[113] marked his position of power in the home. His paternal authority legally extended even to grandchildren and great-grand children,[114] if he lived that long.[115]

Although parental love for children was the expected norm,[116] discipline,[117] often harsh discipline (including flogging),[118] was stressed in the children's education.[119] Although Paul sides with the minority who disapproved of severe discipline (Eph. 6:4),[120] the culture as a whole was much more oriented toward filial obedience and parental authority than ours is today.

It is, of course, valid to say that ministers should not get so involved with the business of the church that they neglect their families. But this is not what Paul meant by this passage, although that is probably the closest application of the principle for our culture. Paul meant that Timothy should especially choose church leaders who had proven their administrative skill in the home, as evidenced by their children's obedience. I do not doubt that he might have allowed exceptions to this policy under unusual circumstances, but unusual circumstances are normally understood rather than *stated* in lists of general qualifications.

Why was Paul so concerned with what people thought? He did not want church leaders falling into "condemnation" (3:6), i.e., into false accusations[121] that would bring reproach against the gospel (3:7). Greco-Roman writers who had spent much time in politics were well-aware of the need, because of one's enemies,

> to live circumspectly, to give heed to one's self, and not to do or say anything carelessly or inconsiderately, but always to keep one's life unassailable as though under an exact regimen.[122]

A new convert had thus to be tested[123] so the church could be certain that the recent convert would not incur personal reproach or bring reproach upon the church through proud carelessness in such matters. But this requirement, valid in the Ephesian church which was over a decade old, is not found in Titus, since the newly formed Cretan church probably *had* only new converts.[124] Paul's list of qualifications had to be adapted to the specific situations his letters addressed.

In other words, most of the items on the list were included because Paul was addressing specific communities with specific kinds of expectations of their leaders.[125] Today we may learn from each of the requirements Paul gives, but the lists for our communities might be different than Paul's list for his readers, just as his lists in 1 Timothy and Titus differ from each other slightly despite the similarity of culture and issues addressed.

What is constant is the importance of being of good reputation in the community. Even this requirement might not be practical in a situation where the church was under persecution; perhaps the opposition to Christians would render *no* one in the church of good reputation. But for stable churches in stable communities, and especially where false rumors could spread about Christianity, this is unquestionably a part of the church's witness to the outside community, just as it was part of the Jewish community's attempt to win a hearing in the Greco-Roman world.[126]

Christian leaders must live "above reproach"; but they should not—and in our culture would not—be reproached for circumstances beyond their control, such as being abandoned or divorced by a spouse without good reason. Nor would anyone in our culture, except those who read selected biblical verses out of context, think twice about someone who had been divorced and/or remarried before their conversion some years ago, but who was now a productive and respectable member of the Christian community.

WHAT SITUATION IS BEING ADDRESSED HERE?

The "faithful sayings" throughout the Pastoral Epistles indicate the importance of the church's tradition, and, with regard to "husband of one wife," if the issue concerned the remarriage of divorced persons, the church tradition could cite the standard set by Jesus and known by the Pauline churches in 1 Corinthians 7. But if this were the referent of "husband of one wife," we would again have to allow the exception found 1 Corinthians 7, which would still render a leader "above reproach."[127]

But the remarriage of divorced people is probably *not* the issue here. First Timothy 3:2–7 is framed by what has been called an *inclusio*, a device that brackets together material of a given subject. The passage begins with the instruction that the overseer be "above reproach" (also 5:7; 6:14) and concludes with the directive that he have "a good testimony (reputation, report) from those outside," which would be some insurance against his falling into reproach. The main issue here may thus be how "those outside view the church,"[128] which is also the apparent motivation for most of the exhortations in the context (2:1–7).

If Paul is concerned about the church's presentation of itself to "those outside," it is next to impossible that he is addressing the remarriage of divorced men, because no one in antiquity, whether Jewish or Greco-Roman, would have looked down on the remarriage of *men*, even if (and this is far from always the case) they thought more highly of women who did not remarry. Whatever the "one-spouse" inscriptions may mean, they praise once-married women, not once-married men. Let us assume, for the sake of argument, that these inscriptions mean that women who avoided remarriage were considered virtuous. Is the reference in 1 Timothy 3:2 to a higher standard than society's, avoiding also the remarriage of *male* widowers and/or divorcees? If so, one would have expected Paul to state this more explicitly; but instead he is more interested in articulating customary exhortations about keeping one's children in line.

What *was* ridiculed in this culture was successive divorce, bigamy (including marriage to a concubine on the side), and marital infidelity. It would be odd if, on one point only, Paul departed from the standard moral exhortations of his culture, and on this point refused to state what he meant clearly enough that his readers would recognize that he meant something totally different from what they would naturally suppose. This is particularly the case since, in that culture, forbidding remarriage would have been perceived as an oddity and would have actually undermined his whole attempt to be "above reproach" to outsiders.

What in particular then is Paul addressing in seeking to be "above" the culture's "reproach"? Understanding ancient society may again help us answer this question. Many Eastern cults had acquired unhealthy—and often undeserved—reputations for destroying traditional Roman family values. Here, as in Ephesians 5:21–6:9 and 1 Peter 3:1–8, the preservation of traditional family values may be intended in part as a witness to "those outside."[129]

In the case of the situation addressed in 1 Timothy, some believers had erred on the side of asceticism (1 Tim. 4:3),[130] and this could have brought the community into reproach just as dangerously as sexual promiscuity would have. The Romans were wary of all sexual irregularities as disruptive to the family,[131] and forsaking marriage would have been viewed as disruptive to the family.[132]

If "husband of one wife" is directed to counter the false teachers and maintain the church's witness, it may actually be requiring church leaders to be married rather than single,[133] *even though* it would have been widely known that Paul was single, and it is possible that Timothy was also. In other words, the instruction is related to the specific social situation addressed. Titus also emphasizes family values and views the threat of the subversion of "households" as a reason for maintaining these standards of leadership (1:10–11). (This passage could just mean that whole families are going off into error, but if the error is substantially different from the error encountered in 1 Timothy, the difference is difficult to detect, since similar language describes the opponents in both letters. So our best guess is that the crisis facing the church in Crete is similar to the one in Ephesus reported in 1 Timothy.)[134]

If it is replied that both 1 Timothy and Titus give "husband of one wife" as a standard, thus it must not be limited to the situation in Ephesus, we may recall in response our earlier suggestion that had this been a universal rule, Timothy and Titus would have already known it. The fact that the two lists diverge slightly also indicates that the list was not an invariable standard for all situations. But even if we insist that what Paul said to his situation must be used in exactly that form in all situations, then we still ought not to be forbidding previously divorced ministers remarriage; we ought to be urging them to establish families as quickly as possible, since "husband of one wife" may well mean that Paul was urging heads of households to take leadership in the church.

CONCLUSION

The requirements in 1 Timothy 3:2–7 and its parallels address a particular cultural situation, and their application must be varied from one community to another. Even if that were not the case, however, it is clear that "husband of one wife" is not directed toward divorced and remarried men. As preceding chapters have shown, a valid divorce does not leave one still married to the preceding wife, and one who remarries after such a divorce is thus not the husband of both wives, but only of one, the second one.[135] Indeed, the requirement here may even be that overseers in those congregations be married and be heads of families, which would have suggested that divorced men needed to be remarried to qualify, although we should not make this a requirement for all church leaders in all situations.

The passage does, of course, indicate the importance of a stable family life, particularly for ministering in a church built around families. It implicitly excludes from ministry those who take marriage lightly, whether by seeking a divorce or by devoting so much time to their ministry that they neglect their families. But this principle more readily excludes a pastor who spends all his or her time away from home than a pastor who had been divorced and remarried ten years before but has a current stable home life. A minister deserted by a spouse might indeed struggle with the sort of pastorate Paul describes in 1 Timothy (as might any single minister), but if the minister had been with the congregation for a long time and was otherwise qualified, Paul probably would have kept that minister there. After all, Paul, Barnabas, and apparently Timothy were all single, even though most apostles were married (1 Cor. 9:5).

As we noted above, it is necessary to be "above reproach" for the sake of the church's witness in the world. But is a policy of refusing ordination to divorced ministers really "above reproach," if those ministers were not at fault or if the divorce happened before their conversion? What happens when the world calls us on the carpet for having "standards" that reflect a Pharisaic legalism rather than belief that the Cross of Christ really cancels our past?[136]

To apply Scripture is not only to ask what Paul said in his situation, but to also ask what he would therefore say in ours. This has been the main failing of most modern interpreters who quote Paul glibly but pay no attention to the issues that Paul himself was addressing.

8 Final Words

This book has examined the New Testament teaching on divorce and has questioned how these insights might be applied today. The chapters on Matthew made it clear that if Jesus did not explicitly allow exceptions for remarriage, they were at least implicit in his words, as his disciples writing under the Spirit's inspiration understood.

Paul draws out a similar but different exception for why divorce is permissible, adding abandonment to adultery as grounds for a valid divorce. He also permits remarriage, because a valid divorce simply renders the innocent party "single" and permits remarriage in the same way that it is permitted for any single person. There are advantages to remaining single, but these apply equally to the divorced person and the never-married person.[1]

Finally we noted that Paul does not exclude divorced and remarried persons from ministry. In the situation he addresses, the best local church leaders would have been respectable heads of households with submissive wives and children whose lives testified that marriage was indeed a viable way to serve God. But the fact that Paul himself was single testifies against the assumption that even this should be made a qualification for all church leaders for all time.

But a few practical questions remain to be considered, since they could not be specifically addressed in our study above. Although the bulk of this book focuses on biblical texts and what their authors meant by them, the relevance of this book is that divorce and remarriage has become a major pastoral issue. The illustrations below are intended to provoke pastoral reflection on the principles articulated in this book.

WHAT ABOUT "OTHER EXCEPTIONS"?

Matthew allows that a spouse's infidelity can dissolve the marital union. This suggests that he permits divorce in the case of unrepentant infidelity, not that he gives an excuse to get out of a difficult marriage even though the bonds might be restored. But infidelity is clearly an exception. Paul, addressing a specific situation where nonbelieving spouses may have wanted to leave the Christian, also allows divorce and remarriage. The tenor of New Testament teaching, however, is that divorce is to be avoided at all costs.

But what happens if divorce occurs for reasons other than these two exceptions? What happens if divorce occurred before conversion? What happens if the guilty party repents, but the marriage has already been dissolved and the other partner has already begun a new relationship? Can a spouse who is physically abused get out of the situation? Can she (or he) divorce if all else fails, and must she (or he) then remain single?

These are hard questions, and they are all too relevant in our society. I have unfortunately encountered most of these situations, and a variety of others, in my limited pastoral experience; we must be ready to address such situations in our culture today. Assuming that Jesus' teaching on the subject is a general principle meant to admit exceptions (as Matthew and Paul demonstrate), and acknowledging the probability that his teaching is hyperbolic, we may allow some exceptions not addressed by Matthew or Paul because they were not specifically relevant to the situations these writers addressed.

With regard to any preconversion sin, the New Testament expressly teaches that a believer in Christ is a new creation; the old sins have passed away and are remembered no more. If Saul of Tarsus, after all he did against the Christians, could be forgiven and welcomed fully into fellowship, then a pre-conversion divorce should no longer be reckoned against the new believer as a sin.[2] This does not, of course, mean that no attempt should be made at reconciliation, if that possibility still lies open. Marriage is sacred, whether contracted before (as in the case of most of the believers in 1 Cor. 7 and 1 Pet. 3) or after conversion. But where reconciliation is impossible, a new life qualifies the new believer to pursue a new relationship in the Lord, provided it is with the understanding that the next marriage must be fully submitted to God's teachings.

If a wife (or, in fewer cases, a husband) is being physically or sexually abused by the spouse, my own pastoral counsel would be for her to get out of the situation. In my opinion, if reconciliation and restoration of the marriage are subsequently impossible (and the innocent partner has tried), the abused person is free to remarry. The fact that the New Testament does not explicitly make an exception for this does not demonstrate that no exception could be made. I do not suppose that spousal abuse never occurred in New Testament times, but I cannot honestly think of any references to it in the ancient literature; and the New Testament writers apparently thus had no immediate need to address it. Can we honestly maintain that a valid marriage exists when one spouse is treated only as an object for venting the other's repressed, violent rage? Is this not infidelity in some sense? And does not Paul's ad hoc exception, addressing a specific situation, point us to the kind of exceptions we must make in analogous situations?

Too often battered wives have been told that it is Christlike to remain in the abusive situation and have been made to bear the guilt and shame of the situation themselves, as if they accomplish some redemptive purpose for their husbands thereby. But although Peter's instructions to wives in 1 Peter 3 is prefaced by the example of our Lord's suffering, it was not addressing the situation of physical abuse. Slaves in Peter's day might have had to endure such affliction, because they could not get out of the situation. But wives today can get out of the situation, and we should not think that Peter wanted slaves to endure beatings if they could have avoided them. The early Christians in fact helped slaves to get out when they could, buying their freedom. (When early Christians used their money to have compassion on those in great need rather than on church buildings, there was for some reason more money to go around.) Paul was right to preach the gospel even in the face of persecution; he was also right to escape that persecution when the opportunity presented itself (e.g., Acts 9:24–25; 14:6; Matt. 10:23).

If it is argued that claims of abuse might be used as a phony excuse for a woman to leave a marriage, it should also be observed that the church's standard against divorce has been used by husbands as an opportunity to continue abusing their wives. Sometimes "taking sides" on whether or not a divorce is legitimate is a tough call; but when the case is genuinely too tough for us to judge, we ought to be humble enough not to judge it at all. But other times the decision is not tough: we just do not want to get involved, and so we give out pat theological formulas: No divorce under any circumstances.

I know of a woman who refused to confess her husband's abuse or be taken to the hospital after a beating; she died from her injuries. In this case she acted out of loyalty to her husband rather than from pastoral advice; but had a pastor advised her to remain in that situation, he would in my opinion share the bloodguilt of her murderer. This is, I confess, strong language. But too many churches have looked the other way while people were being broken, and my reading of the Bible says that calls for strong language: it calls us to repent of not caring enough to move beyond our pet formulas and deal with real human lives for whom Christ died.

In the past I either counseled people to stay together or left the decision entirely to the person seeking my counsel; I have never recommended divorce. But in retrospect, I think on those few occasions when I knew or suspected physical abuse, adultery, or that a parent was giving drugs to the kids, I should have recommended at least a temporary separation. Although I would still maintain that we must do everything possible to hold together a marriage until it is clear that one spouse is bent on dissolving it, there are circumstances where separation, and indeed divorce, is necessary. Some ivory-tower theologians who spend their time picking apart the grammar of New Testament texts without regard to the situations it addressed or the situations with which pastors must grapple today would do well to give attention to texts like these:

> If you had understood what Scripture says, "I want mercy and not sacrifice," you would not have condemned the innocent (Matt. 12:7).

> Whoever causes one of these little ones who believe in me to stumble, it would have been better for him to have had a millstone suspended from his neck, and to have been cast into the open sea (Matt. 18:6).

> They (the scribes and Pharisees) bind together heavy loads and lay them on other people's shoulders, but they themselves won't even push the loads with a finger (Matt. 23:4).

Pastors are shepherds, called to live among the sheep, to feed them and bind up their wounds. Indeed, all of us in the body are called to go after straying or wounded sheep (Matt. 18:10–14); and all of us are called to care for one another as for ourselves (Matt. 22:37–39), nay, to love one another even as Christ loved us, by serving one another to the death (John 13:34–35). Divorce is wrong because it violates a covenant of permanent love made before God to another person made in God's image; condemning the innocent party in a divorce is wrong because it despises the righteousness of Christ and oppresses the person who has already experienced the deepest rejection possible. Rejecting the guilty party or parties in a divorce once they have repented is wrong because it is a denial of the only forgiveness any of us can have before God (Matt. 6:14–15; 18:21–35; Col. 3:13, etc.).

Not all divorces have an innocent party, of course. Often the officially innocent party could have done much more to hold the marriage together. Often "exceptions" can become excuses—one spouse urging the other spouse to commit adultery so he or she can have the excuse to file (this has happened), an unforgiveness that refuses to accept the other's repentance, an angry slap taken as physical abuse. And where do we draw the line? While day after day of subjection to menial labor and cursing is not physical abuse, it is certainly abuse of the severest sort. But then what about arguments (in which most couples engage at times)? What about insensitivity to needs, expressed or unexpressed? Disagreements over the use of money? Disagreements over who should lead in the home? "Psychological abuse" can become a catch-all phrase that permits divorce for almost any reason, as the school of Hillel did (except that either party can now file). Can a man divorce his wife "for any cause," or are there definite limitations?

Jesus' teaching on the matter was stated hyperbolically for a reason. Yes, there may be exceptions. But Jesus' point is that we dare not look for the exceptions—they are only the last resort when all else has failed. A tough marriage is not an excuse to bail out. Indeed, in Jesus' day, marriages were arranged by parents; some marriages started off with more in their favor than others, but Jesus told his followers to make their marriages work, as much as it was in their power. In the same way today, there will always be marriages more and less comfortable than our own, and we, as much as is in our power, must make our marriages healthy and enduring.

The summons of his Kingdom is to be servants, to lay down our own desires and to seek reconciliation and healing (not just repressed hostility) in our marriages. Jesus demands that we make our marriages work. Only God ultimately knows what is in our hearts, but that inward standard is the one by which we will be judged: even if all the world thinks we did our best, if we really were not doing so, he knows. Following the teaching of the Kingdom means holding neither anger nor lust, and it means not looking for ways out of our marriage vows. The exception clause may be increasingly forced upon us in our culture, but we must never forget that it remains an "exception," after all else has failed.[3] The exception may come sooner or later, depending on how the breaking of the marriage is forced upon the faithful partner; but to the extent that it depends on us, we must always do our best to make our marriages alive and strong.

Jesus' message to everyone is plain enough: to those contemplating divorce, don't; to those inclined to condemn without knowing the circumstances, don't; to those near a prospective Christian divorce, offer yourselves as humble agents of reconciliation and healing; to those who have repented and made restitution (insofar as possible) for a sinful choice, trust his forgiveness; to those upon whom dissolution of marriage forced itself without invitation, be healed by God's grace and dare to stand for your freedom in Christ, which no one has the authority to take away from you. And whether his call after the divorce proves to be singleness or marriage, make your life a life of prayer that will minister to all believers with whom you have relationships, harboring no bitterness either against your former spouse or against a church whose fear of human pain often overshadows its willingness to heal it.

CONCLUSION

Is God against divorce? To this we must answer a resounding Yes. But the Yes must be qualified if the other partner has already broken the marriage; Scripture certainly allows making the brokenness of the marriage official if the partner has broken it. And the divorce is made official precisely to allow the innocent party (when there is an innocent party) to remarry, after God's compassion through the body of Christ and time have wrought their healing.[4] It is not legitimate for us to think of divorced people as a category; we must differentiate between the innocent and the guilty, or discard the label altogether. The innocent should be treated as other singles (or married people, if they have remarried); the guilty should be helped first to repent and then to seek reconciliation if it is still possible.

Divorce has become common in Western society. This is a tragedy, and the church is right to take a stand against it. But it is no longer possible to "sacrifice" divorced Christians for the sake of the standard. It was never right, of course, but it has now become a stumblingblock to more and more people. How long will conservative churches be able to continue evangelizing the multitudes in our society who are divorced, while forbidding them to hold offices in the church and often requiring them to remain single? Most churches, regardless of their position on divorce and remarriage, address all too little the acid agony of divorce, the problems faced by the children growing up in single-parent homes, the need of the innocent party for assurance and the need of the guilty party for correction and restoration to right relationship with God and his people. Scripture gives us some guidelines on how to make its teaching practical in our culture, just as it was when its Author first gave it. May we have the courage to obey its guidance.

Appendix A: Several Sayings on Divorce?

As might be expected, there is more than one place in the Gospels where Jesus addresses the issue of divorce. What complicates matters is that we have four Gospels, and several of them record the same conversations and sayings of Jesus in slightly different ways.[1] Of course, this does not bring into question the Gospels' accuracy; in Jesus' day it was considered perfectly natural for the most accurate of writers to put sayings in their own words,[2] to rearrange the order of their sources,[3] and to either delete details or add them from other sources.[4] Since our Gospels draw on oral tradition as well as on written sources, it is all the more natural that they would each include some different details.

But the varying reports of exactly how Jesus said something *do* pose a problem for the reader who wants to know "exactly" what Jesus said on an issue. In one story, which occurs in Mark and Matthew, Jesus debates the grounds for divorce with the religious people of his day;[5] elsewhere, in Luke and Matthew, Jesus forbids divorce as one example of how he has come to intensify the law. It is entirely possible that Jesus taught on divorce in both situations,[6] so the idea that Jesus gave the teaching in two different situations is not problematic; Matthew certainly saw no problem with it, since he reports both settings for the saying.

The real puzzle is that in both passages in Matthew, Jesus allows divorce on certain grounds, whereas in Mark and Luke, no exception is explicitly stated. The question this raises is whether Jesus actually allowed an exception or not.

There are three possible ways to answer this question. The first and least likely possibility is that one or two of the Gospels simply got it wrong. This proposal is unlikely given how close the accounts are in other details; their close correspondence on other points renders an *accidental* oversight here by the Gospel writers unlikely. A second proposal holds that Matthew's exception is really barely an exception at all, and thus not worth being mentioned by Mark or Luke. This is a view taken by many conservative interpreters today, but this position does not adequately explain why *Matthew* would choose to include such a minimal exception. A final possibility, the one we favor in this book, is that Matthew is "translating" the saying as we have it in Mark and Luke—i.e., bringing out its meaning for new situations.[7]

Each of the Gospels portrays Jesus in its own unique language and style, but the final product of each is what we as believers accept as an inspired and therefore authoritative portrayal of Jesus. For this reason, I have written as freely of Jesus speaking in Matthew as I do of Matthew doing so, although Matthew edited and arranged many of the sayings in their present order, as anyone who studies the different Gospels together can see.[8] Because technical scholarly debates about the transmission of traditions are not relevant to most of the readers for whom this book is intended, I do not engage in them in this book.

Because we hold all the Gospel accounts to be inspired, their exact relation to one another and the history of how they arrived in their final form are less important for our present purposes than their meaning as they stand. Because Matthew gives a much more complete context for the sayings, we have focused our attention on his passages and have commented only briefly on the differences between Matthew and the other Gospels.

Appendix B: Jesus' Law in the Sermon on the Mount

In Matthew 5:31–32 and Luke 16:16–18, Jesus' prohibition of divorce and remarriage occurs in a context that stresses that God's law is eternal and that Jesus has come to enforce its true meaning, not to compromise it. Both of these sayings occur in a broader context that indicates what point each writer wishes to emphasize. Luke, on the one hand, emphasizes the radical demands of the Kingdom on disciples' possessions (Luke 16:9–15, 19–25). Matthew, on the other hand, emphasizes how the demands of the Kingdom go deeper than the standard practice of the law followed in Jewish tradition (Matt. 5:17–20). Because Matthew's context is fuller and includes the "exception clause," we have concentrated on his version of the saying in this book.

Matthew, following the standard "topical" way of ordering many ancient biographies, includes most of Jesus' material on the law in his section on the ethics of the Kingdom, in chapters 5–7 of his book.[1] Early Christians, very concerned with what Jesus had said, had collected his teachings, and Matthew arranges them according to subject. In this passage Matthew reports what Jesus taught about the law of Moses.

INTERPRETATIONS OF MATTHEW'S LAW

There is a variety of views on exactly what Matthew 5:21–48 means. One traditional interpretation argues that Jesus here *opposes* the law. As Rudolf Bultmann puts it,[2] Jesus opposes the scribal interpretation of the law, thus "completely destroying . . . the formal authority of Scripture."[3] Bultmann's position is problematic, however, since *many* Jewish groups opposed scribal interpretation without renouncing the formal authority of the law.[4] Bultmann's interpretation simply would not have been the most natural way for an ancient Jewish reader to construe the text. Further, his reading is not the most natural reading of 5:17–20, even today, as my students typically demonstrate on their first reading of this text. It it is moreover clear, as we point out below, that in 5:21–48 Jesus *intensifies*, rather than abandons, the fence around the law.

More scholars today recognize that Jesus was not opposing the writings of Moses, but rather regarded them as God's Word.[5] Nevertheless, among these scholars there remain some differences of opinion. Some writers suggest that Jesus was *radicalizing* the law, making it stricter, as the Essenes did.[6] Others contend that he was just advocating more rigorously observing what was already written.[7] Many scholars think that he was opposing Pharisaic interpretations of the law, which they regard as mere attention to the letter of the law;[8] while others point out *parallels* between the views of Jesus and those of the ancient rabbis.[9] Since there are so many differences of opinion on exactly how to read the context of Jesus' teachings here, it is necessary for us to examine the text in greater detail. Understanding the figures of speech Jesus employs in this passage will help us better hear the text in the way its first hearers did.

Matthew 5:17–20: Not Against the Law

One does not have to read far in Matthew 5 before one realizes that Jesus is not against the law.[10] This is proclaimed in 5:17–20: Jesus came not to annul, but to fulfill[11] the law (v. 17);[12] he is, in fact, dissatisfied with the Pharisees' inadequate performance of it (v. 20). Matthew emphasizes that Jesus does not interpret the law in such a way as to undermine its authority; instead he interprets it in such a way as to uphold its proper meaning, a meaning which is sometimes against the more common Pharisaic interpretation of the passage.[13]

Jesus seems to accept the continuing validity of the law in this passage. He announces in v. 18 that the law will stand until the time when heaven and earth pass away—in other words, until the end of the world (cf. 24:35).[14] Most Jewish readers would have understood this as a figure of speech meaning that the law would stand "forever," a suggestion of the eternality of the covenant.[15] Jesus certainly understands the law to be eternal; its sanctions are executed at the day of judgment (5:19–20).[16]

Indeed, as v. 18 continues, not one *yod* (the smallest Hebrew letter)[17] or marking was to pass from the law. This is not a statement about God using waterproof ink on the Bible, of course; it just means that even the least noticed parts of God's Word are eternally true and valid. Later Jewish teachers often spoke in similar ways about the importance of even the most trivial elements:[18] they spoke of how God would rather uproot a thousand king Solomons than a single *yod* from the Bible;[19] or they told how a *yod* removed from Sarai's name in Genesis cried out to God from generation to generation, until he finally stuck it back into the Bible, in Joshua's name.[20] Although there is no way to know how early these Jewish stories are, they at least illustrate the point that Jesus' readers would have no doubt understood: he was upholding the veracity of even the smallest details of God's Word.

In 5:19,[21] Jesus declares:

> Whoever annuls[22] one of the least of these commandments or teaches[23] others to do so, will be called[24] least[25] in the kingdom of heaven;[26] but whoever practices and teaches the least of these commandments,[27] this one will be called great[28] in the kingdom of heaven.

This is, of course, a strong way of saying that one should keep the commandments. The passage does not answer the sort of questions we are likely to ask about it today, for example: What happens if we break one and keep another? Or, how many of us can be the greatest if we all keep that commandment? Questions like these miss his point. This sort of saying about what is greatest and least was in Jesus' day a standard figure of speech used by Jewish teachers, who often liked to state their points in graphic, extreme terms. One might take as an example of the same way of speaking the praise attributed to a late first-century rabbi:

> If all the wise of Israel were in a scale of a balance, and Eliezer ben Hyrcanus in the other scale, he would outweigh them all; but Abba Saul cited the same rabbi as saying, if all the wise of Israel were in a scale of a balance, and R. Eliezer ben Hyrcanus was included with them, and R. Eliezer ben Arach in the other scale, *he* would outweigh them all.[29]

Obviously Eliezer ben Hyrcanus and Eliezer ben Arach could not have *both* outweighed all the other rabbis; otherwise, each would have had to outweigh the other. But mathematical precision about who weighed most in the Kingdom was not their teacher's point. The point is simply that on different occasions he chose to compliment them both in superlative terms.

Similar extreme language came to be used of matters more directly related to the law: a part of the law could stand for the whole, whether that part were a small or a large commandment. With regard to a large commandment, the Jewish sages said that whoever confesses to idolatry denies the whole law, and whoever denies idolatry confesses to the whole law.[30] They could argue similarly with regard to smaller commandments:

> whoever accepts the religious duties involving just weights affirms the Exodus from Egypt, and whoever denies the religious duties involving just weights denies the Exodus from Egypt.[31]

In this sense, as the rabbis said, "a minor religious duty should be as precious to you as a principal one."[32] Small commands carried with them the promise of large rewards or punishments:[33]

> If a man performs but a single commandment it shall be well with him and he shall have length of days and shall inherit the Land; but if he neglects a single commandment it shall be ill with him and he shall not have length of days and shall not inherit the Land.[34]

Or, in the words of James in the New Testament, "For if anyone is keeping the whole law, yet stumbles on even one point, he has become liable for transgressing the whole thing."[35]

When Jesus condemns breaking even the smallest of commandments, he is espousing an idea that most of his hearers would have readily understood. By the third century many rabbis had even decided *which* commandment was the lightest and which the heaviest.[36] The lightest commandment stated that one who took young birds from a nest should leave the mother alive; the heaviest was to honor one's father and mother. In Scripture, both commandments received the same reward: "life" (Exod. 20:12; Deut. 22:7), which the rabbis interpreted as eternal life. Thus, they reasoned, the reward for keeping even the smallest commandment is eternal life, and the punishment for breaking even the smallest commandment is damnation.[37]

The rabbis thereby affirmed that one who performed a single precept was regarded as if he had kept the whole law,[38] and one suspected of violating one precept could as easily be suspected of violating any other.[39] Indeed, a Jew could not become a Pharisee, and a Gentile could not convert to Judaism if he were unwilling to keep even a single, little-known law.[40] As one scholar points out, "Deliberate rejection of any commandment was, in the later rabbinic formulation, tantamount to rejecting the God who gave it."[41]

The point is not that no one ever breaks a commandment; the rabbis admitted that virtually everyone broke some commandments sometimes.[42] The point is that no one has the right to say, "I like these commandments over here, but those little commandments over there are not worth my attention." To deny that one was responsible to do *whatever* God commanded, no matter how trivial it might seem, was to deny his lordship and to intentionally rebel against his whole law.[43] According to the rabbis, such a person merited damnation.[44]

This is not to say that coveting your neighbor's car and killing him have precisely the same effect on your neighbor; nor is it to equate the value of ritual law with that of moral law,[45] since Jesus himself makes a distinction between the lighter and weightier matters of the law (Matt. 23:23).[46] It is instead to say that we cannot pick and choose which teachings of God we will obey. We must obey everything he says, and to take anything he says lightly is to deny him the right to rule our lives.

But while most Jewish teachers would have agreed with what Jesus had said up to this point, Jesus suggests that their hearts did not match up to what he was saying. Matthew 5:20 challenges the Pharisees, who in Jesus' day were the most respected religious movement in Palestine,[47] and whose successors in Matthew's day had achieved a position of much greater prominence in Palestinian Judaism. The Pharisees and legal scholars are cited because of their strict adherence to the law;[48] but Jesus argues here that their adherence is insufficient. Jewish piety stressed the pure intention of the heart more than outward ritual,[49] but, like much religion today, this emphasis was not always translated into practice.

In the rest of Matthew 5, Jesus goes on to demand a deeper righteousness than he finds in the most religious people of his day;[50] we might call the righteous standard he demands, "heart-law." The key to his interpretation of the law is valuing one's neighbor as oneself (7:12, 22:38). This principle was already accepted in Judaism,[51] but Jesus places this command within a new interpretive framework of "mercy" (9:13; 12:7; 23:23), in the context of his mission (28:19) and community (ch. 18).

The Six "Antitheses": "You have heard it said . . ."

Six times in the Sermon on the Mount Jesus says, "You have heard it said, but I say to you."[52] On the one hand, this phrase is often taken to mean that Jesus is disputing what they have heard—in most cases, verses he cites from the Old Testament;[53] thus these sayings are called "antitheses." These sayings could therefore be taken to mean, "A is false, but B is true," as they would mean if they were really antithetical.

On the other hand, these sayings could be interpreted as meaning, "not only is A the case, but also B is being said here."[54] If they mean that A and B are both true, then Jesus is not correcting the Old Testament, but expounding it. He is demanding an interpretation of the Bible that goes beyond its face-value interpretation and understands the inspired *point* of the text. Rather than stopping with the particular cultural issue a text addresses, we must determine the supracultural principle behind the text.

Given what we have seen above in 5:17–20, this second option is more likely: Jesus is interpreting the law of Moses, not refuting it. In laying his interpretation of the law against a mere face-value interpretation of the law, Jesus stands well within Jewish tradition.[55] In this case, he is not claiming to refute the law, but rather to interpret the law, as any good Jewish teacher would.[56]

Those who think that Jesus opposed the Old Testament law often argue that he contradicts it in this chapter, for instance, by saying that divorce is no longer permissible, although Moses had allowed it. But this suggestion is a thoroughly modern reading of the text, and it betrays a misunderstanding of how first-century Jewish readers would have understood Jesus' words. It was never against the law to be *stricter* than the law;[57] to be stricter was to set a respectful "fence" around the law,[58] a boundary to keep one from breaking its intention. Fulfilling the law's intention sometimes meant overriding its apparent concessions.[59]

Not only did Jewish teachers make the law stricter; sometimes they even made the law more lenient, to adapt it to new situations so that its intent would be fulfilled. This happened, for example, when the interpretation of Sabbath law was changed to allow defensive warfare on the Sabbath,[60] and when a way was found around the command to forgive debts, so the poor could still get loans from creditors afraid to lose their money.[61] Practice of parts of the law could be temporarily suspended, by prophets[62] or sages,[63] when it was necessary for survival. Both main schools of Pharisaic thought were lenient on some points and stricter on others, but as long as a teacher followed either one school or the other (and did not simply follow the more lenient position all the time), one's teaching was acceptable to the later rabbis.[64]

The language that Jesus uses in this passage, "You have heard it said, but I say to you," would not have signified to anyone that he was quoting the law to refute it. To any ancient Jewish reader it would have conveyed nothing stronger than that Jesus was *interpreting* the biblical laws they already knew. The Greek word translated "but" in "*but* I say to you" (as in, e.g., NIV, NRSV, KJV, Phillips, NAB) is a weak "but"; elsewhere the same word is sometimes translated "and," and a much stronger word for "but" was available had Matthew wanted to underscore that Jesus was disagreeing with what the hearers had heard. The phrase "you have heard it said," when used to quote Scripture, could even be understood as a polite way of saying, "God said this to you in the Bible."[65] If this is what Jesus is saying, we can be sure that he would be agreeing with what he said his Father had claimed.

Further, *other* Jewish teachers often said things like, "one (I, or you) might hear" (i.e., might interpret a passage in a certain way), and then went on to give a different or more complete interpretation.[66] One rabbi challenging another rabbi's interpretation could say, "You say such-and-such (but how do you know that you are correct)?"[67] A Jewish teacher could also say things like, "I say," or, "I cite such-and-such a case,"[68] without claiming to refute what had just been said.[69] There is nothing necessarily unusual with the saying, "You have heard it said, but I say to you"; it could have been said by other rabbis as easily as by Jesus. Scholars who have not noticed this and maintain that Jesus' wording is anti-law cannot be said to be simply a few months behind on their scholarly reading; a great modern scholar of ancient rabbinic Judaism, Solomon Schechter, pointed out these parallels in 1900.[70]

This is not to say, of course, that the conjunction of all the features of this discourse would not have provided an impressive image of authority. Jesus is definitely claiming to have the right interpretation of the law and is not citing any other authorities to confirm his position; it is not without reason that his hearers marvel at his authority (7:28–29), which is especially claimed at the end of the Sermon (7:21–27).[71] But this is not the same as saying that Jesus is setting his own authority against that of the Scriptures.

I once debated with a scholar who was arguing that Jesus was against the Old Testament law here. He followed Bultmann's position and regarded my interpretation as a "fundamentalistic" attempt to "save" the Old Testament. But, as I argued (I think successfully, since he finally conceded this point), Matthew's readers would not have thought that Jesus was opposing the law at all. They would have seen him as explaining the law's demands on our hearts, even to the level of our motives and intentions.

In this appendix, we have examined the nature of Jesus' legal sayings in the Sermon on the Mount. Here, too, understanding the specific ways people expressed their teachings in Jesus' day helps us understand more clearly what Jesus meant.

Appendix C: Glossary

Alexandria: A Greek city in northern Egypt, one third of whose population was Jewish
Amoraim: Rabbis after c. AD 220
Dead Sea Scrolls: Documents from a Jewish sect, probably Essenes, who lived in the wilderness by the Dead Sea
Diaspora: The Jewish community in the "Dispersion," i.e., outside Palestine
Greco-Roman Antiquity: The ancient Greek and Roman world; as we use it, especially the culture of the first-century Roman Empire, which had synthesized many elements of Greek and Roman culture
Mishnah: Our earliest record of Palestinian Jewish law by the rabbis, especially those following the teachings of the School of Rabbi Akiba
Pastoral Epistles: 1 & 2 Timothy, and Titus
Rabbis: Jewish teachers who by the late first century began to assume a position of authority in Palestine (in this book, we refer to *ancient* rabbis unless stated otherwise)
Redaction History: The study of how each Gospel writer adapted the earlier traditions to make certain points
Rhetoric: The art or form of proper public speaking
Satirists: writers of witty ridicule (such as Martial, Horace, or Juvenal)
Tannaitic: Rabbinic literature reporting opinions of rabbis who lived before AD 220

Important Names

Akiba: An influential late first and early second-century rabbi
Epictetus: A first-century Stoic philosopher
Hillel: With Shammai, one of the two rabbis most influential by the early first century; generally the more lenient of the two
Josephus: A Jewish historian writing toward the end of the first century AD
Lucian: An early second-century rhetorician

Philo: A first-century AD Jewish philosopher in Alexandria
Plato: An influential pre-Christian Greek philosopher
Seneca: A first-century Stoic philosopher
Shammai: With Hillel, one of the two rabbis most influential by the
early first century; generally the stricter of the two

Abbreviations

MODERN TEXTS

ACR	*Australasian Catholic Record*
AFER	*AFER* (continues *African Ecclesial Review*)
AJAH	*American Journal of Ancient History*
AnaBib	Analecta Biblica
ANET	Ancient Near Eastern Texts Relating to the Old Testament, ed. Pritchard
Ant	*Antonianum*
APP	*Analytic Psychotherapy and Psychopathology*
ASNU	Acta Seminarii Neotestamentici Upsaliensis
ATR	*Anglican Theological Review*
AUSS	*Andrews University Seminary Studies*
BETL	Bibliotheca Ephemeridum Theologicarum Lovaniensium
Bib	*Biblica*
BibR	*Biblia Revuo*
BibSac	*Bibliotheca Sacra*
BiTr	*Bible Translator*
BJS	Brown Judaic Studies
BR	*Biblical Research*
BT	*The Bible Today*
BZ	*Biblische Zeitschrift*
CBQ	*Catholic Biblical Quarterly*
CBQMS	Catholic Biblical Quarterly Monograph Series
CH	*Church History*
ChM	*Churchman*
CIJ	Corpus Inscriptionum Iudaicarum
CIL	Corpus Inscriptionum Latinarum

ColTh	*Collectanea Theologica*
CP	*Classical Philology*
CPJ	Corpus Papyrorum Iudaicarum
CQ	*Classical Quarterly*
CT	*Christianity Today*
DCBCN	The Development of Christian Doctrine before the Council of Nicaea
CTM	*Concordia Theological Monthly*
EglTh	*Eglise et Théologie*
EPROER	Etudes Préliminaires aux Religions Orientales dans l'Empire Romain
ETL	*Ephemerides Theologicae Lovanienses*
EvJ	*Evangelical Journal*
EvT	*Evangelische Theologie*
ExpT	*Expository Times*
FV	*Foi et Vie*
GNS	Good News Studies
HSS	*Harvard Semitic Series*
HUCA	*Hebrew Union College Annual*
ICC	International Critical Commentaries
JANES	*Journal of the Ancient Near Eastern Society of Columbia University*
JBL	*Journal of Biblical Literature*
JBLMS	Journal of Biblical Literature Monograph Series
JCBRF	*Journal of the Christian Brethren Research Fellowship*
JETS	*Journal of the Evangelical Theological Society*
JJS	*Journal of Jewish Studies*
JPFC	The Jewish People in the First Century
JQR	*Jewish Quarterly Review*
JR	*Journal of Religion*
JRS	*Journal of Roman Studies*
JSJ	*Journal for the Study of Judaism*
JSNT	*Journal for the Study of the New Testament*
JSOT	*Journal for the Study of the Old Testament*
JSR	*Journal of Sex Research*
JTS	*Journal of Theological Studies*
KJV	King James Version (Authorized Version)
LEC	Library of Early Christianity
MNTC	Moffatt New Testament Commentary
NAB	New American Bible
NCB	New Century Bible

Neot	*Neotestamentica*
NIBC	New International Biblical Commentary
NICNT	New International Commentary on the New Testament
NIGTC	New International Greek Testament Commentary
NIV	New International Version
NovT	*Novum Testamentum*
NRSV	New Revised Standard Version
NRT	*Nouvelle Revue Théologique*
NTA	New Testament Abstracts
NTM	New Testament Message
NTS	*New Testament Studies*
NTT	*Norsk Teologisk Tidsskrift*
OBT	Overtures to Biblical Theology
OTPS	*Old Testament Pseudepigrapha*, ed. Charlesworth
PAAJR	Proceedings of the American Academy for Jewish Research
Phillips	J. B. Phillips, *The New Testament in Modern English*
POTT	Pittsburgh Original Texts and Translations
RB	*Revue Biblique*
RestQ	*Restoration Quarterly*
RevQum	*Revue de Qumran*
RevRel	*Review of Religion*
RMP	*Rheinisches Museum für Philologie*
RSR	*Recherches de Science Religieuse*
RTP	*Revue de Théologie et de Philosophie*
SBLDS	Society of Biblical Literature Dissertation Series
SBLMS	Society of Biblical Literature Monograph Series
SBLSBS	Society of Biblical Literature Sources for Biblical Study
SBLSS	Society of Biblical Literature Semeia Supplements
ScEsp	*Science et Esprit*
Scr	*Scripture: The Quarterly of the Catholic Biblical Association*
SEÅ	*Svensk Exegetisk Årsbok*
Sem	*Semitica*
SNTSMS	Society for New Testament Studies Monograph Series
TB	*Tyndale Bulletin*
TDGR	Translated Documents of Greece and Rome
TDNT	*Theological Dictionary of the New Testament*
Them	*Themelios*

TPQ	*Theologisch-Praktische Quartelschrift*
TQ	*Theologische Quartelschrift*
TS	*Theological Studies*
TVT	*Tijdschrift voor Theologie*
TZ	*Theologische Zeitschrift*
VC	*Vigiliae Christianae*
VT	*Vetus Testamentum*
WBC	Word Biblical Commentary
WomSt	*Women's Studies*
ZAW	*Zeitschrift für die Alttestamentliche Wissenschaft*
ZNW	*Zeitschrift für die Neutestamentliche Wissenschaft*

ANCIENT LITERATURE

Old Testament, New Testament, and Apocrypha:

Gen	Genesis
Exod	Exodus
Lev	Leviticus
Num	Numbers
Deut	Deuteronomy
Josh	Joshua
Judg	Judges
Ruth	Ruth
1-2 Sam	1-2 Samuel
1-2 Kgs	1-2 Kings
1-2 Chron	1-2 Chronicles
Ezra	Ezra
Neh	Nehemiah
Esth	Esther
Job	Job
Pss	Psalms
Prov	Proverbs
Eccl	Ecclesiastes
Song Sol	Song of Solomon
Isa	Isaiah
Jer	Jeremiah
Lam	Lamentations
Ezek	Ezekiel
Dan	Daniel
Hos	Hosea

Joel	Joel
Amos	Amos
Obad	Obadiah
Jonah	Jonah
Mic	Micah
Nah	Nahum
Hab	Habakkuk
Zeph	Zephaniah
Hag	Haggai
Zech	Zechariah
Mal	Malachi
Matt	Matthew
Mark	Mark
Luke	Luke
John	John
Acts	Acts
Rom	Romans
1-2 Cor	1-2 Corinthians
Gal	Galatians
Eph	Ephesians
Phil	Philippians
Col	Colossians
1-2 Thess	1-2 Thessalonians
1-2 Tim	1-2 Timothy
Titus	Titus
Phlm	Philemon
Heb	Hebrews
Jas	James
1-2 Pet	1-2 Peter
1-2-3 John	1-2-3 John
Jude	Jude
Rev	Revelation
1-2 Esd	1-2 Esdras
Tob	Tobit
Jdt	Judith
Sir	Sirach
Bar	Baruch
1-2 Macc	1-2 Maccabees
3-4 Macc	3-4 Maccabees
Ep Jer	Epistle of Jeremiah
Pr Azar	Prayer of Azariah

Sus	Susanna
Add Esth	Additions to Esther
Wisd	Wisdom of Solomon
4 Ezra	4 Ezra
Bel	Bel and the Dragon
Sg TYM	Song of Three Young Men

Dead Sea Scrolls:

1QH	Thanksgiving Hymns
1QM	War Scroll
1QS	Manual of Discipline
CD	Damascus Document
4QpNah	Pesher commentary on Nahum
4QpHab	Pesher commentary on Habakkuk
4QTemple	Temple Scroll

Rabbinic Texts:

Tractates of Mishnah (m.), Talmud (Babylonian, b.; Palestinian, p.), and/or Tosefta (Tos.):

Ab.	Aboth	Sayings of the Fathers*
Arak.	'Arakin	Estimates (vows)
A.Z.	'Abodah Zarah	Idolatry and idolaters
Bek.	Bekorot	Firstborn
Ber.	Berakot	Benedictions
Bez.	Betzah	Egg (Sabbaths vs. Festivals)
Bik.	Bikkurim	Firstfruits
B. B.	Baba Batra	Real estate
B. K.	Baba Kamma	(direct) Damages
B. M.	Baba Metzia	Property
Dem.	Demai	Doubtful (whether tithed)
Ed.	'Eduyot	Testimonies (of prior teachers)
Erub.	'Eruvin	Overlappings (for Sabbath)
Git.	Gittin	Divorce documents
Hag.	Hagiga	Pilgrimage festivals & offerings

---

*These English summary titles are based especially on H. L. Strack, *Introduction to the Talmud and Midrash* (New York: Atheneum, 1978), and in their brevity may fail to adequately explain or summarize the tractate. But they can give the reader some sense of the general contents of the tractate from which references in this work are taken.

Hor.	Horayot	Ritual errors
Kel.	Kelim	Vessels
Ker.	Keritot	Being cut off (mortal sins)
Ket.	Ketubot	Marriage contracts
Kid.	Kiddushin	Betrothals
Kil.	Kilaim	(on trees)
Kin.	Kinnim	Birds' nests
Hal.	Halla	Heave from the dough
Hul.	Hullin	Profane things (esp. meat)
Maas.	Maaserot	Tithes
Mak.	Makkot	Stripes (corporal punishments)
Maksh.	Makshirin	Liquid-impurities
Meg.	Megilla	Scroll (of Esther)
Meil.	Meilah	Trespassing on sacred things
Men.	Menahot	Meal-offerings
Mid.	Middot	Measurements of Temple
Mik.	Mikvaot	Immersion pools
M. K.	Moed Katan	Inside days of long feasts
M. S.	Maaser Sheni	Second Tithe
Naz.	Nazir	Nazirite vows
Ned.	Nedarim	Vows
Neg.	Negaim	Leprosy
Nid.	Nidda	Menstrual and postpartum imp's
Ohal.	Ohalot	Tents (corpse-impurity)
Par.	Para	Red Heifer
Peah	Peah	Gleanings for poor in field corner
Pes.	Pesahim	Passover
R. H.	Rosh ha-Shanah	New Year's Festival
Sanh.	Sanhedrin	Judicial procedures
Shab.	Shabbat	Sabbath
Sheb.	Shevuot	Oaths
Shebi.	Shebiith	Seventh Year
Shek.	Shekalim	On half-shekel tax
Sot.	Sotah	Suspected adulteress
Suk.	Sukkoth	Tabernacles
Taan.	Taanit	Fasting
Tam.	Tamid	Daily offering
Tem.	Temura	"Changing" offerings
Ter.	Terumot	Heave-offerings
Toh.	Toharot	(Im)purities

Yad.	Yadaim	Hand(washing)s
Yeb.	Yebamot	Levirate marriages
Yoma	Yoma	On Day of Atonement
Zab.	Zabim	Those with impure emissions
Zeb.	Zebahim	Animal offerings

Midrashim and Other Rabbinic Texts:

Ab.R.Nathan, A, B	Aboth d-Rabbi Nathan, Recensions A and B
Mek.	Mekilta
Pisha	Pisha
Bah.	Bahodesh
Nez.	Neizikin
Sifra	Sifra on Leviticus (Tannaitic)
par.; pq.	parashah; pereq
VDDen.	Vayyiqra Dibura Denedabah
VDDeho.	Vayyiqra Dibura Dehobah
Sav	Sav
Sh.	Shemini
Taz.	Tazria
Neg.	Negaim
Mes.	Mesora
Zab.	Zabim
AM	Aharé Mot
Qed.	Qedoshim
Emor, Behor	Emor, Behor
Behuq.	Behuqotai
Sifré Num.	Sifré to Numbers (Tannaitic)
Sifre Deut.	Sifre to Deuteronomy (Tannaitic)
Gen. Rab.	Genesis Rabbah
Ex. Rab.	Exodus Rabbah
Lev. Rab.	Leviticus Rabbah
Num. Rab.	Numbers Rabbah
Deut. Rab.	Deuteronomy Rabbah
Ruth Rab.	Ruth Rabbah
Esther Rab.	Esther Rabbah
Lam. Rab.	Lamentations
Song Rab.	Songs of Songs Rabbah
Koh. Rab.	Ecclesiastes (Kohelet) Rabbah
Pes. Rab. Kah.	Pesikta de-Rab Kahana
Pes. Rab.	Pesikta Rabbati

EARLY CHRISTIAN AND OTHER EARLY JEWISH LITERATURE:

Ahikar	Ahikar (story and sayings)
Apoc. Peter	Apocalypse of Peter
Apoc. Zeph.	Apocalypse of Zephaniah
Arist.	Letter of (Ps.)Aristeas to Philocrates
Asc. Isa.	Ascension of Isaiah
Athenag.	Athenagoras, Plea
Did.	Didache
1 Clem.	1 Clement
1 En.	1 Enoch
4 Ezra	4 Ezra
4 Macc.	4 Maccabees
Gr. Ezra	Greek Apocalypse of Ezra
Herm.	Shepherd of Hermas
Ign. *Trall.*	Ignatius, To the Trallians
Jos.	Josephus
Ant.	Antiquities
Apion	Against Apion
Life	Life of Josephus
War	Jewish War
Jos. & As.	Joseph and Asenath
Jub.	Jubilees
Justin	Justin
1 Apol.	1 Apology
Dial.	Dialogue with Trypho
LXX	Septuagint
Min. Fel. *Oct.*	Minucius Felix, Octavius
Odes Sol.	Odes of Solomon
Philo	Philo
Abr.	De Abrahamo
Aet.	De Aeternitate Mundi
Agr.	De Agricultura
Cher.	De Cherubim
Conf.	De Confusione Linguarum
Cong.	De Congressu Eruditionis gratia
Cont.	De Vita Contemplativa
Decal.	De Decalogo
Det.	Quod Deterius Potiori insidiari soleat
Deus	Quod Deus sit Immutabilis
Ebr.	De Ebrietate

Exsec.	De Exsecrationibus
Fug.	De Fuga et Inventione
Gig.	De Gigantibus
Her.	Quis rerum divinarum heres sit
Jos.	De Josepho
L.A.	Legum Allegoriarum
Mig.	De Migratione Abrahami
Mos.	De Vita Mosis
Mut.	De Mutatione Nominum
Op.	De Opifio Mundi
Plant.	De Plantatione
Post.	De Posteritate Caini
Praem.	De Praemiis et Poenis
Prob.	Quod omnis probus liber
Sac.	De Sacrificiis Abelis et Caini
Sob.	De Sobrietate
Som.	De Somniis
Spec.	De Specialibus Legibus
Virt.	De Virtutibus
Ps-Philo	Pseudo-Philo
Ps.-Phocyl.	Pseudo-Phocylides
Ps. Sol.	Psalms of Solomon
2 Bar.	2 Baruch
2 En.	2 Enoch
Syr. Men. Sent.	Sentences of the Syriac Menander
Sib. Or.	Sibylline Oracles
Tat.	Tatian
Tert. *Apol.*	Tertullian, Apology
Test. Abr.	Testament of Abraham
Test. Job	Testament of Job
Test. Moses	Testament of Moses
Test. Sol.	Testament of Solomon
Testaments of the Twelve Patriarchs	
Test. Asher	Testament of Asher
Test. Benj.	Testament of Benjamin
Test. Dan	Testament of Dan
Test. Gad	Testament of Gad
Test. Iss.	Testament of Issachar
Test. Jud.	Testament of Judah
Test. Jos.	Testament of Joseph
Test. Levi	Testament of Levi
Test. Naph.	Testament of Naphtali

Test. Reub.	Testament of Reuben
Test. Simeon	Testament of Simeon
Test. Zeb.	Testament of Zebulon
Theoph.	Theophilus (Chr.)
3 En.	3 Enoch
3 Macc.	Third Maccabees
Tr. Shem	Treatise of Shem
V. Ad.	Life of Adam and Eve

OTHER GRECO-ROMAN LITERATURE:

Ach. Tat. *Clit.*	Achilles Tatius, Clitophon and Leucippe
Apul. *Metam.*	Apuleius, Metamorphoses (The Golden Ass)
Artem. *Oneir.*	Artemidorus, Oneirocritica
Athen. *Deipn.*	Athenaeus, The Deipnosophists
Aul. Gel., *Att. Nights*	Aulus Gellius, Attic Nights
Chariton *Chaer.*	Chariton, Chaereas and Callirhoe
Cic.	Cicero
De Amic.	De Amicitia
De Legib.	De Legibus
De Offic.	De Officiis
De Part. Or.	De Partitione Oratoria
Tusc. Disp.	Tusculan Disputations
Dio Cass. *Hist. Rome*	Dio Cassius, History of Rome
Dio Chrys., *Disc.*	Dio Chrysostom, Discourses
Alex.	To the People of Alexandria
Beauty	On Beauty
Chrys.	Chryseis
fr.	Fragments
Pop. Opin.	On Popular Opinion
Diog. Laert. *Lives*	Diogenes Laertius, Lives of Eminent Philosophers
Epict.	Epictetus
Disc.	Discourses
Encheir.	Encheiridion
Greek Anth.	Greek Anthology
Herod. *Hist.*	Herodotus, Histories
Hier. *Toward Parents*	Hierocles, How to Conduct Oneself Toward One's Parents
Hor.	Horace

Ep.	Epodes
Odes	Odes
Sat.	Satires
Isoc. (Or.)	Isocrates (Orations)
Antid.	Antidosis
Demon.	To Demonicus
Nicoc.	To Nicocles
Nic./Cyp.	Nicocles/Cyprians
Justin. *Cod.*	Justinian, Codex
Justin. *Instit.*	Justinian, Institutes
Juv. *Sat.*	Juvenal, Satires
Lucian	Lucian
Aff. Heart	Affairs of the Heart
Dem.	Demonax
Doub. Ind.	The Double Indictment
Syr. Godd.	The Syrian Goddess
Vit. Auct.	Vitarum Auctio (Philosophies for Sale)
Lucret. *Nat.*	Lucretius, De Rerum Natura
Marc. *Aur. Med.*	Marcus Aurelius, Meditations
Mart. *Epig.*	Martial, Epigrams
Mus. Ruf. *fr.*	Musonius Rufus, fragments
Paulus *Opin.*	Paulus, Opinions
Petr. *Sat.*	Petronius, Satires
Philost. *V.A.*	Philostratus, The Life of Apollonius of Tyana
Plat. *Rep.*	Plato, Republic
Plut.	Plutarch
Lives:	
Crass.	(Nicias and) Crassus
Numa	(Lycurgus and) Numa
Publ.	(Solon and) Publicola
Rom.	(Theseus and) Romulus
Solon	Solon (and Publicola)
Mor.:	Moralia
Bride	Advice to Bride and Groom
Consol. to Wife	Consolation to his Wife
Dial. on Love	Dialogue on Love (Amatorius)
Dinner	The Dinner of the Seven Wise Men
Div. Veng.	On the Delays of Divine Vengeance
Educ.	The Education of Children
G.Q.	Greek Questions

Isis	Isis and Osiris
Lectures	On Listening to Lectures
Kings	Sayings of Kings and Commanders
Lett. Apoll.	A Letter of Condolence to Apollonius
L. S.	Love Stories
Old Man in Affairs	Whether an Old Man Should Engage in Public Affairs
Pl. Life Imp.	That Epicurus Actually Makes a Pleasant Life Impossible
Profit	How to Profit by One's Enemies
Or. at Delphi	The Oracles at Delphi no longer given in verse
Romans	Sayings of Romans
R. Q.	Roman Questions
Spartans	Sayings of Spartans
Stoic Contr.	Stoic Contradictions
Table-Talk	Table-Talk
Virt. Vice	Virtue and Vice
Pythag. Sent.	The Pythagorean Sentences
Quint.	Quintilian
Rhet. ad Herenn.	Rhetorica ad Herennium (in Cicero, Loeb vol. 1)
Sen.	Seneca
Ben.	De Benefacto
Dial.	Dialogues
Ep. Lucil.	Epistulae ad Lucilium
Suet.	Suetonius
Calig.	Caligula
Claud.	Claudius
Jul.	Julius
Nero	Nero
Tac. *Ann.*	Tacitus, Annals
Theon *Progymn.*	Theon, Progymnasmata
Val. Max. *Mem. Deeds*	Valerius Maximus, Memorable Deeds

Endnotes

NOTES TO PREFACE

1. For instance, I speak of Jewish and Greco-Roman as essentially separate categories and refer to "the rabbis" as a definitive group coextensive with pre-70 Pharisaic teachers.

2. There are different ways to do scholarship, too: many scholars summarize and critique the views of other scholars, whereas others feel more comfortable just reading the NT in light of its own culture. Although both approaches are valid, my training and research incline me heavily toward the latter option.

3. This includes those whom I was trained to think of as among the most conservative: J. E. Adams, *Marriage, Divorce & Remarriage in the Bible* (Grand Rapids: Baker, 1980), pp. 86–87; E. G. Dobson (who worked with Jerry Falwell) *What the Bible Says about Marriage, Divorce, & Remarriage,* foreword by Tim LaHaye (Old Tappan, N.J.: Fleming H. Revell, 1986), p. 68.

4. W. A. Heth and G. J. Wenham, *Jesus and Divorce: The Problem with the Evangelical Consensus* (Nashville: Thomas Nelson, 1984).

5. I note this only to challenge the repeated implication of Heth and Wenham that the modern evangelical view knowingly or unknowingly derives from Erasmus, whereas the second-century church was much stricter. My response to the second-century church is that asceticism was rising within the church, and the NT was read more on the basis of grammar, proof-texts, and a fence-around-the-law type interpretation than according to culture and genre considerations.

NOTES TO CHAPTER 1

1. This is well-documented; see C. E. Lincoln, *Race, Religion, and the Continuing American Dilemma* (New York: Hill & Wang, 1984), p. 23–59. Bonding between slaves and some masters did occur, of course, as one may gather from the poignant *Slave Narratives,* 10,000 pages of interviews with former slaves written down before that generation passed

away. One may sample some of these accounts in books such as *Before Freedom*, ed. by Belinda Hurmence (Bergenfield, N.J.: Mentor, 1990).

2. Responsibility in the Bible could be viewed corporately (Deut. 21:1–9) and intergenerationally (Deut. 23:2–6; 1 Sam. 15:2–3), although there are limitations to this principle (Deut. 24:16; Ezek. 16; cf. Gen. 15:16); as Christians we may share corporate *responsibility* although we may not share corporate *guilt* (the latter being removed at conversion along with personal guilt). That restitution may be required even of another generation if one side in a conflict still profits and another side still is wounded by past injustice, is suggested by 2 Sam. 21:1–9. Ron Sider (*Rich Christians in an Age of Hunger*, 3d ed. [Dallas: Word, 1990], pp. 106–7) suggests that, like the merchants' wives in Amos 4:1–2, many Christians today partake of an unjust economic system without ever stopping to consider the system. My fear is that those who are able to overlook real social issues today would have done the same had they lived in the context of different social issues a century or two ago, no matter how loudly we may protest, "Had we lived in the days of our ancestors" (Matt. 23:30).

3. G. G. Hull, "In the Image of God: Women and Men as Social Equals," *ESA Advocate* 12 (9, Nov. 1990): 14.

4. Steven Myers, "Crown of Beauty Instead of Ashes," pp. 20–25 in *World Christian Summer Reader 1990*, p. 22.

5. For an early example, read *The Autobiography of Malcolm X*, by Malcolm X with Alex Haley (New York: Grove Press, 1965). Christianity as the Bible teaches it is the antithesis of racism, but until white Christians begin listening to the needs of their African-American brothers and sisters in Christ and determine to make restitution for their past failures, the black church in many places will continue to bear the brunt of false accusations.

6. Not her real name. It is my intention here to share the experience of a divorced person from a personal perspective; it is not my intention to bring his wife's behavior into the picture, since I also knew her, and I have purposely abbreviated any material dealing with anyone else as much as possible.

7. Since his first year of Bible college, his favorite game was to have people read verses in the New Testament, and he would give them the chapter and verse. Now it is to have them read the verses in Greek, and he has to identify where the verses are and what their historical context is. He is always useful in a Bible study group.

8. Readers with an astute attention to grammar may note that this prepositional phrase also qualifies "encouragement"; cf. Matt. 19:9?

NOTES TO CHAPTER 2

1. See especially our extensive treatment of this paragraph in Appendix B. Much of what follows in this chapter is dependent on that appendix and the cultural insights presented there, but the appendix is too far afield from the topic of divorce and remarriage per se to include in the body of this book.

2. This could be rendered in more colloquial English, "You've already been taught that God told our ancestors . . . ," if "was said to" is the divine passive. Appeal to the ancients, normally to those who received the law at Mount Sinai, is standard in Jewish texts; it also appears in Greek literature (Epict. *Disc.* 1.18.17; [Ps]Crates 35, to Aper [in A. J. Malherbe, *The Cynic Epistles*, SBLSBS 12 (Atlanta: Scholars, 1977) pp. 88–89]; cf. Test. Zeb. 9:5). Thus I. J. Du Plessis, "The Ethics of Marriage According to Matt. 5:27–32," *Neot* 1 (1967): 18, is probably wrong when he cites later rabbinic evidence suggesting that this passage refers to the older rabbis (following Billerbeck; cf. e.g., Tos. Shab. 1:14; perhaps Sir. 39:1) and thus that Jesus is challenging the rabbis here. The quote is not a rabbinic interpretation but simply Scripture itself, which needs to be more fully interpreted.

3. "Judgment" here probably refers to the punishment executed by a Jewish court, although it was believed that God carried out the sentence in this world or the world to come if the earthly court could not do so (cf. Sib. Or. 3:258–60, probably second century BC; p. Sanh. 11:5, §1; Num. Rab. 18:4). "Judgment" is used with reference to a case coming to trial, e.g., in *CPJ* 1:239–40, §129, line 7. M. Borg, *Conflict, Holiness & Politics in the Teaching of Jesus*, SBEC 5 (New York: Edwin Mellen, 1984) p. 203, compares this with church discipline in Matt. 18, but in Matt. 18 the earthly community acts on the authority of the heavenly one; see below. R. A. Guelich, "Mt 5.22: Its Meaning and Integrity," *ZNW* 64 (112, 1973): 43–44, rightly challenges those who think the "sanhedrin" (supreme court) represents the church.

4. Many MSS read, "without good reason." This reading does have some support; see D. A. Black, "Jesus on Anger: The Text of Matthew 5:22a Revisited," *NovT* 30 (1, Jan. 1988): 1–8. If it should be included, it may well be an extremely literal translation of an Aramaic idiom, which actually would reinforce the point that it is not right to be angry for any reason, instead of providing grounds for anger (see Preben Wernberg-Møller, "A Semitic Idiom in Matt. V.22," *NTS* 3 [1956–1957]: 71–73). The "fellow," literally, "brother," is presumably a fellow-disciple; cf. 5:9, 23; 18:15; 23:10; cf. R. H. Gundry, *Matthew: A Commentary on his Literary and Theological Art* (Grand Rapids: Eerdmans, 1982), pp. 84–85. This *could* suggest that this is a false accusation.

5. Aramaic "Raka," cf. e.g., Ab. R. Nathan B, 32, §69; b. Ber. 22a; cf. the morally negative sense of "empty," e.g., CD 10.18. In Greek one could speak of the "empty-headed" (Sib. Or. 3:430, cf. 590, both probably pre-Christian; cf. the term translated "vainglory," which could relate to "empty thinking" [e.g., Arist. 8]).

6. Lit., the "sanhedrin," the Jewish supreme court (although lower courts could also be called sanhedrins, or assemblies, by the second century AD; see p. Mak. 1:8, §1; Matt. 10:17; cf. m. Sanh. 1:1; Tos. Hag. 2:9; Sanh. 3:1; S. Safrai, "Jewish Self-Government," in *The Jewish People in the First Century: Historical Geography, Political History, Social, Cultural, and Religious Life and Institutions*, (= *JPFC* hereafter), 2 vols., ed. S. Safrai and M. Stern, with D. Flusser and W. C. van Unnik (Assen: Van Gorcum, 1974; Philadelphia: Fortress, 1976) pp. 377–419, esp. p. 403;

cf. D. R. A. Hare, *The Theme of Jewish Persecution of Christians in the Gospel According to St Matthew* [Cambridge: Cambridge, 1967], pp. 102–3).

7. Although this is a standard Greek term (cf. Sir. 19:11), it had come into Semitic Jewish usage as well (cf. Lam. Rab. Proem 31); cf. the connection between the two in Pes. Rab Kah. 14:5. Some scholars (T. W. Manson, *The Sayings of Jesus*, [Grand Rapids: Eerdmans, 1969; London: SCM, 1957] p. 156) stress here the Semitic content of the word, paralleling "Raka," but it is probable that most of Matthew's readers would have read it as the Greek "fool"; this is especially likely given Matthew's normal use of the term (7:26, 23:17, 25:2, 3, 8, cited by Gundry, *Matthew*, p. 84). Cf. Joachim Jeremias, *NT Theology* (New York: Charles Scribner's Sons, 1971), p. 149; Morton Smith, *Tannaitic Parallels to the Gospels* (Philadelphia: Society of Biblical Literature, 1951), p. 2.

8. Matt. 5:21–22, my translation. "Fiery Gehenna" was common enough in Jewish texts (Sib. Or. 1:101–3; 3 En. 44:3); cf. the idea in Judith 16:17; Sir. 7:16 (apparently); 4 Macc. 9:9, 12:12; Ps-Philo 38:4; Ab. R. Nathan B, 32, §69; for a late example (maybe with Christian influence), cf. Gr. Ezra 1:9 (ed. Wall, p. 25). In some texts, Gehenna is the temporary prelude to annihilation or release (Tos. Sanh. 13:4, though eternal for the very wicked, 13:5; Ab. R. Nathan A, 41; Num. Rab. 18:20; Pes. Rab Kah. 10:4; cf. 1QS 4.13–14); in others rabbis argued for a Gehenna as opposed to immediate annihilation (Gen. Rab. 6:6, late second century); there were clearly different views (Ab. R. Nathan 36). In Matthew we read the severest option in Judaism, namely *eternal* punishment (25:46; cf. Jos. *War* 2.9.14, §163). Some scenes closely resemble Greek portrayals of Tartarus (b. Git. 56b–57a; p. Sanh. 6:6, §2; Hag. 2:2, §5; 3 En. 33:4–5; cf. Asc. Isa. 1:2; Gr. Ezra 4:22 [Tartarus]; Sib. Or. 1:10, 101–3, 119, 4:186 [Tartarus, probably c. AD 80], 5:178 [Tartarus, probably by early second century AD]; Apoc. Peter 5–12; Plut. *Div. Veng.* 31, *Mor.* 567DE); it was particularly thought to hold the destiny of the wicked Gentiles (Sifré Num. 40.1.9; Sifre Deut. 311.3.1; Ab. R. Nathan A, 16; Pes. Rab. 11:5, 53:2). "Gehenna" and eschatological "fire" occur throughout Matthew; see 3:10, 5:30, 10:28, 18:8, 23:15, 25:41.

9. Cf. Konrad Köhler, "Zu Mt 5,22," *ZNW* 19 (1919): 91–95.

10. E.g., Gundry, *Matthew*, p. 85. J. P. Meier, *The Vision of Matthew: Christ, Church, and Morality in the First Century*, TI (New York: Paulist, 1979) pp. 244–45 (cf. also J. P. Meier, *Matthew*, NTM [Wilmington, Del.: Michael Glazier, 1980] p. 51), finds a rhetorical heightening "In mock imitation of the hair-splitting casuistry of the Pharisees" in contrast "with the obvious lack of ascending seriousness in the crimes"; while this is plausible, an ironic interpretation should not be suggested unless the more obvious literal interpretation does not fit well.

11. E.g., C. F. D. Moule, "Matthew v.21, 22," *ExpT* 50 (4, Jan. 1939): 189–90, is forced to propose a twofold gloss to get around the problem, by allowing him to omit "supreme court" entirely. Moule much later addressed this passage again; in idem, "Uncomfortable Words—I. The Angry Word: Matthew 5.21f.," *ExpT* 81 (1, Oct. 1969): 11, he cites

second-century rabbinic material in which severe insults were rigorously punished under Jewish law, although he does not think the closest parallel these afford to Matthew is relevant (it is late). But here as well he assumes a heightening of force in Matthew and maintains his view that this involved a marginal gloss (ibid., p. 12).

12. Even though publicly shaming a fellow (or, a haber) warrants exclusion from the life of the world to come (m. Ab. 3:11; b. Sanh. 107a, cf. 101a). Both Pharisees and Sadducees apparently punished false accusers, who spread an evil name about someone without evidence, by a beating; see Samuel Belkin, *Philo and the Oral Law: The Philonic Interpretation of Biblical Law in Relation to the Palestinian Halakah*, HSS 11 (Cambridge: Harvard, 1940), p. 267.

13. E.g., Sib. Or. 1:273–74; 3:34, 56, 91; cf. Jub. 4:31. In Sib. Or. 3:670 (probably second century BC), future divine "judgment" will come on "the unlearned, empty-headed people." In the late text, Gr. Ezra 1:24 (ed. Wall, p. 26), it is coupled with unquenchable flame.

14. Cf. C. S. Keener, "Matthew 5:22 and the Heavenly Court," *ExpT* 99 (2, 1987): 46, although I include here some references I had not yet found when I wrote that article. Ab. R. Nathan A, 32 (late Tannaitic); b. B.M. 86a; p. Sanh. 1:1, §4, 11:5, §1; Pes. Rab Kah. 24:11; Ex. Rab. 12:4; Lev. Rab. 24:2, 29:4; Num. Rab. 3:4; Koh. Rab. 2:12, §1 (purportedly second century); 3 En. 5:10–12, 16:1, ch. 28, especially 28:8, 29:1, 30:1–2; perhaps 3 En. 2:4, 18:16. For a comparison of the heavenly and earthly tribunals, see b. Mak. 13b (purportedly early second-century tradition); Shab. 129b; Git. 68a; Ex. Rab. 30:18 (the two Sanhedrins correspond; late second century); Ruth Rab. 4:3, 5 (the heavenly court approved the earthly court's decree, citing early third-century tradition); perhaps Num. Rab. 18:4; Koh. Rab. 3:14, §1; Pes. Rab. 15:19; cf. Ethelbert Stauffer, *Jesus and His Story*, trans. Richard and Clara Winston (New York: Alfred A. Knopf, 1960), p. 206. God presided in the heavenly court and taught new laws there (Gen. Rab. 49:2, 64:4, probably both late). For the inclusion of deceased pious people in the heavenly academy, seated there as a reward for their piety, cf. b. B.M. 85a (late); Pes. 53b (early third century); Sanh. 92a; Lev. Rab. 11:8 (eschatological). Some other texts are cited in OTPS 1:284, note b. The predominance of later materials on the subject may be due to the nature of the editing; such images are less frequent in earlier rabbinic collections, even when we know popular speculation already had developed the images (as in the case of demonology and astrology).

15. This did not evolve from polytheism, since it predominates in later parts of the OT; but imagery from the pagan heavenly court is probably borrowed (J. Bright, *A History of Israel*, 3rd ed. (Philadelphia: Westminster, 1981) pp. 158–59; see especially F. M. Cross, *Canaanite Myths and Hebrew Epic* [Cambridge: Harvard, 1973], pp. 186–87). The image of a divine assembly around Zeus continues quite late in Greek imagery; cf. Chariton *Chaer.* 5.4.6, following Homer.

16. In 11Q Melch., Melchizedek presides over the divine assembly of Ps. 82:1, made up mainly of angels; see P. J. Kobelski, "Melchizedek and Melchiresa: The Heavenly Prince of Light and the Prince of Darkness

in the Qumran Literature" (Ph.D. dissertation, Fordham University, 1978), p. 123. Other early Jewish literature includes plenty of scenes of heavenly courtrooms before which the deceased are tried, e.g., Test. Abr. 10 B, 12 A. In apocalyptic and prophetic tradition, see further Guy Couturier, "La vision du conseil divin: étude d'une forme commune au prophétisme et à l'apocalyptique," *ScEsp* 36 (1, Jan. 1984): 5–43. This may bear some relation to the idea of heavenly tablets, which in some cases record human deeds and in some God's decrees; cf. 1 En. 81:1, 2, 93:2, 103:2–3, 106:19, 107:1, 108:7; Jub. 3:10, 31, 4:32, 5:13, 6:17, 29, 15:25, 16:3, 9, 28–29, 18:19, 19:9, 23:32, 24:33, 28:6, 30:9, 18–23, 31:32, 32:10 (perhaps 32:21), 28, 33:10, 49:8, 50:13; perhaps CD 3.3–4 (Scripture does not explicitly say this of Isaac and Jacob), and the Qumran fragment in Michel Testuz, "Deux fragments inédits des manuscrits de la mer morte," *Sem* 5 (1955): 38 ("les tables précieuses"); cf. also Bent Noack, "Qumran and the Book of Jubilees," *SEÅ* 2–23 (1957–58): 200.

17. The rabbis spoke of their legislative, and hence judicial, function as interpreters of law as "binding" and "loosing"; given the context of 18:15–17 (a judicial assembly, as in a synagogue court headed by a priest, or later by rabbis), and the probable relation of the "two or three" praying in vv. 19–20 to the two or three witnesses of vv. 16–17 . The earthly court is thus simply ratifying the decree of the heavenly court, by properly interpreting heaven's laws, as in standard Jewish teaching.

18. G. B. Caird, "Expounding the Parables: I—The Defendant (Matthew 5.25f.; Luke 12.58f.)," *ExpT* 77 (2, Nov. 1965): 36–39; Joachim Jeremias, *The Parables of Jesus*, 2d rev. ed. (New York: Charles Scribner's Sons, 1972), p. 96, view it as originally a crisis parable, although in its Matthean context it emphasizes reconciliation (on the special wording, see Gundry, *Matthew*, pp. 86–87; cf. R. A. Guelich, *The Sermon on the Mount*, [Waco: Word, 1982] pp. 191–92). The parabolic image is certainly urgent; Gentile courts allowed creditors to sell debtors into slavery, at least temporarily, if it was the only way to recover their investment (J. E. Stambaugh and D. L. Balch, *The NT in Its Social Environment*, LEC 2 [Philadelphia: Westminster, 1986], p. 73).

19. Cf. similarly Sifre Deut. 309.1.1; cf. Lucian *Doub. Ind.* 17 (in A. J. Malherbe, *Moral Exhortation: A Greco-Roman Sourcebook*, LEC 4 [Philadelphia: Westminster, 1986] p. 55).

20. P. B. K. 8:6, §2 (trans. Neusner, 28:181).

21. C. G. Montefiore, "The Spirit of Judaism," 1:35–81 in *The Beginnings of Christianity*, 5 vols., ed. F. J. Foakes Jackson and Kirsopp Lake (Grand Rapids: Baker, 1979), p. 77; cf. E. E. Urbach, *The Sages: Their Concepts and Beliefs*, 2d ed., 2 vols., trans. I Abrahams (Jerusalem: Magnes, 1979) 1:625. Cf. reconciliation to one another in the world to come in Pes. Rab. 50:6.

22. P. B.K. 8:7, §1.

23. Sifre Deut. 309.1.1, 2.1; b. A.Z. 3a; Ruth Rab. 3:3; Koh. Rab. 1:15, §1; especially for interlocutors: b. Ber. 10a (purportedly second century; a *min*); Yeb. 102b (a *min*); B.B. 115b, end; Erub. 101a (purportedly early but probably not); cf. Philo *Cher.* 23, §75. Cf. the standard Greco-Roman insult: Epict. *Disc.* 1.18.10, 2.21.2; especially for interlocutors:

Epict. *Disc.* 2.16.13; 2.22.4–5 (*aphrōn*); 3.13.17, 22.85; Marc. Aur. *Med.* 5.36.1; Mart. *Epig.* 10.100.1; 1 Cor. 15:36; Gal. 3:1; James 2:20. Epicureans were allegedly most addicted to defamatory rhetoric (Plut. *Pl. Life Imp.* 2, *Mor.* 1086EF; cf. Diog Laert. *Lives* 10.1.7–8).

24. This may be why Matthew has "sanhedrin" rather than a more explicit term for the heavenly court; he wishes to oppose the corrupt earthly "sanhedrin" that rendered false judgment against Jesus (26:59), and whose local namesakes would render false judgment against Matthew's first readers (10:17). Those who condemned Jesus claimed that he was liable to death (26:66); but in light of 5:21–22, they were condemning themselves to eternal death before God's lawcourt.

25. For the witness receiving the same penalty, see especially Deut. 19:16–21; 4QTemple 61:7–11; Sus. 62; m. Mak. 1:7. The concept may also be represented in Greek texts, e.g., Isoc. *To Nicocles* 29, *Or.* 2. One had thus to be careful about witnesses (m. Ab. 1:9; R.H. 2:9–10), and they had to be cross-examined and found deliberately contradictory before they themselves could be convicted (Tos. Sanh. 6:3, 6; Sifre Deut. 93.2.1, 149.1.1–2, 189.1.3, 190.5.1). On the danger of false witnesses bringing death to others, see e.g., evidence in *The Roman Empire: Augustus to Hadrian*, ed. and trans. R. K. Sherk, TDGR 6 (New York: Cambridge, 1988), pp. 25–26, §13, under Augustus.

26. Cf. disciplines of exclusion imposed in the Dead Sea Scrolls for members who utter harsh words to other members or who slander the community (1QS 7.15–17).

27. This could be translated "looks habitually" or "contemplates," referring to a man who not merely notices someone's attractiveness (which is not "looking to lust" here), but who actually wishes to have her for himself (the verb may imply wishing to own her sexually or otherwise for oneself). This probably also refers primarily to desiring a *particular* woman.

28. In this case, a married woman is implied, since this is called "adultery," which always implied the violation of a marriage covenant (so also Guelich, *Sermon*, p. 193; Gundry, *Matthew*, p. 88), but the principle would no doubt apply to an unmarried woman in terms of a "fence" around the law of fornication: desiring someone who will later be married to someone else.

29. Matt. 5:27–29. This is cited also in Justin *1 Apol.* 16.

30. Du Plessis, "Ethics," pp. 19–20, points out that the rabbis judged adultery according to criminal law, not ethical demand, but this is due to the halachic nature of most of our sources.

31. This was pointed out long ago by Hugo Odeberg, *Pharisaism and Christianity*, trans. J. M. Moe (St. Louis: Concordia, 1964, from a 1943 ed. in Swedish). E. P. Sanders and others have rightly pointed to the Christocentric nature of early Christianity, rather than ethics or grace per se, being the main divergence between Christianity and Pharisaism.

32. Diog. Laert. *Lives* 1.36 (Thales).

33. Epict. *Disc.* 2.18.15–18; cf. Marc. Aur. *Med.* 3.2.2. Marc. Aur. *Med.* 2.10, following Theophrastus, felt that offenses (the word the NT uses for sins) of desire were worse than those due to anger, because they indicated that one was dominated by pleasure.

34. Epict. *Disc.* 3.2.8; Marc. Aur. *Med.* 9.40. Epict. *Disc.* 4.9.3, uses the same word for "desire" that Jesus uses in Matthew 5, although it applies to being content and the context suggests not seeking office as well as not desiring a more attractive wife.

35. This is especially true of the Cynics, most notably in traditions about Diogenes: Diog. Laert. *Lives* 6.2.4.6, 6.2.69; Diogenes 35, to Sopolis (*Cynic Epistles*, pp. 146–47). Cf. W. A. Meeks, *The Moral World of the First Christians*, LEC 6 (Philadelphia: Westminster, 1986) p. 55. If p. Nid. 2:1, §1, correctly interprets m. Nid. 2:1, some Jewish circles felt that this could require the cutting off of the hand (cf. also Matt. 5:30?). Some rabbis did debate how "far one could go" before intercourse had taken place (p. Yeb. 6:1, §3), but this was for technical purity reasons.

36. Clitophon for Leucippe in Ach. Tat. *Clit.* 1.4–6. In Ach. Tat. *Clit.* 4.3.1–2, the general's same act is bad only because she has been pledged by the goddess to Clitophon; in Chariton, *Chaer.* 5.7.5–6, planning but not committing adultery seems not so wrong (and is certainly not punishable by a court); cf. similarly 8.8.8. In Chariton *Chaer.* 2.2.8, noble Callirhoe wishes to please no man's eye except Chaereas's. For Greek views about nocturnal sexual dreams, see Artem. *Oneir.* 1.78.

37. E.g., Sib. Or. 4.33–34 (perhaps hellenistic period); Ps. Sol. 4:4; cf. Test. Reub. 4:1; p. Hag. 2:2, §4. Merely thinking of doing evil was bad; see Ep. Arist. 132–33; in early Christian literature, cf. 2 Pet. 2:14; Herm. 1.1.1; Tert. *Apol.* 46:11–12.

38. Sir. 9:8, 41:20–21; Sus. 8; Test. Judah 17:1; Test. Iss. 3:5, 4:4.

39. Test. Reub. 4:8; Test. Iss. 7:2 ("nor did I fornicate by . . . my eyes"); cf. 1QS 1.6–7, CD 2.16 (eyes of lust); and possibly Gen. Rab. 32:7, if lust is intended.

40. B. Shab. 64ab (Soncino, pp. 305–6). Du Plessis, "Ethics," pp. 21–22, notes that most of the material is from the third or fourth century, but Ishmael lived in the early second century and his school (particularly Rabbis Josiah and Jonathan) was mid-second century, and normally excluded from the Mishnah, whose provenance is in Akiban circles. It is, of course, true, that we have no first-century examples, but the nature of rabbinic literature almost precludes that we would have such; we use these examples here to substantiate only that this view was widespread in early Judaism, as conjunction with the non-rabbinic examples seems to imply.

41. B. Nid. 13b.

42. Lev. Rab. 23:12; Pes. Rab. 24:2; so also an anonymous tradition and another third-century rabbi in Pes. Rab. 24:2.

43. B. Hullin 142a, denies that God will punish for the thought in the way he will for the deed.

44. Ps. Sol. 16:7–8; Test. Reub. 3:11–12, 14, 6:3 (one would expect such from Reuben, given his crime!); b. Yeb. 63b, on Sirach. Men noble enough to withstand great temptations are praised, e.g., Ab. R. Nathan A, 2; B, 2, §9; b. Ber. 20a; B.M. 84a; Pes. Rab Kah. Sup. 3:2; though later haggadists warned that even great rabbis could fall prey to such temptations, as in the stories of Akiba and Meir chasing Satan when he disguised himself as a woman.

45. Ben Witherington, III, *Women in the Ministry of Jesus*, SNTSMS 51 (Cambridge: Cambridge, 1984), p. 28; Du Plessis, "Ethics," p 19.

46. He also provides a negative example warning of the danger of making oaths (14:7; against 5:33–37) and of committing adultery with her who had been (or still officially was) the wife of another (14:3, vs. 5:31–32).

47. The rabbis just suggested marriage. See the discussion under 1 Cor. 7, below.

48. H. W. Basser, "The Meaning of 'Shtuth,' Gen.R. 11 in Reference to Matthew 5.29–30 and 18.8–9," *NTS* 31 (1, Jan. 1985): 148–51, argues that Gen. Rab. 11 depends on this passage. He may be right that the tradition of this passage is in view, if the saying of a min has been transferred to a philosopher, but the case is not clear. Johannes Schattenmann, "Jesus und Pythagoras," *Kairos* 21 (2–3, 1979): 215–20, derives the tradition from Neopythagoreanism, since Jews abhorred the idea of self-mutilation; yet we know that they would accept the amputation of appendages for sufficient cause (2 Macc. 7:11), and, as Gundry points out, it was less than the death penalty for the unrepentant (*Matthew*, p. 88).

49. Cf. Col. 3:5; perhaps Sib. Or. 1:154 (*apokopsate*, cut off, the things that are bad).

50. Also Tert. *Apol.* 46:11–12. Philostratus has Apollonius demonstrate that even eunuchs may act sexually with the king's harem.

51. Cf. Heb. 13:4. Love would demands seeking the other person's joy above one's own, but it my suspicion that this gives sexual pleasure its proper role, rather than excludes it.

NOTES TO CHAPTER 3

1. Although I have come to this view through my own research, it has often been proposed before; cf. e.g., R. H. Stein, " 'Is It Lawful for a Man to Divorce His Wife?' " *JETS* 22 (2, June 1979): 119; Myrna and Robert Kysar, *The Asundered: Biblical Teachings on Divorce and Remarriage* (Atlanta: John Knox, 1978), pp. 69–70; cf. pp. 39, 48–49; P. E. Harrell, *Divorce and Remarriage in the Early Church: A History of Divorce and Remarriage in the Ante-Nicene Church* (Austin, Tex.: R. B. Sweet Company, 1967), p. 142.

2. As recognizable also in Jewish texts, e.g., the "village scribe" in 2d century BC Egypt, *CPJ* 1:188–89, §43 (cf. Josephus references in Geza Vermes, *Jesus and the World of Judaism* [Philadelphia: Fortress, 1984; London: SCM, 1983], p. 31, n. 9), or "scribes" in the Ptolemaic administration (*CPJ* 1:157, §21); cf. *CIJ* 1:xcii–xciv, 1:12, §7, 1:18, §18, 1:21, §24, (perhaps) 1:27, §36, 1:70, §99, 1:84, §121, 1:85, §122, 1:88, §125, 1:100, §142, 1:103, §145, 1:104, §146, 1:106, §148, 1:107, §149; 1:130, §180, 1:158, §221, 1:161, §225, 1:196, §279 (19 years old), 1:200, §284, 1:250, §318, 1:275, §351, 1:326, §433 (of the synagogue), 1:337, §456. H. J. Leon, *The Jews of Ancient Rome* (Philadelphia: The

Jewish Publication Society of America, 1960), pp. 184–85, thinks the Roman synagogue inscriptions refer to the secretary of the congregation, not to "scribes" in the way the rabbis used the term. Scribes in preexilic Israelite times were probably civil servants (see Roland de Vaux, *Ancient Israel: Its Life and Institutions*, trans. John McHugh [New York: Mc-Graw-Hill, 1961], p. 50; cf. Ahiqar col. 1, #1, a court scholar) but by the period of Ezra and Nehemiah they were especially interpreters of the law of God, and by the time of Sirach they could be teachers with disciples as well (see Bright, *History*, p. 437; cf. Martin McNamara, *Palestinian Judaism and the NT*, GNS 4 [Wilmington, Del.: Michael Glazier, 1983], pp. 51–54). "Scribes of the people" have a leading role in 1 Macc. 5:42 but its particular nature is unclear.

3. M. Ab. 1:4, 17; Pes. Rab Kah. 27:2; cf. J. T. Townsend, "Ancient Education in the Time of the Early Roman Empire," pp. 139–63 in *The Catacombs and the Colosseum: The Roman Empire as the Setting of Primitive Christianity*, ed. Stephen Benko and J. J. O'Rourke (Valley Forge, Penn.: Judson, 1971), p. 155.

4. John Wilkinson, *Jerusalem as Jesus Knew It* (London: Thames & Hudson, 1978), p. 88; Stambaugh and Balch, *Environment*, p. 99. Enoch is probably given such a role, following Ezra, in pre-Christian tradition; see 1 En. 12:4, 92:1.

5. Wilkinson, *Jerusalem*; G. F. Moore, *Judaism in the First Centuries of the Christian Era*, 2 vols. (New York: Schocken Books, reprint 1971), 1:43.

6. Several pre-70 inscriptions suggest that the title was in some use even before 70; see G. N. Stanton, *The Gospels and Jesus*, OBS (Oxford: Oxford University Press, 1989), p. 185. The term also appears in the Diaspora, also the dates are not always certain, and where verifiable are post-70: *CIJ* 1:438–39, §611, 2:7, §736; cf. 2:339, §1414 (as an archisynagogos). *CIJ* 1:519, §719 (from Argos in Greece) seems to use "wise man" in this manner.

7. See especially C. E. Carlston, "Proverbs, Maxims, and the Historical Jesus," *JBL* 99 (1, 1980): 87–105. Proverbial-type wisdom is not characteristic of most halachic rabbinic literature, but there is an abundance of it in the collection Pirke Aboth.

8. In contrast to the prohibition of lust, which, contrary to much other Jewish tradition, made men responsible for their attitude, or Mark's version of the divorce prohibition (Mark 10:11), which makes sharing a man adulterous, this passage again makes the sharing of a woman (not the sharing of a man) the issue of adultery, as in Palestinian Jewish law (Guelich, *Sermon*, pp. 200–201).

9. R. C. Tannehill, *The Sword of His Mouth*, SBLSS 1 (Missoula, Mont.: Scholars Press, 1975), pp. 72–73, thinks this has more legal force than the abandonment of legal retaliation, too, since its language may be hyperbolic (e.g., if pressed by a Roman soldier into temporary service, one should give twice what the soldier demands).

10. Mishnaic and papyrological evidence suggest that it was not strictly necessary to involve a court unless the wife were guilty of something which would cause her to forfeit her *ketubah* to her husband (S. Safrai,

"Home and Family," pp. 728–92 in *JPFC*, p. 790). The essential rabbinic form of divorce document seems to be very early, as suggested by forms in Hosea and the Elephantine papyri; see M. J. Geller, "The Elephantine Papyri and Hosea 2,3. Evidence for the form of the Early Jewish Divorce Writ," *JSJ* 8 (2, Oct. 1977): 139–48.

11. E.g., the early second century teacher R. Tarfon, who was noted for the vow expression, "May I bury my sons, if." (e.g., Sifra VDDen. par. 4.7.3.2; Tos. Shab. 13:5; Hag. 3:33; p. Hor. 3:2, §13).

12. Cf. examples in Tannehill, *Sword*, e.g., "antithetical aphorisms" (p. 89). Jeremias, *Theology*, pp. 29–36, cites examples of characteristics virtually "unique" to Jesus' sayings in early Christian literature, but many characteristics are shared with other early Jewish teachers (e.g., periphrasis, ibid., pp. 9–11, 179; J. Bonsirven, *Palestinian Judaism in the Time of Jesus Christ* (New York: Holt, Rinehart & Winston, 1964), pp. 5–6; the eschatological correlative, D. E. Aune, *Prophecy in Early Christianity and the Ancient Mediterranean World* [Grand Rapids: Eerdmans, 1983], pp. 168–95; repetition, Tannehill, *Sword*, pp. 39–45, and so on). Many of Jesus' sayings exhibit a poetic structure, although the Aramaic rhythm of the original cannot carry over into the Greek (Maurice Goguel, *The Life of Jesus*, trans. Olive Wyon [New York: Macmillan, 1948], p. 296; Vincent Taylor, *The Formation of the Gospel Tradition*, 2d ed. [London: Macmillan, 1960], p. 89, depending on C. F. Burney, *The Poetry of our Lord* [1925]; cf. Jeremias, *Theology*, pp. 22–27; J. Luyten, "Psaumes et paroles de Jésus," *Questiones Liturgiques* 61 [4, 1980]: 241–62, points out resemblances to the Psalms). M. D. Goulder, *Midrash and Lection in Matthew* (London: S.P.C.K., 1974), pp. 70–92, documents poetic constructions in Matthew and suggests that Matthew improves Markan rhythms; he does acknowledge that Mark contains poetic language, too, although he contrasts this unfavorably with Matthew, whom he believes composed many of Jesus' sayings (rejecting the Q hypothesis in any of its forms). The "Amen, I say to you," seems, if not entirely unique to Jesus (for a double amen, but not in an introductory formula, see p. Kid. 1:5, §8 [the oath formula of Num. 5:22]; Ps-Philo 22:6, 26:5, both replies, the second to a curse invocation), then almost unique (Jeremias, *Theology*, pp. 35–36, 79; F. C. Burkitt, *The Earliest Sources for the Life of Jesus* [Boston: Houghton Mifflin, 1910], p. 18; see qualifications in David Hill, *NT Prophecy* (Atlanta: John Knox, 1979), pp. 64–65; Aune, *Prophecy*, pp. 164–65; against M. E. Boring, *Sayings of the Risen Jesus: Christian Prophecy in the Synoptic Tradition*, SNTSMS 46 [Cambridge: Cambridge University, 1982], p. 132); for distribution, see M. Smith, *Parallels*, p. 6.

13. E.g., m. Ab. 2:8, cited above in Appendix A.

14. Quint. 8.6.73–76.

15. Other scholars have also suggested that Matt. 5:32 is hyperbole, e.g., Stein, "Lawful?"; J. M. Efird, *Marriage and Divorce: What the Bible Says* (Nashville: Abingdon, 1985), p. 57; its purpose is not a new legalistic rule, but to reinforce the sanctity of marriage (ibid., pp. 58–59).

16. See especially G. D. Fee and Douglas Stuart, *How to Read the Bible for All Its Worth* (Grand Rapids: Zondervan, 1981), pp. 188–91, 196–203. The terseness of wisdom sayings was valued by rabbis (B.

Gerhardsson, *Memory and Manuscript*, ASNU 22 (Upssala: C.W.K. Gleerup, 1961), p. 142); condensation and abridgment probably also occurred in communicating and transmitting such sayings (ibid., pp. 136–48).

17. This is pointed out especially by Du Plessis, "Ethics," p. 17, who comments on the use of the *mashal* and that Jesus' hearers would have recognized this manner of speaking.

18. The verb tense at the least indicates that Jesus' community is to be so directed by his presence (18:20) that they will act according to heaven's will in such matters; cf. Gundry, *Matthew*, p. 335 (on 16:19); I. H. Marshall, *Kept by the Power of God: A Study of Perseverance and Falling Away* (Minneapolis: Bethany, 1974; London: Epworth, 1969), p. 87; against Meier, *Matthew*, p. 183. On the earthly court acting in lieu of the heavenly court, see especially the passages about the new moon (Pes. Rab Kah. 5:13; cf. m. R.H. 3:1; p. R.H. 3:1, §17).

19. Their original import, like the teachings in Matt. 5, may well not have been judicial per se, since this may be related to material also found in Luke 17:3–4; cf. R. Bultmann, *The History of the Synoptic Tradition*, 2d ed., trans. J. Marsh (Oxford: Basil Blackwell, 1968), p. 141. 18:17 may be echoed in Polycarp *Phil.* 11, or this may point to common tradition.

20. Reproof was heavily emphasized in rabbinic Judaism; cf. R. Tarfon in Sifra Qed. pq. 4.200.3.3; Sifre Deut. 1.3.2; b. Arak. 16b, bar.; cf. also b. Tam. 28a, bar.; Arak. 16b, Tannaitic tradition (how far reproof: rebuking or beating); Shab. 119b; Gen. Rab. 54:3. Doing it privately was also critical (b. Sanh. 101a).

21. This is extremely similar to Qumran's practice (1QS 5.25–6.1; CD 9.3–4), as many commentators have pointed out (e.g., R. E. Brown, "The Dead Sea Scrolls and the NT," pp. 1–8 in *John and Qumran*, ed. J. H. Charlesworth [London: Geoffrey Chapman, 1972], p. 4; W. D. Davies, *The Sermon on the Mount* [Cambridge: Cambridge University, 1966], p. 79). It is also rabbinic practice; see Sifre Deut. 173.1.2; p. Sanh. 7:6, §2; cf. p. B.K. 8:7, §1; L. Schiffman, *Sectarian Law in the Dead Sea Scrolls*, BJS 33 (Chico, Calif.: Scholars, 1983), pp. 97–98; Moore, *Judaism*, 2:153. Publicly shaming a fellow warrants exclusion from the world to come (m. Ab. 3:11).

22. The two or three witnesses from Deut. 17:6, 19:15, were of course standard in early Jewish discussions of testimony; Jos. *Ant.* 4.8.15, §219; CD 9.17–23; 4QTemple 61:6–7, 64:8; Tos. Sanh. 8:3; Sifre Deut. 148.1.1; 188.2.1–2, 3.1–2; p. Sanh. 6:3, §3; cf. Syriac Men. 142; Test. Ab. 13 A; m. Toh. 5:9; 2 Cor. 13:1; 1 Tim. 5:19; David Daube, "The Law of Witnesses in Transferred Operation," *JANES* 5 (1973): 91–93; J. Neusner, " 'By the Testimony of Two Witnesses' in the Damascus Document IX, 17–22 and in Pharisaic-Rabbinic Law," *RevQum* 8 (30/2, March 1973: 197–217; N. L. Rabinovitch, "Damascus Document IX,17–22 and rabbinic Parallels," *RevQum* 9 (1, 1977): 113–16. Witnesses are also important for legality in Greco-Roman evidence, even though probability was a more standard form of evidence; cf. Chariton, *Chaer.* 2.5.1.

23. Hare, *Persecution*, p. 102; cf. F. F. Bruce, *1 & 2 Corinthians*, NCB 38 (Greenwood, S.C.: Attic Press, 1971), p. 59; R. M. Grant, *Early Christianity and Society: Seven Studies* (San Francisco: Harper & Row, 1977), p. 38. "Binding and loosing" do not usually specify excommunication in rabbinic literature (W. G. Thompson, *Matthew's Advice to a Divided Community: Mt. 17,22–18,35*, AnaBib 44 [Rome: Biblical Institute, 1970], pp. 190–92), but most commentators (e.g., Bultmann, *Tradition*, pp. 138–39, n. 1; Gundry, *Matthew*, p. 336; Meier, *Matthew*, pp. 182–83; Manson, *Sayings*, p. 210; cf. Samuel Sandmel, *Anti-Semitism in the NT?* [Philadelphia: Fortress, 1978], p. 58) are right in seeing a judicial application of rabbinic interpretive and hence legislative language here. The language is extremely frequent in rabbinic literature; cf. e.g., m. Git. 9:1; Tos. Sanh. 7:2; b. A.Z. 7a (bar.); Hul. 39b (bar.); Erub. 17a; Pes. 42a; p. Ter. 11:7; Bez. 3:6, §5, 5:2, §3; Gen. Rab. 7:2, 80:9, 85:5; Num. Rab. 20:24 (for Mosaic period!); Deut. Rab. 2:19. (Jos. *War* 1.5.2, §111, speaks of Pharisees "binding" and "loosing" whom they will in the second century BC, but he could mean imprisoning or setting free.) Ze'ev W. Falk, "Binding and Loosing," *JJS* 25 (1, Feb. 1974): 92–100, suggests that in these Matthean texts the rabbinic competence for absolving vows is exceeded. The demonological use (e.g., Text 14.1–2, 18.1, 19.5–6, etc. [C. D. Isbell, *Corpus of the Aramaic Incantation Bowls*, SBLDS 17 (Missoula, Mont.: Scholars Press, 1975), pp. 50, 58, 61]; curses in M. R. Lefkowitz and M. B. Fant, *Women's Life in Greece and Rome* [Baltimore: Johns Hopkins, 1982], p. 258) is not appropriate in this context (and *probably* not even in 12:29) (against R. H. Hiers, " 'Binding' and 'Loosing': The Matthean Authorizations," *JBL* 104 [2, June 1985]: 233–50). (Cf. the idea of "loosing the bonds of death," H. W. Basser, "Derrett's 'Binding' reopened," *JBL* 104 (2, 1985): 297–300, although he rejects a connection with rabbinic forbidding and permitting.)

24. E.g., Acts 7:58, which also plays on Jewish tradition. According to tradition, the convicted criminal was to be stripped (m. Sanh. 6:3; b. Sanh. 45a [bar.]), but here the executing false witnesses are the ones who strip. Although stripping was practiced in hellenistic society before engaging in strenuous exercise (e.g., Diogenes 37, to Monimus [*Cynic Epistles*, pp. 156–57]), it is presumably mentioned by Luke because he is portraying the executioners as the real criminals (for which reason Stephen, like Jesus in Luke 23, confesses his opponents' sins rather than his own, contrary Jewish law).

25. The two or three in this context must refer back to the witnesses; this has been recognized by others as well, e.g., J. D. M. Derrett, " 'Where two or three are convened in my name . . . ': a sad misunderstanding," *ExpT* 91 (3, 1971): 83–86.

26. This could refer to a prayer for the man's repentance, as suggested by 18:21–35 (cf. 1 John 5:14–16); but it may refer to a prayer for God to execute judgment, similar to Paul's language of "handing over to Satan" in 1 Cor. 5:5 and 1 Tim. 1:20.

27. Many scholars draw attention to the comparable saying about God's presence and Torah in m. Ab. 3:2, 6, Mek. *Bah.* 11.48ff. (cf. a faint parallel in 1QS 6.3?): G. Barth, "Matthew's Understanding of the Law,"

in *Tradition and Interpretation in Matthew,* by G. Bornkamm, G. Barth, and H. J. Held (Philadelphia: Westminster, 1963), pp. 135–36; D. Flusser, *Judaism and the Origins of Christianity* (Jerusalem: Magnes, 1988), p. 515; Gundry, *Matthew,* p. 370; Meier, *Matthew,* p. 206; Daniel Patte, *The Gospel According to Matthew: A Structural Commentary on Matthew's Faith* (Philadelphia: Fortress, 1987), pp. 254–55; Davies, *Sermon,* p. 80; Smith, *Parallels,* pp. 152–53. On the *minyan* idea in this text, cf. 1QS 6.3, 6; m. Ber. 7:3; b. Ber. 6b; Meg. 23b. J. A. Ziesler, "Matthew and the Presence of Jesus (2)," *Epworth Review* 11 (2, 1984): 90–97, speculates that Matthew deemphasizes the Spirit here because of dangerous pneumatics (cf. Matt. 7:22, 24:24), but it seems to me more likely that he is simply continuing a theme from 1:23 through 28:20. Rabbinic literature often calls God "the Place" (*ha-Makom*), the Omnipresent One; cf. e.g., m. Ab. 2:9, 13, 3:14; Tos. Peah 1:4, 3:8; Shab. 7:22, 25, 13:5; Sot. 3–4; R.H. 1:18; Taan. 2:13; B.K. 7:7; Sanh. 1:2, 13:1, 6, 14:3, 10; Sifra VDDen. pq. 2.2.4.2, pq. 4.6.4.1; Sav Mek. DeM. par. 98.7.7; Shem. Mek. deM. 99.1.4, 5, 7, 2.2, 3, 3.9, 11, 5.13; Qed. par. 1.195.2.3, pq. 7.204.1.4; Emor pq. 9.227.2.5; Behuq. pq. 5.266.1.1, 8.269.1.3; Sifré Num. 11.2.3, 3.1, 42.1.2, 2.3, 76.2.2, 78.1.1, 5.1, 80.1.1, 82.3.1, 84.1.1, 5.1, 85.3.1, 4.1, 5.1; Sifre Deut. 1.8.3, 9.2, 10.4; 2.1.1; 11.1.1; 21.1.1; 24.2.1; 26.4.1; 28.1.1; 32.3.2, 5.8; 33.1.1; 37.1.1, 3; 38.1.1, 3; b. Ber. 19a, 35b; Shab. 12ab, 13b; Suk. 29a, 33ab; M.K. 15a; Yoma 86b; Yeb. 62a, 63b (bar.); Ket. 66b (attributed to ben Zakkai), 111a; Ned. 10a; Kid. 30b (bar.), 31b, 68a; Nid. 13a; Sanh. 50a; Sheb. 29a, 34a, 39a, 47b; Zeb. 115b; B.B. 10a (Akiba), 91b (bar.); Erub. 19a; p. Ned. 9:1, 3; Lev. Rab. 2:10; Num. Rab. 1:11, 2:18–21, 23, 3:4, 12, 4:3, 5, 6, 20, 6:10, 9:24, 33, 41, 11:7, 14:6, 10–11, 19:9, 20:6; Deut. Rab. 7:2; Lam. Rab. 1:16, §50, 2:20, §23; Ruth Rab. 3:5; Koh. Rab. 2:18, §1, 3:17, §1, 11:1, §1; 3 En. 18:24, chs. 40–48 passim; cf. the second-century Christian writer Theophilus 2.3. This is true even though some rabbis did not believe that the Shekinah was directly revealed outside the land (e.g., Mek. *Pisha* 1); Diaspora Jews would no doubt have objected to such a restriction (Sib. Or. 3:701, second century BC).

28. E.g., Tos. Sanh. 14:16; Mak. 5:16; cf. Sifra VDDen. pq. 2.2.4.1.

29. The form of Jesus' exposition, if taken as law, is apodictic (like the Ten Commandments) as opposed to casuistic (like most of the civil laws in the law of Moses, which resemble other ancient Near Eastern civil law). It is general moral legislation, the sort found in prophetic pronouncements, as opposed to specific civil legislation, the sort found in case law (although even this required divine sanction in the ancient Near East).

30. One of the two expressions found in Matt. 5:18.

31. Luke 16:17–18.

32. Cf. M. J. Down, "The Sayings of Jesus about Marriage and Divorce," *ExpT* 95 (11, 1984): 332–34, though it is not quite true that Matthew has *misunderstood* Jesus' haggadic teaching as halakic in intention; it is a matter of reapplying Jesus' teaching in a new context (just as acts of rabbis, nonhalakic in themselves, could set precedents, as in the case of discussing the colors of prayer shawls worn by various rabbis).

33. That Mark would have omitted it to have created a more radical challenge to the law, and Luke would have omitted it by following Mark, whereas Matthew knew the clause independently, is entirely possible; it is the lack of Paul's knowledge about the exception clause that weights the case heavily in favor of Matthew's having added it.

34. On these terms, the case of Manfred Lehmann, "Gen 2.24 as the Basis for Divorce in Halakah and NT," *ZAW* 72 (3, 1966): 263–67, is entirely reasonable; so also L. W. Hurtado, *Mark*, NIBC (Peabody, Mass.: Hendrickson, 1989), pp. 166–67. Ulrich Nembach, "Ehescheidung nach alttestamentlichen und jüdischen Recht," *TZ* 26 (3, May 1970): 161–71, notes that the early church viewed it as original and saw no contradiction. It should be noted that if the Matthean clause is original, it would strengthen, not weaken, our case that Jesus intended an exception to his divorce rule.

35. Most, though not all, scholars concur that this is Matthew's addition: Gundry, *Matthew*, p. 90; Stein, "Lawful?" p. 118; W. Stenger, "Zur Rekonstruktion eines Jesusworts anhand der synoptischen Ehescheidungslogion (Mt 5,32; 19,9; Lk 16,16–18; Mark 10,11f)," *Kairos* 26 (3–4, 1984): 194–205; Goulder, *Matthew*, pp. 25, 39; J. C. Fenton, *Saint Matthew* (Philadelphia: Westminster, 1977), p. 90. Guelich, *Sermon*, pp. 206–10, thinks that the phrase is pre-Matthean in the 5:32 tradition and that he added it to the 19:9 tradition; given the connection of 19:9 with the houses debate in m. Git. 9:10, I would be inclined to argue in the opposite direction if it were necessary to make a case in either direction.

36. Quint. 7.6.5 (Loeb 3:138–39). Cf. Aristotle *Rhet* 1.17.1354a.

37. Some have read Deut. 24:1–4 as claiming that a wife who marries a second husband is guilty of adultery and for *that* reason cannot return to her first husband. (If this were true, it would be surprising that only the priests were forbidden to marry divorcées and non-priestly widows.) But if we compare the whole OT law, we find its (cultural?) abhorrence of intercourse with someone already defiled, e.g., the laws on the rape of virgins. Does this mean that only virgins should ever be permitted to marry? Whatever else Deut. 24:1–4 may mean, God's forgiveness in Christ (and in the case of innocent victims, his healing) must go beyond such limits: wives were not to be shared, but this applied as much to fornication (defiling wives to be) as to adultery. That divorced wives who had not remarried could be taken back was taken for granted; cf. Safrai, "Home and Family," p. 791.

38. Also Gundry, *Matthew*, p. 90.

39. It has often been noted that "uncleanness" should mean more than adultery, since adulterers were stoned and thus need not be divorced (e.g., Efird, *Divorce*, p. 40). The Hebrew expression "nakedness" used may imply inappropriate sexual relations, although one interpretation, that it refers to illegitimate marriages between those of forbidden degrees of kinship (Lev. 18) applies to a situation rare enough that it would probably not be covered, particularly in such ambiguous terms. It is less relevant to our discussion precisely what the Hebrew text meant, than how Matthew could have expected his Jewish readers to understand the term.

40. By the father, who gives his daughter in marriage.
41. J. J. Sabatowich, "Christian Divorce and Remarriage," *BT* 25 (4, 1987): 253–55. In the argument of H. G. Coiner, "Those 'Divorce and Remarriage' Passages (Matt. 5:32; 19:9; 1 Cor. 7:10–16)," *CTM* 39 (6, June 1968): 378, the husband putting her away "does not adulterate her because she is adulterated already" (so also Gundry, *Matthew*, p. 90).
42. B. Byron, "The Meaning of 'Except it be for Fornication,' " *ACR* 40 (2, 1963): 90–95. Cf. Bernard Leeming and R. A. Dawson, "Except It Be for Fornication?" *Scr* 8 (3, July 1956): 75–82, on concubinage; but some Roman jurists even felt that concubines could be prosecuted for adultery (J. F. Gardner, *Women in Roman Law and Society* [Bloomington: Indiana University, 1986], p. 58). Cf. also Leonard Ramaroson, "Une nouvelle interprétation de la 'clausule' de Mt 19,9," *SciEsp* 23 (2, 1971): 247–51, on polygamous unions after the initial union. But polygamous marriages were accepted as valid under OT law. Mark Geldard, "Jesus' Teaching on Divorce: thoughts on the meaning of *porneia* in Matthew 5:32 and 19:9," *ChM* 92 (2, 1978): 134–43, suggests that premarital sexual intercourse invalidated the marriage contract and the Matthean clause thus refers to an annulment rather than to a divorce in the modern sense; but this again unnaturally restricts the sense of "immorality."
43. Meier, *Matthew*, p. 53, protests that Matthew would not "relax Jesus' radical morality," and therefore would not make up a real exception (except the very narrow one Meier does indeed allow here); but this neglects the fact that Matthew is radicalizing the law, not radicalizing Mark. In other cases as well (e.g., Matt. 12 and 15), Matthew's narrative is more in line with rabbinic Jewish ideas than Mark's.
44. E.g., B. N. Wambacq, "Matthieu 5,31–32. Possibilité de divorce ou obligation de rompre une union illégitime," *NRT* 104 (1, 1982): 34–49; Gerard Caron, "Did Jesus Allow Divorce? (Mt. 5:31–32). A Preaching Problem," *AFER* 24 (5, Oct. 1982): 312; Claus Schedl, "Zur Ehebruchklausel der Bergpredigt im Lichte der neu gefundenen Tempelrolle," *TPQ* 130 (4, 1982): 362–65; A. D. Macho, "Cristo instituyó el matrimonio indisoluble," *Sefarad* 37 (1–2, 1977): 261–91 (NTA 23:281–82); Leeming and Dawson, "Except for Fornication?" pp. 75–82; F. F. Bruce, *1 & 2 Thessalonians*, WBC 45 (Waco, Tex.: Word, 1982), p. 82. Guelich, *Sermon*, pp. 206–9, concludes that both adultery and incest represent possible interpretations, though he notes (pp. 204–5) that either just fornication or incest are much narrower than the semantic range of *porneia* in this period, and strong contextual support would be needed for the incest interpretation. P. Lamarche, "L'indissolubilité selon Matthieu. Matthieu 19,9," *Christus* 30 (120, 1983): 475–82 (NTA 28:130) thinks the exception is an illicit union, but takes it as a "spiritual statement" rather than as a legal rule.
45. Ben Witherington, III, "Matthew 5.32 and 19.9—Exception or Exceptional Situation?" *NTS* 31 (4, 1985): 571–76.
46. The subject of sexual immorality was often brought up (Sifra Qed. pq. 7.204.1.1–2; Sifre Deut. 258.2.3; p. Taan. 4:5, §13; Num. Rab. 10:1, 13:15; cf. Jos. *Apion* 2.30, §215 [adding to 2.24, §§199, 201]; 1 En. 8:1–2; Jub. 20:4, 30:1–6, 33:20; CD 7.1; Jos. & As. 7:5/6, 21:1/20:8; Test.

Ab. 10, 14 A, 12 B; Test. Reub. 3:3; Test. Levi 17:11; Asc. Isa. 2:5; Ps-Phocyl. 198; etc.; cf. Belkin, *Philo*, pp. 258–59), and of course the minimum punishment was always divorce, as noted below.

47. Particularly in the first-century discussion in m. Git. 9:10, which will be addressed in the next chapter. The language of this discussion is similar enough to the terms in Matthew to warrant comparison.

48. Leeming and Dawson, "Except for Fornication?" p. 82; Caron, "Allow Divorce?" p. 312; Meier, *Matthew*, p. 53.

49. Meier, *Matthew*, pp. 52–53, thinks that "Some rabbis allowed a Gentile to maintain the incestuous union when he entered Judaism"; but he is mistaken. Most of these texts allow a proselyte to *contract* such a union, rather than to preserve it; further, this is theoretical halakah, a late application illustrating the earlier halakic principle that a proselyte has a new life (m. Dem. 6:10; Tos. Dem. 6:12–13; b. Kid. 17b; Yeb. 22a, 62a; Bek. 47a, bar.; Gen. Rab. 18:5; B. Bamberger, *Proselytism in the Talmudic Period* (New York: KTAV, 1968), p. 86; S. B. Hoenig, "Conversion During the Talmudic Period," pp. 33–66 in *Conversion to Judaism*, ed. D. M. Eichhorn [New York: KTAV, 1965], p. 54; J. Jeremias, *Jerusalem in the Time of Jesus* (London: SCM, 1969), p. 324; Tac. *Hist.* 5.5); this had an analogy in Roman law for becoming a citizen (*CIL* 2.1963, AD 82–84, in *Empire*, ed. Sherk, p. 138, 97). The assumption that Gentiles favored incest may be found in Sifra Qed. par. 4.206.1.2; p. Kid. 1:1, §4; Gen. Rab. 18:5, 52:11 (brother-sister); cf. Tert. *Apol.* 9.16; Tat. 28. Sib. Or. 5:390–91 (probably late first to early second century AD Egypt) attributes it to many Romans—but also pederasty (387) and bestiality (393). The charge of incest against early Christians was likewise false (Min. Fel. *Oct.* 31.1; Theoph. 3.4), as was Theophilus' accusation against Stoics (3.6).

50. E.g., b. Yeb. 60b, attributed to R. Simeon ben Yohai (second century): a proselyte converted by the age of 3 years and 1 day may be expected to be a virgin. A proselyte has no certain way to recognize his father (b. Yeb. 98a; Sanh. 58a, bar.; Gen. Rab. 18:5, bar.) (although the words could be taken instead as simply allowing Gentile rules on brother-sister marriages, concessions on Lev. 18 would be unlikely for rabbis who demanded divorce even for barrenness). In some traditions even Israel had practiced brother-sister marriages (though not parent-child marriages) until Moses (Gen. 20:12 [though he lied according to Gen. Rab. 52:11] vs. Lev. 18:9, 11 and Deut. 27:22; Gen. ch. 30 with Lev. 18:18; Sifré Num. 90.1.1; cf. p. Sanh. 5:1, §4; Yeb. 11:2, §3 [earlier comments]); but the sages followed the biblical laws of incest firmly (more demanding, e.g., p. Ned. 2:1, §4; Taan. 4:5, §8 [second century]; Deut Rab. 2:21; less demanding, e.g., Sifre Deut. 246.1.2), and incest was generally considered repulsive in early Judaism (cf. Gen. 19:30–38, 49:3–4; Jub. 16:8–9, 33:1–14, 41:23–26; Ps-Phocyl. 179–81; Test. Reub. 1:6–10; Philo *Spec.* 3.3, §§13, 19; Jos. *Ant.* 17.13.1, §341, 20.2.1, §18; Gr. Ezra 4:24).

51. Classical Greek plays on Oedipus (still alluded to in our period: Epict. *Disc.* 1.24.16; Mart. *Epig.* 10.4.1; cf. Sib. Or. 11:143–44; Justin *1 Apol.* 27); Herod. *Hist.* 3, §31; Plut. *RestQ* 108, *Mor.* 289D; Juv. *Sat.* 2:32–33, 4:8–9; Tac. *Ann.* 12.2, 16.8; Suet. *Calig.* 23–24; *Claud.* 39;

Nero 28, 34; Diog. Laert. *Lives* 7.7.188; Apul. *Metam.* 10.3; Philost. *V.A.* 1, §10. Cic. *De Legib.* 2.9.22 suggested that incest should be punishable by death; but its normal punishment, like that of *stuprum* and *adulterium*, was banishment (Paulus *Opin.* 2.26.1–17 in Lefkowitz and Fant, *Life*, p. 182, 193; Gardner, *Women*, pp. 36–37, 126–27). The only significant (cf. Ach. Tat. *Clit.* 1.3.1–2) exception would have been in Egypt (Gardner, *Women*, p. 36), which is not likely to have been in view for the readers of Luke–Acts or Matthew, any more than for any of Paul's epistles. Meier, *Matthew*, p. 53, cites 1 Cor. 5:1 in *favor* of his position, because it uses "immorality" to mean incest; but here it is specifically said to be a particular *kind* of immorality, which appears as part of a larger discussion of broader immorality in the Corinthian church (chs. 5–7, especially 5–6).

52. T. Considine, "Except it be for Fornication," *ACR* 33 (1956): 214–23 (NTA 1:177). In Tobit 4:12 "immorality" may refer to intermarriage with a pagan, but this is again a specific *example* of immorality, not its meaning.

53. As agreed by many of the commentators, e.g., Gundry, *Matthew*, p. 91; D. A. Carson, "Matthew," 8:3–599 in *The Expositor's Bible Commentary*, ed. Frank Gaebelein (Grand Rapids: Zondervan, 1984), p. 414.

54. Harrell, *Divorce*, pp. 36–40, argues convincingly for its commonness in other strata of society as well, though our data is sparser there. Cf. also Jérôme Carcopino, *Daily Life in Ancient Rome: The People and the City at the Height of the Empire*, ed. H. T. Rowell, trans. E. O. Lorimer (New Haven: Yale, 1940), pp. 101–3, who thinks male slaves may have increased the occurrence.

55. Seneca *Ben.* 1.9.4; 3.16.3; *Dial.* 12.16.3 (to Helvia); Juv. *Sat.* 6.133–41. One may also survey the examples with which Apuleius peppers his novel about Lucius the ass. But honorable Roman men were rarely *caught* in adultery; the activity was never so popular that very many people could carry it on in public (Beryl Rawson, "The Roman Family," pp. 1–57 in *The Family in Ancient Rome: New Perspectives*, ed. Beryl Rawson [Ithaca, N.Y.: Cornell, 1986], p. 33). Amy Richlin, "Approaches to the Sources on Adultery at Rome," *WomSt* 8 (1–2, 1981): 225–50, offers a balanced study of the various strands of evidence, and warns that the moralistic accounts in many of our documents are slanted in a certain direction (ibid., pp. 235–37; for gossip and satire, pp. 237–42); each genre dictated certain features to be reported. Her article also appears in pp. 379–404 in *Reflections of Women in Antiquity*, ed. H. P. Foley (New York: Gordon and Breach Science Publishers, 1981).

56. This is true despite the fact that the main motivation behind Augustus' laws was to increase the birthrate among the nobility (Harrell, *Divorce*, p. 39); see Seneca *Dial.* 2.18.2; Epict. *Disc.* 2.10.18; 2.18.15; Plutarch *Bride* 42, *Mor.* 144B, 46, *Mor.* 144EF; *G.Q.* 2, *Mor.* 291F; Athen. *Deipn.* 4.167e. The offensiveness of the act may be somewhat gauged by its occurrence in the satirists; cf. Horace *Sat.* 1.2.38, 49, 64–110 (cf. also his *Ep.* 1.2.25–26; *Ode* 1.15.19–20); Martial *Epig.* 2.47, 49, 3.26.6, 6.45.4, 91; 9.2, 20; Juv. *Sat.* 1.77–78, 2.27, 29, 68, 6.231–41, 8.144–45. Of course, Zeus, inflamed by Cupid, broke the adultery laws—but even the gods were *supposed* to obey them (e.g., Apul. *Metam.*

6.22); according to most philosophers, it was absurd for Zeus to be portrayed as adulterous (Seneca *Dial.* 7.26.6). Theodorus in Diog. Laert. *Lives* 2.99 is an exception to the disdain for adultery, but even here the offense is grouped with theft and sacrilege as *normally* considered immoral; the earliest Spartans (1200–800 BC) may have also constituted an exception (S. B. Pomeroy, *Goddesses, Whores, Wives, and Slaves: Women in Classical Antiquity* [New York: Schocken, 1975], p. 37). In Jewish texts, of course, adultery was one of the standard epitomizations of evil deeds (Ps-Philo 2:8; James 2:11; Syriac Menander Sentences 240–51; cf. ibid., 45–46; Tr. Shem 7:15, 9:9, 10:16; Num. Rab. 9:11 [purportedly citing a first-century Tanna]).

57. Epict. *Disc.* 2.4.

58. Petr. *Sat.* 79 (Encolpius is angry that Ascyltus stole his boyfriend Giton); Epict. *Disc.* 1.18.11–12, 3.3.12 (similar to thief, but let both take what they want); Artem. *Oneir.* 3.11; Sib. Or. 1.178 and 3.38 (*lektroklopoi*, probably literally, "bed-stealers"), 3.204 and 5.430 ("wifestealers"); Ps-Phocylides 3 (*gamoklopeein*, "wife-stealing"); 1 Thess. 4:6. Thus fornication was not viewed as wrong like adultery; a king discovered just in time that the woman in whom he was interested was married (Alexander #3 in Plutarch *Kings, Mor.* 179E). In early Judaism and Christianity, of course, fornication was an offense against someone's future spouse, and hence was analogous to adultery.

59. Women's chastity—not so much men's—was highly valued in the ancient Mediterranean; Pomeroy, *Goddesses*, pp. 209–14; see the second or third century BC Pythagorean treatise in Lefkowitz and Fant, *Life*, p. 104, 107, and Justin. *Cod.* 9.1 in ibid., p. 182, 193. In Judaism, see especially J. R. Wegner, *Chattel or Person? The Status of Women in the Mishnah* (New York: Oxford, 1988), pp. 50–54; cf. Harrell, *Divorce*, pp. 62–63, 75. Bruce, *1 & 2 Thessalonians*, p. 87, is among the commentators who note the double standard prevalent in antiquity (and unfortunately, we might add, to some extent, today). But cf. Diog. Laert. *Lives* 8.1.21, where Pythagoras reports as tortured in the afterlife those who would not *syneinai* their wives (have intercourse, associate, or live with); cf. especially Isoc. *Nic/Cyp* 40 (3.35).

60. Seneca *Ben.* 6.32.1; laws cited in Richlin, "Adultery," p. 228; Lefkowitz and Fant, *Life*, p. 182, 193; Tigellinus in records cited in *Empire*, ed. R. K. Sherk, TDGR 6 (New York: Cambridge, 1988), 60, p. 101. In Ach. Tat. *Clit.* 6.5.3–4, a landowner wishes to imprison a man for lying with his wife.

61. Quint. 7.1.7; Paulus, *Opin.* 2.26.1–17 in Lefkowitz and Fant, *Life*, pp. 181–82, 193, cf. p. 187; Richlin, "Adultery," pp. 227–28; Gardner, *Women*, p. 7; Rawson, "Family," pp. 33–34; Pomeroy, *Goddesses*, p. 159; cf. Apul. *Metam.* 9.27–29; Chariton, *Chaer.* 1.4.7, 11–12; under the Republic, Aul. Gel. *Att. Nights* 10.23, in Lefkowitz and Fant, *Life*, p. 175, 189; in classical Athens, Antisthenes in Diog. Laert. *Lives* 6.1.4, Plutarch, *Solon* 23.1, and the text in Lefkowitz and Fant, *Life*, pp. 41–47, 75. For lesser punishments, cf. Mart. *Epig.* 2.40, 83, 3.85. Epict. *Disc.* 1.18.5–6, recommends rehabilitation rather than punishment. In Jewish tradition, cf. e. g., Prov. 2:18, 5:5, 23, 7:27, 9:18; b. Ned. 91b; the death

penalty was supposed to be left to the court, however (Jub. 30:8–9; Ps-Philo 25:10; Sifra Qed. pq.10.208.2.4; other references in Harrell, *Divorce*, n. 107 on p. 81). What men did not avenge, God would; cf. Ps. Sol. 8:8–10; Sib. Or. 3:765–66, 5:430; 1 Thess. 4:6; Test. Ab. 12 B; b. Sot. 5b (as cited in Harrell, *Divorce*, p. 63); Num. Rab. 9:1; Acts of John 35.

62. The Julian laws, in Richlin, "Adultery," p. 228.

63. Cf. e.g., Apul. *Metam.* 9.27–29; the Egyptian marriage contract in Greek, 13 BC, in BGU 1052 (cited in *Empire*, ed. Sherk, 185, p. 243); Julius Caesar divorced his wife Pompeia because she was *rumored* to be in adultery, which was, of course, harmful to his political aspirations (Suet. *Jul.* 6, 74); for classical Athenian law, see Pomeroy, *Goddesses*, p. 86; K. J. Dover, "Classical Greek Attitudes to Sexual Behaviour," pp. 143–58 in *Women in the Ancient World: The Arethusa Papers*, ed. John Peradotto and J. P. Sullivan (Albany, N.Y.: State University of New York, 1984), p. 146. Roman law, of course, did not require grounds for divorce—only the insistence of either party. This will be discussed in much greater detail under 1 Cor. 7, below.

64. Gardner, *Women*, p. 89; Justin. *Digest* 48.5.1.pr. in Lefkowitz and Fant, *Life*, p. 184, 193.

65. Safrai, "Home and Family," p. 762 (citing Tos. Ket. 7:6; m. Ket. 7:6; cf. b. Git. 90ab; p. Git. 9.50d); S. S. Smalley, "Redaction Criticism," pp. 181–95 in *New Testament Interpretation: Essays on Principles and Methods*, ed. I. H. Marshall (Grand Rapids: Eerdmans, 1977), p. 190; F. Hauck and S. Schulz, "*Pornē*," 6:579–95 in *TDNT*, p. 592. R. Akiba and R. Ishmael (early second century) (Num. Rab. 9:12), or R. Eliezer and R. Joshua (late first to early second century) (p. Sot. 1:1, §2) are reputed to have debated whether a suspicious husband must or simply may test his wife with the bitter waters (the law of the accused wife in Num. 5 is the subject of the tractate Sotah in Mishnaic literature). Harrell, *Divorce*, p. 59, shows that this is one possible way to construe the Hebrew conditional sentence in Deut. 24.

66. So also *Herm.* 2.4.1, which allows him to receive her back, if she repents, only once. This document does not allow the innocent spouse to remarry, and is the first instance I know of this practice in ancient literature; it appears in a mid-second century document which also condemns those guilty of more than one postbaptismal sin. I confess that I am grateful to God that this document failed to make it into the canon. Heth and Wenham, *Divorce*, pp. 37–38, summarize the "early Christian consensus" against the view we here take, but Hermas is the earliest evidence they are able to cite.

67. Gardner, *Women*; Paulus *Opin.* 2.26 (in Lefkowitz and Fant, *Life*, p. 182, 193).

68. The charge was officially called *lenocinium*; see Gardner, *Women*, pp. 131–32; Richlin, "Adultery," p. 227; J. J. O'Rourke, "Roman Law and the Early Church," pp. 165–86 in *Catacombs*, p. 182. The same idea appears in the Jewish text Ps-Phocyl., 177–78.

69. Pomeroy, *Goddesses*, p. 158; the fraction of dowry withheld depended on the severity of her crime.

70. Safrai, "Home and Family," p. 790.

71. Leeming and Dawson, "Except for Fornication," p. 76; Meier, *Matthew*, p. 52.

72. "Immorality" (*porneia*) might be used to mean sexual passion of any sort in Tobit 8:7, but even though this is possible (Josephus thinks the law allows married sex only for the purpose of procreation, *Apion* 2.24, 199), it probably just contrasts a moral union ("in truth," i.e., purity) with an immoral kind.

73. Degrees of sexual activity were recognized by Roman society; for example, fathers might execute their daughters for unchastity, but would punish them much more leniently for only kissing (Gardner, *Women*, p. 7).

74. Palestinian Jewish women were to keep their heads covered, at least according to what came to be rabbinic law (Sifré Num. 11.2.2; Gen. Rab. 17:8; cf. 3 Macc. 4:6; Jos. & As. 15:1–2, 18:6), under certain penalty of divorce (m. Ket. 7:6; Num. Rab. 9:12; Belkin, *Philo*, p. 230); uncovered hair came to be associated with prostitution (Gen. Rab. 85:8; cf. elsewhere 12th century BC Middle Assyrian Laws, Tablet A 40, trans. T. J. Meek, *ANET* p. 183), male lust (Sifré Num. 11:2.1, 3; p. Sanh. 6:4, §1; Num. Rab. 18:20; cf. Test. Jos. 9:5; Chariton, *Chaer.* 6.4.5), and adulterous promiscuity (b. Sot. 9a; p. Sot. 1:5, §5; Num. Rab. 9:16; Pes. Rab. 26:1/2; cf. Test. Sol. 13:1). By the second century the rabbis were agreed that the law compelled a man to divorce a wife who "appeared in public in torn clothing or bathed together with men, as was the Roman custom" (Safrai, "Home and Family," p. 762).

75. Belkin, *Philo*, pp. 230–31. Although some of his material is from Amoraic sources, it purports to be Tannaitic in substance (a baraita in p. Git. 50d; Sot. 16b) and is supported by his Mishnah reference (m. Ket. 5:5).

76. Ibid., p. 231.

77. Cf. F.-J. Leenhardt, "Les femmes aussi . . . à propos du billet de répudiation," *RTP* 19 (1, 1969): 31–40; Edward Schweizer, *The Good News According to Matthew*, trans. D. E. Green (Atlanta: John Knox, 1975), p. 124; perhaps Patte, *Matthew*, pp. 80, 266 (though he does not dispute Meier in p. 108, n. 27).

78. Cf. Matt. 8:22. 28:4 might come into view if Matthew uses his language on the narrative level here in a symbolic sense. Cf. M. Christiaens, "Pastoraal van de echtscheiding volgens Matteüs. Vragen rond de 'ontuchtclausule,' " *TVT* 23 (1, 1983): 3–23, on the Jewish idea of the woman's misbehavior making her "dead" to her husband, meaning that the marriage no longer actually existed (as reported in NTA 27:255).

79. Lehmann, "Gen 2.24," p. 265 (using p. Kid. 1:1). On pp. 266–67 he argues that Paul opposes divorce because he is writing to Gentiles. The same argument, appealing to the Noahic laws (in b. Sanh. 58a), is found in Harvey Falk, *Jesus the Pharisee: A New Look at the Jewishness of Jesus* (New York/Mahwah: Paulist Press, 1985), p. 154.

80. Gentiles grafted into the covenant community were considered spiritually, though not ethnically, Jewish (Rom. 2:27–29, chs. 4, 11; Gal. 3:14–29), and therefore could be exhorted not to live like the Gentiles (1 Thess. 4:5).

81. T. V. Fleming, "Christ and Divorce," *TS* 24 (1, 1963): 106–20. It should be noted that there are a number of private explanations in Mark, though this need not make them the interpretations of the early Church (against B. S. Easton, "Divorce in the NT," *ATR* 22 [2, April 1940]: 81).

82. E.g., J. J. Kilgallen, "To what are the Matthean Exception-Texts (5,32 and 19,9) an Exception?" *Bib* 61 (1, 1980): 102–5, noting (p. 105) that this enables Matthew to fit Mark and Luke better.

83. Gundry, *Matthew*, p. 377; Coiner, "Passages."

84. Heth and Wenham, *Divorce*, p. 198.

85. This is also true of Greek law; cf. e.g., the deed of divorce (13 BC) in *BGU* 1103, translated in *Empire*, trans. Sherk, p. 246, 189, which decrees the marriage agreement henceforth invalid.

86. W. F. Luck, *Divorce and Remarriage: Recovering the Biblical View* (San Francisco: Harper & Row, 1987), p. 102; cf. pp. 84, 86. Efird, *Divorce*, p. 42, argues that Mal. 2:13–16 is no exception to this, addressing specifically the situation of Jewish husbands divorcing Jewish wives to marry pagans (thus the reference to "godly offspring"), similar to the situation depicted in Ezra and Nehemiah.

87. Cf. 8:3; 9:12–13; 11:28–12:14; 15:3–20; 23:4; 23:24; 24:49; 25:40, 45. While it is true that Jesus demands his followers give up possessions, security, and, when necessary, family ties, he addresses this to all his disciples across the board; he does not indefinitely forbid something to only a particular group of disciples who have experienced misfortune, as opposed to others. Believers might lose family ties for following Christ, but it is understood that the body of Christ will supply new family ties (Matt. 19:29).

88. Wegner, *Chattel*, pp. 45–50, shows that in Mishnaic law divorce, or the disposition of a wife, functions like property transactions. Wegner argues that this relates only to her sexuality; it is a legal argument from analogy rather than a statement on women's worth. Cf. also Easton, "Divorce," p. 82.

89. Luck, *Divorce*, pp. 103–7.

90. Ibid., pp. 107–8.

91. Efird, *Divorce*, p. 61, proposes a different explanation: the husband causes her to commit adultery by becoming someone's second wife (polygamy) or worse.

NOTES TO CHAPTER 4

1. Some scholars have pointed to the form of the debate as reflecting actual rabbinic controversy patterns, e.g., B. Fjärstedt, "Fråga och svar i Matt. 19, 3–12," *SEÅ* 33 (1968): 118–40 (NTA 14:37); H. Zimmerman, "*Mé epi porneia* (Mt 19,9)—ein literarisches Problem. Zur Komposition von Mt 19,3–12," *Catholica* 16 (4, 1962): 293–99 (NTA 7:311).

2. Gundry, *Matthew*, p. 377, suspects that the Markan form of the question was an attempt to lure Jesus into condemning Herod Antipas, thus jeopardizing himself politically; while this is plausible, there is no

immediate reference to Antipas in the context. Another possibility would be that the Pharisees knew Jesus' views on divorce from a previous statement and they wished to challenge them; but there is no evidence for this in Mark itself. This is not to suggest that Matthew's narrative is prior to Mark's here (although some notable scholars have thought so), but to argue that Matthew rightly reconstructed the sort of issue Jesus was addressing in its own Palestinian Jewish terms. Gundry, *Matthew*, agrees that *Matthew's* text is to be construed in these terms.

3. E.g., F. V. Filson, *A Commentary on the Gospel According to St. Matthew* (New York: Harper & Row, 1960), p. 206; A. W. Argyle, *The Gospel According to Matthew* (Cambridge: Cambridge University, 1963), pp. 51–52; cf. John Lightfoot, *A Commentary on the New Testament from the Talmud and Hebraica*, 4 vols. (Grand Rapids: Baker, 1979; Oxford: Oxford University, 1859), 2:260–63 (the original of which volume was completed in 1658).

4. M. Git. 9:10 (trans. Danby, p. 321). Although Neusner has shown that the form of such passages has been redacted to create consistent structures (see especially *The Rabbinic Traditions About the Pharisees Before 70*, 3 vols. [Leiden: E. J. Brill, 1971]), the comments of R. Akiba from a more controlled period of transmission suggest that the opinions of these schools reported in this text had become fixed by his time.

5. Sifre Deut. 269.1.1 (trans. Neusner, 1:206). The particular argument of the school of Hillel, encapsulated in the Mishnah, is here expanded.

6. M. Shab. 1:4–5; Tos. Shab. 1:16; b. Bez. 20a; cf. also W. D. Davies, *Paul and Rabbinic Judaism: Some Rabbinic Elements in Pauline Theology*, 4th ed. (Philadelphia: Fortress, 1980), p. 9; perhaps suggested by the example in Belkin, *Philo*, pp. 230–31 (although to *me* Philo's view on this matter seems closer to the Hillelite position); against Jeremias, *Jerusalem*, p. 321.

7. M. Dem. 3:1; Tos. Ed. 2:3; cf. also Neusner, *Rabbinic Traditions*, 1:339; Louis Finkelstein, *Akiba: Scholar, Saint and Martyr* (New York: Atheneum, 1970), p. 127 (although his sociological analysis may not be correct). The majority opinion of Sages was considered normative (Tos. Ber. 4:15; b. Ber. 37a, purportedly late first century; p. M. K. 3:1, §6; Gen. Rab. 79:6; Koh. Rab. 10:8, §1; Song Rab. 1:1, §5; Pes. Rab Kah. 11:17), even though "majority opinion" changed from one generation to the next (Urbach, *Sages*, 1:586).

8. So Safrai, "Home and Family," p. 790.

9. Ibid., citing Sir. 7:19, 26; 25:25–26. In a second-century parable in Ab. R. Nathan 1, a husband divorces his wife for disobeying something he had ordered (which appears to have been designed to tempt her?)

10. Meier, *Matthew*, p. 215; cf. idem, *Vision*, pp. 248–53.

11. Jesus' refutation of the Sadducees in 22:31–32 is similar to those posed in rabbinic literature; see especially b. Sanh. 90b, 91b–92a (including R. Meir, second century); b. Pes. 68a, bar.; cf. e.g., Sifre Deut. 306.28.3, 329.2.1; Gen. Rab. 20:10 (second century); Deut. Rab. 3:15 (third century); Koh. Rab. 9:5, §1; Moore, *Judaism*, 2:383; cf. b. Meg. 15a; Ex. Rab. 1:8; Pes. Rab. 1:2; 4 Macc. 7:18–19, 16:25, 18:17–19; F. G. Downing, "The Resurrection of the Dead: Jesus and Philo," *JSNT* 15

(1982): 42–50; against D. M. Cohn-Sherbok, "Jesus' Defence of the Resurrection of the Dead," *JSNT* 11 (1981): 64–73.

12. Cf. e.g., Bonsirven, *Judaism*, p. 29; C. G. Montefiore and H. Loewe, *A Rabbinic Anthology* (New York: Schocken, 1974; London: Macmillan, 1938), p. 111, §291; Test. Iss. 5:6; Test. Dan 5:3. Flusser, *Judaism*, p. 474, on Jub. 36 and here: midrashic technique would naturally combine the two Torah commandments opening with *ve'ahavta*.

13. Belkin, *Philo*, p. 231.

14. In 19:7, as Patte, *Matthew*, p. 265, points out, the Pharisees end up challenging his citation of the law; in Mark, they give *their* citation first.

15. This may be an especially Matthean rub, not being in Mark's version.

16. "From the beginning" was often understood in this sense, with reference to the general time of creation (1 En. 69:18; Ps-Philo 32:7; Test. Moses 1:12–13, 12:4; Text 20:11–12 in Isbell, *Incantation Bowls*, pp. 64–65; Rom. 1:20; cf. Diog. Laert. *Lives* 10.1.75, on Epicurus): in 4 Ezra 4:30 it refers to no earlier than the sixth day, whereas in 6:38 it refers to the first day; in Ps-Philo 1:1 it refers to the general era of Adam (when he begets children, *initium Mundi*).

17. The Markan version, which does not explicitly separate the two verses, is slightly closer to the LXX, possibly reflecting Matthew's community's skillful eclecticism with texts (see Krister Stendahl, *The School of St. Matthew and Its Use of the OT* [Philadelphia: Fortress, 1968], p. 59; though, as my colleague Chris Stanley has recently shown in his dissertation, outside of rabbinic circles it was not common to cite texts with attention to exact wording). The attribution of the second Scripture text to God in Matthew, although it was not directly spoken by him, reflects Matthew's respect for Scripture as inspired, a view he shares with early Judaism (although the practice of attributing Scripture quotes directly to God is rare [Sifre Deut. 45.1.3 refers to what he said in Gen. 8:21], attributing them to the Holy Spirit, which the rabbis considered to be his agent of inspiration, is common: e.g., Sifra VDDen. par. 1.1.3.3, 5.10.1.1; Shem. Mek. deM. 99.5.12; Behuq. pq. 6.267.2.1; Sifre Deut. 355.17.1–6, 356.4.1; b. Meg. 7a, bar.; cf. 4 Ezra 14:22; 1QS 8.16; Justin *Dial.* 25).

18. They became one flesh in marriage (Gen. 2:24) because they were originally male and female (1:27) and *began* as one flesh (2:23); for the Hebrew idiom, cf. 29:14; Judg. 9:2; 2 Sam. 5:1; 19:13; 1 Chr. 11:1.

19. Ab. R. Nathan 1 A; 8, §§23, 37, §94 B; Gen. Rab. 8:1, 14:7; David Daube, *The NT and Rabbinic Judaism* (New York: Arno, 1973; London: University of London, 1956), p. 72; idem, "The Gospel and the Rabbis," *The Listener* 56 (Sept. 6, 1956): 343, 346; cf. Richard Batey, "The MIA SARJ Union of Christ and the Church," *NTS* 13 (3, April 1967): 280. Hermaphrodites were an established legal category despite their probable rarity: e.g., Tos. Bik. 2:7; Sifra VDDen. pq. 18.31.2.1 (animals); Neg. par. 5.138.1.1; b. Nid. 28b; Hag. 4a; p. Hag. 1:1, §§5–6; Yeb. 8:6, §3. For hermaphrodites in the Greek mythological tradition, see W. K. C. Guthrie, *Orpheus and Greek Religion: A Study of the Orphic Movement*, 2d

ed. (New York: W. W. Norton & Company, 1966), p. 101. The concept of the adrogynous man is developed in Gnostic texts, e.g., "Eugnostos the Blessed" and "The Sophia of Jesus Christ," trans. D. M. Parrott, pp. 216–17 in *The Nag Hammadi Library in English*, ed. J. M. Robinson (San Francisco: Harper & Row, 1977).

20. The ideal of unity in marriage is also reflected in some Greek and Latin texts, e.g., Hierocles (a Stoic) in Malherbe, *Exhortation*, p. 100; Plut. *Bride* 34, *Mor.* 142EF; Cic. *De Amic.* 21.81. The concept of "one flesh" (Jub. 3:6–7; Life of Adam 3:2; Jos. & As. 20:4/3; p. Ket. 11:3, §2; Pes. Rab. 8:5; 1 Clem. 6; Samaritan ketubah in John Bowman, *Samaritan Documents Relating to their History, Religion and Life*, POTT 2 [Pittsburgh: Pickwick, 1977], p. 311) is mainly but perhaps not strictly Jewish (cf. Plut. *Bride* 33, *Mor.* 142E; Ach. Tat. *Clit.* 1.3.4).

21. E. P. Sanders, *Jesus and Judaism* (Philadelphia: Fortress, 1985), p. 257, argues that this is probably valid tradition; Jesus would naturally have given an argument to defend his position.

22. Carson, "Matthew," p. 417, concurs that the violation of the sexual union in "one flesh" constitutes a de facto exception to the anti-divorce rule, since the "one flesh" would already have been broken.

23. CD 4.20.

24. The Genesis texts on marriage were normally used to advocate abundant procreativity, which in normal ancient thought would encourage at least quick remarriage after divorce (see our chapter on marriage in 1 Cor. 7, below). See m. Yeb. 6:6, a Houses dispute and thus presumably first-century.

25. Our Hebrew text of Genesis, the Targum and Jubilees all omit "they *two* shall be one flesh"; but this idea is inserted into the Septuagint (the Greek translation of the Old Testament) and the Samaritan recension of the Pentateuch, in keeping with the view prevalent in the Greek world (Daube, *Judaism*, p. 81).

26. Viewing it as "fornication" or "harlotry."

27. It is usually cited as a proof-text against both divorce *and* polygamy (Matthew Black, *The Scrolls and Christian Origins* [London: Thomas Nelson & Sons, 1961], p. 123; cf. Kurt Schubert, "Ehescheidung im Judentum zur Zeit Jesu," *TQ* 151 [1, 1971]: 27), perhaps modeled on a certain reading of Matthew and Mark.

28. This is also the position of Geza Vermes, "Sectarian Matrimonial Halakah in the Damascus Rule," *JJS* 25 (1, 1974): 197–202; cf. D. E. Nineham, *Saint Mark* (Philadelphia: Westminster, 1977), p. 265.

29. CD 5.2; the sealed book of the law was still in the ark, so this was not judged as sin till the coming of Zadok. One may parallel the time of stricter accounting that comes with Jesus.

30. 4Q Temple 56.18–19. Yigael Yadin, "L'attitude essénienne envers la polygamie et le divorce," *RB* 79 (1, 1972): 98–99, uses this against Jerome Murphy-O'Connor's suggestion that CD applies to remarriage even after the death of a spouse; Murphy-O'Connor responds that the Damascus Document and the Temple Scroll may not be referring to the same thing ("Remarques sur l'exposé du Professeur Y. Yadin," *RB* 79 [1, 1972]: 99–100). The documents may indeed be saying something differ-

ent, but we should not suppose them to be doing so when the Damascus Document itself can be read as simply prohibiting polygamy.

31. Against J. R. Mueller, "The Temple Scroll and the Gospel Divorce Texts," *RevQum* 10 (2, 1980): 247–56; McNamara, *Judaism*, p. 145. This is also noticed by Gundry, *Matthew*, p. 91.

32. Against, e.g., Leeming and Dawson, "Except Fornication?" p. 76.

33. P. Meg. 1:5, §4; Hag. 2:2, §2; Pes. Rab Kah. Sup. 5:3; cf. b. Shab. 104a; Peter Schäfer, "Die Torah der messianischen Zeit," *ZNW* 65 (1–2, 1974): 27–42; Moore, *Judaism*, 1:271–72; Barth, "Understanding," pp. 154–56; H. M. Teeple, *The Mosaic Eschatological Prophet*, JBLMS 10 (Philadelphia: Society of Biblical Literature, 1957), pp. 14–27; Urbach, *Sages*, 1:297–302; Bonsirven, *Judaism*, p. 219; I. Abrahams, *Studies in Pharisaism and the Gospels*, 2d ser. (Cambridge: Cambridge University, 1924), p. 126, n. 2. W. D. Davies, *Torah in the Messianic Age and/or the Age to Come*, JBLMS 7 (Philadelphia: Society of Biblical Literature, 1952), gives the fullest summary of evidence for a new, messianic Torah, which reveals its sparse and late character, though this is a point on which Davies in his later work seemed less convinced (*Paul*, p. 72; *Sermon*, p. 54).

34. The *git*, or divorce document, is dealt with in m. Gittin and the Tosefta and Talmuds structured around it; cf. also m. Yeb. 5:1ff. For a Samaritan bill of divorce and notes on it, see Bowman, *Documents*, pp. 328–30. They need not be executed by a court (Safrai, "Home and Family," p. 790).

35. Cf. S. Sandmel, *Judaism and Christian Beginnings* (New York: Oxford University, 1978), pp. 194–95; Gundry, *Matthew*, p. 380; Hurtado, *Mark*, pp. 166–67; Coiner, "Passages," pp. 368–69. Support settlements were not to be neglected (p. B.M. 1:5, §4).

36. Certain commandments were understood as obligations only should the occasion to fulfill them arise (Ab. R. Nathan 24, §49 B).

37. E. Rivkin, *A Hidden Revolution* (Nashville: Abingdon, 1978), p. 91, reads the Markan version as Jesus attacking the law; Matthew aimed to correct any such misimpressions. That God commanded that his whole law be kept is accepted throughout Jewish texts (e.g., Sib. Or. 3:258, probably second century BC); but this particular application of that standard teaching was presumably to trap Jesus into a position of opposing Moses.

38. Gundry, *Matthew*, p. 380, observes that Matthew reverses Mark's usage, making it more precise technically.

39. David Daube, "Concessions to Sinfulness in Jewish Law," *JJS* 10 (1–2, 1959): 1–13; see especially the prozbul (ibid., p. 10), which was instituted no later than Hillel. It is possible that marriage is permitted as a concession to human weakness in 19:11–12, but unlikely, since this would undercut the appeal to the Genesis narrative.

40. For Epictetus, too, engaging in what might be considered hardheartedness (*sklēros*) toward a relative was less important than seeking the "good" (*Disc.* 3.3.5); although Epictetus is not actually opposed to his father here, it is clear that philosophical inquiry rather than compassion prevails as a hermeneutical principle.

41. P. Git. 1:1, §4 (trans. Neusner, 25:19).

42. The form parallels the "antithesis" of 5:32; cf. Mark 10:11. Occurring immediately after the quote from Moses, this again suggests Jesus' authority as a legal interpreter superior to his opponents.

43. G. J. Wenham, "Matthew and Divorce: An Old Crux Revisited," *JSNT* 22 (1984): 95–107; idem, "The Syntax of Matthew 19.9," *JSNT* 28 (1986): 17–23; Heth and Wenham, *Divorce*, p. 117.

44. Heth and Wenham, *Divorce*, p. 114.

45. Ibid.

46. Ibid., pp. 115–16.

47. Ibid. Other places to put the clause, it is argued, would have served the point even less well. It could be asked, however, why Matthew did not simply lengthen the sentence and clarify the point unambiguously, if this were to produce a sense different than the one naturally read in 5:32 (cf. for this point John Murray, *Divorce* [Philadelphia: The Committee on Christian Education, The Orthodox Presbyterian Church, 1953], pp. 39–43).

48. Murray, *Divorce*, pp. 40–41.

49. Variation is a common rhetorical and literary technique in ancient texts: *Rhet. ad Herenn.* 4.28.38; Carcopino, *Life*, p. 115; cf. also H. J. Cadbury, "Four Features of Lukan Style," pp. 87–102 in *Studies in Luke–Acts: Essays in honor of Paul Schubert*, ed. L. E. Keck and J. L. Martyn (Nashville: Abingdon, 1966), p. 92; Burchard on Joseph and Asenath (OTPS 2:186).

50. Jeremias, *Jerusalem*, p. 217, citing m. Yeb. 10:3; Sifra Lev. 21.7, 47b.

51. E.g., Murray, *Divorce*, p. 42.

52. Heth and Wenham, *Divorce*, p. 59; Gundry, *Matthew*, pp. 377, 381.

53. Cf. similarly Meier, *Matthew*, pp. 216–17.

54. In contrast, perhaps, to the Old Testament priests, who alone among the Israelites were forbidden to marry divorcées or widows of anyone but other priests.

55. The idea of different measures in 13:11, 25:14–30; cf. 10:40–42, and passages about the least and greatest in the Kingdom could be, but probably are not, relevant here, because of the nature of Jesus' (and other ancient wisdom teachers') rhetoric. 24:45–51 is one illustration of the greater responsibility of one group within the early church, i.e., the church leaders; 13:52 apparently refers to converted scribes.

56. 13:9 is addressed to the crowds in Matthew, but the disciples already hear (13:12–13, 16–17).

57. To take them as saying, "not to remarry," after taking 19:9 as calling all remarriage adulterous, is nonsensical.

58. P.-R. Côté, "Les eunuques pour le Royaume (Mt 19,12)," *EglTh* 17 (3, 1986): 321–34, sees them as married men who had had to leave their wives for the Kingdom's sake, and then remain single; cf. Tannehill, *Sword*, p. 136 (both married and unmarried men). Jesus did indeed call disciples to value him over family, but his strong saying on divorce suggests to me that the spouse unwilling to live out or tolerate one living out the values of the Kingdom would have to be the one leaving, which would *allow* the disciple remarriage under the Pauline exception, below.

59. Cf. Tannehill, *Sword*, pp. 136–37; cf. B. J. Malina, *The NT World: Insights from Cultural Anthropology* (Atlanta: John Knox, 1981), pp. 5–6. For eunuchs "by nature" or God, see e.g., Tos. Yeb. 10:3; Sifre Deut. 247.1.3; p. Yeb. 8:5, §1; cf. Gen. Rab. 86:3 (in which God saves Joseph from being used for sodomy by emasculating him). For eunuchs by men, e.g., Ps-Phocyl. 187; Test. Jud. 23:4. "Eunuch" when used metaphorically generally bore a negative sense (Ach. Tat. *Clit.* 5.22.5), as when it was used more literally (Ach. Tat. *Clit.* 6.21.3; Juv. *Sat.* 1.22; Ps-Lucian, *Aff. Heart* §21.)
60. Sirach 20:4, 30:20.
61. Cf. similarly Manson, *Sayings*, pp. 215–16.
62. Suggested by e.g., Gundry, *Matthew*, p. 381.
63. It is generally accepted that Mark has adapted the form of Jesus' saying to address his Roman readers (e.g., Ernest Best, *Mark: The Gospel as Story* [Edinburgh: T. & T. Clark, 1983], p. 36), although Mark 10:12 also fits Hellenistic law (Greek law in the eastern Mediterranean after Alexander; Hugh Anderson, *The Gospel of Mark* [London: Oliphants, 1976], p. 27).
64. This could be hard on the women, and there was "a certain stigma" attached to being the son of a divorced woman (Safrai, "Home and Family," p. 791). For a negative (perhaps too negative) assessment of the social status of women in rabbinic sources, see Jeremias, *Jerusalem*, pp. 359–76.
65. Cf. e.g., Luck, *Divorce*, p. 109; Kysar, *Asundered*, p. 43.
66. C. D. Osburn, "The Present Indicative in Matthew 19:9," *RestQ* 24 (4, 1981): 193–203, calls it a gnomic present.

NOTES TO CHAPTER 5

1. Carcopino, *Life*, pp. 95–100; William Baird, *The Corinthian Church—A Biblical Approach to Urban Culture* (New York: Abingdon, 1964), p. 64; cf. examples in Harrell, *Divorce*, pp. 32–33.
2. Gardner, *Women*, p. 261.
3. Plut. *Rom.* 22.3.
4. It was not curtailed until Christianity became powerful enough in the empire to begin to affect Roman law (Tenney Frank, *Aspects of Social Behavior in Ancient Rome* [Cambridge: Harvard, 1932], p. 26). The ante-Nicene church gradually redefined "divorce" to mean " 'separation' from bed and board," not allowing remarriage; the pre-Christian morals of catechumens were not, however, judged (Harrell, *Divorce*, p. 226; for various ante-Nicene views, see ibid., pp. 157–220).
5. *Virt. Vice* 2, *Mor.* 100E (Loeb 2:96–97). The word translated "slave" was commonly used by Epictetus and other moralists for one whose nature was enslaved to passion rather than liberated by truth.
6. The specific period when Roman women gained this right is in dispute (e.g., Myles McDonnell, "Divorce Initiated by Women in Rome: The Evidence of Plautus," *AJAH* 8 [1, 1983]: 54–80: not as early as the Middle Republic), but it is agreed that women could initiate divorces by

the Roman imperial period, the time of the NT (W. L. Lane, *The Gospel According to Mark*, NICNT [Grand Rapids: Eerdmans, 1974] p. 358, accepts 50–40 BC).

7. Officially, she still needed her guardian's help; but she could easily enough change guardians; see D. C. Verner, *The Household of God: The Social World of the Pastoral Epistles*, SBLDS 71 (Chico, Calif.: Scholars Press, 1983), p. 40; cf. W. A. Meeks, *The First Urban Christians: The Social World of the Apostle Paul* (New Haven: Yale, 1983), p. 71.

8. M. Cary and T. J. Haarhoff, *Life and Thought in the Greek and Roman World*, 4th ed. (London: Methuen & Co., 1946), p. 144; W. G. Hardy, *The Greek and Roman World* (Cambridge: Schenkman Publishing Company, 1962), p. 88; Pomeroy, *Goddesses*, p. 158. Also in the Hellenistic world, according to ibid., p. 129. Abrahams, *Studies* (1), p. 69, argues for the same practice in early Judaism, but this is not what our sources indicate, and we may expect that matters had not been much more lenient before the Hillelites prevailed.

9. O'Rourke, "Roman Law," p. 181; cf. Easton, "Divorce," pp. 78–79, who demonstrates that the civil, as opposed to private, conception of marriage does not generally predate the second millennium AD.

10. Pomeroy, *Goddesses*, p. 64.

11. Many commentators, e.g., Hans Conzelmann, *1 Corinthians: A Commentary on the First Epistle to the Corinthians*, trans. J. W. Leitch, ed. G. W. MacRae (Philadelphia: Fortress, 1975), p. 120; Lane, *Mark*, p. 358; C. F. D. Moule, *The Gospel According to Mark* (Cambridge, 1965), p. 77, Don Williams, *The Apostle Paul and Women in the Church* (Glendale, Calif.: Regal Books, 1977), p. 56, point out this difference.

12. Witherington, *Women*, p. 5; Harrell, *Divorce*, p. 64; de Vaux, *Ancient Israel*, p. 35; J. D. M. Derrett, *Jesus's Audience: The Social and Psychological Environment in which He Worked* (New York: Seabury, 1973), pp. 37–38. Some writers have taken these few exceptions to reflect a more normative practice (B. J. Brooten, "Konnten Frauen im alten die Seheidung betreiben? Überlegungen zu Mark 10,11–12 und 1 Kor 7,10–11," *EvT* 42 [1, Jan. 1982]: 65–80; idem, "Zur Debatte über das Scheidungsrecht der jüdischen Frau," *EvT* 43 [5, Sept. 1983]: 466–78), but their proposal has not gained wide acceptance (see E. Schweizer, "Scheidungsrecht der jüdischen Frau? Weibliche Jünger Jesu?" *EvT* 42 [3, 1982]: 294–300; Hans Weder, "Perspektive der Frauen?" *EvT* 43 [2, 1983]: 175–78). Exceptions by the wealthy aristocracy (Jos. *Ant.* 20.7.2, §143, 3, §§146–47) are noteworthy precisely because they show the powerful following Greek rather than Jewish custom. For grounds on which the wife could demand divorce, see Z. W. Falk, "Jewish Private Law," 1:504–34 in *JPFC*, p. 517.

13. Safrai, "Home and Family," p. 791.

14. The word translated "depart" can mean "divorce" in first-century business documents; see Adolf Deissmann, *Bible Studies*, trans. Alexander Grieve (Peabody, Mass.: Hendrickson, 1988; reprint of Edinburgh: T. & T. Clark, 1901), p. 247.

15. Harrell, *Divorce*, p. 127; in greater detail, David Wenham, "Paul's Use of the Jesus Tradition: Three Samples," pp. 7–37 in *Gospel Perspec-*

tives, vol. 5: *The Jesus Tradition Outside the Gospels*, ed. David Wenham (Sheffield: JSOT Press, 1984), p. 12.

16. Quint. 7.4.11.

17. Rawson, "Roman Family," p. 32.

18. Harrell, *Divorce*, p. 32, citing Plut. *Cicero* 41.187–89.

19. Plut. *Bride* 22, *Mor.* 141A.

20. A deed of divorce in which at least one of the parties was Jewish, dating to March 10, 13 BC, is "couched in terms typical of Hellenistic deeds of this kind. No trace of the influence of the Jewish law of divorce is to be seen in it" (*CPJ* 2:10–12, §144).

21. Jewish law nevertheless did provide some protection for some categories of women, e.g., an insane wife (Falk, "Law," p. 517; C. G. Montefiore, *The Synoptic Gospels*, 2 vols. [New York: KTAV, 1968], 1:225ff); and the laws of dowry meant to protect a woman in a divorce probably were developed before the Christian period (b. Shab. 14b). On laws meant to discourage divorce in Judaism, see also Harrell, *Divorce*, pp. 68–71; Bonsirven, *Judaism*, p. 147

22. Sirach 25:26, my translation; though one should not cast away an obedient wife (Sir. 7:26). Lane, *Mark*, p. 355, is probably right that the "flesh" reflects the "one flesh" of Gen. 2:24.

23. P. Ket. 11:3, §2; Gen. Rab. 17:3; Lev. Rab. 34:14. As the story goes, he later became financially secure and was able to help her and her new husband.

24. Harrell, *Divorce*, p. 61.

25. *Dial.* 5.4.4 (Loeb 1:264–65). The second-century Stoic philosopher and Roman emperor, Marcus Aurelius, may also have disliked divorce, although the saying attributed to him (Saying 7, in Loeb pp. 362–65, from *Capit.* 19.8) is circumstantial and probably spurious (he elsewhere praises his wife).

26. B. Sanh. 22a. Montefiore and Loewe, *Rabbinic Anthology*, p. 509, §1436, cites b. Git. 90b as saying the same. Cf. Abrahams, *Studies* (1), pp. 69, 71.

27. Martin Dibelius, *From Tradition to Gospel*, trans. Bertram Lee Woolf (Cambridge: James Clarke & Company, 1971), p. 39; Wenham, "Jesus Tradition," p. 5:8; Anderson, *Mark*, p. 12; Günther Bornkamm, *Paul*, trans. D. M. G. Stalker (New York: Harper & Row, 1971), p. 110; Williams, *Paul and Women*, p. 55. D. L. Balch, "Backgrounds of I Cor. VII: Sayings of the Lord in Q; Moses as an Ascetic *theios anēr* in II Cor. III," *NTS* 18 (3, April 1972): 351–64, suggests that even "the Corinthians' asceticism was formed by certain sayings of the Lord that were under discussion at Corinth" (p. 358); cf. Matt. 19:11–12. E. P. Sanders has noted that the rabbis usually regarded the "words of the scribes" as less authoritative than the words of Torah, and I would suggest that Paul views his extrapolation of Jesus' teaching analogously—though much like the sages, he still thinks that he is right.

28. See Meeks, *World*, p. 115; for rabbinic procedure here, see Peter Richardson, " 'I Say, not the Lord': Personal opinion, Apostolic Authority, and the Development of Early Christian Halakah," *TB* 31 (1980): 65–86; Birger Gerhardsson, *The Origins of the Gospel Traditions* (Philadelphia: Fortress, 1979), p. 34.

29. Which is not to say that it is not an accurate opinion; an ancient letter of advice, as opposed to a commanding letter, gave reasoned arguments, but still wanted the reader to come to the same conclusion as the writer (see S. K. Stowers, *Letter Writing in Greco-Roman Antiquity*, LEC 5 [Philadelphia: Westminster, 1986], p. 109). The wording in 7:10, with reference to Jesus' saying, is of course much stronger (cf. Epict. *Disc.* 2.9.13 for the teachings of the philosophers).

30. Intermarriage with pagans was forbidden in the OT (Deut. 7; Ezra 9:2–3; Neh. 13:23–29) and Jewish tradition (Jub. 20:4, 22:20). Intermarriage was, of course, a religious rather than an ethnic problem, as the book of Ruth shows; Paul, with his radical opposition to any required boundaries between Jews and Gentiles, would certainly have opposed any restrictions on *racial* intermarriage (cf. 1 Cor. 12:13; Gal. 3:28; Eph. 2:11–22), which was probably fairly common in his churches (cf. Acts 16:3), despite the cultural differences involved. The only possible objection to an interracial marriage in the Bible was raised by Aaron and Miriam, when Moses married an Ethiopian woman (Num. 12:1), and in that case God strongly disagreed with their opinion (Num. 12:1–15).

31. Ach. Tat. *Clit.* 1.3.2; baraitha in b. Yeb. 62b; cf. Jub. 28:6–7; Safrai, "Home and Family," p. 755. Cf. the suitors imploring a father for his daughter (following the motif of wicked suitors as early as the Odyssey) in (Ps?)Plut. *L.S.* 4, *Mor.* 774E.

32. Marriages could be arranged by parents at the suggestion of children "in love"; see Chariton *Chaer.* 1.1.8–9. In imperial Roman society children sometimes also refused marriages (Ach. Tat. *Clit.* 1.8.1; Suzanne Dixon, *The Roman Mother* [Norman, Okla.: Oklahoma University Press, 1988] pp. 27, 62–63, 177; cf. Gardner, *Women*, pp. 10, 41–43). In Palestinian Jewish practice, a minor girl could exercise the right of refusal with regard to getting pregnant (p. Yeb. 1:2, §§4–5, especially the second century material), and Tobias was said to have married piously without his father's knowledge (Tobit 7:13–15).

33. The degree of parental authority over children's decisions was disputed even among the rabbis; it was said that some rabbis allowed a father to impose Nazirite vows on his sons, while others forbade it (a Houses dispute reported in R. Meir's name in p. Sot. 3:8, §2).

34. Jean Héring, *The First Epistle of Saint Paul to the Corinthians*, trans. A. W. Heathcote and P. J. Allcock (London: Epworth, 1962), p. 52, also thinks these are pre-Christian marriages.

35. One could argue that some rabbis saw intermarriage as a missionary tool, based on their view that Solomon married foreign wives "to draw them to the teachings of Torah and to bring them under the wings" of the Shekinah (p. Sanh. 2:6, §2, translated in Neusner 31:89); but this tradition was created to exonerate Solomon's violation of Torah, not to advocate "missionary dating."

36. And as Henry Chadwick, " 'All Things to All Men' (I Cor. ix.22)," *NTS* 1 (4, May 1955): 266, notes, "the Christian ethic cannot be imposed upon the pagan partner."

37. Luke 18:29 and some MSS of Matt. 19:29 include "wife." Since this follows quickly upon the passage prohibiting divorce in all three of

these Gospels, it would have been natural for Mark and probably Matthew to have omitted it.

38. My colleague Byron McCane has argued persuasively that this passage refers to the Jewish practice of secondary burial (" 'Let the Dead Bury their own Dead': Secondary Burial and Matt. 8:21–22," *HTR* 83 (1, 1990): 31–45. The father had died some time before, and the son wished to wait out the year so he could gather up the father's bones and place them in an ossuary. This had no doubt acquired the same sense of religious duty as burial of the father in general (see the piety of this in Tobit), but it was not a biblical commandment.

39. H.-U. Willi, "Das Privilegium Paulinum (1 Kor 7,15f)—Pauli eigene Lebenserinnerung? (Rechtshistorische Anmerkungen zu einer neueren Hypothese)," *BZ* 22 (1, 1978): 100–108. Faith in Jesus would not have been viewed by most first-century Jews as apostasy, even if some, like Paul himself before his conversion, had viewed it as worthy of synagogue discipline.

40. Jerome Murphy-O'Connor, "The Divorced Woman in 1 Cor. 7:10–11," *JBL* 100 (4, Dec. 1981): 601–6. But Murphy-O'Connor seems to me to be undeniably correct to conclude that Paul in 7:10–11 refuses the divorce because he considers the grounds inadequate, whereas in 7:15 he permits it because the grounds are sufficient (p. 606).

41. See D. L. Balch, *Let Wives be Submissive: The Domestic Code in 1 Peter*, SBLMS 26 (Chico: Scholars Press, 1981), chs. 5–6, for a thorough discussion of the situation addressed in 1 Pet. 3:1–7; for a shorter summary, see Stambaugh and Balch, *Environment*, p. 124.

42. Cf. Plut. *Bride* 19, *Mor.* 140D; Balch, *Wives*, passim; for a brief summary of such a social situation, cf. my suggestions on p. 10 of "Is Paul's Teaching 'Sexist'?" *The Crucible* 1 (1, Fall 1990): 4–11 (dependent here especially on Balch's work).

43. 1 Esdras 9:9, LXX.

44. Harrell, *Divorce*, p. 67, cf. p. 126. His appeal to the earlier m. Git. 9:8 is possible but it does not clearly support his point.

45. Sirach 25:13–26 makes it a necessity; cf. b. Yeb. 63b.

46. P. Ket. 7:6, §1. A baraitha in b. Pes. 49a advises young men to marry the daughters of scholars, rather than of *amme haaretz*, the uneducated masses.

47. Tos. Demai 3:9.

48. Belkin, *Philo*, p. 258.

49. Often noted in current literature: Hoenig, "Conversion," p. 54; Moore, *Judaism*, 1:335; Rudolf Schnackenburg, *Baptism in the Thought of St. Paul* (Oxford: Basil Blackwell, 1964), p. 15.

50. Mekilta *Nez.* 1:47ff. (Lauterbach, 3:5), R. Ishmael; b. Yeb. 47b; Moore, *Judaism*, 1:328, 333–34; Hoenig, "Conversion," pp. 48, 54; Bamberger, *Proselytism*, p. 60. Legal standing, of course, does not mean that he was received as a *social* equal.

51. B. Pes. 92a, a Babylonian Amora interpreting a mishnah of Beth Hillel; b. Yeb. 47b.

52. Usually the later rabbis addressed the issue only with regard to inheritance rights; to my knowledge, the issue of a *marriage's* continuing

validity on grounds of one partner's conversion to Judaism did not come up. It is presented here only as a possible extension of Jewish thinking on the subject.

53. Josephus tells us that many women in Syria and Rome had converted to Judaism, arousing the ire of their husbands; but he is careful to argue that Judaism is not subversive and that it does not undermine traditional Roman family values of the wife's submission.

54. Diog. Laert. *Lives* 1.78–81; 1.92; Plut. *Educ.* 19, *Mor.* 13F-14A; cf. Ps-Phocyl. 199–200.

55. Official Roman marriages were only granted to citizens, though the majority of the people in the empire still practiced their marriages unrecognized by official Roman law. See Gardner, *Women*, p. 32. Free women who cohabited with slaves could become slaves of the owner, although in some cases, as with a slave of the emperor, this act would guarantee upward social mobility (Stambaugh and Balch, *Environment*, p. 116).

56. As noted above, this would not have been a reservation that Paul would have shared.

57. Meeks, *Urban Christians*, p. 101, rightly notes the preference of Pauline Christians for "group endogamy"—marrying fellow-Christians (1 Cor. 9:5); but he notes that the rule against divorce "takes precedence over the preference for group endogamy."

58. See Wegner, *Chattel* pp. 64–70.

59. See I. H. Marshall, "The Meaning of Reconciliation," pp. 117–32 in *Unity and Diversity in New Testament Theology: Essays in Honor of George E. Ladd*, ed. Robert Guelich (Grand Rapids: Eerdmans, 1978), pp. 121, 127.

60. Safrai, "Home and Family," p. 791.

61. Though then, as now, the children obviously would not be kept by both parents. Under Roman law, children normally remained with their fathers (Pomeroy, *Goddesses*, pp. 158, 169).

62. I have tried to bring out the meaning in this translation as adequately as possible. "Brother" may be "husband" here; the manuscripts disagree, but the meaning of the text is the same either way.

63. Gardner, *Women*, p. 32.

64. Ulpian *Rules* 5.8–9 (3d century AD Rome), in Lefkowitz and Fant, *Life*, p. 192, §195. If she were a citizen, however, the child took whatever status was inferior (ibid.). For a much more thorough examination of marriages between people of different legal status, see P. R. C. Weaver, "The Status of Children in Mixed Marriages," pp. 145–69 in *The Family in Ancient Rome*, ed. Rawson.

65. Weaver, "Status," pp. 149–51.

66. Tos. Sanh. 4:7 (Neusner, 4:208). This is, of course, merely one example among many.

67. P. Ket. 1:5, §2 (Neusner 22:41). See especially p. Yeb. 6:1–9:8.

68. P. Kid. 1:1, §8.

69. P. Git. 1:4, §2.

70. Tos. Sanh. 13:2; Ab. R. Nathan 36 A. It was sometimes thought that Jewish parents' sins could affect children who died as minors; see A. Marmorstein, *The Doctrine of Merits in Old Rabbinical Literature* (New

York: KTAV, 1968; reprint of a 1920 ed.), pp. 40–41, although this may all be later tradition.

71. B. Sanh. 58a; Richard R. De Ridder, *Discipling the Nations* (Grand Rapids: Baker, 1971), pp. 98, 107.

72. P. Kid. 3:12, §8, early third century.

73. Bruce, *1 & 2 Corinthians*, p. 70, citing m. Yeb. 9:2. This reference does not demonstrate his case, but given the connection between holiness and Israel in Jewish literature, he is probably right.

74. Bonsirven, *Judaism*, p. 56, citing m. Ket. 4:3, which says the child would be "a daughter of Israel in every respect."

75. Esther Rab. 8:3. The rabbi cited lived in the third century, but two opposing views are here cited in his name.

76. As R. E. O. White, *The Biblical Doctrine of Initiation* (Grand Rapids: Eerdmans, 1960), p. 213, n. 2, and p. 362, notes, this would undercut Paul's entire polemic against the traditional Jewish view of salvation by virtue of one's membership in Israel. And as A. D. Nock, *St. Paul* (New York: Harper & Row, 1963), p. 151, observes, "Such transferred holiness is not salvation—it is only the possibility of salvation: even those fully in Christ could lapse." Their "specialness" in some sense might be suggested if an allusion is being made to the story of children brought to Jesus, which follows immediately upon the divorce pericope in the Jesus tradition as we have it in Mark (Wenham, "Jesus Tradition," p. 9); but the evidence for an allusion to that passage here is not very strong.

77. Against Alan Richardson, *An Introduction to the Theology of the NT* (New York: Harper & Row, 1958), p. 359. M. P. Nilsson, *The Dionysiac Mysteries of the Hellenistic and Roman Age* (Lund: C. W. K. Gleerup, 1957), pp. 106–15, may be correct in finding the dedication of babies and small children in the cult of Dionysus in the Greek East of the Roman period, but his written evidence is sparser and later than the more ambiguous artwork on which much of his case is based, and he acknowledges that this practice was unique to the cult of Dionysus among the Mysteries (ibid., p. 110).

78. G. Walther, "Übergreifende Heiligkeit und Kindertaufe im Neuen Testament," *EvT* 25 (11, 1965): 668–74.

79. 7:15 and 7:16 should be taken together; cf. Sakae Kubo, "I Corinthians VII.16: Optimistic or Pessimistic?" *NTS* 24 (4, July 1978): 539–44. The hope of v. 16 is that the unbeliever may yet come to salvation, and thus one should stay in the marriage (Bruce, *1 & 2 Corinthians*, p. 70, examining the LXX construction).

80. This is argued along lines of Jewish purity codes. The impurity of menstruants was transferrable in Leviticus, and this came to be transferred to other classes of impurity in early Judaism (cf. e.g., E. P. Sanders, *Jewish Law from Jesus to the Mishnah: Five Studies* [London: SCM; Philadelphia: Trinity, 1990], p. 190). Gentiles, who on converting to Judaism needed to undergo proselyte baptism to remove impurity, could be thought to convey some level of contamination. By analogy, some Christians may have feared becoming impure through contact with unbelieving spouses.

81. Williams, *Paul and Women*, p. 57, argues from 1 Cor. 6:15–16 that the Christian brings Christ into the marital union and so exercises a superior influence on the children.

82. I am therefore in agreement with Stein, " 'Lawful?' " p. 120, who notes that just as Paul and Matthew found exceptions to Jesus' general principle, we must allow for some further exceptions in certain situations which none of these teachers had occasion to address in our extant texts.

83. An argument from different Greek words used for being "bound" in Paul is fallacious; they are used interchangeably, unless one excludes categories so as to have so few examples left as to be able to argue whatever one wishes; see Luck, *Divorce*, p. 173.

84. J. C. Laney, "Paul and the Permanence of Marriage in 1 Corinthians 7," *JETS* 25 (3, Sept. 1982): 283–94; J. Zateski, "Problem 'wyjatku' w 1 Kor 7,15–16 (Le problème de 'l'exception' en 1 Cor 7:15–16)," *ColTh* 53 (3, 1983): 43–63 (NTA 28:268).

85. Harrell, *Divorce*, p. 71; cf. p. 128, citing m. Git. 9:3.

86. Danby's translation, p. 319.

87. E.g., the deed of divorce of 13 BC, in which at least one of the participants in Jewish, stipulating permission to remarry (*CPJ* 2:10–12, §144), and the Jewish deed of divorce from Wadi Murabba'at, probably AD 72, using the same language of release for remarriagability (in *Inscriptions Reveal: Documents from the time of the Bible, the Mishna and the Talmud*, ed. Efrat Carmon, trans. R. Grafman [Jerusalem: Israel Museum, 1973], §189, pp. 90–91, 200–1); this was a normal part of such documents. Rom. 7:2 applies the language of "binding" and "loosing" to marriage and its termination (in this case, by the death of the spouse) as well. On a more popular level, Guy Duty, *Divorce and Remarriage* (Minneapolis: Bethany, 1967), pp. 39–44, argues this same point from the Greek term used.

88. E.g., Epict. *Disc.* 1.14; 3.24.109; Marc. Aur. *Med.* 4.25, 5.27.

89. *Disc.* 3.5.6.

90. 1 Macc. 1:15–16; Test. Moses 8:3 (probably first century AD); b. Sanh. 44a; p. Sanh. 10:1, §1; Sheb. 1:6, §5 (citing R. Judah ha-Nasi, c. AD 200); Gen. Rab. 46:13 (also citing R. Judah); Lev. Rab. 19:6; Pes. Rab Kah. Sup. 5:2; cf. J. B. Lightfoot, *Notes on the Epistles of St Paul* (Winona Lake, Ind.: Alpha, n.d.), p. 228 (citing 1 Macc. 1:15; Jos. *Ant.* 12.5.1); James Moffatt, *The First Epistle of Paul to the Corinthians*, MNTC (London: Hodder & Stoughton, 1938), p. 86 (citing 1 Macc. 1:15; 4 Macc. 5:2). On the historical situation of the early references, see Bright, *History*, p. 420; Moore, *Judaism*, 1:49. The characteristic, physical identifying feature of Jews was circumcision (e.g., Petr. *Sat.* 102), and when Antiochus Epiphanes wished to de-Judaize the Jewish people he forbade them to circumcize their infants (Jos. *War* 1.1.2, §34).

91. Falk, *Jesus the Pharisee*, p. 17, cites the accurate teaching of R. Jacob Emden (1697–1776) on this verse, with regard to the practice of ancestral customs.

92. This is similar again to Stoic language (e.g., Epict. *Disc.* 1.1.23), except that it is Christ and not philosophy that liberates.

93. It is possible that this text means that, just as a former slave owed continuing allegiance to the patron who freed him or her, so also the spiritually freed person owes obligations to Christ as "the Lord's freed-

man" (Francis Lyall, "Roman law in the Writings of Paul—The Slave and the Freedman," *NTS* 17 [1, Oct. 1970]: 79).

94. *Demon.* 29, *Or.* 1 (Loeb 1:20–21).

95. Cf. Sir. 14:11.

96. Epictetus, in fact, received his freedom from slavery, though he had been content; many Jews had also been freed from slavery by fellow-Jews (Leon, *Jews of Rome*, p. 237); on forms of manumission, see S. S. Bartchy, *Mallon Chrēsai: First-Century Slavery and the Interpretation of 1 Corinthians 7:21*, SBLDS 11 (Missoula, Mont.: SBL, 1973), pp. 87–125. One could not impose one's position on ancient society without either extreme violence or a gradual change in public morality; no one seriously attempted the former course, but Stoicism and Christianity worked for the latter one. But even as emperor, the Stoic Marcus Aurelius did not force his views of equality (Marc. Aur. *Med.* 1.14) onto the state, maintaining earlier Stoic (and ultimately Aristotelian) household codes that emphasized hierarchy; he praises Pius for using moderation with public spectacles (Marc. Aur. Med. 1.16.7), but no one thought to shut them down.

97. Against Lightfoot, *Notes*, p. 231.

98. It was of paramount importance for women to remain virgins until marriage, even in the Greek world where the same standard was not required of men; cf. Ach. Tat. *Clit.* 5.18.6; 5.27. In Jewish inscriptions, it appears to function as a designation of age, 14–19 years old (*CIJ* 1:cxvii; cf. 1:31, §45, 1:252, §320 [no age listed], 1:297, §381, 1:300, §386, 1:429, §588; though cf. also 1:598, §733).

99. The concept is not completely without parallel, although the parallels are later; cf. Ach. Tat. *Clit.* 5.20.5; Jos. & As. 4:7/9, 8:1; Rev. 14:4. Many scholars see primarily men as in view here: J. C. Hurd, *The Origin of 1 Corinthians* (London: S.P.C.K., 1965), p. 68 (male and female); J. F. Bound, "Who Are the 'Virgins' Discussed in 1 Corinthians 7:25–38?" *EvJ* 2 (1, 1984): 3–15 (men, excluding the feminine article before "virgin"); Black, *Scrolls*, p. 84 (paralleling the Essenes).

100. This could refer to the final period of suffering before the end of the age (F. L. Arrington, *Paul's Aeon Theology in 1 Corinthians* [Washington, D.C.: University Press of America, 1978], pp. 122–23; cf. Archibald Robertson and Alfred Plummer, *A Critical and Exegetical Commentary on the First Epistle of St Paul to the Corinthians*, 2d ed., ICC [Edinburgh: T. & T. Clark, 1914], p. 152), but it need not be (cf. Herman Ridderbos, *Paul: An Outline of His Theology*, trans. John Richard De Witt [Grand Rapids: Eerdmans, 1975], pp. 311–13). Chadwick, "All Things," p. 268, suggests that ascetic, eschatological, and Stoic-Cynic ideas about being undisturbed are fused in this passage; Conzelman, *1 Corinthians*, p. 133, rejects the Stoic component. Helmut Koester, *Introduction to the NT*, vol. 2: *History and Literature of Early Christianity* (Philadelphia: Fortress, 1982), p. 124, thinks Paul here counters their ascetic view based on realized eschatology.

101. 2 Bar. 10:13–15; cf. Test. Job 33:4.

102. This has Stoic parallels (Robertson and Plummer, *First Corinthians*, p. 157). When Paul wants them to be "free from worry" in 7:32, he means from worldly care, not from the concern for the Lord he describes

as more natural to single people; the word translated "concern" has good (2 Cor. 11:28; Sib. Or. 3:234–35; Anacharsis to Hipparchus Ep. 3.6 [*Cynic Epistles*, pp. 40–41]) as well as negative (Matt. 6:34) senses. But as Héring, *1 Corinthians*, p. 60, notes, even the preoccupation with spouse is not pejorative here as "worry" is in Matt. 6; it is, rather, natural that a husband should care for his wife and her needs, and vice versa, and *this* is what Paul is saying. But this commitment takes time, and those not in need of the married lifestyle could devote more time to God as singles. Marriage also carries its own cares, as suggested in Jer. 16:2–4, because it involves attachments and hence griefs which singleness does not.

103. See Ach. Tat. *Clit.* 5.13.3.

104. Moore, *Judaism*, 2:127; in Jewish marriage contracts, his duties included support, hers, household chores. Ancient writers insisted that a woman should desire to please only her husband (e.g., Ps-Melissa To Kleareta, in Malherbe, *Exhortation*, p. 83).

105. Cf. Du Plessis, "Ethics," p. 26 (one who does not want to marry, rather than one who cannot, is the one with the gift). Cf. Pes. Rab Kah. 27:1 for a story about R. Johanan's willingness to forsake everything for the study of Torah. Of course, the Gospels make forsaking possessions much more normative than they make going without marriage (Luke 14:33, etc.).

106. Diog. Laert. *Lives* 6.7.96 (Loeb 2:100–1).

107. Diog. Laert. *Lives* 6.7.97 (Loeb 2:100–1).

108. Ps-Crates 32, To Hipparchia (*Cynic Epistles*, pp. 82–83).

109. See David Balch, "1 Cor 7:32–35 and Stoic Debates about Marriage, Anxiety, and Distraction," *JBL* 102 (3, Sept. 1983): 429–39.

110. *Divorce*, p. 129.

NOTES TO CHAPTER 6

1. Apparently some well-to-do members of the congregation—for only those of higher social status could expect much justice from the courts— had been engaging in lawsuits. Given the context, it is at the very least possible that their disputes involved sexual affairs (cf. Peter Richardson, "Judgment in Sexual Matters in 1 Corinthians 6:1–11," *NovT* 25 [1, 1983]: 37–58), since this was one of the few categories of offense tried by jury courts (Stambaugh and Balch, *Environment*, p. 32). On the other hand, the context of the church executing judgment may be sufficient to explain the placement of these verses, and they may refer, as by themselves they would most likely appear to refer, to property disputes (cf. 6:7).

2. Diog. Laert. *Lives* 7.1.121, citing Zeno; cf. Antisthenes in 6.1.11. The Mandean commands to marry (E. S. Drower, *The Mandaeans of Iraq and Iran: Their Cults, Customs, Magic, Legends, and Folklore* [Leiden: E. J. Brill, 1962], pp. 59–72; F. C. Burkitt, *Church and Gnosis* [Cambridge, 1932], p. 113) are far too late to warrant our discussion here.

3. See also Plato (e.g., Diog. Laert. *Lives* 3.78), Aristotle, and Epictetus in Verner, *Household*, pp. 71–72, 78.

4. Fragment 14. I have cited this from Meeks, *World*, p. 51.

5. Cf. the early Augustan poem of Propertius, 4.11, in Marjorie Lightman and William Ziesel, "Univira: An Example of Continuity and Change in Roman Society," *CH* 46 (1, March 1977): 21; Cicero in Rawson, "Roman Family," p. 9. For evidence concerning the early empire, see Harrell, *Divorce*, p. 29. Some have attributed the low birth-rate in Rome to the daily Roman practice of hot baths; see A. M. Devine, "The Low Birth-Rate in Ancient Rome: A Possible Contributing Factor," *RMP* 128 (3–4, 1985): 313–17.

6. Harrell, *Divorce*, p. 29; Dixon, *Mother*, pp. 22, 24, 71–103; Gardner, *Women*, p. 77; Ludwig Friedländer, *Roman Life and Manners Under the Early Empire*, 4 vols., trans. Leonard A. Magnus (New York: Barnes & Noble, 1907), 1:232–33.

7. Gardner, *Women*, p. 82. To escape extra taxes, she had to remarry within 18 months (O'Rouke, "Roman Law," p. 180).

8. Apul. *Metam.* 4.32.

9. E.g., Achilles Tatius; Joseph and Asenath.

10. In Lefkowitz and Fant, *Life*, p. 11, §21. For tomb inscriptions of the poor commemorating the joys of their marriages in Roman imperial times, see Cary and Haarhoff, *Life*, p. 147.

11. Hipponax, *Fr.* 68, in Lefkowitz and Fant, *Life*, p. 16, §31. The context is lost, and consequently the text could be interpreted other than the way we have read it above.

12. Cf. Plut. *Dinner* 21, *Mor.* 164B.

13. The view espoused by Clinias in Ach. Tat. *Clit.* 1.8.1–2; the topic of debate is common, as early as Plato's *Symposium*. It should be noted, however, that most Greeks involved in homosexual activity were bisexual, and the widespread character of Greek homosexuality does not normally exclude marriage and childbearing.

14. For the honor attached to this office, cf. e.g., Tarquinia, in Plutarch *Publ.* 8.4.

15. Plutarch *R.Q.* 96, *Mor.* 286EF. Charges of intimacy with a Vestal were still prosecuted in the time of Crassus; see Plut. *Crass.* 1.2.

16. Plutarch *R.Q.* 83, *Mor.* 284A–C.

17. Mary Beard, "The Sexual Status of Vestal Virgins," *JRS* 70 (1980): 12–27, argues that the Vestals were viewed partly as virgins and partly as matrons, and maybe partly as men, and that this role ambiguity gave them power, according to Mary Douglas's anthropological approach to purity and danger. I am not entirely persuaded by her argument; all the matronal imagery she cites could be alternatively understood as simply virgin imagery. For an older study of the Virgins, see T. Cato Worsfold, *The History of the Vestal Virgins of Rome*, 2d ed. (London: Rider & Co., 1934); for several excerpts on them, Lefkowitz and Fant, *Life*, pp. 249–50. For virginity and spirituality, cf. perhaps Acts 21:9; for asexual virginal spirituality, Orphic Hymn 32.7, 10, 42.4 (though these are late); Sib. Or. 5:395–96 (probably late first to early second century AD Egypt) link the punishment of the Vestals with the sexual sins of the Roman people (5:386–94). "The Virgin" can refer to Minerva (Mart. *Epig.* 9.23.1) or Diana (10.92.8).

18. Apul. *Metam.* 11.19.

19. None of the evidence cited by Harrell, *Divorce*, pp. 28–29, contradicts this. Various forms of food abstinence were also practiced by the priests, but only during certain periods of time (Plut. *Isis* 5, *Mor.* 352F, 6, *Mor.* 353B). The chastity required of the earlier priestesses of Artemis (E. E. Barthell, Jr., *Gods and Goddesses of Ancient Greece* [Coral Gables, Fla.: University of Miami Press, 1971], p. 27) seems to have been more demanding.

20. Cf. the temple inscriptions in F. C. Grant, ed., *Hellenistic Religions: The Age of Syncretism* (Indianapolis: Bobbs-Merrill, 1953), pp. 6 (temporary, within marriage), 29 (outside of marriage). Moffatt, *1 Corinthians*, p. 76, cites some mystery-cults and also Jewish abstention on Yom Kippur (m. Yoma 8.1; cf. also Bonsirven, *Judaism*, p. 160, citing Gen. Rab. 35.9.8–9); cf. the Sabbath in Jub. 50:8, though not everyone would have agreed (p. M.K. 3:5, §20). In Greek-speaking Judaism, cf. Test. Naph. 8:8 (cited also by Moffatt, Kelly, and Bruce); J. N. D. Kelly, *A Commentary on the Epistles of Peter and Jude* (Grand Rapids: Baker, 1981), p. 134, compares 1 Pet. 3:7 and our text.

21. Lucian *Syr. Godd.* 51 (Grant, *Religions*, p. 118); Lucret. *Nat.* 2.614–15; *Rhet. ad Herenn.* 4.49.62; Epict. *Disc.* 2.20.17, 19. This becomes a frequent butt of crude satire: Hor. *Sat.* 1.2.120–21; Juv. *Sat.* 2.110–16, 6.514–16; Martial *Epig.* 1.35.15; 3.24.13, 91; 9.2.13–14; 13.64. Cf. *Greek Anth.* 6.220; G. S. Gasparro, *Soteriology and Mystic Aspects in the Cult of Cybele and Attis,* EPROER 103 (Leiden: Brill, 1985), pp. 26–28, 53; Walter Burkert, *Ancient Mystery Cults* (Cambridge: Harvard, 1987), pp. 6, 36. Joscelyn Godwin, *Mystery Religions in the Ancient World* (San Francisco: Harper & Row, 1981), p. 20, seems to give a psychoanalytic interpretation to the practice. Cf. the disappearance of Osiris' phallus in the Isis myth; Plut. *Isis* 18, *Mor.* 358B.

22. The cult was thus forbidden to Roman citizens; see Robert M. Grant, *Gods and the One God,* LEC 1 (Philadelphia: Westminster, 1986), p. 33.

23. Epict. *Disc.* 3.1.31; Heraclitus 9 (*Cynic Epistles,* pp. 212–13). Cf. M. J. Vermaseren, *Cybele and Attis: the Myth and the Cult,* trans. A. M. H. Lemmers (London: Thames & Hudson, 1977), pp. 96–101.

24. With W. M. Ramsay, *A Historical Commentary on St. Paul's Epistle to the Galatians* (Grand Rapids: Baker, 1979; reprint of New York: G. P. Putnam's Sons, 1900), pp. 437–39; Hans Dieter Betz, *A Commentary on Paul's Letter to the Churches in Galatia,* Hermeneia (Philadelphia: Fortress, 1979), p. 270, against J. B. Lightfoot, *St Paul's Epistle to the Galatians,* 3d ed. (London & Cambridge: Macmillan & Co., 1869), p. 204. What is instead in view is probably the fact that emasculated men were excluded from the congregation; Deut. 23:1, Sifre Deut. 247.1.1–2. What would have given Paul's rhetoric there extra force was the fact that the pagans sometimes saw circumcision as a form of castration; indeed, Hadrian later implemented Domitian's anti-castration law against circumcision (e.g., M. D. Herr, "Sybwtyw sl mrd br-kwkb' [The Causes of the Bar-Kokhba War]," *Zion* 43 [1–2, 1978]: 1–11 [NTA 24:169]). Accidental mutilation during circumcision must have been extremely

rare, but if it ever occurred it led to exclusion from Israel (p. Yeb. 8:1, §11, where it is worse than death).

25. Diog. Laert. *Lives* 6.1.3. One of these sayings is also attributed to Bion (3d century BC) in 4.48; whether it was transferred or spoken by both is now hard to say.

26. E.g., Plato *Phaedo* 64CE, 67C. In the *Republic*, however, he proposes group marriage, with procreative efficiency.

27. Diog. Laert. *Lives* 2.33 (Loeb 1:162–63).

28. Diog. Laert. *Lives* 6.2.54 (Loeb 2:54–55); cf. 6.2.29. On Cynics in general on nonmarriage (to avoid distraction), see Epict. *Disc.* 3.22.69–76; Crates' marriage to Hipparchia is allowed as an exception because she was "herself another Crates."

29. Diogenes 47, to Zeno (*Cynic Epistles*, pp. 178–79). He goes on to note that it is of no consequence even should all agree and the human race thus die out. Cf. also Diogenes 44, to Metrocles (*Cynic Epistles*, pp. 174–75). With regard to those who were married, he advocated community of wives (Diog. Laert. *Lives* 6.2.72; cf. similarly Plato).

30. E.g., Diogenes in Diog. Laert. *Lives* 6.2.46, 69; cf. Diogenes 35, to Sopolis (*Cynic Epistles*, pp. 146–47). Diogenes does, however, seem to have a low opinion of stylish prostitutes (*hetairai*) in Diog. Laert. *Lives* 6.2.61, 62, 66.

31. Diog. Laert. *Lives* 8.1.9. For subsequent Pythagoreans, see R. McL. Wilson, *Gnosis and the NT* (Oxford: Basil Blackwell, 1968), p. 41; cf. the late Neoplatonic source cited by Harrell, *Divorce*, p. 28. This might apply to other philosophical schools as well; the Skeptic Pyrrho (c. 360–270 BC) is said to have lived with his sister and not to have married, because he viewed manner of life as a matter of indifference (Diog. Laert. *Lives* 9.11.66).

32. Diog. Laert. *Lives* 10.119, citing Epicurus' works no longer extant. Cf. the opposition of the Epicurean Lucretius to passion (*Nat.* 4.1073–1148).

33. Epict. *Disc.* 3.7.19 (Loeb 2:54–55).

34. Epict. *Encheir.* 33.8; cf. an apparently stronger position in Mus. Rufus *fr.* 12 (Malherbe, *Exhortation*, p. 153), and weaker positions in Diog. Laert. *Lives* 2.69, 74 (Aristippus); Ps-Plut. *Educ.* 7DE (Malherbe, *Exhortation*, p. 31, cf. pp. 152–54). A purportedly Pythagorean treatise lists chastity especially among female qualities (3d/2d century BC, in Lefkowitz and Fant, *Life*, p. 104, §107). The Roman idea that comes closest to immoral premarital sex is "*stuprum*," between those of higher social status; men were, however, allowed to do as they wished with lower-class women to whom no one was married (Rawson, "Roman Family," p. 34; Gardner, *Women*, p. 124). The rabbis supposed the Gentiles to be naturally promiscuous, so that Simeon ben Yohai (second century) doubted that a gentile girl converted after the age of 3 would still be a virgin (b. Yeb. 60b).

35. Hierocles *On Duties. On Marriage* 4.22.21–24 (in Malherbe, *Exhortation*, pp. 102–3); cf. Zeno in Diog. Laert. *Lives* 7.1.21 (whether the other person represents a precise philosophical position or simply a specific attitude). This is true despite the fact that Epictetus waited until old

age to marry, and that some Stoics would abstain from intercourse if love were not present (Diog. Laert. *Lives* 7.1.130).

36. Also Tob. 8:6; Jub. 3:4. This may help explain the *kalon* of 1 Cor. 7:1, suggesting that it might not refer to getting married.

37. A third-century rabbi in Pes. Rab Kah. 26:9.

38. Koh. Rab. 11:9, §1. Given the lateness of this document, this story could actually be later than the second century unless earlier parallels (which I have not yet noticed) exist.

39. 175–76 (OTPS 2:580; Greek, p. 109).

40. R. Hiyya in b. Yeb. 63ab (Soncino, p. 422). Cf. b. Kid. 29b–30a.

41. B. Yeb. 63b (Soncino, p. 423).

42. B. Kid. 29b; some rabbis, however, held the opposite view, because marriage had its own distractions, as Paul also notes in 1 Cor. 7:32–33.

43. B. Yeb. 64b. It is possible that something else (such as restraining waste fluid) is meant, here; but if the restraint of semen is in view, the biological inaccuracy of the statement only confirms that young marriages and regular sexual activity during the clean part of the wife's month were the norm.

44. B. Pes. 113b (p. 584).

45. Gen. Rab. 17:2, on Gen. 2:8. Several third-century Palestinian rabbis add some more details to this tradition.

46. A late third- or early fourth-century rabbi observes correctly that God called both the man and woman Adam, and infers from this that an unmarried man is incomplete in what was intended for his full humanity (Gen. Rab. 17:2). Parallel passages are cited in Moore, *Judaism*, 2:119; cf. Urbach, *Sages*, 1:478.

47. Marriage ages vary from one society to another; for instance, the average age among the Nuer is 17 or 18 (E. E. Evans-Pritchard, *Kinship and Marriage Among the Nuer* [Oxford: Clarendon, 1951], p. 57). Ronald L. Koteskey, "Growing Up Too Late, Too Soon: The Invention of Adolescence," *CT* (March 13, 1981): 25–26, provides some other examples; he argues that modern adolescence is a cultural phenomenon of the period following the industrial revolution, and later marriages are an adjustment to this phenomenon.

48. W. Den Boer, *Private Morality in Greece and Rome: Some Historical Aspects* (Leiden: E. J. Brill, 1979), pp. 38, 41, however, thinks Spartan men married at age 18, and girls at age 12.

49. Ibid., p. 269.

50. *Laws* 6.785BC, in Pomeroy, *Goddesses*, p. 118.

51. See B. D. Shaw, "The Age of Roman Girls at Marriage: Some Reconsiderations," *JRS* 77 (1987): 30–46, depending primarily on epigraphic evidence. Cf. Plut. *Bride* 2, *Mor.* 138D; and such inscriptions as a first century BC inscription of the freedwoman, unmarried by age 14, in Lefkowitz and Fant, *Life*, p. 133, §135 (*ILS* 5213); Epicydilla, in the first century, was married at fifteen and lived with her husband fifty years (Pleket 10 in Lefkowitz and Fant, *Life*, p. 136, §140). Many were married in early teens, however, as other scholars have chosen to emphasize (Verner, *Social World*, p. 41).

52. Epict. *Encheir.* 40 (Loeb 2:524–25).

53. Pref. 4 (Loeb 2:374–75).

54. Pomeroy, *Goddesses*, p. 164; Gardner, *Women*, p. 38; Rawson, "Roman Family," p. 21; Friedländer, *Roman Life*, 1:232; cf. Paulus *Opin.* 2.1–9 in Lefkowitz and Fant, *Life*, p. 193, §196. Shaw, "Age," pp. 42–43, observes that 12 for girls and 14 for boys were minimum ages, not the usual age; though our indicators are few, they point often to the late teens (p. 43).

55. Pomeroy, *Goddesses*, p. 164, argues that this is true of *most* first marriages for girls; cf. similarly Friedländer, *Roman Life*, 4:123–31 (usually between 13 and 16). Stambaugh and Balch, *Environment*, p. 111, concur that twelve was a normal age for a girl's marriage.

56. Gardner, *Women*, p. 39. The figures she cites from the Egyptian census declarations, however, indicate a commonly higher marriage age, although these need not all be first marriages.

57. Rawson, "Roman Family," p. 22.

58. B. Pes. 113a (third century); Yeb. 62b (baraita, perhaps second century); Pes. Rab Kah. 11:6; cf. Sirach 7:23–25.

59. cf. Wegner, *Chattel*, p. 37

60. Although the danger of early pregnancy was not completely unknown, and contraception (such as it was) was permitted for girls who were afraid (Safrai, "Home and Family," p. 764).

61. Sirach 7:23; Test. Levi 9:10 (OTPS 1:792)/9:9(Charles p. 47). Cf. also above.

62. B. Sot. 22a; Ta'an. 24a; cf. Meg. 15a. This is, of course, unfair to the woman; Jesus in Matt. 5 lays the fault for lust squarely on the man who does it.

63. B. Kid. 29b–30a, mainly later Babylonian Amoraim, but citing the school of R. Ishmael. Also Koh. Rab. 3:2, §3. Cf. Safrai, "Home and Family," p. 755, citing b. Sot. 44a.

64. M. Aboth 5:21. Marriage was a yoke that should be assumed in one's youth, according to anonymous tradition in the late document Lam. Rab. 3.27, §9. For youthful marriage, see Ab. R. Nathan 3 A; 4, §16 B, and the diverse evidence in Safrai, "Home and Family," p. 748.

65. The leader in one Diaspora synagogue seems to have been married at about the age of 22 (*CIJ* 1:409, §553; is "Juda" in "Alfius Juda" a conversion name?) T. C. G. Thornton, "Jewish Bachelors in NT Times," *JTS* 23 (2, Oct. 1972): 444–45, points out a number of significant exceptions: Josephus married at 30, Philo prescribes 40, Paul and Jesus were not married and certain figures in the Testaments of the Twelve Patriarchs married late.

66. Gardner, *Women*, p. 38.

67. R. P. Saller, "Men's Age at Marriage and Its Consequences in the Roman Family," *CP* 82 (1, 1987): 21–34.

68. Cf. L. S. Sussman, "Workers and Drones; Labor, Idleness and Gender Definition in Hesiod's Beehive," pp. 79–93 in *Women in the Ancient World: The Arethusa Papers*, ed. John Peradotto and J. P. Sullivan (Albany, N.Y.: State University of New York, 1984). But in Plato, *Timaeus* 91 (excerpts in Lefkowitz and Fant, *Women's Life*, p. 81, §91), men and women are both moved by a virtually unstoppable desire for procreation.

69. In practice, of course, there was much resistance; see Dixon, *Mother*, pp. 22–23, and the sources she cites.

70. *Pythag. Sent.* 29 (in Malherbe, *Exhortation*, p. 111); Hierocles, *On Duties. On Marriage* (in ibid., p. 100); Rawson, "Roman Family," p. 9. Cf. Dio Cass. *Hist. Rome* 54.16.1–2, in Lefkowitz and Fant, *Life*, p. 181, §191. Dio Cassius wrote in the third century AD, but he writes of first-century attitudes.

71. *Bride* 42, *Mor.* 144B.

72. Ibid. This remark is directed especially against adultery.

73. Plut. *Bride* 34, *Mor.* 142F; cf. Diogenes 21, to Amynander (*Cynic Epistles*, pp. 114–15); Hierocles *On Duties. On Marriage* (in Malherbe, *Moral Exhortation*, p. 101).

74. The ancient references to child abandonment are frequent; e.g., Quint. 8.1.14; Juv. *Sat.* 6.602–9; and others in *Empire*, ed. Sherk, p. 245, §188A–E; cf. Dixon, *Mother*, pp. 19, 23, 95; Beryl Rawson, "Children in the Roman *Familia*," pp. 170–200 in *Family in Ancient Rome*, p. 172. Tarn argues for high levels of female infanticide in the hellenistic period (W. W. Tarn, *Hellenistic Civilisation*, 3d rev. ed., rev. W. W. Tarn and G. T. Griffith [New York: New American Library, 1974], p. 101; cf. Pomeroy, *Goddesses*, pp. 227–28), but this has been disputed; by the Roman period there seems to be no imbalance of the sexes (Rawson, "Roman Family," p. 18). Donald Engels, "The Problem of Female Infanticide in the Greco-Roman World," *CP* 75 (2, April 1980): 112–20, has argued that the rate of female infanticide must have been far lower than 10%. This may be correct, although the data is not as complete as we might like; see the response of W. V. Harris, "The Theoretical Possibility of Extensive Infanticide in the Graeco-Roman World," *CQ* 32 (1, 1982): 114–16. Engels' reply ("The Use of Historical Demography in Ancient History," *CQ* 34 [2, 1984]: 386–93) is well-reasoned but again may rely too heavily on assumptions about extant data; for instance, if most abandoned infants were adopted as slaves, population levels might not be fair indicators of child exposures. Natural infant mortality was, however, high; an aristocrat like Plutarch had already lost three of his five young children (*Consol. to Wife, Mor.* 608C, 609D, 611D); a brief perusal of *CIJ* will indicate how many of those buried had died in childhood, though cf. the caution of Leon, *Jews of Rome*, p. 230. As Dixon, *Mother*, p. 113, suggests, wealthy parents tended to invest less attachment to newborns, since they often would not survive. For direct killing of children, perhaps in the case of deformity, see Gardner, *Women*, p. 155; Boer, *Morality*, pp. 98–99; in other cultures, e.g., John Dawson, "Urbanization and Mental Health in a West African Community," pp. 305–42 in *Magic, Faith, and Healing: Studies in Primitive Psychiatry Today*, ed. Ari Kiev (New York: Free Press, 1964), p. 324.

75. Thus Hierocles and the Stoics condemned child exposure (Malherbe, *Exhortation*, p. 99).

76. On Jewish opposition to infant exposure, besides the references combined with abortion in the next note, see Sib. Or. 3:765–66 (probably second century BC Alexandria); Safrai, "Home and Family," p. 750

(citing m. Maksh. 2:7, Tos. Maksh. 1:8); cf. Ps-Philo 2:10, 4:16 (on the evils of killing infants).

77. Jos. *Apion* 2.24, §202; Sib. Or. 2:281–82 (although this may be part of a Christian interpolation); Ps-Phocyl. 184–85 (see further references in OTPS 2:580, note i; cf. Safrai, "Home and Family," p. 750); cf. 1 En. 69:12; Michael J. Gorman, *Abortion and the Early Church: Christian, Jewish, and Pagan Attitudes in the Greco-Roman World* (Downers Grove, Ill.: InterVarsity, 1982), pp. 33–45; J. David Bleich, "Abortion and Jewish Law," pp. 405–19 in *New Perspectives on Human Abortion*, ed. T. W. Hilgers, D. J. Horan, and David Mall (Frederick, Md.: University Publications of America, 1981); Germain Grisez, *Abortion: The Myths, the Realities, and the Arguments* (New York: Corpus Books, 1970), pp. 127–35; cf. a different view in Urbach, *Sages*, 1:242–43, who too quickly dismisses some of the contrary evidence he cites. Early Christian writers also unanimously opposed abortion (Did. 2; Athenag. 35; Tert. *Apol.* 9:8; see further Gorman, *Abortion*, passim). Sander J. Breiner, "Child abuse patterns: Comparison of ancient Western civilization and traditional China," *APP* 2 (1, 1985): 27–50 (from sociofile abstracts), tries to show a correspondence between child abuse and societies less favorable toward women and affection, ranking the Hebrews above the Chinese, and Chinese above Greek and Roman societies.

78. Heraclitus 7, to Hermodorus (*Cynic Epistles*, pp. 202–3).

79. Cf. the clause in the Hippocratic oath (Boer, *Morality*, pp. 272–73). Gorman, *Abortion*, pp. 19–32, argues that medical ethicists were more likely to oppose nontherapeutic abortion, and social and philosophical ethics to endorse it.

80. Paulus *Sententiae* 5.23.14, in *Empire*, ed. Sherk, p. 206, §161B. D. B. Gregor, "Abortige en la antikva mondo," *BibR* 17 (4, 1981): 71–90, argues that it was not punished under any Greek or Roman laws (NTA 26:288).

81. Chariton *Chaer.* 2.8.6–9.5; the heroine's ultimate decision, involving a narrative praise of motherly love, is to keep the child (9.6–11); Juv. *Sat.* 6.595–601. Many references to the public male attitude are provided in Dixon, *Mother*, pp. 94–95. Women had more access to abortion; the fathers of the family were the only ones authorized to dispose of a child once born (Gardner, *Women*, pp. 6, 154–55).

82. Theon *Progymn.* 2.96–99. Chrysippus thought that the fully human soul was received only at birth (Plut. *Stoic Contr.* 41, *Mor.* 1052EF); but later Stoics condemned abortion (Boer, *Morality*, p. 272). That it was a common practice, however, is not much in dispute; see Gorman, *Abortion*, pp. 14–18.

83. Jos. *Apion* 2.24, §199, saw procreation as the only proper reason for intercourse, and attributed this view to the law! For prayers for help in procreation in many pseudepigraphic texts, see Norman B. Johnson, *Prayer in the Apocrypha and Pseudepigrapha*, JBLMS 2 (Philadelphia: Society of Biblical Literature, 1948), p. 19.

84. B. Yeb. 62b, probably from Tannaitic tradition.

85. *Divorce*, p. 62, citing j. Ket. 5:7.

86. B. Ber. 10a.

87. B. Nid. 13a.

88. Starting with Adam, Gen. Rab. 23:4. One thus could not get married on festival days when one could not perform this function properly; see p. Git. 4:5, §2. For references from the Schools of Hillel and Shammai in m. Yeb. 6:6, Git. 4:5, see Urbach, *Sages*, 1:253; cf. Safrai, "Home and Family," p. 750.

89. E.g., Pes. Rab Kah. 22:2.

90. Attributed to R. Eleazar b. Azariah, a late first-century rabbi, in Gen. Rab. 34:14.

91. E.g., Ex. Rab. 1:13. All Abel's destined descendants died in him when Cain murdered him (Ab. R. Nathan 31 A).

92. Cf. Harrell, *Divorce*, p. 62, citing m. Yeb. 6:6; b. Yeb. 64a, 65b. Roman law permitted but did not require divorce on these grounds; see Rawson, "Home and Family," p. 32; Gardner, *Women*, p. 81; Pomeroy, *Goddesses*, p. 158. Many of the societies which disallow divorce for barrenness have less severe penalties for adultery; cf. P. C. Rosenblatt and W. J. Hillabront, "Divorce for Childlessness and the Regulation of Adultery," *JSR* 8 (2, May 1972): 117–27.

93. Ibid., on Yeb. 65b; Safrai, "Home and Family," pp. 750, 791 (citing also Tos. Yeb. 6:4, b. Yeb. 64a); cf. also the earlier rabbinic teaching in Ex. Rab. 37:4; Pes. Rab Kah. 22:2, following m. Yeb. 6:6.

94. *Life* 426, §76 (Loeb 1:156–57). Only an aristocrat would have so complained; the infant mortality rate among Egyptian peasants must have approached 50%.

95. Ps-Philo 42:1.

96. Philo *Spec.* 3.6 §36 (Loeb 7:496–97).

97. Pes. Rab Kah. 22:2. The story is told of the second-century rabbi Simeon ben Yohai, but it is undoubtedly later than R. Simeon. Cf. Sir. 16:3: it is better for a man to die childless than to have ungodly children; but the wording implies that it was also considered a terrible thing to die childless.

98. S. Safrai, "Education and the Study of the Torah," pp. 945–70 in *JPFC*, p. 965, citing Aboth de R. Nathan A, 6; b. Ket. 62b. It was hard on wives when husbands would be away for long periods, and thus often becomes the subject of parables in which kings go off to far countries (e.g., Pes. Rab Kah. 22:3).

99. Sandmel, *Judaism*, pp. 246–47, citing b. Ned. 50a. This left the tradition with the problem of disposing of the impossible number of disciples, which it did ingeniously but by destroying the true worth of Akiba's accomplishment (they all died due to sin, except for seven): Ab. R. Nathan 12, §29 B; b. Yeb. 62b; Gen. Rab. 61:3; Koh. Rab. 11:6, §1.

100. That he is said to be over 40 when he starts, however, may suggest that his wife had already completed her childbearing years (e.g., Ab. R. Nathan 6 A).

101. Gen. Rab. 95 (MSV).

102. Mark 1:18–20/par, 10:28–29/par.

103. Tos. Yeb. 8:7 (Neusner, 3:28–29); see also b. Yeb. 63b; Gen. Rab. 34:14.

104. B. Shab. 33b. This was based on prior Jewish tradition that women tended to be unreliable and unstable; cf. Jos. *Ant.* 4.8.15, §219; Philo

Prob. 18, §117; *Syr. Men. Sent.* 118–21, 336–39; Gen. Rab. 45:5, 80:5, reflecting wider Greco-Roman male perspectives (cf. Plut. *Bride* 48, *Mor.* 145C; Marc. Aur. *Med.* 5.11). Thus Josephus rejects their testimony (*Ant.* 4.8.15, §219; cf. Sifra VDD pq.7.45.1.1).

105. P. Taan. 1:6, §8; the attributions are, however, late. In Num. Rab. 14:12, Noah postponed the duty of procreation *before* building the ark, due to the wickedness of his generation.

106. Geza Vermes, *Jesus the Jew: A Historian's Reading of the Gospels* (Philadelphia: Fortress, 1973), pp. 100–101, on b. Shab. 87a, Sifré Num. 99, and Philo *Mos.* 2, §§68–69. He observes, however, that the rabbis held that this excuse was no longer valid for their own time. Another parallel, with Moses, may be adduced from Ab. R. Nathan 2 A; 2, §10 B.

107. Cf. the questions raised in Harvey McArthur, "Celibacy in Judaism at the Time of Christian Beginnings," *AUSS* 25 (2, Summer 1987): 163–81.

108. Alfred Marx, "Les racines du célibat essénien," *RevQum* 7 (3, Dec. 1970): 323–42, cites texts in 1 Enoch and Philo. R. A. Horsley, "Spiritual Marriage with Sophia," *VigChr* 33 (1, 1979): 30–54, finds in Philo the concept of a spiritual marriage with Wisdom and a related tendency toward sexual asceticism, apparent particularly in the Therapeutae; he links this with certain pagan parallels.

109. Ps-Philo 9:2.

110. Jub. 25:4.

111. *Enkrateian,* as in 1 Cor. 7:9.

112. Test. Iss. 2:1–2.

113. See Lev. 15:18 and the development of this in later Jewish tradition (e.g., Ab. R. Nathan 2 A; 2, §§9–10 B).

114. Further, the passage in Ex. Rab. 1:13, cited above, regards this as impious; even in Ps-Philo, Amram wants his wife to conceive and bear a deliverer (Moses) (9:5).

115. In Jub. 25:4–10, he promises not to marry a foreign wife. And Jubilees also concurs with Genesis that man should be married (Jub. 3:4).

116. In Test. Reub. 2:8, married sexuality is good, but (in good Stoic style) it can lead to a dangerous attraction to pleasure. The date of the Testaments is in question, but there is no reason to suppose that either of these references betray particularly Christian influence.

117. 2 Bar. 56:6. This contradicts the Genesis chronology in which the command to "Be fruitful and multiply" preceded the Fall and was part of the natural order God instituted.

118. The dispute on this matter in the interpretation of the Scrolls is acknowledged by Conzelmann, *1 Corinthians,* p. 114; cf. Henry Chadwick, *The Early Church* (New York: Penguin, 1967), p. 11, n. 1. But many other scholars, like McNamara, *Judaism,* p. 142, assume the celibacy of the Essenes to have been established.

119. No one was to lie with a woman in the sanctuary city (CD 12.1–2); the Qumran community seems to have viewed itself as the present surrogate for the temple.

120. See S. J. Cohen, *From the Maccabees to the Mishnah,* LEC 7 (Philadelphia: Westminster, 1987), p. 152; 1QS "envisions a society of

celibate men living in isolation from their fellow Jews," while CD "envisions a community of men, women, and children living among Jews (and gentiles!) who are not members of the group"; so also the Temple Scroll scatters women with men throughout the eschatological land except for the temple city. Given what we observed above, that the Scrolls oppose second marriages, it is not likely they opposed first marriages.

121. *War* 2.8.2, §§120–21 (Loeb 2:368–69), 13 (2:384–85). Josephus, who himself speaks of women's weakness, notes that these first Essenes "wish to protect themselves against women's wantonness," certain that women cannot be faithful to their husbands. In *Ant.* 18.1.5, §21, he omits reference to non-celibate Essenes.

122. Marx, "célibat essénien," pp. 323–42, points out that celibacy may have been practiced in one period there, but notes several references suggesting begetting of children. Hans Hübner, "Zölibat in Qumran?" *NTS* 17 (2, Jan. 1971): 153–67 observes that the texts speak of "descendants," etc.; though this may have been due to metaphorical use of OT language.

123. F. M. Cross, *The Ancient Library of Qumran and Modern Biblical Studies*, rev. ed. (Grand Rapids: Baker, 1980), p. 97. J. M. Baumgarten, "4Q 502, Marriage or Golden Age Ritual?" *JJS* 34 (2, Autumn 1983): 125–35, does not think the text he examines refers to marriage, but he does argue that it shows elderly women in the community.

124. Barbara Thiering, "The Biblical Source of Qumran Asceticism," *JBL* 93 (3, Sept. 1974): 429–44, derives it ultimately from the Israelite prophetic tradition rather than Hellenistic sources.

125. Commentators rightly emphasize that Paul is here replying to specific questions (e.g., H. C. Kee, *Christian Origins in Sociological Perspective: Methods and Resources* (Philadelphia: Westminster, 1980), p. 131; Hurd, *Origin*, pp. 290–91; Conzelmann, *1 Corinthians*, p. 115). Thus *peri de* ("now concerning") in 1 Cor. 7–16 may mark answers to questions from the Corinthians (S. S. Smalley, "Spiritual Gifts and I Corinthians 12–16," *JBL* 87 [4, Dec. 1968]: 432, following Hurd); it is used by other writers as a transition device (e.g., Theon *Progymn.* 1.60, 5.442; Artem. *Oneir.* 1.1; cf. 1 Thess. 4:9a), although not usually consistently.

126. A familiar sort of phrase; e.g., Tob. 12:6–8 (*kalos* and *agathos* are used interchangeably here); cf. Gen. 2:18 (*lo' tob*) and the repetition of the phrase in Gen. 1. Williams, *Paul and Women*, p. 53, argues that it means "advantageous" rather than morally good, although he also takes "touch" as a euphemism for intercourse. For expediency as a test of soundness, see 6:12 (possibly refuted in the following verses), and Seneca *Dial.* 7.8.2; Epict. *Disc.* 1.18.2, 22.1, 28.5, 2.7.4, 4.7.9; Marc. Aur. *Med.* 6.27; Diog. Laert. *Lives* 7.1.98–99 (Stoics); 10.150.31, 33, 151.36, 152.37, 153.38 (Epicurus); Sirach 37:28; in Plato, R. C. Lodge, *Plato's Theory of Ethics* (New York: Harcourt, Brace & Company, 1928), pp. 62–63; in rhetoric, cf. Theon, *Progymn.* 8.45, Burton L. Mack, "Elaboration of the Chreia in the Hellenistic School," pp. 31–67 in *Patterns of Persuasion in the Gospels*, by Burton Mack and Vernon K. Robbins (Sonoma, Calif.: Polebridge, 1989), p. 38.

127. The phrase probably means "touch" sexually; Gordon Fee (*The First Epistle to the Corinthians*, NICNT [Grand Rapids: Eerdmans, 1987],

p. 275) provides a thorough examination of the evidence supporting this position (cf. also 4 Macc. 17:1, though a different word is used). (In idem, "1 Corinthians 7:1 in the NIV," *JETS* 23 [4, Dec. 1980]: 307–14, he suggests that the intercourse issue addresses overrealized eschatology, a point probably less certain than that intercourse is in view.) Other *possibilities* for interpretation exist: in Test. Ab. 15 A, touching implies touching for harm; Ab. R. Nathan 2 A reports the evil of an otherwise righteous man who *touched* but did *not* have intercourse with his menstruating wife; it could also have ascetic connotations (cf. Col. 2:21; 1 Tim. 4:3; Gen. 3:3 and comments, such as Ab. R. Nathan 1 A). But if it addresses intercourse, as is most likely, it carries over the thought of 6:12–20; if it has ascetic connotations, it is probably a Corinthian slogan. In favor of the former explanation is the fact that *haptō* in the middle can mean "burn," and given 7:9, it could here mean to "ignite a woman's passions."

128. See especially Chadwick, "All Things," pp. 264–65 (Paul addressing ascetics in the community); this view is also held by Bruce (cited below), Longenecker, *Paul*, pp. 235–39, and others. 7:1 is thus often viewed as a Corinthian slogan which Paul rejects; cf. William E. Phipps, "Is Paul's Attitude toward Sexual Relations Contained in 1 Cor 7.1?" *NTS* 28 (1, Jan. 1982): 125–31; C. H. Giblin, "1 Corinthians 7—A Negative Theology of Marriage and Celibacy?" *BT* 41 (1969): 2839–55. G. E. Harpur, "A Comment on Abstinence Mentioned in 1 Corinthians," *JCBRF* 27 (1975): 30–40, is among many who argue that Paul here opposes abstention within marriage. Héring, *1 Corinthians*, p. 45, who thinks Paul is opposing ascetic gnostics, suggests that their argument may have been that as physical union with a prostitute affects one's union with Christ (ch. 6), so also could physical union with a spouse.

129. Jeremy Moiser, "A Reassessment of Paul's View of Marriage with reference to 1 Cor. 7," *JSNT* 18 (June 1983): 103–22, feeling that Paul's view is based on the eschatological situation and human weakness rather than opposition to marriage or sex. R. F. Collins, "The Unity of Paul's Paraenesis in 1 Thess. 4:3–8, 1 Cor. 7.1–7, and Significant Parallels," *NTS* 29 (3, July 1983): 420–29, rightly shows Paul's emphasis on purity in both; but 1 Thess. 4:6 indicates, in my opinion, that the Thessalonians passage addresses adultery specifically.

130. F. F. Bruce, " 'All Things to All Men': Diversity in Unity and Other Pauline Tensions," pp. 82–99 in *Unity and Diversity in NT Theology: Essays in Honor of G. E. Ladd*, ed. R. A. Guelich (Grand Rapids: Eerdmans, 1978), p. 89. Plummer and Robertson, *1 Corinthians*, p. 130, title 7:1–7, "Celibacy is Good, but Marriage is Natural."

131. E.g., Dio Chrys. *21st Disc.*, *Beauty* (Loeb 2:271–89), *61st Disc.*, *Chrys.* (5:1–21), *67th Disc.*, *Pop. Opin.* (5:117–25); Epict. *Disc.* 1.1.23–25, 1.28; Seneca *Ben.* 4.5.1, 21.6; *Dial.* 3.6.1, 8.6; *Ep. ad Lucil.* 14.1, 42.2; Hor. *Sat.* 101–2; Cicero *Tusc. Disp.* 3.23.55, 5.36.103; *Rhet. ad Herenn.* 4.16.23–24; Mekilta *Pisha* 1.35 (Lauterbach 1:3) (at least on the redactional level); p. Sanh. 6:1, §1; and Paul, throughout Romans (see Stanley Kent Stowers, *The Diatribe in Paul's Letter to the Romans*, SBLDS 57 [Chico: Scholars Press, 1981], on diatribe in Paul). This is related to

the question and answer dialogue format probably introduced by Plato (cf. Diog. Laert. *Lives* 3.24; and in *The Apology*, where Socrates cannot dialogue, he asks questions of his opponents and answers for them [e.g., 27C]), and interlocutors often function in stories to permit the hero to give a witty comeback (Diog. Laert. *Lives* 1.35).

132. The singular, anarthrous form of the phrase in Tob. 8:7 presumably means that Tobias did not marry Sara on the basis of lust, but rather, in true purity.

133. Mart. *Epig.* 3.33, 5.37; Artem. *Oneir.* 1.78; Apul. *Metam.* 3; Ach. Tat. *Clit.* 6.20; Mus. Rufus *fr.* 12 (in Malherbe, *Exhortation*, pp. 153–54); Paulus *Opin.* 2.1–9 (cohabitation) (in Lefkowitz and Fant, *Life*, p. 193, §196); Justin. *Cod.* 9.25 (Lefkowitz and Fant, *Life*, p. 184, §193); Val. Max. *Mem. Deeds* 6.7.1 (Lefkowitz and Fant, *Life*, p. 145, §153); *ILS* 7479 (*Empire*, ed. Sherk p. 237, §178E); cf. Gardner, *Women*, pp. 118, 206–9, 221; Friedländer, *Roman Life*, 1:243–44. This is also true in Jewish texts: Sir. 41:22; m. Ab. 2:7 (Hillel); Tos. Hor. 2:11; p. Hor. 3:5, §1; Pes. Rab Kah. 20:6; Pes. Rab Kah. Sup. 3:2; Syr. Men. Sent. 347–53. Slaves could not contract their own marriages, but were joined at their masters' discretion (noted even in Jewish texts, e.g., Pes. Rab Kah. 2:4). Slaves were often used for prostitution (Apul. *Metam.* 7.9; Mart. *Epig.* 9.6.7, 8; Dover, "Attitudes," pp. 147–48; cf. Pomeroy, *Goddesses*, pp. 140–41, 192).

134. Plut. *Educ.* 7, *Mor.* 5; cf. Artem. *Oneir.* 1.78; Athen. *Deipn.* 13.596b; Justin. *Cod.* 9.20, 22, 29 (in Lefkowitz and Fant, *Life*, pp. 183–84, §193); texts in *Empire*, ed. Sherk, pp. 210–11, 227; §§165, 173; Ramsay MacMullen, *Roman Social Relations: 50 B.C. to A.D. 284* (New Haven: Yale, 1974), pp. 86–87; Lionel Casson, *Travel in the Ancient World* (London: George Allen & Unwin, 1974), pp. 206–7, 211; Dover, "Attitudes," pp. 147–48; Gardner, *Women*, pp. 32, 130, 133; Pomeroy, *Goddesses*, pp. 88–92, 201. Jewish texts provide abundant warnings against this practice: Deut. 23:17 (though cf. Gen. 38:15–16); Sir. 9:6, 19:2, 41:20; Jos. *Ant.* 4.8.9, §206; 1QS 4.10 (if literal), CD 4.17, 8.5; Ab. R. Nathan 48, §132 B (also b. Men. 44a); Sifré Num. 115.5.7; Ex. Rab. 43:7; Num. Rab. 9:24, 20:7; cf. 2 Macc. 6:4; Sib. Or. 5:388 (probably late first-century AD Egypt); Belkin, *Philo*, p. 256. Slave-girls were commonly used for prostitution (Apul. *Metam.* 7.9; Mart. *Epig.* 9.6.7, 8; Dover, "Attitudes," pp. 147–48; Pomeroy, *Goddesses*, pp. 140–41, 192; Gardner, *Women*, p. 132; cf. Ab. R. Nathan 8 A).

135. B. Pes. 113a; Yeb. 63a and other texts above. In some Greco-Roman texts, prostitution could be viewed as a deterrent from adultery (*Greek Anth.* 7.403), though even in Greco-Roman texts it rarely appears in an unambiguously positive light (e.g., Hor. *Sat.* 2.7.46–47).

136. See Fee, *1 Corinthians*, p. 278. Cf. Tob. 8:7, where Tobias takes (*lambanō*) Sara, meaning that they slept together as man and wife.

137. This is usually not reciprocal in the texts I have seen, although 6:12 (compare how Fotis gains control of Lucius through her affections) indicates that the man can also be subjected to the woman by his passion (this was pointed out to me by Dr. Dale Martin of Duke University); and in Sir. 47:19, Solomon was "brought under the authority" of his wives

by his body. Artem. *Oneir.* 1.44 says the husband rules his wife's body (different term); Plut. *Bride* 6, *Mor.* 139A ridicules women who wish to have power over their husbands (through magical spells), saying they control only fools, when they ought to be heeding wise men.

138. Plut. *R.Q.* 7, *Mor.* 265E; also not from in-laws, 8, *Mor.* 266A. Presumably gift-giving would make division of property difficult or unfair under a later divorce settlement. Cf. Gardner, *Women*, p. 74.

139. Plut. *Bride* 20, *Mor.* 140F. The context is a theoretical "sharing" in marriage.

140. Ibid. 12, *Mor.* 139DE. The context is that if she would just not resist him, she would probably get her way.

141. Gardner, *Women*, p. 68, cf. pp. 97, 103.

142. For one example with stipulations easily located, see C. K. Barrett, *The New Testament Background: Selected Documents* (New York: Harper & Row, 1961), pp. 37–38.

143. Verner, *Social World*, p. 37.

144. Ibid. For a marriage contract providing maintenance of the wife, see *BGU* 1052 (in *Empire*, ed. Sherk, p. 243, §185), from 13 BC.

145. Ibid., p. 38.

146. M. J. Geller, "New Sources for the Origins of the Rabbinic Ketubah," *HUCA* 49 (1978): 227–45, points out similarities to Akkadian texts before the first century BC, but to old demotic forms in the rabbinic texts. Joseph Klausner, *Jesus: His Life, Times, & Teaching*, trans. Herbert Danby (New York: Menorah, 1979; n.p.: Macmillan, 1925), p. 195, points out that "similar contracts occur in the Aramaic documents of Elephantine dating from the time of Ezra." The extant Samaritan ketubah is similar to the Jewish except it requires "absolute obedience" from the wife (Bowman, *Documents*, p. 311).

147. B. B.M. 17b, 104b; Witherington, *Women*, p. 3; Sandmel, *Judaism*, pp. 194–95; for circumstances under which she could forfeit her ketubah, see Wegner, *Chattel*, pp. 80–85. On the dowry in ancient Israel, see de Vaux, *Ancient Israel*, pp. 26ff. In this chapter we use ketubah both in the sense of "dowry" and in the sense of "marriage contract."

148. M. Ket. 4:4 (where, as in Roman *patria potestas*, she is under the authority of either her father or, after her marriage, her husband); Gen. Rab. 52:12, and texts in Witherington, *Women*, p. 4; Sandmel, *Judaism*, pp. 194–95; Harrell, *Divorce*, pp. 66–67. The document in *CPJ* 1:236–38, §128, dated May 11, 218 BC, may reflect Greek custom, but certainly reinforces the antiquity of this right in a Jewish contract. Fathers also were required to support their children; Safrai, "Home and Family," pp. 769–70.

149. Falk, "Private Law," p. 516, citing b. Ket. 61a; Safrai, "Home and Family," p. 763, citing p. Ket. 5,30a; b. Ket. 48a, 61a.

150. Safrai, "Home and Family," p. 761, citing m. Ket. 5:8–9; Tos. Ket. 5:8.

151. Safrai, "Home and Family," pp. 790–91. Cf. b. Git. 57a, in a story about a betrothed Jewish couple who refrained from intercourse till the husband's death because they were unable to procure a ketubah, even though pagans had married them according to pagan law.

152. M. Ket. 5:5; Gen. Rab. 52:12; Safrai, "Home and Family," p. 761; cf. p. Ket. 5:8, §1.

153. See Wegner, *Women*, pp. 11, 74–76. For reciprocal rights and duties, see e.g., p. Ket. 5:3–9:1.

154. M. Ket. 5:6; Sifre Deut. 213.2.1–2; p. Ket. 5:7, §5. Cf. b. Sanh. 107a, where an Amora notes that even while ill David carried out his duties to his eighteen wives.

155. E.g., a virgin might not have pleasure at first, but she would acquire this by continuing the practice with her husband (Apul. *Metam.* 5.4). To dream of one's wife's willing submission to intercourse was a good omen (Artem. *Oneir.* 1.78). Spouses should avoid quarreling in the bedchamber (Plut. *Bride* 39, *Mor.* 143E). Social level may have determined some concepts of propriety, of course; Plutarch says that while the husband can make advances to his wife, the reverse is not proper (*Bride* 18, *Mor.* 140CD), but Apuleius' Lucius seems intrigued with Fotis the slave-girl's brazen sexual advances in *Metam.* 3.

156. M. Sot. 3:4; one may compare the mythical debate between Zeus and Hera, each arguing that the other's gender enjoyed sex more, until Tiresias, who had been both genders, came down on the side of Zeus (and thus incurred Hera's wrath); or the portrayal of the slave-girl's sexual appetites in the previous note. Pomeroy, *Goddesses*, p. 87, notes that in classical Athens law, citizens were to give wives "sexual attention" three times a month, for purposes of procreation; she suggests that in classical Greece women received little pleasure (pp. 143–44), but that their situation improved in this regard in hellenistic literature (p. 146). Boer, *Morality*, p. 267, notes that sexual satisfaction was usually portrayed from the man's point of view in the literature, but there were exceptions. Dover, "Attitudes," p. 149, thinks that it was generally believed that women enjoyed sex more and were more likely to fall under the other person's power through it. In m. Ket. 5:7, however, if a woman refused to consent to intercourse, the husband could reduce her ketubah.

157. M. Ket. 5:6. Cf. also m. Ed. 4:10; p. Ket. 5:7, §4. In contrast to stories of Akiba and his disciples told above, Mishnaic law stipulated that "even for Torah study a married man was not allowed to leave home for more than thirty days" (m. Ket. 5:6; p. Ket. 5:7, §2; Safrai, "Home and Family," p. 763, on m. Ket. 13:10, 5:6).

158. T. K. Seim, "Seksualitet og ekteskap, skilsmisse og gjengifte i 1. Kor. 7," *NTT* 81 (1, 1980): 1–20 (NTA 25:37), observes this mutuality in much of the chapter, despite what the writer perceives as Paul's partial chauvinism.

159. It was also permitted during certain stages of the pregnancy (Safrai, "Home and Family," p. 765, citing b. Nid. 31a; compare similar taboos in other cultures).

160. Concessions to weakness, to avoid succumbing to the evil impulse, are an established legal category; see Daube, "Concessions," pp. 1–13, especially p. 12, although his argument on our passage is not quite the same as the one I have argued. Cf. p. M.K. 3:5, §20, where R. Samuel makes a legal concession allowing sex during a mourning period on the Sabbath, but when one of his disciples actually takes advantage of the

concession, he warrants death. Cf. also the baraitha in b. Git. 52a (Soncino, p. 233): "Women, slaves and minors should not be made guardians: if, however, the father of the orphans chooses to appoint one, he is at liberty to do so" (Rule B overrules Rule A; Do A, but if B, acceptable).

161. One could read the passage as suggesting that Paul is only allowing intercourse as a matter of concession, but this would contradict what he says in 7:2–5.

162. B. Kid. 81ab tells stories of famous rabbis, notably Akiba and Meir, who were overpowered by Satan's sexual temptation, no doubt just to illustrate the greatness of the danger. But third-century rabbis could also appreciate the virtue of a bachelor who willfully avoided temptation (b. Pes. 113a).

163. This, rather than the gift of singleness vs. the gift of marriage; see Ridderbos, *Paul*, p. 310; Conzelmann, *1 Corinthians*, p. 118.

164. The connection, or probably dependence, on Jesus' saying about eunuchs for the kingdom of God who are "able to receive it" has not been missed by scholars; cf. Wenham, "Jesus Tradition," p. 9. Cf. Philost. *V.A.* 1, §§33, 36 (Loeb 1:94–97, 104–5): "true chastity" does not reside in physical eunuchs, who may still have passion, but in those with self-control.

165. We are taking "unmarried" here with reference to first marriages, although it could naturally include the divorced. Since he only begins to address virgins directly in v. 25, some have thought that only divorced persons are meant here, but Paul could have said this had this been his intention.

166. Assuming that "unmarried" here refers to first marriages, unmarried and widows were often distinguished in first-century Jewish practice, e.g., the day of the week on which they were married (b. Ber. 16a; Safrai, "Home and Family," pp. 757, 760); cf. also the aged vs. the unmarried virgin in CD 14.13–16. There appears to be a distinction in brideprice in Samaritan ketuboth (cf. Bowman, *Documents*, pp. 312–28). In Philo *Spec. Leg.* 3, §64 "widow" includes those bereaved through divorce as well as through a husband's death (Belkin, *Philo*, p. 257). Older customs discouraging the remarriage of widows in the Greco-Roman world were themselves played down in the time of Augustus (Rawson, "Roman Family," p. 31), as we shall see in our chapter on 1 Tim. 3:2.

167. For a similar use of "It is better," cf. e.g., Philo *Det.* 48, §176 (Loeb 2:316–17): "It is better to be made a eunuch than to be mad after illicit unions." Philo no doubt shared the standard Jewish horror of castration, however, so it is a preference only by comparison.

168. Cf. Hierocles *On Duties. On Marriage* (in Malherbe, *Exhortation*, p. 100): Nature urges marriage.

169. M. L. Barré, "To Marry or to Burn: *pyrousthai* in 1 Cor 7:9," *CBQ* 36 (2, April 1974): 193–202; K. C. Russell, "That Embarrassing Verse in First Corinthians!" *BT* 18 (5, 1980): 338–41; cf. Bruce, *1 & 2 Corinthians*, p. 68. M. Ab. 1:5 cites a pre-Christian sage as saying that one who talks too much with women will "inherit Gehenna"; so also the Tannaitic tradition in b. Ber. 61a claims that one who lusts after a woman counting change into his hand will not escape Gehenna. Gehenna is probably also

meant by the "fire" consuming transgressors of Torah in b. B.B. 79a. B. Sota 17a, cited in Urbach, *Sages*, 1:43, and Daube, *Judaism*, pp. 368–69, could refer either to Gehenna or to unnatural passions. In Jub. 30:7 a woman who sought a gentile husband was to be burned with literal fire (cf. the burning of priest's daughter in OT, detailed in m. Sanh. 7:2; b. Pes. 75a, and a betrothed adulteress in b. Sanh. 50b), but this is certainly not what Paul means here! For fire of passions *and* punishment, cf. in "The Book of Thomas the Contender," trans. J. D. Turner, in *The Nag Hammadi Library in English*, ed. James M. Robinson (San Francisco: Harper & Row, 1977), pp. 188ff.

170. Chariton *Chaer.* 1.1.8, 15, 2.3.8, 4.7, 4.7.6, 5.9.9, 6.3.3, 4.5, 7.1; Ach. Tat. *Clit.* 1.5.5–6, 11.3, 17.1, 2.3.3, 4.6.1, 7.4, 5.15.5, 25.6, 6.18.2; Apul. *Metam.* 2.5, 7 (Lucius for Fotis); 5.23.

171. Plut. *Table-Talk* 1.2.6, *Mor.* 619A (*antilēpsontai*); *Dial. on Love* 16, *Mor.* 759B; Athen. *Deipn.* 1.10d (*phlegmonēn*); Sir. 9:8; Test. Jos. 2:2; cf. b. Sanh. 69a, 108b; p. Hor. 2:6, §3 (?). "Burning" can also refer to non-sexual cravings or feelings (Cic. *Tusc. Disp.* 1.19.44; Sir. 28:10–12; Jos. *Life* 263, §51; 2 Cor. 11:29; Luke 24:32). Plut. *Bride* 4, *Mor.* 138F, however, does not think being on "fire" is adequate grounds for marriage; but he does not see the burning itself as sinful, as Paul does.

172. (Ps?)Plut. *L.S.* 1, *Mor.* 772C; Plut. *Or. at Delphi* 20, *Mor.* 403F–404A. For the pain of sexual passion, cf. Athen. *Deipn.* 13.598d ("pangs," *odynas*, smitten by [Cupid's] bow); Chariton *Chaer.* 1.1.7 (a "wound"); "bow" is also in some of the passages above (Chariton *Chaer.* 4.7.6), so that Eros's/Cupid's arrows may have been seen as flaming darts (cf. Eph. 6:16, from Roman warfare practices); Susanna 10. In b. Sanh. 75a; p. A.Z. 2:2, §3, a man is said to have been dying from unfulfilled sexual passion, but the rabbis thought it better that he die than be permitted to sin.

173. Cf. 7:36, if the man refers to the fiancé and not the father, although this is not clear. He reflects the Jewish tradition as found in Jesus' teaching, treated in our first chapter, and the danger of burning with passion in Sir. 23:16.

NOTES TO CHAPTER 7

1. Some might argue this by an analogy with the Old Testament priesthood, whose marital prospects were restricted. Priests could not marry widows other than those of priests, or divorcées, but this may be part of the cleanliness laws, analogous to forms of ritual purification, or it may relate to the hereditary nature of the priesthood and entangling of lineages. Though this practice still obtained after the NT period (Tos. Terum. 10:18; p. Yeb. 2:2, §2; cf. Jeremias, *Jerusalem*, p. 217), Paul nowhere applies the priesthood to Christian clergy in particular (1 Cor. 9:13 is an analogy with apostles).

2. Of all the Pauline letters in the NT, it is the authorship of the Pastoral Epistles—1 and 2 Timothy and Titus—that is most disputed, even by

some evangelicals. Since the general consensus among evangelical scholars remains that Paul is the author, however, my argument will assume (rather than attempt to demonstrate) Pauline authorship; for the arguments, see especially G. D. Fee, *1 & 2 Timothy, Titus*, NIBC 13 (Peabody, Mass.: Hendrickson, 1988), pp. 23–26.

3. Bishops are distinguished from elders as early as Ign. *Trall.* 3, but not in any of the NT evidence. For a study of patristic sources, see J. B. Lightfoot, *St. Paul's Epistle to the Philippians* (Grand Rapids: Zondervan, 1953; London: Macmillan, 1913), pp. 181–269.

4. There is very little evidence that pastors had to double as patrons; see A. J. Malherbe, *Social Aspects of Early Christianity*, 2d ed. (Philadelphia: Fortress, 1983), p. 99.

5. Cf. Leon, *Jews of Rome*, p. 167, on a similar problem in inscriptions concerning lists of synagogue officers; the texts were intended for those who were already familiar with these offices and consequently had no need to explain what the terms meant. Philippians 1:1, normally thought to be the earliest NT reference to overseers and deacons, does not supply any clues as to their functions, nor does the one earlier Pauline reference to administrative giftings (1 Cor. 12:28; also Rom. 12:8).

6. Many towns were run by elders of the upper class, though later Palestinian rabbis thought themselves their towns' real guardians (p. Hag. 1:7, §2).

7. Some have noted the parallel term in the Dead Sea Scrolls (1QS 6.12; CD 9.18–19, 22; Cross, *Library*, pp. 232–33; Brown, "Scrolls," p. 7; B. E. Thiering, "*Mebaqqer* and *Episkopos* in the Light of the Temple Scroll," *JBL* 100 [1, March 1981]: 72; Jean Daniélou, *The Theology of Jewish Christianity*, trans. J. A. Baker, DCBCN [London: Darton, Longman & Todd, 1964], p. 349; McNamara, *Judaism*, pp. 139–40; Leonhard Goppelt, *Apostolic and Post-Apostolic Times*, trans. Robert Guelich [Grand Rapids: Baker, 1980], pp. 188–89; J. N. D. Kelly, *A Commentary on the Pastoral Epistles* [London: Adam & Charles Black, 1972], pp. 73–74), although differences can be pointed out (cf. B. J. Humble, "The Mebaqqer in the Dead Sea Scrolls," *RestQ* 7 [1–2, 1963]: 33–38; Thiering, "*Mebaqqer*," notes that the *mebaqqer* was a Levitical priest); there may be links with other Jewish titles (G. R. Driver, *The Judaean Scrolls: The Problem and a Solution* [Oxford: Basil Blackwell, 1965], p. 522). The term is also used for various officials in the Greco-Roman world (Plut. *Numa* 9.5; Martin Dibelius and Hans Conzelmann, *The Pastoral Epistles*, trans. Philip Buttolph and Adela Yarbro [Philadelphia: Fortress, 1972], pp. 54–55; Kelly, *Pastoral Epistles*, p. 73; cf. Goppelt, *Times*, p. 188); as E. G. Selwyn (*The First Epistle of St. Peter*, 2d ed. [New York: Macmillan, 1946], p. 230) also notes, one may compare the role of the "guardian" in Plato (on which cf. e.g., Lodge, *Ethics*, pp. 389–90). It was a natural general term for leaders (e.g., 1 Macc. 1:51; Jub. 40:4, from Lat. *speculatores*; Epict. *Disc.* 3.22.72).

8. This is presumably the faithful saying of 3:1a; see P. Ellingworth, "The 'true saying' in 1 Timothy 3.1," *BiTr* 31 (4, 1980): 443–45; G. W. Knight, III, *The Faithful Sayings in the Pastoral Epistles* (Grand Rapids: Baker, 1979), p. 54. The conjunction of a wish with qualifications seems

to have also occurred in official legal documents; cf. the municipal charter of Salpensa, AD 82–84, in *CIL* 2.1963, in *Empire*, ed. Sherk, pp. 138–40, §97; for the availability of certain spiritual gifts to those who would seek them, cf. 1 Cor. 12:31, 14:1.

9. Keener, " 'Sexist'?" pp. 5–7.

10. W. Lock, *A Critical and Exegetical Commentary on the Pastoral Epistles*, ICC (Edinburgh: T. & T. Clark, 1924), p. 36, cites other commentators' comparisons of Stoic lists for the ideal wise man and the requirements for a general; he and Fee, *Timothy*, p. 84, both argue for a common milieu rather than dependence in the latter case.

11. E.g., Stowers, *Letter-Writing*, p. 77.

12. Dibelius and Conzelmann, *Pastoral Epistles*, p. 50, discuss especially rhetorical praise of a subject's virtues and its relation to moral paranesis, which would contribute to the idea of qualifications.

13. Isoc. *Nicocl.* 31, *Or.* 2; Antisthenes in Diog. Laert. *Lives* 6.1.6, 8.

14. Aristeas 32 (Hadas, p. 111); cf. also Arist. 39, 269, 280; 2 Macc. 14:37.

15. On 1QM 7:1, Yigael Yadin, *The Scroll of the War of the Sons of Light against the Sons of Darkness*, trans. Batya and Chaim Rabin (Oxford: Oxford University, 1962), p. 290, translates the title of military leaders as "prefects" (ages 40–50); in 1QM 2:4 leaders of tribes (over 50) are meant. CD 10.6–7 refers to "judges of the congregation" (knowledgeable in the law as interpreted by the community, ages 25–60); CD 14.7, the ruling priest (30–60), and 14.9, so the *mebaqqer*. With short lists of qualifications such as these, compare, e.g., Acts 6:3, which may be modeled on Deut. 1:13.

16. Tos. Hag. 2:9 (trans. Neusner, 2:315); paralleled in Tos. Sanh. 7:1; partly in Tos. Shek. 3:27. This no doubt represents second-century tradition idealizing an earlier time—judges were presumably not all sages, certainly not in the later rabbinic sense, though they should have been learned in the law. Compare the idea of testing the leader first in 1 Tim. 3:10.

17. Compare the ideal of the honorable life in Isoc. *Demon.* 16, *Or.* 1; *Nic/Cyp* 44, *Or.* 3.35–36; Plut. *Educ.* 7DE. Cf. Dibelius and Conzelmann, *Pastoral Epistles*, p. 52.

18. *Chaer.*, 5.7.2 (p. 77; cf. Greek, p. 77). Cf. Acts 23:1, 24:16; Phil. 3:6; in a stronger sense, John 8:46.

19. *CIJ* 1:13, §9, 1:57, §82, 1:66, §93, 1:81, §117, 1:83, §119, 1:91, §130, 1:102, §144, 1:276, §353, 1:372, §509, 1:398, §537. Cf. the blameless (*amomos*) priests chosen in 1 Macc. 4:42; cf. Luke 1:6.

20. Justin. *Cod.* 9.18 (in Lefkowitz and Fant, *Life*, p. 183, §193); Gardner, *Women*, p. 92.

21. Gardner, *Women*, p. 93.

22. So also Diogenes the Cynic, according to Diog. Laert. *Lives* 6.2.72; Zeno in ibid., 8.1.33.

23. Diog. Laert. *Lives* 7.1.131 attributes the practice to the Stoics, citing Zeno and Chrysippus, but it seems not to have been practiced by Stoics in the imperial period; we know that Seneca had but one wife, and Epictetus married one wife in old age. Epictetus *Disc.* 2.4.8 notes indeed

that women are "common property," but continues that while a pig is also common property, once it has been divided you do not take another man's share (he uses this to oppose adultery).

24. *Vit. Auct.*, in Loeb 2:482–83.

25. Harrell, *Divorce*, p. 53, observes that the Romans made an exception for them (Justin. *Instit.* 1.10.6).

26. E.g., in parables as in b. B.K. 60b; or the hypothetical five wives in b. Erub. 73a (baraita). Justin uses this as a basis for polemic in *Dial.* 134.1.

27. M. Sanh. 2:4 and other references in Jeremias, *Jerusalem*, p. 90; cf. pp. 93–94, 370; see Safrai, "Home and Family," p. 749. Derrett, *Jesus' Audience*, p. 37, argues that polygamy was only permitted for rulers; even princes were not permitted to take a second wife before divorcing the first.

28. B. Pes. 113a. The note in the Soncino Talmud suggests that the third wife is to reveal the plots of the other two; given the context, however, the redactional point is to keep from having an even number of wives, since even numbers attract demons!

29. Finkelstein, *Akiba*, p. 76.

30. Jos. *War* 1.28.4. The count here is nine because he had already murdered Mariamne. See further Emil Schürer, *A History of the Jewish People in the Time of Jesus*, ed. N. N. Glatzer (New York: Schocken, 1961), p. 151.

31. M. Ab. 2:7. Lucius' host's wife at the beginning of Apuleius' *Golden Ass* may not be representative, but this saying does not have a particularly high view of women's behavior.

32. Ab. R. Nathan 2, §9 B; b. Yeb. 65a. One Amora insists that one must divorce one's first wife before marrying a second; the other permits additional wives provided one can support them all.

33. Safrai, "Home and Family," pp. 749–50. Falk, *Jesus the Pharisee*, p. 53, notes some of the same data, but implausibly proposes that the school of Shammai favored polygamy and is the object of the Dead Sea Scrolls' polemic.

34. Cf. the documents discussed above, CD 4.20–5.2; 4QTemple 56:18–19; Vermes, "Halakah," pp. 197–202.

35. Cf. *CIJ* 1:cxii: "Bien qu'en principe la polygamie ne fût pas interdite aux Juifs, les inscriptions donnent l'impression que, pratiquement, c'est le marriage monogame qui existe chez eux."

36. Also Verner, *Household*, p. 129, 131.

37. For the inscription, see Grant, *Religions*, p. 29.

38. Athen. *Deipn.* 13.556b–57e.

39. Paulus *Opin.* 2 (in Lefkowitz and Fant, *Life*, p. 193, §196); cf. also Gardner, *Women*, pp. 56–57.

40. Safrai, "Home and Family," pp. 748–49.

41. See in Lock, *Epistles*, p. 37.

42. Gardner, *Women*, p. 57.

43. Ibid., p. 58.

44. Of course, the only actually legal marriages under Roman law were those between Roman citizens, with certain exceptions. But marriage still worked functionally for the provincials within the confines of their own cultures. But while "concubinary unions had no legal standing, custom

demanded that they be more than mere transitory affairs" (O'Rourke, "Roman Law," p. 182).

45. Gardner, *Women*, pp. 58, 143; O'Rourke, "Roman Law," p. 182.

46. This was a long time to wait, and romances were consequently more readily forgiven (Fabius Maximus 4, in Plut. *Romans, Mor.* 195EF), though it was best to avoid them (cf. Scipio the Elder 2, in Plut. *Romans, Mor.* 196B).

47. *ILS* 1986/*CIL* 16.1, in *Empire*, ed. Sherk, pp. 99–100, §58, from AD 52; so also the edict of Trajan, AD 98, in *CIL* 16.42 in *Empire*, ed. Sherk, p. 154, §111.

48. Ps-Phocyl. 181 (OTPS 2:580; Greek, p. 109).

49. Lock, *Epistles*, p. 37, mentions this as *part* of the text's point.

50. Cf. Plut. *Old Man in Affairs, Mor.* 783B–797F, for the timeliness of the issue.

51. E. R. Hardy, "The Priestess in the Greco-Roman World," *Churchman* 84 (4, Winter 1970): 264–70, compares the Vestal Virgins on this point of upholding the community by prayers.

52. E.g., E. F. Scott, *The Pastoral Epistles*, MNTC (London: Hodder & Stoughton, 1936), p. 57; G. M. M. Pelser, "Women and Ecclesiastical Ministries in Paul," *Neot* 10 (1976): 105.

53. The term is elsewhere used in its monetary, remunerative sense, e.g., Plut. *Bride* 33, *Mor.* 142DE. But cf. p. Ket. 4:14, §1.

54. Cf. the OT understanding of widows (noted, e.g., in P.-G. Duncker, " ' . . . quae vere viduae sunt' [1 Tim. 5,3]," *Angelicum* 35 [2, 1958]: 121–38); though cf. also Sifre Deut. 281.1.2.

55. The first two, since Aristotle, are husband-wife and father-children relations; the third normally addressed the slavemaster, so the *pater familias*, the head of the household, knew how to relate to all members of the home; see especially Balch, *Wives*, and Verner, *Household*.

56. *CIJ* 1:xcv–xcvi; 1:66, §93, 1:250–51, §319, 1:360, §494, 1:372, §§508–9, 1:373, §510, 1:393, §533, 1:397, §535 (?), 1:398, §537, 1:462, §645, 1:463, §646, 1:505, §694, 1:520, §720, 2:9, §739. The title was probably "purely an honorary one, probably involving no active duties" (Leon, *Jews of Rome*, p. 186). Cf. the honorary use of "father of the Jews" in 2 Macc. 14:37, and the use of "fathers" for Roman senators (Plut. *R. Q.* 58, *Mor.* 278D), and for leaders in the Mithraic cult (Burkert, *Cults*, p. 42). Merely being older men, however, was grounds for showing them respect (e.g., 1 Pet. 5:5; Tos. Meg. 3:24; A.Z. 1:19; 4 Bar. 5:20; Ps-Phocyl. 220–22; Syr. Men. Sent. 11–14, 76–93 [but cf. 170–72]; Lycurgus 14 in Plut. *Spartans, Mor.* 227F; Pythagoras in Diog. Laert. *Lives* 8.1.22–23); for older women, cf. the wicked old woman of Apul. *Metam.* 4.26 who is nevertheless *sancta*, venerable because of her age.

57. *CIJ* 1:118, §166, 1:362, §496, 1:384, §523, 1:457, §639. See especially B. J. Brooten, *Women Leaders in the Ancient Synagogue* (Chico, Calif.: Scholars Press, 1982), pp. 57–72, who argues that this may represent an actual office in ancient synagogues. She also deals with women elders (pp. 41–55), although admitting that they were rare. The widowed mother who urged her seven sons to die for Torah is called "Mother of

the nation" as an address of honor in 4 Macc. 15:29; Deborah, as leader, is similarly addressed in Ps-Philo 33:4 (cf. 33:1).

58. E.g., Diog. Laert. *Lives* 1.37; Hierocles *On Duties. On Marriage* 4.22.21–24 (Malherbe, *Exhortation*, pp. 101, 103), *Toward Parents* 4.25.53 (ibid., p. 92); Quint. 7.6.5; Gen. Rab. 100:2; cf. Sib. Or. 2:273–75 (Christian interpolation?), 11:148 (ancient tradition of Aeneas carrying his father on his shoulders in a Jewish text, maybe late first century BC); Moore, *Judaism*, 2:170. Epigraphic evidence suggests that the nuclear family was more of an emphasis than one might guess from the literary and legal evidence for the extended family (R. P. Saller and B. D. Shaw, "Tombstones and Roman Family Relations in the Principate: Civilians, Soldiers and Slaves," *JRS* 74 [1984]: 124–56), but grandchildren are under *patria potestas* as much as children, if the father lived this long (Gardner, *Women*, pp. 5–6).

59. I argued in Keener, " 'Sexist'?" pp. 4–7, that the women are in danger in this congregation because of the lack of education for women in Torah, rather than that we should think Paul (or, on a non-Pauline authorship view, pseudo-Paul) believed all women incapable of sound doctrine.

60. The term was originally in use only among the social elite, but it came to be used by all classes; see Lightman and Zeisel, "Univira," pp. 22–25, with abundant epigraphic evidence.

61. Lightman and Zeisel, "Univira," pp. 19–20, following Tertullian; cf. Gardner, *Women*, pp. 50–51.

62. Lightman and Zeisel, "Univira," p. 20, apparently still especially dependent on Tertullian.

63. Gardner, *Women*, pp. 22–23. The still-married requirement figured at least in the one case she cites from Tac. *Ann.* 2.86.2.

64. *R.Q.* 50, *Mor.* 276D (Loeb 4:82–83).

65. So Callirhoe in Chariton, *Chaer.*, 3.6.6; cf. Virgil *Aeneid* 4.28, cited in Harrell, *Divorce*, p. 30; perhaps Judith 16:22.

66. See Dixon, *Mother*, p. 22.

67. Petr. *Sat.* 111 (Loeb pp. 228–29); although Petronius is a satirist (see the soldier seeking to assault her virtue in 112), he is here employing motifs borrowed from the romance genre, which appears in fuller form in extant works of subsequent centuries.

68. Harrell, *Divorce*, p. 30.

69. Ibid., p. 31.

70. Cf. Dixon, *Mother*, p. 22; Stambaugh and Balch, *Environment*, pp. 111–12. This was directed primarily toward the upepr classes, but its effects were no doubt felt throughout society. Because men tended to be older than their wives at the age of marriage, their wives often survived them, although the reverse is often true (particularly since women often died in childbirth). Quick remarriage was not as highly valued beyond childbearing years (Dionysius the Elder 6 in Plut. *Mor.* 175F; O'Rourke, "Roman Law," p. 181).

71. Gardner, *Women*, p. 56.

72. See *CIJ* 1:56, §81, 1:114, §158 (perhaps), 1:303, §392, 1:401, §541; also Leon, *Jews of Rome*, p. 232. J. B. Frey, "La Signification des termes *monandros* et *univira*: coup d'oeil sur la Famille Romaine aux

Premiers siècles de Notre ère," RSR 20 (1930): 51, observes that the term is rare in Jewish inscriptions; he thinks that when it occurs it means that the wife had not given the husband occasion to divorce her (ibid., p. 59).
73. OTPS 2:581.
74. Cf. e.g., Tos. A.Z. 2:7; p. Ket. 9:8, §4.
75. Lightman and Zeisel, "Univira," p. 32; cf. Frey, "Signification," pp. 54–55.
76. Lightman and Zeisel, "Univira," p. 26.
77. Kelly, *Pastoral Epistles*, p. 75. Dibelius and Conzelmann, *Pastoral Epistles*, p. 52, are not certain that this is relevant here.
78. Kelly, *Pastoral Epistles*; Verner, *Household*, p. 130.
79. Cf. Frey, "Signification," p. 59, as cited above.
80. Verner, *Household*, p. 129. Although Frey ("Signification," p. 55) admits that the verb may be used to exclude adultery, he thinks fidelity is not in view; rather, he thinks it is in opposition to the prevalent divorce of the Greco-Roman world (ibid., p. 60)—although the evidence he has cited does not support his conclusion.
81. See especially the argument of Harrell, *Divorce*, pp. 131–34: in Judaism, Gentiles were not expected to follow all Jewish ethics, and Christians would not have held unbelievers responsible for living according to Christian ethics prior to their conversion.
82. Also favoring the marital fidelity interpretation are Fee, *Timothy*, pp. 80–81; Dibelius and Conzelmann, *Pastoral Epistles*, p. 75.
83. E.g., Isoc. *Nic/Cyp* 36–37, Or. 3.34.
84. The Pastorals require church leaders to be able to *gently* instruct even those in serious error (2 Tim. 2:24–26), and to avoid unnecessary controversies, which often deal only with semantics or peripheral matters (1 Tim. 1:6, 6:4, etc.); this was normally the meaning of such exhortation: Isoc. *Nicoc.* 39, Or. 2 (though cf. *Antid.* 261–65, Or. 15); Zeno in Diog. Laert. *Lives* 7.1.18; other Stoics in ibid., 7.1.59; Hor. *Ep.* 1.18.15–16; Sen. *Ep. ad Lucil.* 45.5, 48, 49.12; Quint. 8.pref. 18; Lucian *Dem.* [Loeb 1:158–59]; Plut. *Lectures* 4, *Mor.* 39CD; Philo *Prob.* 13, §88; against such as Protagoras (Diog. Laert. *Lives* 9.8.52); for worldly chatter as opposed to spiritual talk, cf. CD 10.18; Lev. Rab. 12:1. The rabbis also agreed that someone with a quick temper should not teach (m. Ab. 2:5, attributed to Hillel).
85. The Qumran community also required leaders to know the book of the law (for the purpose of judging properly); in CD 13.2–3, a priest rules each group of ten, if he knows the law; but if a Levite knows it better, he should be used. Dibelius and Conzelmann, *Pastoral Epistles*, p. 53, point to a partial parallel in Philo on Abraham.
86. E.g., Fee, *Timothy*, p. 81.
87. Also stressed as a requirement for leadership in ancient texts, e.g., Plato *Rep.* 3.390B; Dio Chrys. *fr.* (in Loeb 5:350–51); Philo *Virt.* 3, §14. Naturally respectability was widely valued in terms of the class-consciousness of Greco-Roman society.
88. The homeless, in Ps-Phocyl. 24 (where it parallels leading the blind); cf. especially m. Ab. 1:5 (attributed to Jose ben Jochanan of Jerusalem, pre-Christian).

89. Although usage and context, not etymology, determine meaning, it is significant in conjunction with the usage that the term literally means "friendship to strangers."

90. Epict. *Disc.* 1.28.23; cf. Cic. *De Part. Or.* 23.80; *De Offic.* 2.18.64; *Rhet. ad Herenn.* 3.3.4; the satire on poor hospitality in Apul. *Metam.* 1.26; Fee, *Timothy*, p. 81. Malherbe, *Aspects*, p. 95, observes that the practice may have declined a little by this period, but not much.

91. Tob. 7:8–9; m. Ab. 1:15 (attributed to Shammai, and perhaps applying to friendliness as well), probably 3:12 (early second century); a second-century rabbi in b. Ber. 63b; for a variety of other references, see John Koenig, *NT Hospitality: Partnership with Strangers as Promise and Mission*, OBT 17 (Philadelphia: Fortress, 1985), p. 16; cf. 1 Pet. 4:9. It was only praiseworthy to extend this to sages and their disciples, however, not to Gentiles or dangerous people (Sifre Deut. 1.10.1; cf. Sir. 11:29, 34).

92. E.g., Gen. Rab. 48:9, 50:4; Num. Rab. 10:5; Song Rab. 1:3, §3; see Koenig, *Hospitality*, pp. 15–20. Heb. 13:2 may well allude to this event. Abraham as a desert dweller would have no doubt considered the visit of strangers a special occasion. On Job's hospitality, possibly derivative from this tradition, see Test. Job 10:1–4.

93. The importance of protecting travelers may be symbolized by Zeus as the patron of "strangers" (*Greek Anth.* 7.516); travel conditions were not entirely safe (Socrates 2, to Xenophon [*Cynic Epistles*, pp. 226–27]).

94. See especially Meeks, *Urban Christians*, p. 29, citing Philo; Stambaugh and Balch, *Environment*, p. 38.

95. James Moffatt, *A Critical and Exegetical Commentary on the Epistle to the Hebrews*, ICC (Edinburgh: T. & T. Clark, 1924), pp. 224–25; idem, *The General Epistles: James, Peter, and Judas*, MNTC (Garden City, N.Y.: Doubleday, 1928), p. 153.

96. E.g., Socrates 2, to Xenophon (*Cynic Epistles*, pp. 226–27). Cf., much earlier, Tobit's special hospitality when he learns the stranger shares kinship ties (5:10–15).

97. B. Kid. 29b; p. Meg. 3:3, §5 (both late, but one is Babylonian and one Palestinian).

98. The very strict might, of course, object to staying in a home of questionable purity with regard to demai: Tos. Demai 3:9.

99. Cf. Tobit 10:6–10; this narrative may be modeled after the display of hospitality in Judg. 19:1–9 (which is intended to contrast the proper reception the Levite received from David's ancestral town with the later indignity he suffered from Saul's). According to later tradition, it was the wife who was particularly responsible for keeping the guests happy (references in Safrai, "Home and Family," p. 762).

100. E. A. Judge, "The Early Christians as a Scholastic Community: Part II," *Journal of Religious History* 1 (1960): 130; R. F. Hock, *The Social Context of Paul's Ministry: Tentmaking and Apostleship* (Philadelphia: Fortress, 1980), pp. 29–31.

101. Perhaps some would attack my friend's credibility, even though his wife is with him whenever they take in prostitutes; some enemies of Christianity seize upon any excuse to undermine the church's witness.

102. E.g., Chilon in Diog. Laert. *Lives* 1.70; Marc. Aur. *Med.* 1.9.
103. Isoc. *Nic/Cyp* 41, *Or.* 3.35; *Nicoc.* 19, *Or.* 2; *Demon.* 35, *Or.* 1; Sen. *Ben.* 4.27.5; cf. Chilon in Plut. *Bride* 144CD (in Malherbe, *Exhortation*, pp. 107–8); *Dinner* 12, *Mor.* 155D; Marc. Aur. *Med.* 1.16.4; Verner, *Household*, p. 152; Malherbe, *Aspects*, p. 99, n. 21; Dibelius and Conzelmann, *Pastoral Epistles*, p. 53. For the necessity of managerial abilities in general, cf. J. G. Gager, "Religion and Social Class in the Early Roman Empire," pp. 99–120 in *Catacombs and Colosseum*, pp. 100–101.
104. Plut. *Bride* 17, *Mor.* 140C; cf. Verner, *Household*, pp. 38, 65, 134. The satirist Martial frequently ridicules men by mocking their wives (e.g., Mart. *Epig.* 2.56: his wife is adulterous), and Judaism also felt that one's honor or disgrace affected one's family or tribe (Sifra Emor par. 14.242.1.11) or ancestors (4 Macc. 9:2).
105. E.g., R. Akiba in Sifre Deut. 32.5.12; Stilpo in Diog. Laert. *Lives* 2.114, defending himself.
106. Cf. Malherbe, *Aspects*, pp. 98–99; Fee, *Timothy*, p. 82–83.
107. Isoc. *Demon.* 14, 16, *Or.* 1; Thales in Diog. Laert. *Lives* 1.37; Solon in ibid., 1.60; Diogenes the Cynic in ibid., 6.2.65; Stoics in ibid., 7.1.120; Pythagoras in ibid., 8.1.22–23; Epicurus in ibid., 10.1.9; Epict. *Disc.* 3.11.5; Hierocles *On Duties. Toward One's Parents* 4.25.53 (in Malherbe, *Exhortation*, p. 91–93), *On Fraternal Love* 4.27.20 (ibid., p. 94); cf. Moses Hadas, *Aristeas to Philocrates* (New York: Harper & Brothers, for the Dropsie College for Hebrew and Cognate Learning, 1951), p. 189 (citing Plato *Laws* 4.717B); Cic. *De Amic.* 8.27; Socrates in Diog. Laert. *Lives* 2.29; Dixon, *Mother*, pp. 6–7.
108. Isoc. *Nic/Cyp* 57, *Or.* 3.37; Muson. Ruf. 16 in Meeks, *World*, p. 51; Dixon, *Mother*, pp. 180–82, 227, 234.
109. *Honor*: Sir. 3:8; Syr. Men. Sent. 9–10, 20–24, 94–98; Ps-Phocyl. 8, 180; Arist. 228, 238; Jos. *Apion* 2.27, §206; Philo *Ebr.* 5, §17; *Spec.* 2.42, §§234–36; *Prob.* 12, §87; Sib. Or. 1:74–75, 2:275–76 (if not interpolated); Jub. 7:20, 35:1–6, 11–13; Mekilta *Pisha* 1.28, *Bah.* 8.28ff; Sifre Deut. 81.4.1–2; b. Sanh. 66a (baraita); Kid. 31ab; Gen. Rab. 1:15, 36:6; Deut. Rab. 1:15; cf. Gen. Rab. 94:5; Safrai, "Home and Family," p. 771; Moore, *Judaism*, 2:131–32; Urbach, *Sages*, 1:346; Montefiore and Loewe, *Anthology*, pp. 500–506; Bonsirven, *Judaism*, p. 109. *Obedience also*: Sir. 3:7; Test. Ab. 5 B; Test. Jud. 1:4–5; Pes. Rab. 23/24:2; cf. b. Kid. 31ab, above.
110. W. K. Lacey, "Patria Potestas," pp. 121–44 in *Family in Rome*, argues that assumptions related to *patria potestas* affected Roman society as a whole; it may, however, be possible that they both simply reflect common cultural assumptions.
111. Gardner, *Women*, p. 6; on indenturing children, see Dixon, *Mother*, pp. 233–34; Cary and Haarhoff, *Life*, p. 143.
112. Gardner, *Women*, p. 7.
113. Quint. 7.1.14; Juv. *Sat.* 6.602–9. For the Jewish antipathy toward the pagan practice, see Ps-Philo 2:10, 4:16. For further references, see the note on child abandonment and infanticide in our chapter on marriage in 1 Cor. 7.
114. Gardner, *Women*, pp. 5–6.

115. R. P. Saller, review article in *CP* 83 (3, July 1988): 264; idem, "Men's Age at Marriage and its Consequences in the Roman Family," *CP* 82 (1, Jan. 1987): 21–34, thinks that the practice must always have been rare, since few men would have living fathers when entering adulthood (based on epigraphic longevity evidence; we may suspect that life expectancy was somewhat higher in upper classes).

116. Stoics in Diog. Laert. *Lives* 7.1.120; Agasicles 2, in Plutarch *Spartans, Mor.* 208B; cf. Hor. *Sat.* 1.1.84–87; Dixon, *Mother*, p. 27; Gardner, *Women*, p. 5; Frank, *Behavior*, p. 25.

117. Crates 33, to Hipparchia (*Cynic Epistles*, pp. 82–83); Petr. *Sat.* 4; Quint. 2.2.4; cf. Christopher Gill, "The Question of Character-Development: Plutarch and Tacitus," *Classical Quarterly* 33 (2, 1983): 469–87; and the general Greek emphasis on paideia, e.g., Epict. *Disc.* 1.2.6, 22.9, 2.19.29, 21.9; Dio Chrys. *32d Disc., Alex.* §3; Arist. 8; Eph. 6:4; 2 Tim. 3:16; Heb. 12:5–11; cf. John Gould, *The Development of Plato's Ethics* (Cambridge: Cambridge University, 1955), pp. 142–53; Martin Hengel, *Judaism and Hellenism: Studies in their Encounter in Palestine during the Early Hellenistic Period*, 2 vols., trans. John Bowden (Philadelphia: Fortress, 1974), 1:65.

118. Ahiqar 81 (saying 3); cf. Ps-Theano, *To Eubule* (Malherbe, *Exhortation*, p. 83); Syr. Men. Sent. 27–44; Pes. Rab Kah. 15:4; Stambaugh and Balch, *Environment*, p. 124; Carcopino, *Life*, p. 105; J. T. Townsend, "Ancient Education," pp. 139–63; Safrai, "Home and Family," pp. 770–71; idem, "Education and the Study of the Torah," pp. 945–70 in *JPFC*, p. 954. Protests against excessive harshness do, however, appear, as indicated below.

119. For which the fathers were primarily responsible: Sir. 7:23; Arist. 248; Malherbe, *Exhortation*, p. 23; Meeks, *World*, p. 61; Safrai, "Home and Family," p. 770.

120. Quint. 1.3.13–14, 2.4.10; Ps-Phocyl. 150, 207.

121. On guarding against false accusations elsewhere in Paul, cf. Rom. 12:17; 2 Cor. 8:21; and perhaps 1 Thes. 5:22; Rom. 14; 1 Cor. 8.

122. Plut. *Profit* 3, *Mor.* 87D (Loeb 2:12–13). He uses the term *anepilēpton*, "above reproach."

123. On testing new recruits, cf. Tos. Demai 2:12, on the haberim; Tos. Shek. 3:27; Hag. 2:9; Sanh. 7:1, on judges; and 1 QS 6 on new candidates for the Qumran community. On the development of philosophical/moral novices, see Plutarch in Malherbe, *Exhortation*, p. 60. Jos. *Ant.* 4.8.15, §219, requires that witnesses' lifestyles be used to evaluate their credibility.

124. Kelly, *Pastoral Epistles*, p. 78.

125. Generosity (Jub. 37:15; emperors in *Empire*, ed. Sherk, pp. 111, 134, §§71, 92), nonaddiction to wine (Fee, *Timothy*, p. 81; Kelly, *Pastoral Epistles*, p. 77), avoidance of greed (Test. Levi 14:6; cf. how traveling teachers must always guard against the charge, e.g., Dio Chrys.) and quarrelsomeness (Epict. *Disc.* 2.95) were all virtues in the culture at large, and some may counter qualities of the false teachers in Ephesus (6:3–10; so Fee, *Timothy*, p. 81).

126. Cf. especially 3 Macc. 3:5.

127. Readers would naturally simply assume exceptions to general rules, and Roman law was argued on this premise: see Quint. 7.6.5, cited above on the Matthean exception.

128. This is also found in earlier Pauline texts, e.g., 1 Thess. 4:12, *perhaps* 1 Cor. 6:6.

129. The parallels drawn with Josephus' *Against Apion* may not carry all the weight assigned to them, since Josephus' work is an apology, whereas Ephesians, 1 Peter, and 1 Timothy are intra-community documents; but these documents emphasize the impact of the readers' lifestyle on their witness to the world outside, so they do have an ultimately apologetic function in the broadest sense of the term.

130. See the notes on 1 Cor. 7 for the social context of this problem.

131. See especially Balch, *Wives*, on the Roman concern for familial disruption by Eastern religions.

132. See above in our chapter on marriage and remarriage in 1Cor. 7.

133. Contrast Harrell, *Divorce*, p. 100. Given the heavy stress on marriage and childbearing in rabbinic Judaism, we may note the list of those excluded from judging on a court of elders in m. Hor. 1:4, which includes an elder without children.

134. It is admittedly the case that Paul may address different issues in similar language which is on his mind; 1 Cor. 8 and Rom. 14 use similar language, but the former seems to address status divisions in the Corinthian church, whereas the latter addresses a Jewish-Gentile conflict in the Roman church. His use of the language of baptism into one body shows a similar problem.

135. Cf. R. L. Saucy, "The Husband of One Wife," *BibSac* 131 (523, 1974): 229–40; Ed Glasscock, " 'The Husband of One Wife' Requirement in 1 Timothy 3:2," *BibSac* 140 (559, July 1983): 244–58.

136. As E. P. Sanders and others have shown, the Pharisees as a group have sometimes received a bad reputation from modern interpreters on their interpretation methods. I use the term in its colloquial sense to make the point. That Pharisees were often personally legalistic despite official Jewish teachings about grace is, of course, probable; modern Christendom unfortunately offers abundant samples of the same tendency, as we suggest in the first chapter of this book.

NOTES TO CHAPTER 8

1. There may be emotional reasons unmentioned by Paul that differentiate between the two, but they seemingly level out. A divorced person must work through some deep hurts before being ready to adjust fully to a new relationship; but this person also may bring to a marriage some experience and maturity, provided he or she was the innocent party and worked hard to preserve the union. It may also be more *difficult* for a divorced person, who has tasted the blessing of intimacy, to remain single than for a Christian who has never tasted that blessing.

2. Those who argue that people still have to pay for earlier crimes, for instance, if they are in jail, skew the analogy badly. *God and his church* do *not* enforce such "laws" or discipline the repentant; this is done by civil magistrates. We have not a single instance in the New Testament of the church disciplining someone already repentant.

3. I greatly appreciate the vitally important material written today on building strong marriages, such as by H. Norman Wright, James Dobson, Ed and Gaye Wheat, and others. Having been part of communities besides middle-class white North Americans, I think that there is now a great need for literature to be written that will address the marriage dynamics of Christians in different cultures, but this does not diminish my appreciation for what has already been written in marriage enrichment and counseling.

4. It is my belief, based on inference from New Testament texts about forgiveness, that the guilty parties or party are also allowed to remarry if they have genuinely repented and done their best to make any necessary restitution. But this point is not as easily argued on the basis of explicit statements in Scripture, and I do not wish anyone to confuse it with my argument from Scripture above, which I think *explicitly* allows remarriage for the innocent party.

NOTES TO APPENDIX A

1. Of course, Jesus probably used some illustrations more than once (sometimes the same rabbis would even express different opinions at different times, cf. p. B.K. 2:6, §3); but sometimes his sayings or acts appear at exactly the same place in different Gospels in slightly different words.

2. It was a rhetorical exercise to paraphrase sayings in as many different ways as possible (cf. Theon *Progymn.* 1.93–171; e.g., Epict. *Disc.* 1.9.23–25; cf. Bruce Chilton, "Targumic Transmission and Dominical Tradition," 1:21–45 in *Gospel Perspectives: Studies of History and Tradition in the Four Gospels*, ed. R. T. France and David Wenham [Sheffield: JSOT Press, 1980], comparing the transmission of the Gospel traditions to that of Targumic traditions). Since many of Jesus' sayings may have originally been in Aramaic, and were later translated into Greek, we should expect variations for this reason as well. It was also considered good writing to vary the contents of a narrative for literary effect. The exact extent to which literary adaptations could be made and the extent to which this is found in the Gospels is disputed by different scholars and is not relevant to the purposes of this book.

3. Ancient biographies were quite different than biographies today. There were basically two types; one followed, as best as possible, chronological order, as Luke seems to follow the sequence of his sources; the other followed a more topical order, as Matthew does. The latter is the non-Peripatetic type; see D. E. Aune, *The NT in its Literary Environment*, LEC 8 (Philadelphia: Westminster, 1987), pp. 31–32.

4. It was not uncommon to make up some details altogether, but this varied from writer to writer and depended partially on the completeness of available sources. Given how carefully Matthew and Luke use Mark and the other material they have in common, we may guess that they used their other sources very reliably also. On the Gospels and ancient biography, see especially the discussion in Aune, *Environment*; also idem, "Greco-Roman Biography," pp. 107–26 in *Greco-Roman Literature and the NT: Selected Forms and Genres*, ed. D. E. Aune, SBLSBS 21 (Atlanta: Scholars Press, 1988); cf. P. L. Shuler, *A Genre for the Gospels: The Biographical Character of Matthew* (Philadelphia: Fortress, 1982); C. H. Talbert, *What Is a Gospel? The Genre of the Canonical Gospels* (Philadelphia: Fortress, 1977) (on whom I would be less hard than is D. E. Aune, "The Problem of the Genre of the Gospels: A Critique of C. H. Talbert's What Is a Gospel?" 2:9–60 in Gospel Perspectives: Studies of History and Tradition in the Four Gospels, ed. R. T. France and David Wenham [Sheffield: JSOT Press, 1981]); G. N. Stanton, *Jesus of Nazareth in NT Preaching* (Cambridge: Cambridge University, 1974), pp. 117–36 (though cf. idem, *The Gospels and Jesus* [Oxford: Oxford, 1989], pp. 19–20). Those who claim the Gospels are generically "wholly unique" (e.g., Harald Riesenfeld, *The Gospel Tradition* [Philadelphia: Fortress, 1970], p. 2) are not entirely correct.

5. These must both represent the same story; they even occur at the same point in the narrative (just before the blessing of children and the rich young ruler).

6. Wenham, "Jesus Tradition," pp. 7–15. Sanders, *Judaism*, p. 15, points out the variations in his critique of Gerhardsson's view of meticulously careful transmission; but while Sanders is right to critique Gerhardsson, the differences are not impossibly great, given Gerhardsson's allowance for haggadic-type application and modification of an essentially stable Ur-text (p. 14); the application to women in Mark and Paul may be natural extrapolations of Jesus' teachings in a milieu where women would be freer to initiate divorce. Such adaptation would also be possible in a Hellenistic context (Malherbe, *Exhortation*, p. 65).

7. There are two main ways to approach differences in the Gospel accounts. One is by starting with what biblical scholars call "redaction history," that is, by seeing how each writer edited his available material. Redaction history, when used in this way, can be useful in helping us to discover what the different inspired authors intended when they wrote their Gospels. But discussing it would involve some complex comparisons that would be more technical than necessary for a book of this nature. The other method will be to just examine the passages in their own cultural and literary context, i.e., to just study what they say and how a first-century Christian would have read them. It is mainly this method we have followed here.

8. E.g., sayings from Mark 13 appearing in Matt. 10 instead of Matt. 24 (see F. F. Bruce, *The Message of the NT* [Grand Rapids: Eerdmans, 1981], p. 68; R. E. Morosco, "Redaction Criticism and the Evangelical:

Matthew 10 as a Test Case," *JETS* 22 [4, Dec. 1979]: 323–31); the grouping together of miracle-stories in Matt. 8–9 from Mark 1–6, while the parables (Mark 4) appear later (Matt. 13); the consolidation of the stages of the fig tree's withering (Matt. 21:19/Mark 11:14, 20). These differences can be explained on the basis of ancient historiographic and literary conventions and would not have been thought "contradictions" by ancient readers.

NOTES TO APPENDIX B

1. The gathering together of related sayings on a subject, called an epitome, was common enough in Greek rhetoric; cf. the *Encheiridion* of Epictetus by Arrian and the anthology of maxims in Sentences of the Syriac Menander, or, for an epitomization of Jewish laws in the Torah, see the Temple Scroll of Qumran. Many scholars have compared the Sermon on the Mount to the hellenistic epitome (H. D. Betz, "The Sermon on the Mount: Its Literary Genre and Function," *JR* 59 [3, July 1979]: 285–97; Meeks, *World*, p. 138; Malherbe, *Exhortation*, p. 85). This does not rule out the possibility that some of the structure of 5:17–48 may be older than Matthew (Flusser, *Judaism*, p. 494).

2. On 5:21–48.

3. *Jesus and the Word*, trans. L. P. Smith and E. H. Lantero (New York: Charles Scribner's Sons, 1958), p. 89, cf. p. 91. Contrast Gundry, *Matthew*, p. 83. It could be true that in Jesus' life-setting such statements were directed against the Pharisees (Guelich, "Mt 5, 22," p. 52), but this would still not support Bultmann's point; different schools of Pharisees argued the meaning of law with one another and with other interpretive groups within Judaism.

4. Cf. the sectarian writers in the Dead Sea Scrolls who condemned the "speakers of smooth things" (4QpNah), probably charging Pharisaic interpreters with too much leniency; see Cecil Roth, "The Subject Matter of Qumran Exegesis," *VT* 10 (1, Jan. 1960): 65; idem, "A Talmudic Reference to the Qumran Sect?" *RevQum* 2 (2, 1960): 261–65; J. L. Kugel and R. A. Greer, *Early Biblical Interpretation*, LEC 3 (Philadelphia: Westminster, 1986), p. 79; cf. Saul Lieberman, "Light on the Cave Scrolls from Rabbinic Sources," *PAAJR* 20 (1951): 395–404 (although none of his three major lines of argument seem particularly persuasive). It is inherently likely that the two groups were aware of one another's existence; although liturgical parallels may be due to a common milieu (Sh. Talmon, "The Emergence of Institutionalized Prayer in Israel in the Light of the Qumran Literature," pp. 265–84 in *Qumrân: Sa piété, sa théologie et son milieu*, ed. M. Delcor, BETL 46 [Paris: Gembloux, Leuven U., 1978], pp. 283–84) and there are clear differences in the halakah of the two groups (e.g., Jacob Neusner, "Testimony of Witnesses": pp. 197–217; on similarities for ages of witnesses [probably a cultural given], cf. Schiffman, *Law*, p. 36), there are parallels which indicate a common base of very old tradition or else some interaction, or both; cf. Schiff-

mann, *Law,* passim (differences and similarities); J. M. Baumgarten, "Qumran Studies," *JBL* 77 (1958): 256. (The Qumran sectarians were not, however, simply slightly heterodox Pharisees; cf. André Dupont-Sommer, *Les Manuscrits de la Mer Morte et le Problème des Origines Chrétiennes* [Paris: Editions Estienne, 1969], p. 33; contrast Ralph Marcus, "The Qumran Scrolls and Early Judaism," *BR* 1 [1956]: 25–28.

5. David Wenham, "Jesus and the Law: An Exegesis on Matthew 5:17–20," *Them* 4 (3, 1979): 92–96; Daniel Marguerat, "Jésus et la Loi," *FV* 78 (3, June 1979): 53–76.

6. Meeks, *World,* p. 139; cf. P. F. Ellis, *Matthew: His Mind and His Message* (Collegeville, Minn.: Liturgical Press, 1974), p. 37 (the "paradise will of God" for the end time; cf. p. 150: love is the most radical form of the law).

7. Benno Przybylski, *Righteousness in Matthew and his World of Thought,* SNTSMS 41 (Cambridge: Cambridge, 1980), p. 83.

8. Eduard Schweizer, *Jesus,* trans. D. E. Green (London: SCM, 1971), p. 31. Stephen Westerholm, "Jesus, the Pharisees, and the Application of Divine Law," *EglTh* 13 (2, 1982): 191–210, is more generous in noting that Pharisaism was more concerned with communal behavior, whereas Jesus' teaching focuses more on personal piety.

9. F. Manns, "La Halakah dans l'Evangile de Matthieu," *Ant* 53 (1–2, 1978): 3–22; cf. Sanders, Jesus, p. 55. As Günther Bornkamm, "End-Expectation and Church in Matthew," pp. 15–51 in *Tradition and Interpretation in Matthew,* by G. Bornkamm, G. Barth, and H. J. Held (Philadelphia: Westminster, 1963), p. 24, and others point out, Jesus' problem was more with Pharisaic practice than with Pharisaic opinion (Matt. 23:3).

10. Michael Wyschogrod, "Judaism and Evangelical Christianity," pp. 34–52 in *Evangelicals and Jews in Conversation on Scripture, Theology, and History,* ed. M. H. Tanenbaum, M. R. Wilson, and J. A. Rudin (Grand Rapids: Baker, 1978), p. 43, notes with satisfaction the correspondence between Jesus' position in 5:17–20 and that of rabbinic Judaism.

11. "Fulfilling" commandments included doing them (e.g., Test. Napht. 8:7); it should be understood in the standard Jewish sense (Barth, "Understanding," pp. 58–164 in *Tradition and Interpretation,* p. 65). Meier, *Matthew,* pp. 46–48 (cf. idem, *Vision,* pp. 222–39; Guelich, *Sermon,* p. 148) argues that this passage means Jesus fulfills the law prophetically rather than that he obeys it, and he argues that the turning of the ages here allows Jesus to reinterpret the law. Roger Mohrlang, *Matthew and Paul: A Comparison of Ethic Perspectives,* SNTSMS 48 (Cambridge: Cambridge, 1984), p. 8, rightly observes that this is the least likely of the proposed solutions. Presumably "fulfilling the law" is illustrated in 5:21ff (F. J. A. Hort, *Judaistic Christianity,* ed. J. O. F. Murray [Grand Rapids: Baker, 1980], p. 18).

12. Sanders, *Jesus,* p. 261, suggests that Jesus may not have really offered such pro-law statements; otherwise how could Paul have been allowed with a more ambivalent posture toward the law? But Paul actually supports the moral intention of the law, as Sanders agrees on texts such

as Rom. 13:8–10; and this seems to be how Matthew takes Jesus' sayings here; for a comparison of Matthew and Paul, see Mohrlang, *Matthew and Paul*, pp. 111–25 on inward obedience, and cf. p. 17. Others have seen Matthew's statement as opposing Paul (Urbach, *Sages*, 1:293), or see this as a peculiarly Matthean motif (cf. Goulder, *Matthew*, pp. 133, 24–25) originating with Matthew (Leonhard Goppelt, *Theology of the NT*, 2 vols., trans. J. E. Alsup, ed. Jürgen Roloff [Grand Rapids: Eerdmans, 1981– 82], 2:224) or perhaps from the conservative Palestinian Jewish Christians (Bultmann, *Tradition*, p. 138). O. L. Cope, *Matthew: A Scribe Trained for the Kingdom of Heaven*, CBQMS 5 (Washington, D.C.: Catholic Biblical Association of America, 1976), p. 127, shows that Matthew wishes to keep both Jesus and Scripture and so predicates Jesus' "violations" of the law on the teaching of Scripture itself.

13. Flusser, *Judaism*, p. 495, including n. 4. Different views are summarized in Guelich, *Sermon*, pp. 139–41; our interpretation is closer to the second one listed by him.

14. Cf. the language of the end with Jer. 31:35–37, in the context of the new covenant; Sib. Or. 3:570–72 (probably 2d century BC). Compare also 24:34 (Gundry, *Matthew*, p. 79, actually sees this as a source for the formulation in 5:18). Since early Jewish writers stressed the eternality of the law (e.g., Ps-Philo 11:5), Matthew's Jewish readers would have most naturally read his text as saying the same thing, unless he had clarified his point otherwise. "All things come to pass" elsewhere can include the temple's destruction (24:34; cf. 23:36) and perhaps cosmic signs (cf. 24:34); this at the very least carries its fulfillment beyond the end of Matthew's narrative at the resurrection.

15. Deut. 11:21; Ps. 72:5, 89:36–37; Jer. 31:36, 33:25. Jeremiah 17:4 and Hosea 1:6 might at first sight seem to contradict this, until they are taken in the overall context of their documents (e.g., Jer. 31:3, Hosea 2:23). The language of the immutable covenant was assumed to have literal ramifications in ancient Judaism, and if Matthew meant his language otherwise he would have needed to clarify this difference.

16. Cf. also 4:17; 5:3b, 10b, 13b, 22b–26.

17. A rabbi in Pes. Rab. 11:7 derives special meaning from the *yod* being the least letter of the Hebrew alphabet.

18. Cf. e.g., b. Men. 29b, where a second-century rabbi suggests that God created the future world by means of the letter *yod*.

19. An early third-century rabbi in p. Sanh. 2:6, §2.

20. A late second-century rabbi in Gen. Rab. 47:1, and third-century rabbis in p. Sanh. 2:6, §2; Lev. Rab. 19:2; Num. Rab. 18:21. Joshua's name change is in Num. 13:16.

21. Arguing especially from the Lukan parallel to parts of this passage, Heinz Schürmann, " 'Wer daher eines dieser geringsten Gebote auflöst ...' Wo fand Matthäus das Logion Mt 5,19?" *BZ* 4 (2, 1960): 238–50, thinks this belongs to the oldest levels of tradition.

22. Presumably this phrase means by how one lives, as it normally means in Jewish texts (cf. Rom. 3:31; m. Ber. 10:5; Mek. *Pisha* 1:124; CD 9.7; 1QM 13.7); it could also be translated "looses" or "destroys." These may not have quite the force of techical terms (cf. R. W.

Thompson, "The Alleged Rabbinic Background of Rom 3,31," *ETL* 63 [1, 1987]: 136–48; C. T. Rhyne, *Faith Establishes the Law*, SBLDS 55 [Chico, Calif.: Scholars Press, 1981], pp. 73–74; cf. Sandmel, *Judaism*, p. 356, n. 18), although scholars have pointed to NT connections (Gerhardsson, *Memory and Manuscript*, p. 287; Manson, *Sayings*, p. 154).

23. Some second-century rabbis decided that if someone taught error but nevertheless lived according to the law, he would not be punished for his teaching (Tos. Sanh. 14:12). On the other hand, making the masses sin could be worse than just sinning on one's own (b. R.H. 17a; cf. b. Sanh. 90a, baraita). On the positive side, an early second-century teacher (said himself to have gone into error) reputedly "used to say: If one makes his fellow carry out some commandment, Scripture accounts it as though he had done it himself" (Ab. R. Nathan A, 24, p. 104).

24. Possibly a "divine passive"—a standard Jewish way of saying, "*God* will deem this person least in the Kingdom."

25. Cf. the saying of a second-century rabbi in Ab. R. Nathan A, 28, p. 118 (whoever gives first place to Torah will be first in the world to come; whoever makes it secondary will be secondary in the world to come). The issue of greatness in the Kingdom continues throughout the Gospel (10:42, 11:11, 18:1–4, 23:11, 25:40, perhaps 2:6; elsewhere in the Jesus tradition as well).

26. A standard Jewish synonym for "kingdom of God," referring to his sovereign rule, here particularly with reference to the age to come; see especially the works on the Kingdom by G. E. Ladd (e.g., *The Gospel of the Kingdom* [Grand Rapids: Eerdmans, 1978]).

27. "The least of these commandments" is the implied object of the verbs, which would not need to be repeated in the second "the one who" clause; I have translated it here because it is implied.

28. Matthew's way of saying "greatest" is with the simple form "great," as in 22:34. G. Mussies, "Greek in Palestine and the Diaspora," pp. 1040–64 in *JPFC*, p. 1042 mentions the "increasing obsolescence of the superlative except in its 'elative' aspect ('very . . . ')" in Koine Greek.

29. My free translation of m. Aboth 2:8, on a saying attributed to R. Johanan ben Zakkai.

30. Sifre Deut. 54.3.2 (trans. Neusner, 1:178); the traditions in this document are primarily from the second century.

31. Sifra Qed. pq.8.205.2.6 (trans. Neusner, 3:130); probably second century. Sifra Behor. par. 5.255.1.10 says the same about "the prohibition of usury" (trans. Neusner, 3:331). In Ab. R. Nathan A, 27, whoever denies a single law is not fit for the world to come.

32. Sifre Deut. 96.3.2 (trans. Neusner, 1:253), probably interpreting Deuteronomy accurately at this point. Again at 115.1.2; also in second century material in m. Ab. 2:1, 4:2. Cf. Ab. R. Nathan A, ch. 2; Flusser, *Judaism*, p. 495.

33. Pes. Rab Kah. 8:4, citing a mid-third century rabbi; cf. Pes. Rab. 23/24:2 (anonymous). Cf. Gen. Rab. on Gen. 23:18, cited in Manson, *Sayings*, p. 184, on Matt. 10.

34. M. Kid. 1:10, second century AD (trans. Danby, p. 323).

35. James 2:10; cf. Gal. 5:3. This could also be accepted by readers influenced by Stoic ethics; see Diog. Laert. *Lives* 7.1.120; Cicero *Parad. Stoic.* 20–26; Epict. *Disc.* 2.21.1–7; Pliny *Ep.* 8.2.3; cf. M. O'R. Boyle, "The Stoic Paradox of James 2:10," *NTS* 31 (4, Oct. 1985): 611–17; J. B. Mayor, *The Epistle of St. James*, 3d rev. ed. (n.p.: Macmillan, 1913; reprinted by Minneapolis: Klock & Klock Christian Publishers, 1977), p. cxxv. The Epicurean view opposed this (Diog. Laert. *Lives* 10.120), and occasionally Stoics departed from applying it strictly (Marc. Aur. *Med.* 2.10).

36. The principle of lighter and heavier commandments, of course, is earlier; see below.

37. Urbach, *Sages*, 1:350; most accessibly, cf. Montefiore and Loewe, *Rabbinic Anthology*, p. 205, §555.

38. B. Kid. 39b. In Ab. R. Nathan B, 35, §77 (p. 205), "everyone who preserves one thing from the Torah [by memorization], preserves his life, and everyone who loses one thing from the Torah, loses his life ..."

39. R. Meir (late second century), in b. Bek. 30a, although the other Sages disagree with him. In Test. Asher 2:2–8, anyone who breaks any of God's laws, though he keeps the others, is wholly evil, because his heart is evil; in 3:1, such people are "double-faced."

40. Second-century tradition in b. Bek. 30b; I am assuming that *haber* here means Pharisee, although this is not beyond dispute. I am also taking the schematized tradition of Hillel accepting a proselyte on more lenient terms as reflecting only a temporary concession to win the proselyte, since he ultimately accepts the whole law. One later rabbi adds that even the words of the scribes must be accepted in detail. Cf. Bamberger, *Proselytism*, pp. 61–62; Jeremias, *Jerusalem*, p. 323; Longenecker, *Paul*, pp. 41–42; Martin Dibelius, *Paul*, ed. W. G. Kümmel (Philadelphia: Westminster, 1953), p. 21; idem, *James: A Commentary on the Epistle of James*, rev. Heinrich Greeven, trans. M. A. Williams (Philadelphia: Fortress, 1976), p. 144; Peter Davids, *The Epistle of James: A Commentary on the Greek Text*, NIGTC (Grand Rapids: Eerdmans, 1982), p. 116; Sophie Laws, *A Commentary on the Epistle of James* (San Francisco: Harper & Row, 1980), p. 111; Bonsirven, *Judaism*, p. 95.

41. E. P. Sanders, *Paul, the Law, and the Jewish People* (Philadelphia: Fortress, 1983), p. 103; cf. idem, *Jesus*, pp. 56–57; Flusser, *Judaism*, p. 495; also Bright, *History*, p. 439, citing 4 Macc. 5:19–21; Sirach 41:17–23.

42. See Moore, *Judaism*, 1:467–68; Sandmel, *Beginnings*, p. 187; I. Abrahams, *Studies in Pharisaism and the Gospels*, 1st ser. (New York: KTAV, 1967; Cambridge, 1917), p. 42; Bonsirven, *Judaism*, p. 114; with a different understanding of the *yetzer hara*, cf. Solomon Schechter, *Aspects of Rabbinic Theology* (New York: Schocken, 1961; New York: Macmillan, 1909), p. 262. Some of the Dead Sea Scrolls emphasize human depravity more regularly, especially in 1QH; see e.g., Flusser, *Judaism*, p. 62. Some extra-rabbinic claims to be a sinner may be by comparison only (Test. Ab. 9 A), but wholly righteous people were very rare (4 Ezra 7:138–40; Test. Ab. 10 A; Apoc. Zeph. 7:8; perhaps 1 Esdras 4:37–38 [which may be concessive rather than assertive]). Some Greek

philosophers lamented the badness of most people (Bion in Diog. Laert. *Lives* 1.88; Epict. *Disc.* 4.12.19), but the concept was more intellectual than moral per se (Epict. *Disc.* 1.18; Marc. Aur. *Med.* 9.4; cf. P. E. Matheson, *Epictetus: The Discourses and Manual Together with Fragments of his Writings,* 2 vols. [Oxford: Clarendon, 1916], p. 36; J. F. Hansman, "Some Possible Classical Connections in Mithraic Speculation," pp. 601–12 in *Mysteria Mithrae,* ed. Ugo Bianchi, EPROER 80 [Leiden: E. J. Brill, 1979], p. 611).

43. Sifra Behuq. par. 2.264.1.2. A deliberate act carried much more liability than an inadvertent one (e.g., Sifré Num. 28.2.2; cf. the discipline in p. Nazir 4:3, §1).

44. Sifre Deut. 48.1.3; p. Sanh. 10:1, §1.

45. There seems to be OT precedent for weighing one more heavily than another (1 Sam. 15:22; Ps. 4:5, 40:6, 50:8–15, 23, 51:16, 69:30–31; Prov. 21:3; Isa. 1:11–17; Jer. 11:15; Hos. 6:6; Amos 5:21–27; Mic. 6:6–8), although this does not mean that the prophets sought to abolish sacrifice. (This much is true to whatever extent Sanders, *Jesus,* p. 249, is correct that the typical modern distinction in this regard is anachronistic, as opposed to the ancient distinction between humanward and Godward commandments).

46. A distinction also recognized in early Judaism; SifraVDDeho. par. 1.34.1.3, par. 12.65.1.3; Ab. R. Nathan B, 1, §8; etc.; see Flusser, *Judaism,* p. 496; cf. Gustaf Dalman, *Jesus-Jeshua: Studies in the Gospels* (New York: Macmillan, 1929), p. 64; H. A. Wolfson, *Philo: Foundations of Religious Philosophy in Judaism, Christianity, and Islam,* 2 vols., 4th rev. ed. (Cambridge: Harvard, 1968), 2:277. R. M. Johnston, " 'The Least of the Commandments': Deuteronomy 22:6–7 in Rabbinic Judaism and Early Christianity," *AUSS* 20 (3, Autumn 1982): 207, attributes the distinction to the school of Hillel, and the emphasis on equal weight to the school of Shammai, although both were ultimately worked into rabbinic thinking.

47. This is stressed frequently in Josephus.

48. E.g., Rivkin, *Revolution,* p. 87. That there is also an attack on the Pharisees here is, of course, probable, given the animosity reflected between Matthew's readers and the Pharisees throughout the rest of Matthew; for a sample of this emphasis, see Sjef van Tilborg, *The Jewish Leaders in Matthew* (Leiden: E. J. Brill, 1972). In Matthew Jesus and his community stand in continuity with the real intent of the law and prophets (cf. R. N. Longenecker, *Biblical Exegesis in the Apostolic Period* [Grand Rapids: Eerdmans, 1975], pp. 140–52, 206–9, for Matthew's christocentric hermeneutic); his persecuted readers are heirs of the prophets (e.g., 5:12; 10:41–42; 23:21–36).

49. Tos. Peah 1:4; R.H. 2:7; cf. p. Ter. 1:1; B. S. Jackson, "Liability for Mere Intention in Early Jewish Law," *HUCA* 42 (1971): 197–225; Rivkin, *Revolution,* pp. 296–311. Receiving stolen property could make one a thief just as easily as stealing the property would have, since the same motives were involved (Ps-Phocyl. 135–36). Cf. kavanah also in prayer; M. Maher, "Service of the Heart: The Quest for Authentic Prayer in Judaism," *Rev Rel* 40 (1, 1981): 40–47 (I have from NTA 25:286).

R. Isaac thought that searching for the *intention* of laws could lead one astray, but other rabbis pursued this objective nonetheless (Urbach, *Sages*, 1:382). Intention in laws was also debated in Roman lawcourts (e.g., Quint. 7.6.1).

50. N. J. McEleney, "The Principles of the Sermon on the Mount," *CBQ* 41 (4, Oct. 1979): 552–70, thinks that 5:17 points toward 5:21–48, while 5:20 points toward 6:1–7:12. It is not impossible that Matthew would supply some of what he would cover in his thesis, but even if 5:20 points mainly to ch. 6, the theme of inward righteousness is certainly a part of ch. 5 as well as of ch. 6. As Meier, *Matthew*, p. 46, observes, it is a useful transition between 5:17–19 and 5:21–48.

51. Jub. 20:2; R. Akiba in Sifra Qed. pq. 4.200.3.7; Gen. Rab. 24:7; cf. Jub. 7:20, 36:4; CD 6.20–21; m. Ab. 1:12 (attributed to Hillel); Test. Iss. 7:6, Benj. 3:5 (though cf. H. D. Slingerland, "The Nature of *Nomos* within the Testaments of the Twelve Patriarchs," *JBL* 105 [1, March 1986]: 39–48); Marc. Aur. *Med.* 11.1.2; Stoics in Diog. Laert. *Lives* 7.1.124 (though cf. Boer, *Morality*, pp. 62–72). For one or two (or ten) rules epitomizing the rest, cf. Philo *Decal.* 29, §154; Geza Vermes, "Pre-mishnaic Jewish Worship and the Phylacteries from the Dead Sea," *VT* 9 (1, 1959): 65–72; Epict. *Disc.* 1.20.14–15; Antisthenes in Diog. Laert. *Lives* 6.1.11; Plut. *Lett. Apoll.* 28, *Mor.* 116CD.

52. Scholars debate whether they were all spoken on the same occasion or where Matthew got his material; e.g., Georg Strecker, "Die Antithesen der Bergpredigt (Mt 5:21–48 par)," *ZNW* 69 (1–2, 1978): 36–72, who, with many others, believes that only half the antitheses were in pre-Matthean sources. Meeks, *World*, p. 139, argues that the three with parallels in Luke do not have antithetical form in Luke, and that therefore the form is redactional.

53. Bultmann, *Jesus and Word*, pp. 89–91. Cf. Strecker, "Antithesen," p. 71, for whom Jesus disputes the commandments, standing within Judaism but nevertheless not in the same way Jamnian rabbis did.

54. Sanders, *Jesus*, p. 260, though he is not persuaded of their authenticity; Borg, *Conflict*, pp. 76–77; Gundry, *Matthew*, p. 83.

55. Sanders, *Jesus*, p. 272, against Bornkamm (on the rabbinic practice of actually setting one text against another, to challenge a face-value interpretation of that text); pp. 9–10 (against Käsemann), 57, 248. Cf. similarly Cohen, *Maccabees*, p. 181.

56. Flusser, *Judaism*, p. 494.

57. Sanders, *Jesus*, pp. 9–10. On pp. 256–57, Prof. Sanders observes that "Moses did not command divorce, he permitted it," and that making the rule stricter is not the same thing as defying the law. Such a position is in contrast to that of Joachim Jeremias, *The Sermon on the Mount*, trans. Norman Perrin (Philadelphia: Fortress, 1963), p. 27, and, to a lesser extent, Meier, *Matthew*, p. 51.

58. Pirke Aboth 1:1, claiming to be from the oldest possible tradition, and other sources (e.g., ibid., 3:14; Ab. R. Nathan A, ch. 2; B, chs. 2–3; Sifre Deut. 48.1.5; Ruth Rab. 2:2; cf. Arist. 139, 142; CD 5.9–11, 20–21, 20.25; purportedly Tannaitic examples of the practice, without the term, in m. Ber. 1:1; b. Shab. 12b; Erub. 7a), though one must not make *too*

much of a fence lest people stumble over the fence and the law together (Ab. R. Nathan A ch. 1). Przybylski, *Righteousness*, pp. 81–83 also suggests that Matthew is in agreement with the rabbinic principle of building a fence around the law. The moral principle is known in Greek tradition, although it is couched in different language (Plut. *Compliancy* 6, *Mor.* 531D).

59. We address this point further in our discussion of Matthew 19.

60. 1 Macc. 2:41, after Antiochus IV Epiphanes had slaughtered a thousand Israelites, men, women, and children, who had refused to defend themselves on the Sabbath (2:34–38).

61. The prozbul (e.g., m. Sheb. 10:3–6; Tos. Sheb. 8:7–10), attributed in many of the sources to Hillel. Cf. Mussies, "Greek," p. 1050.

62. Sifre Deut. 175.1.3.

63. Sifre Deut. 221.1.1. See Wallace Greene, "Extra-legal Juridical Prerogatives," *JSJ* 7 (2, Sept. 1976): 152–76.

64. Tos. Ed. 2:3.

65. The so-called divine passive, a periphrasis; Meier, *Vision*, pp. 63–64.

66. E.g., Mek. *Pisha* 1:2, 17. Sanders, *Jewish Law*, p. 93, makes a similar case, citing also a form of halachic ruling in Qumran texts.

67. Mek. *Pisha* 1:35, where the challenger probably functions as an imaginary interlocutor, allowing the respondent to develop his case. Cf. in 1:62, where a valid tradition is cited, "And there are also those who say . . . " Cf. Sifré Num. 112.1.2 (these are randomly selected examples among many).

68. Used by the imaginary interlocutor in Mek. *Pisha* 1:58.

69. The particular formulation, "I say," without citing other authorities, does of course imply special authority, at least as a decisive interpreter of the law; but this need not imply a refutation of what has gone before.

70. "Some Rabbinic Parallels to the NT," *JQR* 12 (1900): 427; cf. Abrahams, *Studies* (1), pp. 16–17; R. A. Guelich, "The Antitheses of Matthew v.21–48: Traditional or Redactional?" *NTS* 22 (4, July 1976): 455; idem, *Sermon*, p. 185, accepts some validity to the parallel but argues that it is inadequate, since Jesus here sets his demand against the immutable law; but this objection's force depends on the premise that Jesus is actually doing that here. Gundry, *Matthew*, p. 84, appeals to Matthew's typical style to argue that rabbinic parallels here are inadequate; he is right that in Matthew's context, the language heightens Jesus' authority far more than that of a normal rabbi (cf. also 7:29); but my point is that his is the language of interpretation, not of refutation. Of course, it should not be suggested that no one "unique" in rabbinic literature could talk this way, either; Schechter points out on p. 428 that God himself sometimes talked this way in rabbinic texts.

71. Sanders, *Jewish Law*, p. 127, argues that the Pharisees did not impose their fence around the law on others as equivalent to the written law itself.

Bibliography of
Sources Cited

Abrahams, I. *Studies in Pharisaism and the Gospels.* 1st Series. Prolegom-
enon by Morton S. Enslin. Library of Biblical Studies. Edited by
Harry M. Orlinsky. New York: KTAV Publishing House, 1967;
Cambridge: Cambridge University Press, 1917.
_____. *Studies in Pharisaism and the Gospels.* 2d Series. Cambridge:
Cambridge University Press, 1924.
Achilles Tatius. *Clitophon and Leucippe.* Translated by S. Gaselee. Loeb
Classical Library. London: Wm. Heinemann; New York: G. P. Put-
nam's Sons, 1917.
Adams, Jay E. *Marriage, Divorce & Remarriage in the Bible.* Grand
Rapids: Baker Book House, 1980.
Anderson, Hugh. *The Gospel of Mark.* New Century Bible. London:
Oliphants (Marshall, Morgan & Scott), 1976.
*The Ante-Nicene Fathers: Translations of the Writings of the Fathers down
to A.D. 325.* 10 vols. Edited by Alexander Roberts and James
Donaldson. Revised by A. Cleveland Coxe. Grand Rapids: Wm. B.
Eerdmans Publishing Company, 1975.
"Apocalypse of Zephaniah." Translated by O. S. Wintermute. 1:497–
515 in *The Old Testament Pseudepigrapha.* 2 vols. Edited by James H.
Charlesworth. Garden City, N.Y.: Doubleday & Company, 1983–
1985.
Apuleius. *The Golden Ass.* Translated by W. Adlington. Revised by S.
Gaselee. Loeb Classical Library. Cambridge: Harvard University
Press, 1915.
Argyle, A. W. *The Gospel According to Matthew.* Cambridge: Cambridge
University Press, 1963.
"Aristeas, Letter of." Translated by R. J. H. Shutt. 2:7–34 in *The Old
Testament Pseudepigrapha.* 2 vols. Edited by James H. Charles-
worth. Garden City, N.Y.: Doubleday & Company, 1983–1985.
Aristeas to Philocrates (Letter of Aristeas). Edited and translated by
Moses Hadas. New York: Harper & Brothers, for The Dropsie
College for Hebrew & Cognate Learning, 1951.

Arrington, French L. *Paul's Aeon Theology in 1 Corinthians.* Washington, D.C.: University Press of America, 1978.

Artemidori Daldiani. *Onirocriticon Libri.* V. Bibliotheca Scriptorum Graecorum et Romanorum Teubneriana. Lipsiae: B. G. Teubneri, 1963.

Artemidorus. *The Interpretation of Dreams (Oneirocritica).* Translation and commentary by Robert J. White. Noyes Classical Studies. Park Ridge, N.J.: Noyes Press, 1975.

Athenaeus. *The Deipnosophists.* 7 vols. Translated by Charles Burton Gulick. Loeb Classical Library. London: Wm. Heinemann; New York: G. P. Putnam's Sons, 1927–1937.

Aune, David E. "Greco-Roman Biography." Pp. 107–26 in *Greco-Roman Literature and the NT: Selected Forms and Genres.* Edited by David E. Aune. Society of Biblical Literature Sources for Biblical Study 21. Atlanta: Scholars Press, 1988.

_____. *The New Testament in Its Literary Environment.* Library of Early Christianity 8. Philadelphia: Westminster Press, 1987.

_____. "The Problem of the Genre of the Gospels: A Critique of C. H. Talbert's What Is a Gospel?" 2:9–60 in *Gospel Perspectives: Studies of History and Tradition in the Four Gospels.* Edited by R. T. France and David Wenham. Sheffield: JSOT Press, 1981.

_____. *Prophecy in Early Christianity and the Ancient Mediterranean World.* Grand Rapids: Wm. B. Eerdmans Publishing Company, 1983.

The Babylonian Talmud. Edited by Isidore Epstein. London: Soncino Press, 1948.

Baird, William. *The Corinthian Church—A Biblical Approach to Urban Culture.* New York: Abingdon Press, 1964.

Balch, David L. "Backgrounds of I Cor. VII: Sayings of the Lord in Q; Moses as an Ascetic *theios anēr* in II Cor. III." *New Testament Studies* 18 (3, April 1972): 351–64.

_____. "1 Cor 7:32–35 and Stoic Debates about Marriage, Anxiety, and Distraction." *Journal of Biblical Literature* 102 (3, September 1983): 429–39.

_____. *Let Wives be Submissive: The Domestic Code in 1 Peter.* Society of Biblical Literature Monograph 26. Chico, Calif.: Scholars Press for the Society of Biblical Literature, 1981.

Bamberger, Bernard J. *Proselytism in the Talmudic Period.* Foreword by Julian Morgenstern. New York: KTAV Publishing House, 1968.

Barré, Michael L. "To Marry or to Burn: *pyrousthai* in 1 Cor 7:9." *Catholic Biblical Quarterly* 36 (2, April 1974): 193–202.

Barrett, C. K. *The New Testament Background: Selected Documents.* New York: Harper & Row, 1961; London: S.P.C.K., 1956.

Bartchy, S. Scott. *Mallon Chrēsai: First-Century Slavery and the Interpretation of 1 Corinthians 7:21.* Society of Biblical Literature Dissertation 11. Missoula, Mont.: Society of Biblical Literature, 1973.

Barth, Gerhard. "Matthew's Understanding of the Law." Pp. 58–164 in *Tradition and Interpretation in Matthew.* By G. Bornkamm, G. Barth, and H. J. Held. Philadelphia: Westminster Press, 1963.

Barthell, Edward E., Jr. *Gods and Goddesses of Ancient Greece.* Coral Gables, Fla.: University of Miami Press, 1971.

Basser, Herbert W. "Derrett's 'Binding' reopened." *Journal of Biblical Literature* 104 (2, 1985): 297–300.

_____. "The Meaning of 'Shtuth,' Gen.R. 11 in Reference to Matthew 5.29–30 and 18.8–9." *New Testament Studies* 31 (1, January 1985): 148–51.

Batey, Richard A. "The *mia sarx* Union of Christ and the Church." *New Testament Studies* 13 (3, April 1967): 270–81.

Baumgarten, Joseph M. "4Q 502, Marriage or Golden Age Ritual?" *Journal of Jewish Studies* 34 (2, Autumn 1983): 125–35.

_____. "Qumran Studies." *Journal of Biblical Literature* 77 (1958): 249–57.

Beard, Mary. "The Sexual Status of Vestal Virgins." *Journal of Roman Studies* 70 (1980): 12–27.

Belkin, Samuel. *Philo and the Oral Law: The Philonic Interpretation of Biblical Law in Relation to the Palestinian Halakah.* Harvard Semitic Series 11. Cambridge: Harvard University Press, 1940.

Best, Ernest. *Mark: The Gospel as Story.* Studies of the New Testament and Its World. Edinburgh: T. & T. Clark, 1983.

Betz, Hans Dieter. *A Commentary on Paul's Letter to the Churches in Galatia.* Hermeneia Commentaries. Philadelphia: Fortress Press, 1979.

_____. "The Sermon on the Mount: Its Literary Genre and Function." *Journal of Religion* 59 (3, July 1979): 285–97.

Black, David Alan. "Jesus on Anger: The Text of Matthew 5:22a Revisited." *Novum Testamentum* 30 (1, January 1988): 1–8.

Black, Matthew. *The Scrolls and Christian Origins.* London: Thomas Nelson & Sons, 1961.

Bleich, J. David. "Abortion and Jewish Law." Pp. 405–19 in *New Perspectives on Human Abortion.* Edited by Thomas W. Hilgers, Dennis J. Horan, and David Mall. Frederick, Md.: University Publications of America, 1981.

Boer, W. Den. *Private Morality in Greece and Rome: Some Historical Aspects.* Mnemosyne: Bibliotheca Classica Batava, Supplementum Quinquagesimum Septimum. Leiden: E. J. Brill, 1979.

Bonsirven, Joseph. *Palestinian Judaism in the Time of Jesus Christ.* New York: Holt, Rinehart & Winston, 1964.

Borg, Marcus J. *Conflict, Holiness & Politics in the Teachings of Jesus.* Studies in the Bible and Early Christianity 5. New York: Edwin Mellen Press, 1984.

Boring, M. Eugene. *Sayings of the Risen Jesus: Christian Prophecy in the Synoptic Tradition.* Society for New Testament Studies Monograph 46. Cambridge: Cambridge University Press, 1982.

Bornkamm, Günther. "End-Expectation and Church in Matthew." Pp. 15–51 in *Tradition and Interpretation in Matthew.* By G. Bornkamm, G. Barth, and H. J. Held. Philadelphia: Westminster Press, 1963.

_____. *Paul.* Translated by D. M. G. Stalker. New York: Harper & Row, 1971.

Bound, J. F. "Who Are the 'Virgins' Discussed in 1 Corinthians 7:25–38?" *Evangelical Journal* 2 (1, 1984): 3–15.

Bowman, John, translator and editor. *Samaritan Documents Relating to Their History, Religion and Life.* Pittsburgh Original Texts and Translations 2. Pittsburgh, Penn.: The Pickwick Press, 1977.

Boyle, Marjorie O'Rourke. "The Stoic Paradox of James 2:10." *New Testament Studies* 31 (4, October 1985): 611–17.

Breiner, Sander J. "Child abuse patterns: Comparison of ancient Western civilization and traditional China." *Analytic Psychotherapy and Psychopathology* 2 (1, 1985): 27–50.

Bright, John. *A History of Israel.* 3d ed. Philadelphia: Westminster Press, 1981.

Brooten, Bernadette J. "Zur Debatte über das Scheidungsrecht der jüdischen Frau." *Evangelische Theologie* 43 (5, September 1983): 466–78.

_____. "Konnten Frauen im alten die Seheidung betreiben? Überlegungen zu Mk 10,11–12 und 1 Kor 7,10–11." *Evangelische Theologie* 42 (1, January 1982): 65–80.

_____. *Women Leaders in the Ancient Synagogue: Inscriptional Evidence and Background Issues.* Chico, Calif.: Scholars Press, 1982.

Brown, Raymond E. "The Dead Sea Scrolls and the New Testament." Pp. 1–8 in *John and Qumran.* Edited by James H. Charlesworth. London: Geoffrey Chapman, 1972.

Bruce, F. F. " 'All Things to All Men': Diversity in Unity and Other Pauline Tensions." Pp. 82–99 in *Unity and Diversity in New Testament Theology: Essays in Honor of George E. Ladd.* Edited by Robert A. Guelich. Grand Rapids: Wm. B. Eerdmans Publishing Company, 1978.

_____. *1 & 2 Corinthians.* New Century Bible 38. Greenwood, S.C.: The Attic Press, 1971.

_____. *1 & 2 Thessalonians.* Word Biblical Commentary 45. Waco, Tex.: Word Books, 1982.

_____. *The Message of the New Testament.* Grand Rapids: Wm. B. Eerdmans Publishing Company, 1981.

Bultmann, Rudolf. *The History of the Synoptic Tradition.* 2d ed. Translated by John Marsh. Oxford: Basil Blackwell, 1968.

_____. *Jesus and the Word.* Translated by Louise Pettibone Smith and Erminie Huntress Lantero. New York: Charles Scribner's Sons, 1958.

Burkert, Walter. *Ancient Mystery Cults.* Carl Newell Jackson Lectures. Cambridge: Harvard University Press, 1987.

Burkitt, F. Crawford. *Church and Gnosis: A Study of Christian Thought and Speculation in the Second Century.* The Morse Lectures for 1931. Cambridge: Cambridge University Press, 1932.

_____. *The Earliest Sources for the Life of Jesus.* Boston: Houghton Mifflin Company, 1910.

Byron, B. "The Meaning of 'Except it be for Fornication'." *Australasian Catholic Record* 40 (2, 1963): 90–95.

Cadbury, Henry J. "Four Features of Lukan Style." Pp. 87–102 in *Studies in Luke–Acts: Essays in honor of Paul Schubert*. Edited by Leander E. Keck and J. Louis Martyn. Nashville: Abingdon Press, 1966.

Caird, George B. "Expounding the Parables: I—The Defendant (Matthew 5.25f.; Luke 12.58f.)" *Expository Times* 77 (2, November 1965): 36–39.

Carcopino, Jérôme. *Daily Life in Ancient Rome: The People and the City at the Height of the Empire*. Edited by Henry T. Rowell. Translated by E. O. Lorimer. New Haven: Yale University Press, 1940.

Carlston, Charles E. "Proverbs, Maxims, and the Historical Jesus." *Journal of Biblical Literature* 99 (1, 1980): 87–105.

Carmon, Efrat, editor. *Inscriptions Reveal: Documents from the time of the Bible, the Mishna and the Talmud*. Translated by R. Grafman. Jerusalem: Israel Museum, 1973.

Caron, Gerard. "Did Jesus Allow Divorce? (Mt. 5:31–32). A Preaching Problem." *AFER* 24 (5, October 1982): 309–16.

Carson, D. A. "Matthew." 8:3–599 in *The Expositor's Bible Commentary*. Edited by Frank Gaebelein. Grand Rapids: Zondervan Publishing House, 1984.

Cary, M., and Haarhoff, T. J. *Life and Thought in the Greek and Roman World*. 4th ed. London: Methuen & Company, 1946.

Casson, Lionel. *Travel in the Ancient World*. London: George Allen & Unwin, 1974.

Chadwick, Henry. " 'All Things to All Men' (I Cor. ix.22)." *New Testament Studies* 1 (4, May 1955): 261–75.

_____. *The Early Church*. New York: Penguin Books, 1967.

Charitonis Aphrodisiensis: De Chaerea et Callirhoe Amatoriarvm Narrationvm Libri Octo. Oxford: Clarendon Press; London: Humphrey Milford, 1938.

Chariton's Chaereas and Callirhoe. Translated by Warren E. Blake. Ann Arbor, Mich.: University of Michigan Press; London: Humphrey Milford, Oxford University Press, 1939.

Charles, R. H., editor. *The Apocrypha and Pseudepigrapha of the Old Testament in English*. 2 vols. Oxford: Clarendon Press, 1913.

Chilton, Bruce. "Targumic Transmission and Dominical Tradition." 1:21–45 in *Gospel Perspectives: Studies of History and Tradition in the Four Gospels*. Edited by R. T. France and David Wenham. Sheffield: JSOT Press, 1980.

Christiaens, M. "Pastoraal van de echtscheiding volgens Matteüs. Vragen rond de 'ontuchtclausule'." *Tijdschrift voor Theologie* 23 (1, 1983): 3–23. (NTA 27:255)

Cicero. *Works*. 28 vols. Translated by Harry Caplan et al. Loeb Classical Library. Cambridge: Harvard University Press, 1913–1977.

Clark, Elizabeth A. *Women in the Early Church*. Message of the Fathers of the Church 13. Wilmington, Del.: Michael Glazier, 1983.

Cohen, Shaye J. D. *From the Maccabees to the Mishnah*. Library of Early Christianity 7. Philadelphia: Westminster Press, 1987.

Cohn-Sherbok, Daniel M. "Jesus' Defence of the Resurrection of the Dead." *Journal for the Study of the New Testament* 11 (1981): 64–73.

Coiner, Harry G. "Those 'Divorce and Remarriage' Passages (Matt. 5:32; 19:9; 1 Cor. 7:10–16)." *Concordia Theological Monthly* 39 (6, June 1968): 367–84.

Collins, Raymond F. "The Unity of Paul's Paraenesis in 1 Thess. 4:3–8, 1 Cor. 7.1–7, and Significant Parallels." *New Testament Studies* 29 (3, July 1983): 420–29.

Considine, T. "Except it be for Fornication." *Australasian Catholic Record* 33 (1956): 214–23. (NTA 1:177)

Conzelmann, Hans. *1 Corinthians: A Commentary on the First Epistle to the Corinthians.* Translated by James W. Leitch. Bibliography and references by James W. Dunkly. Edited by George W. MacRae. Philadelphia: Fortress Press, 1975.

Cope, O. Lamar. *Matthew: A Scribe Trained for the Kingdom of Heaven.* Catholic Biblical Quarterly Monograph 5. Washington, D.C.: Catholic Biblical Association of America, 1976.

Corpus Inscriptionum Iudaicarum: Recueil des Inscriptions Juives qui vont du IIe Siècle de Notre ère. 3 vols. Edited by P. Jean-Baptiste Frey. Rome: Pontifio Instituto di Archeologia Cristiana, 1936–1952.

Corpus Papyrorum Judaicarum. 3 vols. Edited by Victor A. Tcherikover, with Alexander Fuks; vol. 3: edited by Tcherikover, Fuks, and Menahem Stern, with David M. Lewis. Cambridge: Harvard University Press, for the Magnes Press, Hebrew University, 1957–1964.

Côté, Pierre-Rene. "Les eunuques pour le Royaume (Mt 19,12)." *Eglise et Théologie* 17 (3, 1986): 321–34.

Couturier, Guy. "La vision du conseil divin: étude d'une forme commune au prophétisme et à l'apocalyptique." *Science et Esprit* 36 (1, January 1984): 5–43.

Cross, Frank Moore. *The Ancient Library of Qumran & Modern Biblical Studies.* Rev. ed. Grand Rapids: Baker Book House, 1980; Garden City, N.Y.: Doubleday & Company, 1961.

_____. *Canaanite Myths and Hebrew Epic.* Cambridge: Harvard University Press, 1973.

The Cynic Epistles: A Study Edition. Edited by Abraham J. Malherbe. Society of Biblical Literature Sources for Biblical Study 12. Missoula, Mont.: Scholars Press, 1977.

Dalman, Gustaf. *Jesus-Jeshua: Studies in the Gospels.* New York: Macmillan, 1929.

Daniélou, Jean. *The Theology of Jewish Christianity.* Translated and edited by John A. Baker. The Development of Christian Doctrine Before the Council of Nicea 1. London: Darton, Longman & Todd, 1964; Chicago: Henry Regnery Company, 1964.

Daube, David. "Concessions to Sinfulness in Jewish Law." *Journal of Jewish Studies* 10 (1–2, 1959): 1–13.

_____. "The Gospels and the Rabbis." *The Listener* 56 (September 6, 1956): 342–46.

_____. "The Law of Witnesses in Transferred Operation." *Journal of the Ancient Near East Society of Columbia University* 5 (1973): 91–93.

_____. *The New Testament and Rabbinic Judaism*. New York: Arno Press, 1973; London: University of London, 1956.

Davids, Peter. *The Epistle of James: A Commentary on the Greek Text*. New International Greek Testament Commentary. Grand Rapids: Wm. B. Eerdmans Publishing Company, 1982.

Davies, W. D. *Paul and Rabbinic Judaism: Some Rabbinic Elements in Pauline Theology*. 4th ed. Philadelphia: Fortress Press, 1980.

_____. *The Sermon on the Mount*. Cambridge: Cambridge University Press, 1966.

_____. *Torah in the Messianic Age and/or the Age to Come*. Journal of Biblical Literature Monograph 7. Philadelphia: Society of Biblical Literature, 1952.

Dawson, John. "Urbanization and Mental Health in a West African Community." Pp. 305–42 in *Magic, Faith, and Healing: Studies in Primitive Psychiatry Today*. Edited by Ari Kiev. New York: Free Press, 1964.

Deissmann, G. Adolf. *Bible Studies: Contributions Chiefly from Papyri and Inscriptions to the History of the Language, the Literature, and the Religion of Hellenistic Judaism and Primitive Christianity*. Translated by Alexander Grieve. Peabody, Mass.: Hendrickson Publishers, 1988; Edinburgh: T. & T. Clark, 1901.

De Ridder, Richard R. *Discipling the Nations*. Grand Rapids: Baker Book House, 1971.

Derrett, J. Duncan M. *Jesus's Audience: The Social and Psychological Environment in which He Worked*. New York: Seabury Press, 1973.

_____. " 'Where two or three are convened in my name . . .': a sad misunderstanding." *Expository Times* 91 (3, 1971): 83–86.

Devine, A. M. "The Low Birth-Rate in Ancient Rome: A Possible Contributing Factor." *Rheinisches Museum für Philologie* 128 (3–4, 1985): 313–17.

Dibelius, Martin. *From Tradition to Gospel*. Translated by Bertram Lee Woolf. Greenwood, S.C.: The Attic Press; Cambridge: James Clarke & Company, 1971.

_____. *James: A Commentary on the Epistle of James*. Revised by Heinrich Greeven. Translated by Michael A. Williams. Edited by Helmut Koester. Hermeneia Commentaries. Philadelphia: Fortress Press, 1976.

_____. *Paul*. Edited and completed by Werner Georg Kümmel. Philadelphia: Westminster Press, 1953.

Dibelius, Martin, and Hans Conzelmann. *The Pastoral Epistles: A Commentary on the Pastoral Epistles*. Translated by Philip Buttolph and Adela Yarbro. Edited by Helmut Koester. Hermeneia Commentaries. Philadelphia: Fortress Press, 1972.

Dio Chrysostom. *Orations*. 5 vols. Translated by J. W. Cohoon and H. Lamar Crosby. Loeb Classical Library. Cambridge: Harvard University Press, 1932–1951.

Diogenes Laertius. *Lives of Eminent Philosophers*. 2 vols. Translated by R. D. Hicks. Loeb Classical Library. Cambridge: Harvard University Press, 1925.

Dixon, Suzanne. *The Roman Mother.* Norman, Okla.: Oklahoma University Press, 1988.

Dobson, Edward G. *What the Bible Really Says About Marriage, Divorce & Remarriage.* Old Tappan, N.J.: Fleming H. Revell, 1986.

Dover, K. J. "Classical Greek Attitudes to Sexual Behaviour." Pp. 143–58 in *Women in the Ancient World: The Arethusa Papers.* Edited by John Peradotto and J. P. Sullivan. Albany, N.Y.: State University of New York, 1984.

Down, M. J. "The Sayings of Jesus about Marriage and Divorce." *Expository Times* 95 (11, August 1984): 332–34.

Downing, F. Gerald. "The Resurrection of the Dead: Jesus and Philo." *Journal for the Study of the New Testament* 15 (1982): 42–50.

Driver, G. R. *The Judaean Scrolls: The Problem and a Solution.* Oxford: Basil Blackwell, 1965.

Drower, E. S. *The Mandaeans of Iraq and Iran: Their Cults, Customs, Magic, Legends, and Folklore.* Leiden: E. J. Brill, 1962.

Duncker, P.-G. " ' . . . quae vere viduae sunt' (1 Tim. 5,3)." *Angelicum* 35 (2, 1958): 121–38. (NTA 3:56)

Du Plessis, I. J. "The Ethics of Marriage According to Matt. 5:27–32." *Neotestamentica* 1 (1967): 16–27.

Dupont-Sommer, André. *Les Manuscrits de la Mer Morte et le Problème des Origines Chrétiennes.* Paris: Editions Estienne, 1969.

Duty, Guy. *Divorce and Remarriage.* Minneapolis: Bethany Fellowship, 1967.

Easton, Burton Scott. "Divorce in the NT." *Anglican Theological Review* 22 (2, April 1940): 78–87.

Efird, James M. *Marriage and Divorce: What the Bible Says.* Nashville: Abingdon Press, 1985.

Ellingworth, P. "The 'true saying' in 1 Timothy 3.1." *Bible Translator* 31 (4, 1980): 443–45.

Ellis, Peter F. *Matthew: His Mind and His Message.* Collegeville, Minn.: The Liturgical Press, 1974.

Engels, Donald. "The Problem of Female Infanticide in the Greco-Roman World." *Classical Philology* 75 (2, April 1980): 112–20.

_____. "The Use of Historical Demography in Ancient History." *Classical Quarterly* 34 (2, 1984): 386–93.

Epictetus. *The Discourses as Reported by Arrian, the Manual, and Fragments.* 2 vols. Translated by W. A. Oldfather. Loeb Classical Library. London: William Heinemann; New York: G. P. Putnam's Sons, 1926–1928.

The Ethiopic Book of Enoch: A New Edition in the Light of the Aramaic Dead Sea Fragments. Edited and translated by Michael A. Knibb, in consultation with Edward Ullendorf. 2 vols. Oxford: Clarendon Press, 1978.

"Eugnostos the Blessed" and "The Sophia of Jesus Christ." Translated by D. M. Parrott. Pp. 216–17 in *The Nag Hammadi Library in English.* Edited by James M. Robinson. San Francisco: Harper & Row, 1977.

Evans-Pritchard, E. E. *Kinship and Marriage Among the Nuer.* Oxford: Clarendon, 1951.

Falk, Harvey. *Jesus the Pharisee: A New Look at the Jewishness of Jesus.* New York/Mahwah: Paulist Press, 1985.

Falk, Ze'ev W. "Binding and Loosing." *Journal of Jewish Studies* 25 (1, February 1974): 92–100.

_____. "Jewish Private Law." 1:504–34 in *The Jewish People in the First Century: Historical Geography, Political History, Social, Cultural and Religious Life and Institutions.* 2 vols. Edited by S. Safrai and M. Stern with D. Flusser and W. C. van Unnik. Section 1 of Compendia Rerum Iudaicarum ad Novum Testamentum. Vol. 1: Assen: Van Gorcum & Co. B.V., 1974; vol. 2: Philadelphia: Fortress Press, 1976.

The Fathers According to Rabbi Nathan. Translated by Judah Goldin. Yale Judaica Series 10. New Haven: Yale University Press, 1955.

The Fathers According to Rabbi Nathan (Abot de Rabbi Nathan) Version B. Translation and commentary by Anthony J. Saldarini. Studies in Judaism in Late Antiquity 11. Leiden: E. J. Brill, 1975.

Fee, Gordon D. *1 & 2 Timothy, Titus.* New International Biblical Commentary 13. Peabody, Mass.: Hendrickson Publishers, 1988.

_____. *The First Epistle to the Corinthians.* New International Commentaries on the New Testament. Grand Rapids: Wm. B. Eerdmans Publishing Company, 1987.

_____. "1 Corinthians 7:1 in the NIV." *Journal of the Evangelical Theological Society* 23 (4, December 1980): 307–14.

Fee, Gordon D., and Douglas Stuart. *How to Read the Bible for All Its Worth.* Grand Rapids: Zondervan Publishing House, 1981.

Fenton, J. C. *Saint Matthew.* Philadelphia: Westminster Press, 1977.

Filson, Floyd V. *A Commentary on the Gospel According to St. Matthew.* New York: Harper & Row, 1960.

Finkelstein, Louis. *Akiba: Scholar, Saint and Martyr.* New York: Atheneum, 1970.

"1 (Ethiopic Apocalypse of) Enoch." Translated by E. Isaac. 1:5–89 in *The Old Testament Pseudepigrapha.* 2 vols. Edited by James H. Charlesworth. Garden City, N.Y.: Doubleday & Company, 1983–1985.

Fjärstedt, B. "Fråga och svar i Matt. 19, 3–12." *Svensk Exegetisk Årsbok* 33 (1968): 118–40. (NTA 14:37)

Fleming, T. V. "Christ and Divorce." *Theological Studies* 24 (1, 1963): 106–20.

Flusser, David. *Judaism and the Origins of Christianity.* Jerusalem: The Magnes Press, The Hebrew University, 1988.

"The Fourth Book of Ezra." Translated by Bruce M. Metzger. 1:517–59 in *The Old Testament Pseudepigrapha.* 2 vols. Edited by James H. Charlesworth. Garden City, N.Y.: Doubleday & Company, 1983–1985.

Frank, Tenney. *Aspects of Social Behavior in Ancient Rome.* Cambridge: Harvard University Press, 1932.

Frey, J. B. "La Signification des termes *monandros* et *univira*: coup d'oeil sur la Famille Romaine aux Premiers siècles de Notre ère." *Recherches de Science Religieuse* 20 (1930): 48–60.

Friedländer, Ludwig. *Roman Life and Manners Under the Early Empire.* 4 vols. Translated by Leonard A. Magnus. New York: Barnes & Noble, 1965.

Gager, John G. "Religion and Social Class in the Early Roman Empire." Pp. 99–120 in *The Catacombs and the Colosseum: The Roman Empire as the Setting of Primitive Christianity.* Edited by Stephen Benko and John J. O'Rourke. Valley Forge, Penn.: Judson, 1971.

Gardner, Jane F. *Women in Roman Law & Society.* Bloomington, Ind.: Indiana University Press, 1986.

Gasparro, Giulia Sfameni. *Soteriology and Mystic Aspects in the Cult of Cybele and Attis.* Études Préliminaires aux Religions Orientales dans l'Empire Romain 103. Leiden: E. J. Brill, 1985.

Geldard, Mark. "Jesus' Teaching on Divorce: thoughts on the meaning of *porneia* in Matthew 5:32 and 19:9." *Churchman* 92 (2, 1978): 134–43.

Geller, Markham J. "The Elephantine Papyri and Hosea 2,3. Evidence for the form of the Early Jewish Divorce Writ." *Journal for the Study of Judaism* 8 (2, October 1977): 139–48.

_____. "New Sources for the Origins of the Rabbinic Ketubah." *Hebrew Union College Annual* 49 (1978): 227–45.

Gerhardsson, Birger. *Memory and Manuscript: Oral Tradition and Written Transmission in Rabbinic Judaism and Early Christianity.* Acta Seminarii Neotestamentici Upsaliensis 22. Upssala: C. W. K. Gleerup, 1961.

_____. *The Origins of the Gospel Traditions.* Philadelphia: Fortress Press, 1979.

Giblin, C. H. "1 Corinthians 7—A Negative Theology of Marriage and Celibacy?" *Bible Today* 41 (1969): 2839–55.

Gill, Christopher. "The Question of Character-Development: Plutarch and Tacitus." *Classical Quarterly* 33 (2, 1983): 469–87.

Glasscock, Ed. " 'The Husband of One Wife' Requirement in 1 Timothy 3:2." *Bibliotheca Sacra* 140 (559, July 1983): 244–58.

Godwin, Joscelyn. *Mystery Religions in the Ancient World.* San Francisco: Harper & Row, 1981.

Goguel, Maurice. *The Life of Jesus.* Translated by Olive Wyon. New York: Macmillan, 1948.

Goppelt, Leonhard. *Apostolic and Post-Apostolic Times.* Translated by Robert Guelich. Grand Rapids: Baker Book House, 1980.

_____. *Theology of the New Testament.* 2 vols. Translated by John E. Alsup. Edited by Jürgen Roloff. Grand Rapids: Wm. B. Eerdmans Publishing Company, 1981–1982.

Gorman, Michael J. *Abortion and the Early Church: Christian, Jewish, and Pagan Attitudes in the Greco-Roman World.* Downers Grove, Ill.: InterVarsity Press, 1982.

Gould, John. *The Development of Plato's Ethics.* Cambridge: Cambridge University, 1955.

Goulder, M. D. *Midrash and Lection in Matthew*. The Speaker's Lectures in Biblical Studies 1969–71. London: S. P. C. K., 1974.

Grant, Frederick C., editor. *Hellenistic Religions: The Age of Syncretism*. The Library of Liberal Arts. Indianapolis: Bobbs-Merrill Company, Liberal Arts Press, 1953.

Grant, Robert M. *Early Christianity and Society: Seven Studies*. San Francisco: Harper & Row, 1977.

_____. *Gods and the One God*. Library of Early Christianity 1. Philadelphia: Westminster Press, 1986.

The Greek Anthology. 5 vols. Translated by W. R. Paton. Loeb Classical Library. Cambridge: Harvard University Press, 1916–?.

"Greek Apocalypse of Ezra." Translated by Michael E. Stone. 1:561–79 in *The Old Testament Pseudepigrapha*. 2 vols. Edited by James H. Charlesworth. Garden City, N.Y.: Doubleday & Company, 1983–1985.

The Greek Version of the Testaments of the Twelve Patriarchs, edited from nine mss. Together with the variants of the Armenian and Slavonic versions and some Hebrew fragments. Edited by R. H. Charles. Oxford: Clarendon Press, 1908.

Greene, Wallace. "Extra-legal Juridical Prerogatives." *Journal for the Study of Judaism* 7 (2, September 1976): 152–76.

Gregor, D. B. "Abortige en la antikva mondo." *Biblia Revuo* 17 (4, 1981): 71–90. (NTA 26:288)

Grisez, Germain. *Abortion: The Myths, the Realities, and the Arguments* New York: Corpus Books, 1970.

Guelich, Robert A. "The Antitheses of Matthew v.21–48: Traditional or Redactional?" *New Testament Studies* 22 (4, July 1976): 444–57.

_____. "Mt 5, 22: Its Meaning and Integrity." *Zeitschrift für die Neutestamentliche Wissenschaft* 64 (1/2, 1973): 39–52.

_____. *The Sermon on the Mount: A Foundation for Understanding*. Waco, Tex.: Word Books, 1982.

Gundry, Robert H. *Matthew: A Commentary on his Literary and Theological Art*. Grand Rapids: Wm. B. Eerdmans Publishing Company, 1982.

Guthrie, W. K. C. *Orpheus and Greek Religion: A Study of the Orphic Movement*. 2d ed. New York: W. W. Norton & Company, 1966.

Hansman, J. F. "Some Possible Classical Connections in Mithraic Speculation." Pp. 601–12 in *Mysteria Mithrae*. Edited by Ugo Bianchi. Études Préliminaires aux Religions Orientales dans l'Empire Romain 80. Leiden: E. J. Brill, 1979.

Hardy, Edward Rochie. "The Priestess in the Greco-Roman World." *Churchman* 84 (4, Winter 1970): 264–70.

Hardy, W. G. *The Greek and Roman World*. Cambridge: Schenkman Publishing Company, 1962.

Hare, Douglas R. A. *The Theme of Jewish Persecution of Christians in the Gospel According to St Matthew*. Cambridge: Cambridge University Press, 1967.

Harpur, G. E. "A Comment on abstinence mentioned in 1 Corinthians." *Journal of the Christian Brethren Research Fellowship* 27 (1975): 30–40.

Harrell, Pat Edwin. *Divorce and Remarriage in the Early Church: A History of Divorce and Remarriage in the Ante-Nicene Church.* Austin, Tex.: R. B. Sweet Company, 1967.

Harris, W. V. "The Theoretical Possibility of Extensive Infanticide in the Graeco-Roman World." *Classical Quarterly* 32 (1, 1982): 114–16.

Hauck F., and S. Schulz. *"Pornē."* 6:579–95 in *Theological Dictionary of the New Testament.* 10 vols. Edited by Gerhard Kittel and Gerhard Friedrich. Translated by Geoffrey W. Bromiley. Grand Rapids: Wm. B. Eerdmans Publishing Company, 1964–1976.

Hengel, Martin. *Judaism and Hellenism: Studies in their encounter in Palestine during the early Hellenistic period.* 2 vols. Translated by John Bowden. Philadelphia: Fortress Press, 1974.

Héring, Jean. *The First Epistle of Saint Paul to the Corinthians.* Translated by A. W. Heathcote and P. J. Allcock. London: The Epworth Press, 1962.

Herodotus. *Histories.* Translated by A. D. Godley. Loeb Classical Library. Cambridge: Harvard University Press, 1920–1925.

Herr, M. D. "Sybwtyw sl mrd br-kwkb' [The Causes of the Bar-Kokhba War]." *Zion* 43 (1–2, 1978): 1–11. (NTA 24:169)

Heth, William A., and Gordon J. Wenham. *Jesus and Divorce: The Problem with the Evangelical Consensus.* Nashville: Thomas Nelson Publishers, 1984.

Hiers, Richard H. " 'Binding' and 'Loosing': The Matthean Authorizations." *Journal of Biblical Literature* 104 (2, June 1985): 233–50.

Hill, David. *New Testament Prophecy.* New Foundations Theological Library. Atlanta: John Knox Press, 1979.

Hock, Ronald F. *The Social Context of Paul's Ministry: Tentmaking and Apostleship.* Philadelphia: Fortress Press, 1980.

Hoenig, Sidney B. "Conversion During the Talmudic Period." Pp. 33–66 in *Conversion to Judaism: A History and Analysis.* Edited by David Max Eichhorn. New York: KTAV Publishing House, 1965.

Horace. *The Odes and Epodes.* Translated by C. E. Bennett. Loeb Classical Library. Cambridge: Harvard University Press; London: Heinemann, 1914.

_____. *Satires, Epistles and Ars Poetica.* Translated by H. Rushton Fairclough. Loeb Classical Library. New York: G. P. Putnam's Sons; London: Heinemann, 1926.

Horsley, Richard A. "Spiritual Marriage with Sophia." *Vigiliae Christianae* 33 (1, 1979): 30–54.

Hort, Fenton John Anthony. *Judaistic Christianity.* Edited by J. O. F. Murray. Grand Rapids: Baker Book House, 1980.

Hübner, Hans. "Zölibat in Qumran?" *New Testament Studies* 17 (2, January 1971): 153–67.

Hull, Gretchen Gaebelein. "In the Image of God: Women and Men as Social Equals." *ESA Advocate* 12 (9, Nov. 1990): 14–15.

Humble, B. J. "The Mebaqqer in the Dead Sea Scrolls." *Restoration Quarterly* 7 (1–2, 1963): 33–38.

Hurd, John Coolidge, Jr. *The Origin of 1 Corinthians.* London:S.P.C.K., 1965.

Hurmence, Belinda, editor. *Before Freedom: 48 Oral Histories of Former North and South Carolina Slaves.* New York: Penguin Books, 1990.

Hurtado, Larry. *Mark.* New International Biblical Commentary 2. Peabody, Mass.: Hendrickson, 1989.

Isbell, Charles D. *Corpus of the Aramaic Incantation Bowls.* Society of Biblical Literature Dissertation 17. Missoula, Mont.: Scholars Press for the Society of Biblical Literature, 1975.

Isocrates. *Orations.* 3 vols. Translated by George Norlin and Larue van Hook. Loeb Classical Library. London: Wm. Heinemann; New York: G. P. Putnam's Sons, 1928–1961.

Jackson, B. S. "Liability for Mere Intention in Early Jewish Law." *Hebrew Union College Annual* 42 (1971): 197–225.

Jeremias, Joachim. *Jerusalem in the Time of Jesus.* London: SCM Press, 1969.

———. *New Testament Theology.* New York: Charles Scribner's Sons, 1971.

———. *The Parables of Jesus.* 2d rev. ed. New York: Charles Scribner's Sons, 1972.

———. *The Sermon on the Mount.* Translated by Norman Perrin. Philadelphia: Fortress Press, 1963.

Johnson, Norman B. *Prayer in the Apocrypha and Pseudepigrapha.* Journal of Biblical Literature Monograph Series 2. Philadelphia: Society of Biblical Literature, 1948.

Johnston, Robert M. " 'The Least of the Commandments': Deuteronomy 22:6–7 in Rabbinic Judaism and Early Christianity." *Andrews University Seminary Studies* 20 (3, Autumn 1982): 205–15.

"Joseph and Asenath." Translated by C. Burchard. 2:177–247 in *The Old Testament Pseudepigrapha.* 2 vols. Edited by James H. Charlesworth. Garden City, N.Y.: Doubleday & Company, 1983–1985.

Joseph et Aséneth: Introduction, Texte Critique, Traduction et Notes. Edited by Marc Philonenko. Studia Post-Biblica. Leiden: E. J. Brill, 1968.

Josephus. *The Jewish War.* Edited by Gaalya Cornfeld with Benjamin Mazar and Paul L. Maier. Grand Rapids: Zondervan Publishing House, 1982.

———. *Works.* 10 vols. Translated by H. St. J. Thackeray, Ralph Marcus, Allen Wikgren, and Louis H. Feldman. Loeb Classical Library. Cambridge: Harvard University Press, 1926–1965.

"Jubilees." Translated by Orval S. Wintermute. 2:35–142 in *The Old Testament Pseudipgrapha.* 2 vols. Edited by James H. Charlesworth. Garden City, N.Y.: Doubleday & Company, 1983–1985.

Judge, E. A. "The Early Christians as a Scholastic Community: Part II." *Journal of Religious History* 1 (1960): 125–37.

Juvenal. *Satires.* Rev. ed. Translated by G. G. Ramsay. Loeb Classical Library. Cambridge: Harvard University Press, 1940.

Kee, Howard Clark. *Christian Origins in Sociological Perspective: Methods and Resources.* Philadelphia: Westminster Press, 1980.

Keener, C. S. "Is Paul's Teaching 'Sexist'?" *The Crucible* 1 (1, Fall 1990): 4–11.

_____. "Matthew 5:22 and the Heavenly Court." *Expository Times* 99 (2, 1987): 46.

Kelly, J. N. D. *A Commentary on the Epistles of Peter and Jude.* Thornapple Commentaries. Grand Rapids: Baker Book House, 1981.

_____. *A Commentary on the Pastoral Epistles.* London: Adam & Charles Black, 1972.

Kilgallen, John J. "To what are the Matthean Exception-Texts (5,32 and 19,9) an Exception?" *Biblica* 61 (1, 1980): 102–5.

Klausner, Joseph. *Jesus: His Life, Times, & Teaching.* Translated by Herbert Danby. New York: Menorah, 1979; n.p.: Macmillan, 1925.

Knight, George W., III. *The Faithful Sayings in the Pastoral Epistles.* Grand Rapids: Baker Book House, 1979.

Kobelski, Paul Joseph. "Melchizedek and Melchiresa: The Heavenly Prince of Light and the Prince of Darkness in the Qumran Literature." Ph.D. Dissertation, Department of Theology, Fordham University, 1978.

Köhler, Konrad. "Zu Mt 5,22." *Zeitschrift für die Neutestamentliche Wissenschaft* 19 (1919): 91–95.

Koenig, John. *New Testament Hospitality: Partnership with Strangers as Promise and Mission.* Overtures to Biblical Theology 17. Philadelphia: Fortress Press, 1985.

Koester, Helmut. *Introduction to the New Testament.* 2 vols. Hermeneia Foundations and Facets Series. Philadelphia: Fortress Press, 1982. Vol. 1: *History, Culture, and Religion of the Hellenistic Age.* Vol. 2: *History and Literature of Early Christianity.*

Koteskey, Ronald L. "Growing Up Too Late, Too Soon: The Invention of Adolescence." *Christianity Today* (March 13, 1981): 25–26.

Kubo, Sakae. "I Corinthians VII.16: Optimistic or Pessimistic?" *New Testament Studies* 24 (4, July 1978): 539–44.

Kugel, James L., and Rowan A. Greer. *Early Biblical Interpretation.* Library of Early Christianity 3. Philadelphia: Westminster Press, 1986.

Kysar, Myrna and Robert. *The Asundered: Biblical Teachings on Divorce and Remarriage.* Atlanta: John Knox Press, 1978.

Lacey, W. K. "Patria Potestas." Pp. 121–44 in *The Family in Ancient Rome: New Perspectives.* Edited by Beryl Rawson. Ithaca, N.Y.: Cornell University Press, 1986.

Ladd, George Eldon. *The Gospel of the Kingdom.* Grand Rapids: Wm. B. Eerdmans Publishing Company, 1978.

Lamarche, P. "L'indissolubilité selon Matthieu. Matthieu 19,9." *Christus* 30 (120, 1983): 475–82. (NTA 28:130)

Lane, William L. *The Gospel According to Mark.* New International Commentaries on the New Testament. Grand Rapids: Wm. B. Eerdmans Publishing Company, 1974.

Laney, J. Carl. "Paul and the Permanence of Marriage in 1 Corinthians 7." *Journal of the Evangelical Theological Society* 25 (3, September 1982): 283–94.

Laws, Sophie. *A Commentary on the Epistle of James.* Harper's New Testament Commentaries. San Francisco: Harper & Row, 1980.

Leeming, Bernard and R. A. Dawson. "Except It Be for Fornication?" *Scripture: The Quarterly of the Catholic Biblical Association* 8 (3, July 1956): 75–82.

Leenhardt, F.-J. "Les femmes aussi . . . à propos du billet de répudiation." *Revue de Théologie et de Philosophie* 19 (1, 1969): 31–40.

Lefkowitz, Mary R., and Maureen B. Fant. *Women's Life in Greece and Rome.* Baltimore: Johns Hopkins University Press, 1982.

Lehmann, Manfred R. "Gen 2.24 as the Basis for Divorce in Halakah and New Testament." *Zeitschrift für die Alttestamentliche Wissenschaft* 72 (3, 1966): 263–67.

Leon, Harry J. *The Jews of Ancient Rome.* The Morris Loeb Series. Philadelphia: Jewish Publication Society of America, 1960.

Lieberman, Saul. "Light on the Cave Scrolls from Rabbinic Sources." *Proceedings of the American Academy for Jewish Research* 20 (1951): 395–404.

"Life of Adam and Eve." Translated by M. D. Johnson. 2:249–95 in *The Old Testament Pseudepigrapha.* Edited by James H. Charlesworth. Garden City, N.Y.: Doubleday & Company, 1983–1985.

_____. Greek text of the Vita of Adam and Eve, and the Apocalypse of Moses. Pp. 1–23 in *Apocalypses Apocryphae.* Edited by Konstantin von Tischendorf. Hildesheim: Georg Olms, 1966.

Lightfoot, J. B. *Notes on the Epistles of St Paul.* Winona Lake, Ind.: Alpha Publications, n.d.

_____. *St Paul's Epistle to the Galatians.* 3d ed. London: Macmillan & Company, 1869.

_____. *St. Paul's Epistle to the Philippians.* Grand Rapids: Zondervan Publishing House, 1953; London: Macmillan & Company, 1913.

Lightfoot, John. *A Commentary on the New Testament from the Talmud and Hebraica.* 4 vols. Grand Rapids: Baker Book House, 1979; Oxford: Oxford University, 1859.

Lightman, Marjorie, and William Zeisel. "Univira: An Example of Continuity and Change in Roman Society." *Church History* 46 (1, March 1977): 19–32.

Lincoln, C. Eric. *Race, Religion, and the Continuing American Dilemma.* New York: Hill & Wang, 1984.

Lindenberger, J. M. "Ahiqar." 2:479–507 in *The Old Testament Pseudepigrapha.* 2 vols. Edited by James H. Charlesworth. Garden City, N.Y.: Doubleday & Company, 1983–1985.

Lock, Walter. *A Critical and Exegetical Commentary on the Pastoral Epistles.* International Critical Commentaries. Edinburgh: T. & T. Clark, 1924.

Lodge, R. C. *Plato's Theory of Ethics: The Moral Criterion and the Highest Good.* New York: Harcourt, Brace & Company; London: Kegan Paul, Trench, Trubner & Company, 1928.

Lohse, Eduard. *Die Texte aus Qumran.* München: Kösel-Verlag, 1971.

Longenecker, Richard N. *Biblical Exegesis in the Apostolic Period.* Grand Rapids: Wm. B. Eerdmans Publishing Company, 1975.

_____. *Paul, Apostle of Liberty.* Grand Rapids: Baker Book House, 1976.

Lucian. *Works.* 8 vols. Translated by A. M. Harmon, K. Kilburn, and M. D. Macleod. Loeb Classical Library. Cambridge: Harvard University Press, 1913–1967.

Luck, William F. *Divorce and Remarriage: Recovering the Biblical View.* San Francisco: Harper & Row, 1987.

Lucretius. *De Rerum Natura.* 3d rev. ed. Translated by W. H. D. Rouse. Loeb Classical Library. Cambridge: Harvard University Press, 1937.

Luyten, J. "Psaumes et paroles de Jésus," *Questiones Liturgiques* 61 (4, 1980): 241–62. (NTA 25:230)

Lyall, Francis. "Roman law in the Writings of Paul—The Slave and the Freedman." *New Testament Studies* 17 (1, October 1970): 73–79.

McArthur, Harvey. "Celibacy in Judaism at the Time of Christian Beginnings." *Andrews University Seminary Studies* 25 (2, Summer 1987): 163–81.

McCane, Byron R. " 'Let the Dead Bury Their Own Dead': Secondary Burial and Matt 8:21–22," *Harvard Theological Review* 83 (1, 1990): 31–43.

McDonnell, Myles. "Divorce Initiated by Women in Rome: The Evidence of Plautus." *American Journal of Ancient History* 8 (1, 1983): 54–80.

McEleney, Neil J. "The Principles of the Sermon on the Mount." *Catholic Biblical Quarterly* 41 (4, October 1979): 552–70.

Macho, A. D. "Cristo instituyó el matrimonio indisoluble." *Sefarad* 37 (1–2, 1977): 261–91. (NTA 23:281–82)

Mack, Burton L. "Elaboration of the Chreia in the Hellenistic School." Pp. 31–67 in *Patterns of Persuasion in the Gospels.* By Burton Mack and Vernon K. Robbins. Sonoma, Calif.: Polebridge, 1989.

MacMullen, Ramsay. *Roman Social Relations: 50 B.C. to A.D. 284.* New Haven: Yale University Press, 1974.

McNamara, Martin. *Palestinian Judaism and the New Testament.* Good News Studies 4. Wilmington, Del.: Michael Glazier, 1983.

Maher, M. "Service of the Heart: The Quest for Authentic Prayer in Judaism." *Review of Religion* 40 (1, 1981): 40–47. (NTA 25:286)

Malcolm X. *The Autobiography of Malcolm X.* With the assistance of Alex Haley. New York: Grove Press, 1965.

Malherbe, Abraham J. *Moral Exhortation, a Greco-Roman Sourcebook.* Library of Early Christianity 4. Philadelphia: Westminster Press, 1986.

_____. *Social Aspects of Early Christianity.* 2d ed. Philadelphia: Fortress Press, 1983.

Malina, Bruce J. *The New Testament World: Insights from Cultural Anthropology.* Atlanta: John Knox Press, 1981.

Manns, Fréderic. "La Halakah dans l'Evangile de Matthieu." *Ant* 53 (1–2, 1978): 3–22.

Manson, T. W. *The Sayings of Jesus.* Grand Rapids: Wm. B. Eerdmans Publishing Company, 1979; London: SCM Press, 1957.

Marcus, Ralph. "The Qumran Scrolls and Early Judaism." *Biblical Research* 1 (1956): 9–47.

Marcus Aurelius. *The Communings with himself of Marcus Aurelius Antoninus, Emperor of Rome, together with his speeches and sayings.* Edited and translated by C. R. Haines. Loeb Classical Library. Cambridge: Harvard University Press, 1916.

Marguerat, Daniel. "Jésus et la Loi." *Foi et Vie* 78 (3, June 1979): 53–76.

Marmorstein, A. *The Doctrine of Merits in Old Rabbinical Literature.* New York: KTAV Publishing House, 1968.

Marshall, I. Howard. *Kept by the Power of God: A Study of Perseverance and Falling Away.* Minneapolis, Minn.: Bethany Fellowship, 1974; London: Epworth Press, 1969.

_____. "The Meaning of Reconciliation." Pp. 117–32 in *Unity and Diversity in New Testament Theology: Essays in Honor of George E. Ladd.* Edited by Robert Guelich. Grand Rapids: Wm. B. Eerdmans Publishing Company, 1978.

Martial. *Epigrams.* Translated by Walter C. A. Ker. 2 vols. Loeb Classical Library. New York: G. P. Putnam's Sons; London: Heinemann, 1920.

"The Martyrdom and Ascension of Isaiah." Translated by M. A. Knibb. 2:143–76 in *The Old Testament Pseudepigrapha.* 2 vols. Edited by James H. Charlesworth. Garden City, N.Y.: Doubleday & Company, 1983–1985.

Marx, Alfred. "Les racines du célibat essénien." *Revue de Qumran* 7 (3, December 1970): 323–42.

Matheson, P. E. *Epictetus: The Discourses and Manual Together with Fragments of his Writings.* 2 vols. Oxford: Clarendon, 1916.

Mayor, Joseph B. *The Epistle of St. James.* 3d rev. ed. N.p.: Macmillan & Company, 1913; Minneapolis: Klock & Klock Christian Publishers, 1977.

Mbiti, John S. *African Religions and Philosophy.* Garden City, N.Y.: Doubleday & Company, 1970.

Meeks, Wayne A. *The First Urban Christians: The Social World of the Apostle Paul.* New Haven: Yale University Press, 1983.

_____. *The Moral World of the First Christians.* Library of Early Christianity 6. Philadelphia: Westminster Press, 1986.

Meier, John P. *Matthew.* New Testament Message: A Biblical Theological Commentary 3. Wilmington, Del.: Michael Glazier, 1980.

_____. *The Vision of Matthew: Christ, Church, and Morality in the First Gospel.* Theological Inquiries. New York: Paulist Press, 1979.

Mekilta de-Rabbi Ishmael. 3 vols. Translated by Jacob Z. Lauterbach. Philadelphia: Jewish Publication Society of America, 1933–1935.

"Middle Assyrian Laws." Translated by Theophile J. Meek. Pp. 180–88 in *Ancient Near Eastern Texts Relating to the Old Testament.* Edited by James B. Pritchard. Princeton: Princeton University Press, 1955.

The Midrash Rabbah. 5 vol. Edited by Harry Freedman and Maurice Simon. Foreword by I. Epstein. New York: Soncino Press, 1977.

Minucius Felix. *Octavius.* Translated by Gerald H. Randall. Loeb Classical Library. Cambridge: Harvard University Press, 1931.

The Mishnah. Translated by Herbert Danby. London: Oxford University Press, 1933.

The Mishnah. 7 vols. 2d ed. Pointed Hebrew text, introductions, translations, notes, and supplements by Philip Blackman. New York: Judaica Press, 1963.

Moffatt, James. *A Critical and Exegetical Commentary on the Epistle to the Hebrews.* International Critical Commentaries. Edinburgh: T. & T. Clark, 1924.

_____. *The First Epistle of Paul to the Corinthians.* The Moffatt New Testament Commentary. London: Hodder & Stoughton, 1938.

_____. *The General Epistles: James, Peter, and Judas.* The Moffatt New Testament Commentary. Garden City, N.Y.: Doubleday, Doran & Company, 1928.

Mohrlang, Roger. *Matthew and Paul: A Comparison of Ethical Perspectives.* Society for New Testament Studies Monograph 48. Cambridge: Cambridge University Press, 1984.

Moiser, Jeremy. "A Reassessment of Paul's View of Marriage with reference to 1 Cor. 7." *Journal for the Study of the New Testament* 18 (June 1983): 103–22.

Montefiore, C. G. "The Spirit of Judaism." 1:35–81 in *The Beginnings of Christianity.* 5 vols. Edited by F. J. Foakes Jackson and Kirsopp Lake. Grand Rapids: Baker Book House, 1979.

_____. *The Synoptic Gospels.* 2 vols. Library of Biblical Studies. New York: KTAV Publishing House, 1968.

Montefiore, C. G., and Herbert Loewe. *A Rabbinic Anthology.* New York: Schocken Books, 1974.

Moore, George Foot. *Judaism in the First Centuries of the Christian Era.* 2 vols. New York: Schocken Books, 1971.

Morosco, Robert E. "Redaction Criticism and the Evangelical: Matthew 10 as a Test Case." *Journal of the Evangelical Theological Society* 22 (4, December 1979): 323–31.

Moule, C. F. D. *The Gospel According to Mark.* Cambridge: Cambridge University Press, 1965.

_____. "Matthew v.21, 22." *Expository Times* 50 (4, January 1939): 189–90.

_____. "Uncomfortable Words—I. The Angry Word: Matthew 5.21f." *Expository Times* 81 (1, October 1969): 10–13.

Mueller, James R. "The Temple Scroll and the Gospel Divorce Texts." *Revue de Qumran* 10 (2, 1980): 247–56.

Murphy-O'Connor, Jerome. "The Divorced Woman in 1 Cor. 7:10–11." *Journal of Biblical Literature* 100 (4, December 1981): 601–6.

_____. "Remarques sur l'exposé du Professeur Y. Yadin." *Revue Biblique* 79 (1, January 1972): 99–100.

Murray, John. *Divorce.* Philadelphia: The Committee on Christian Education, The Orthodox Presbyterian Church, 1953.

Mussies, G. "Greek in Palestine and the Diaspora." Pp. 1040–64 in *The Jewish People in the First Century: Historical Geography, Political History, Social, Cultural and Religious Life and Institutions.* 2 vols. Edited by S. Safrai and M. Stern with D. Flusser and W. C. van Unnik. Section 1 of Compendia Rerum Iudaicarum ad Novum Testamentum. Vol. 1: Assen: Van Gorcum & Co. B.V., 1974; vol. 2: Philadelphia: Fortress Press, 1976.

Myers, Steven. "Crown of Beauty Instead of Ashes." Pp. 20–25 in *World Christian Summer Reader 1990.* Pasadena: World Christian, Inc., 1990.

Nembach, Ulrich. "Ehescheidung nach alttestamentlichen und jüdischen Recht." *Theologische Zeitschrift* 26 (3, May 1970): 161–71.

Neusner, Jacob. " 'By the Testimony of Two Witnesses' in the Damascus Document IX,17–22 and in Pharisaic-Rabbinic Law." *Revue de Qumran* 8 (30/2, March 1973): 197–217.

_____. *The Rabbinic Traditions About the Pharisees Before 70.* 3 vols. Leiden: E. J. Brill, 1971.

New Testament Apocrypha. 2 vol. Translated by Edgar Hennecke. Edited by Wilhelm Schneemelcher and R. McL. Wilson. Philadelphia: Westminster Press, 1963–1965.

Nilsson, Martin P. *The Dionysiac Mysteries of the Hellenistic and Roman Age.* Skrifter Utgivna Av Svenska Institutet I Athen, 8°, 5. Lund: C. W. K. Gleerup, 1957.

Nineham, D. E. *Saint Mark.* Philadelphia: Westminster Press, 1977; Baltimore: Penguin Books, 1963.

Noack, Bent. "Qumran and the Book of Jubilees." *Svensk Exegetisk Årsbok* 22–23 (1957–58): 191–207.

Nock, Arthur Darby. *Early Gentile Christianity and Its Hellenistic Background.* New York: Harper & Row, 1964.

_____. *St. Paul.* New York: Harper & Row, 1963.

Odeberg, Hugo. *Pharisaism and Christianity.* Translated by J. M. Moe. St. Louis: Concordia Publishing House, 1964.

Die Oracula Sibyllina. Edited by Johannes Geffcken. Leipzig, 1902.

O'Rourke, J. J. "Roman Law and the Early Church." Pp. 165–86 in *The Catacombs and the Colosseum: The Roman Empire as the Setting of Primitive Christianity.* Edited by Stephen Benko and John J. O'Rourke. Valley Forge, Penn.: Judson, 1971.

The Orphic Hymns: Text, Translation and Notes. Translated by Apostolos N. Athanassakis. Society of Biblical Literature Texts and Translations, 12. Graeco-Roman Religion Series 4. Missoula, Mont.: Scholars Press, 1977.

Osburn, Carroll D. "The Present Indicative in Matthew 19:9." *Restoration Quarterly* 24 (4, 1981): 193–203.

Patte, Daniel. *The Gospel According to Matthew: A Structural Commentary on Matthew's Faith.* Philadelphia: Fortress Press, 1987.

Pelser, G. M. M. "Women and Ecclesiastical Ministries in Paul." *Neotestamentica* 10 (1976): 92–109.

Pesikta de-Rab Kahana: R. Kahana's Compilation of Discourses for Sabbaths and Festival Days. Translated by William G. Braude and Israel J. Kapstein. Philadelphia: Jewish Publication Society of America, 1975.

Pesikta Rabbati. 2 vols. Translated by William G. Braude. Yale Judaica Series 18. New Haven: Yale University Press, 1968.

Petronius. *Satyricon, Fragments, and Poems.* Translated by W. H. D. Rouse. Loeb Classical Library. London: Wm. Heinemann; New York: G. P. Putnam's Sons, 1913.

Philo. Works. 10 vols. Translated by F. H. Colson and G. H. Whitaker. Loeb Classical Libarry. Cambridge: Harvard University Press, 1929–1962. Supplementary volumes 1 and 2, translated by Ralph Marcus, 1953.

Philostratus. *The Life of Apollonius of Tyana*. 2 vols. Translated by F. C. Conybeare. Loeb Classical Library. Cambridge: Harvard University Press, 1912.

Phipps, William E. "Is Paul's Attitude toward Sexual Relations Contained in 1 Cor 7.1?" *New Testament Studies* 28 (1, January 1982): 125–31.

Plato. *Works*. 12 vols. Translated by Harold North Fowler et al. Loeb Classical Library. Cambridge: Harvard University Press, 1914–1926.

Pliny. *Letters and Panegyricus*. 2 vols. Translated by Betty Radice. Loeb Classical Library. Cambridge: Harvard University Press, 1969.

Plutarch. *Lives*. 11 vols. Translated by Bernadotte Perrin. Loeb Classical Library. London: Wm. Heinemann; New York: G. P. Putnam's Sons, 1914–?.

_____. *Moralia*. 16 vols. Translated by Frank Cole Babbit et al. Loeb Classical Library. London: Wm. Heinemann; New York: G. P. Putnam's Sons, 1927–1969.

Pomeroy, Sarah B. *Goddesses, Whores, Wives, & Slaves: Women in Classical Antiquity*. New York: Schocken Books, 1975.

Przybylski, Benno. *Righteousness in Matthew and his World of Thought*. Society for New Testament Studies Monograph 41. Cambridge: Cambridge University Press, 1980.

"Pseudo-Philo." Translated by D. J. Harrington. 2:297–377 in *The Old Testament Pseudepigrapha*. 2 vols. Edited by James H. Charlesworth. Garden City, N.Y.: Doubleday & Company, 1983–1985.

Pseudo-Philo's Liber Antiquitatum Biblicarum. Edited by Guido Kisch. Publications in Mediaeval Studies, University of Notre Dame. Notre Dame, Ind.: University of Notre Dame, 1949.

"Pseudo-Phocylides." Translated by P. W. van der Horst. 2:565–82 in *The Old Testament Pseudepigrapha*. 2 vols. Edited by James H. Charlesworth. Garden City, N.Y.: Doubleday & Company, 1983–1985.

Quintilian. *Works*. 4 vols. Translated by H. E. Butler. Loeb Classical Library. Cambridge: Harvard University Press, 1920–1922.

Rabinovitch, N. L. "Damascus Document IX,17–22 and Rabbinic Parallels." *Revue de Qumran* 9 (1, 1977): 113–16.

Ramaroson, Leonard. "Une nouvelle interprétation de la 'clausule' de Mt 19,9." *Science et Esprit* 23 (2, 1971): 247–51.

Ramsay, William M. *A Historical Commentary on St. Paul's Epistle to the Galatians*. Grand Rapids: Baker Book House, 1979; New York: G. P. Putnam's Sons, 1900.

Rawson, Beryl. "Children in the Roman *Familia*." Pp. 170–200 in *The Family in Ancient Rome: New Perspectives*. Edited by Beryl Rawson. Ithaca, N.Y.: Cornell University Press, 1986.

_____. "The Roman Family." Pp. 1–57 in *The Family in Ancient Rome: New Perspectives*. Edited by Beryl Rawson. Ithaca, N.Y.: Cornell University Press, 1986.

Rhyne, C. Thomas. *Faith Establishes the Law*. Society of Biblical Literature Dissertation 55. Chico, Calif.: Scholars Press, 1981.

Richardson, Alan. *An Introduction to the Theology of the New Testament.* New York: Harper & Brothers Publishers, 1958.

Richardson, Peter. " 'I Say, not the Lord': Personal opinion, Apostolic Authority, and the Development of Early Christian Halakah." *Tyndale Bulletin* 31 (1980): 65–86.

_____. "Judgment in Sexual Matters in 1 Corinthians 6:1–11," *Novum Testamentum* 25 (1, 1983): 37–58.

Richlin, Amy. "Approaches to the Sources on Adultery at Rome." Pp. 379–404 in *Reflections of Women in Antiquity.* Edited by H. P. Foley. New York: Gordon and Breach Science Publishers, 1981.

_____. "Approaches to the Sources on Adultery at Rome." *Women's Studies* 8 (1–2, 1981): 225–50.

Ridderbos, Herman. *Paul: An Outline of his Theology.* Translated by John Richard De Witt. Grand Rapids: Wm. B. Eerdmans Publishing Company, 1975.

Riesenfeld, Harald. *The Gospel Tradition.* Foreword by W. D. Davies. Philadelphia: Fortress Press, 1970.

Rivkin, Ellis. *A Hidden Revolution.* Nashville: Abingdon Press, 1978.

Robertson, Archibald, and Alfred Plummer. *A Critical and Exegetical Commentary on the First Epistle of St Paul to the Corinthians.* 2d ed. International Critical Commentaries. Edinburgh: T. & T. Clark, 1914.

Rosenblatt, Paul C., and Walter J. Hillabront. "Divorce for Childlessness and the Regulation of Adultery." *Journal of Sex Research* 8 (2, May 1972): 117–27.

Roth, Cecil. "The Subject Matter of Qumran Exegesis." *Vetus Testamentum* 10 (1, January 1960): 51–68.

_____. "A Talmudic Reference to the Qumran Sect?" *Revue de Qumran* 2 (2, 1960): 261–65.

Russell, K. C. "That Embarrassing Verse in First Corinthians!" *Bible Today* 18 (5, 1980): 338–41.

Sabatowich, J. J. "Christian Divorce and Remarriage." *Bible Today* 25 (4, 1987): 253–55.

Safrai, S. "Education and the Study of the Torah." Pp. 945–70 in *The Jewish People in the First Century: Historical Geography, Political History, Social, Cultural and Religious Life and Institutions.* 2 vols. Edited by S. Safrai and M. Stern with D. Flusser and W. C. van Unnik. Section 1 of Compendia Rerum Iudaicarum ad Novum Testamentum. Vol. 1: Assen: Van Gorcum & Co. B.V., 1974; vol. 2: Philadelphia: Fortress Press, 1976.

_____. "Home and Family." Pp. 728–92 in *The Jewish People in the First Century: Historical Geography, Political History, Social, Cultural and Religious Life and Institutions.* 2 vols. Edited by S. Safrai and M. Stern with D. Flusser and W. C. van Unnik. Section 1 of Compendia Rerum Iudaicarum ad Novum Testamentum. Vol. 1: Assen: Van Gorcum & Co. B.V., 1974; vol. 2: Philadelphia: Fortress Press, 1976.

_____. "Jewish Self-Government," pp. 377–419 in *The Jewish People in the First Century: Historical Geography, Political History, Social,*

Cultural and Religious Life and Institutions. 2 vols. Edited by S. Safrai and M. Stern with D. Flusser and W. C. van Unnik. Section 1 of Compendia Rerum Iudaicarum ad Novum Testamentum. Vol. 1: Assen: Van Gorcum & Co. B.V., 1974; vol. 2: Philadelphia: Fortress Press, 1976.

Saller, Richard P. "Men's Age at Marriage and Its Consequences in the Roman Family." *Classical Philology* 82 (1, 1987): 21–34.

_____. Review article. *Classical Philology* 83 (3, July 1988): 263–69.

Saller, Richard P., and Brent D. Shaw. "Tombstones and Roman Family Relations in the Principate: Civilians, Soldiers and Slaves." *Journal of Roman Studies* 74 (1984): 124–56.

Sanders, E. P. *Jesus and Judaism.* Philadelphia: Fortress Press, 1985.

_____. *Jewish Law from Jesus to the Mishnah: Five Studies.* London: SCM Press; Philadelphia: Trinity Press International, 1990.

_____. *Paul, the Law, and the Jewish People.* Philadelphia: Fortress Press, 1983.

Sandmel, Samuel. *Anti-Semitism in the New Testament?* Philadelphia: Fortress Press, 1978.

_____. *Judaism and Christian Beginnings.* New York: Oxford University Press, 1978.

Saucy, Robert L. "The Husband of One Wife." *Bibliotheca Sacra* 131 (523, 1974): 229–40.

Schäfer, Peter. "Die Torah der messianischen Zeit." *Zeitschrift für die Neutestamentliche Wissenschaft* 65 (1–2, 1974): 27–42.

Schattenmann, Johannes. "Jesus und Pythagoras." *Kairos* 21 (2–3, 1979): 215–20.

Schechter, Solomon. *Aspects of Rabbinic Theology.* New York: Schocken Books, 1961; London: Macmillan Company, 1909.

_____. "Some Rabbinic Parallels to the NT." *Jewish Quarterly Review* 12 (1900): 415–33.

Schedl, Claus. "Zur Ehebruchklausel der Bergpredigt im Lichte der neu gefundenen Tempelrolle." *Theologisch-Praktische Quartelschrift* 130 (4, 1982): 362–65.

Schiffman, Lawrence H. *Sectarian Law in the Dead Sea Scrolls: Courts, Testimony and the Penal Code.* Brown Judaic Studies 33. Chico, Calif.: Scholars Press, 1983.

Schnackenburg, Rudolf. *Baptism in the Thought of St. Paul.* Oxford: Basil Blackwell, 1964.

Schubert, Kurt. "Ehescheidung im Judentum zur Zeit Jesu." *Theologische Quartalschrift* 151 (1, 1971): 23–27.

Schürer, Emil. *A History of the Jewish People in the Time of Jesus.* Edited by Nahum N. Glatzer. New York: Schocken Books, 1961.

Schürmann, Heinz. " 'Wer daher eines dieser geringsten Gebote auflöst . . .' Wo fand Matthäus das Logion Mt 5,19?" *Biblische Zeitschrift* 4 (2, 1960): 238–50.

Schweizer, Eduard. *The Good News According to Matthew.* Translated by David E. Green. Atlanta: John Knox Press, 1975.

_____. *Jesus.* Translated by David E. Green. New Testament Library. London: SCM Press, 1971.

_____. "Scheidungsrecht der jüdischen Frau? Weibliche Jünger Jesu?" *Evangelische Theologie* 42 (3, 1982): 294–300.

Scott, E. F. *The Pastoral Epistles.* Moffatt New Testament Commentary. London: Hodder & Stoughton, 1936.

"2 (Syriac Apocalypse of) Baruch." Translated by A. F. J. Klijn. 1:615–52 in *The Old Testament Pseudepigrapha.* 2 vols. Edited by James H. Charlesworth. Garden City, N.Y.: Doubleday & Company, 1983–1985.

Seim, T. K. "Seksualitet og ekteskap, skilsmisse og gjengifte i 1. Kor. 7." *Norsk Teologisk Tidsskrift* 81 (1, 1980): 1–20. (NTA 25:37)

Selwyn, Edward Gordon. *The First Epistle of St. Peter: The Greek Text with Introduction, Notes and Essays.* 2d ed. London: Macmillan Press, 1947.

Seneca. *Ad Lucilium, Epistulae Morales.* 3 vols. Translated by Richard M. Gummere. Loeb Classical Library. Cambridge: Harvard University Press, 1934.

_____. *Moral Essays.* 3 vols. Translated by John W. Basore. Loeb Classical Library. Cambridge: Harvard University Press, 1928–1935.

"The Sentences of the Syriac Menander." Translated by T. Baarda. 2:583–606 in *The Old Testament Pseudepigrapha.* 2 vols. Edited by James H. Charlesworth. Garden City, N.Y.: Doubleday & Company, 1983–1985.

Septuaginta. Edited by Alfred Rahlfs. Stuttgart: Deutsche Bibelgesellschaft Stittgart, 1935.

Shaw, Brent D. "The Age of Roman Girls at Marriage: Some Reconsiderations." *Journal of Roman Studies* 77 (1987): 30–46.

Sherk, Robert K., translator and editor. *The Roman Empire: Augustus to Hadrian.* Translated Documents of Greece and Rome 6. New York: Cambridge University Press, 1988.

Shuler, Philip P. *A Genre for the Gospels: The Biographical Character of Matthew.* Philadelphia: Fortress Press, 1982.

"The Sibylline Oracles." Translated by J. J. Collins. 1:317–472 in *The Old Testament Pseudepigrapha.* 2 vols. Garden City, N.Y.: Doubleday & Company, 1983–1985.

Sider, Ronald J. *Rich Christians in an Age of Hunger.* 3d ed. Foreword by Kenneth S. Kantzer. Dallas: Word Books, 1990.

Sifra: An Analytical Translation. 3 vols. Translated by Jacob Neusner. Brown Judaic Studies 138–140. Atlanta: Scholars Press, 1988.

Sifre to Deuteronomy: An Analytical Translation. 2 vols. Translated by Jacob Neusner. Brown Judaic Studies 98 and 101. Atlanta: Scholars Press, 1987.

Sifré to Numbers: An American Translation and Explanation. 2 vols. Translated by Jacob Neusner. Brown Judaic Studies 118 and 119. Atlanta: Scholars Press, 1986.

Slingerland, H. Dixon. "The Nature of *Nomos* within the Testaments of the Twelve Patriarchs." *Journal of Biblical Literature* 105 (1, March 1986): 39–48.

Smalley, Stephen S. "Redaction Criticism." Pp. 181–95 in *New Testament Interpretation: Essays on Principles and Methods.* Edited by

I. Howard Marshall. Grand Rapids: Wm. B. Eerdmans Publishing Company, 1977.

_____. "Spiritual Gifts and I Corinthians 12–16." *Journal of Biblical Literature* 87 (4, December 1968): 427–33.

Smith, Morton. *Tannaitic Parallels to the Gospels.* Philadelphia: Society of Biblical Literature, 1951.

Stambaugh, John E., and David L. Balch. *The New Testament in Its Social Environment.* Library of Early Christianity 2. Philadelphia: Westminster Press, 1986.

Stanton, Graham N. *The Gospels and Jesus.* Oxford Bible Series. Oxford: Oxford University Press, 1989.

_____. *Jesus of Nazareth in New Testament Preaching.* Cambridge: Cambridge University Press, 1974.

Stauffer, Ethelbert. *Jesus and His Story.* Translated by Richard and Clara Winston. New York: Alfred A. Knopf, 1960.

Stein, Robert H. " 'Is It Lawful for a Man to Divorce His Wife?' " *Journal of the Evangelical Theological Society* 22 (2, June 1979): 115–21.

Stendahl, Krister. *The School of St. Matthew and its Use of the Old Testament.* Philadelphia: Fortress Press, 1968.

Stenger, W. "Zur Rekonstruktion eines Jesusworts anhand der synoptischen Ehescheidungslogion (Mt 5,32; 19,9; Lk 16,16–18; Mk 10,11f)." *Kairos* 26 (3–4, 1984): 194–205.

Stowers, Stanley Kent. *The Diatribe and Paul's Letter to the Romans.* Society of Biblical Literature Dissertation 57. Chico, Calif.: Scholars Press for The Society of Biblical Literature, 1981.

_____. *Letter Writing in Greco-Roman Antiquity.* Library of Early Christianity 5. Philadelphia: Westminster Press, 1986.

Strack, Hermann L. *Introduction to the Talmud and Midrash.* New York: Atheneum, 1978.

Strecker, Georg. "Die Antithesen der Bergpredigt (Mt 5:21–48 par)." *Zeitschrift für die Neutestamentliche Wissenschaft* 69 (1–2, 1978): 36–72.

Suetonius. *The Twelve Caesars.* Translated by Robert Graves. Baltimore: Penguin Books, 1957.

Sussman, Linda S. "Workers and Drones; Labor, Idleness and Gender Definition in Hesiod's Beehive." Pp. 79–93 in *Women in the Ancient World: The Arethusa Papers.* Edited by John Peradotto and J. P. Sullivan. Albany, N.Y.: State University of New York, 1984.

Tacitus. *The Complete Works of Tacitus.* Translated by Alfred John Church and William Jackson Brodribb. New York: The Modern Library, Random House, 1942.

Talbert, Charles H. *What Is a Gospel? The Genre of the Canonical Gospels.* Philadelphia: Fortress Press, 1977.

Talmon, Sh. "The Emergence of Institutionalized Prayer in Israel in the Light of the Qumran Literature." Pp. 265–84 in *Qumrân: Sa piété, sa théologie et son milieu.* Edited by M. Delcor. Bibliotheca Ephemeridum Theologicarum Lovaniensium 46. Paris: Gembloux, Leuven U., 1978.

Talmud of the Land of Israel: A Preliminary Translation and Explanation. 34 vols. Translated by Jacob Neusner et al. Chicago: University of Chicago Press, 1982–.

Tannehill, Robert C. *The Sword of His Mouth.* Society of Biblical Literature Semeia Supplements 1. Missoula, Mont.: Scholars Press, 1975.

Tarn, W. W. *Hellenistic Civilisation.* 3d rev. ed. Rev. by W. W. Tarn and G. T. Griffith. New York: New American Library, 1974.

Taylor, Vincent. *The Formation of the Gospel Tradition.* London: Macmillan & Company, 1960.

Teeple, H. M. *The Mosaic Eschatological Prophet.* Journal of Biblical Literature Monograph 10. Philadelphia: Society of Biblical Literature, 1957.

The Temple Scroll. An Introduction, Translation and Commentary. Translated and edited by Johann Maier. Journal for the Study of the Old Testament Supplement 34. Sheffield: Journal for the Study of the Old Testament Press, 1985.

Tertullian. *Apology and De Spectaculis.* Translated by T. R. Glover. Loeb Classical Library. Cambridge: Harvard University Press, 1931.

The Testament of Abraham: The Greek Recensions. Translated by Michael E. Stone. Society of Biblical Literature Texts and Translations 2. Pseudepigrapha Series 2. Missoula, Mont.: Society of Biblical Literature, 1972.

"The Testament of Job." Translated by Russell P. Spittler. 1:829–68 in *The Old Testament Pseudepigrapha.* 2 vols. Edited by James H. Charlesworth. Garden City, N.Y.: Doubleday & Company, 1983–1985.

The Testament of Job According to the SV Text. Edited by Robert A. Kraft with Harold Attridge, Russell Spittler, and Janet Timbie. Society of Biblical Literature Texts and Translations 5. Pseudepigrapha Series 4. Missoula, Mont.: Scholars Press, 1974.

"Testament of Moses." Translated by J. Priest. 1:919–34 in *The Old Testament Pseudepigrapha.* 2 vols. Edited by James H. Charlesworth. Garden City, N.Y.: Doubleday & Company, 1983–1985.

"The Testament of Solomon." Translated by D. C. Duling. 1:935–87 in *The Old Testament Pseudepigrapha.* 2 vols. Edited by James H. Charlesworth. Garden City, N.Y.: Doubleday & Company, 1983–1985.

The Testament of Solomon. (Greek text.) Edited by Chester Charlton McCown. Leipzig: J. C. Hinrichs'sche Buchhandlung, 1922.

"Testaments of the Twelve Patriarchs." Translated by Howard Clark Kee. 1:775–828 in *The Old Testament Pseudepigrapha.* 2 vols. Edited by James H. Charlesworth. Garden City, N.Y.: Doubleday & Company, 1983–1985.

Testuz, Michel. "Deux fragments inédits des manuscrits de la mer morte." *Semitica* 5 (1955): 37–39.

Theognis, Ps.-Pythagoras, Ps.-Phocylides, Chares, Anonymi Avlodia, Fragmentvm Teliambicvm. Bibliotheca Scriptorvm Graecorvm et Romanervm Tevbneriana. Leipzig: BSB B. G. Teubner Verlaggesellschaft, 1971.

Theon, Aelius. *The Progymnasmata of Theon: a new text with translation and commentary.* By James R. Butts. Ann Arbor, Mich.: University Microfilms International, 1989.

Thiering, Barbara. "The Biblical Source of Qumran Asceticism." *Journal of Biblical Literature* 93 (3, September 1974): 429–44.

_____. "*Mebaqqer* and *Episkopos* in the Light of the Temple Scroll." *Journal of Biblical Literature* 100 (1, March 1981): 59–74.

"3 (Hebrew Apocalypse of) Enoch." Translated by P. Alexander. 1:223–315 in *The Old Testament Pseudepigrapha.* 2 vols. Edited by James H. Charlesworth. Garden City, N.Y.: Doubleday & Company, 1983–1985.

"The Book of Thomas the Contender." Translated by John D. Turner. Pp. 188–94 in *The Nag Hammadi Library in English.* Edited by James M. Robinson. San Francisco: Harper & Row, 1977.

Thompson, Richard W. "The Alleged Rabbinic Background of Rom 3,31." *Ephemerides Theologicae Lovanienses* 63 (1, 1987): 136–48.

Thompson, William G. *Matthew's Advice to a Divided Community: Mt. 17,22–18,35.* Analecta Biblica 44. Rome: Biblical Institute Press, 1970.

Thornton, Timothy Charles Gordon. "Jewish Bachelors in NT Times." *Journal of Theological Studies* 23 (2, October 1972): 444–45.

Tilborg, Sjef van. *The Jewish Leaders in Matthew.* Leiden: E. J. Brill, 1972.

The Tosefta. 6 vols. Translated by Jacob Neusner, with Richard S. Sarason on vol. 1. New York: KTAV Publishing House, 1977–86.

Townsend, John T. "Ancient Education in the Time of the Early Roman Empire." Pp. 139–63 in *The Catacombs and the Colosseum: The Roman Empire as the Setting of Primitive Christianity.* Edited by Stephen Benko and John J. O'Rourke. Valley Forge, Penn.: Judson, 1971.

"Treatise of Shem." Translated by James H. Charlesworth. 1:473–86 in *The Old Testament Pseudepigrapha.* 2 vols. Edited by James H. Charlesworth. Garden City, N.Y.: Doubleday & Company, 1983–1985.

Urbach, Ephraim E. *The Sages: Their Concepts and Beliefs.* 2d ed. 2 vols. Translated by Israel Abrahams. Jerusalem: Magnes Press, Hebrew University, 1979.

Vaux, Roland de. *Ancient Israel: Its Life and Institutions.* Translated by John McHugh. New York: McGraw-Hill Books Company, 1961.

Vermaseren, Maarten J. *Cybele and Attis: the Myth and the Cult.* Translated by A. M. H. Lemmers. London: Thames & Hudson, 1977.

Vermes, Geza. *Jesus and the World of Judaism.* Philadelphia: Fortress Press, 1984; London: SCM Press, 1983.

_____. *Jesus the Jew: A Historian's Reading of the Gospels.* Philadelphia: Fortress Press, 1973.

_____. "Pre-mishnaic Jewish Worship and the Phylacteries from the Dead Sea." *Vetus Testamentum* 9 (1, 1959): 65–72.

_____. "Sectarian Matrimonial Halakah in the Damascus Rule." *Journal of Jewish Studies* 25 (1, 1974): 197–202.

Verner, David C. *The Household of God: The Social World of the Pastoral Epistles.* Society of Biblical Literature Dissertation 71. Chico, Calif.: Scholars Press, 1983.

Walther, G. "Übergreifende Heiligkeit und Kindertaufe im Neuen Testament." *Evangelische Theologie* 25 (11, 1965): 668–74.

Wambacq, B. N. "Matthieu 5,31–32. Possibilité de divorce ou obligation de rompre une union illégitime." *Nouvelle Revue Théologique* 104 (1, 1982): 34–49.

Weaver, P. R. C. "The Status of Children in Mixed Marriages." Pp. 145–69 in *The Family in Ancient Rome: New Perspectives.* Edited by Beryl Rawson. Ithaca, N.Y.: Cornell University Press, 1986.

Weder, Hans. "Perspektive der Frauen?" *Evangelische Theologie* 43 (2, 1983): 175–78.

Wegner, Judith Romney. *Chattel or Person? The Status of Women in the Mishnah.* New York: Oxford University Press, 1988.

Wenham, David. "Jesus and the Law: An exegesis on Matthew 5:17–20." *Themelios* 4 (3, 1979): 92–96.

_____. "Paul's Use of the Jesus Tradition: Three Samples." Pp. 7–37 in *Gospel Perspectives.* 5 vols. Vol. 5: *The Jesus Tradition Outside the Gospels,* Edited by David Wenham. Sheffield: JSOT Press, 1984.

Wenham, Gordon J. "Matthew and Divorce: An Old Crux Revisited." *Journal for the Study of the New Testament* 22 (1984): 95–107.

_____. "The Syntax of Matthew 19.9." *Journal for the Study of the New Testament* 28 (1986): 17–23.

Wernberg-Møller, Preben. "A Semitic Idiom in Matt. V.22." *New Testament Studies* 3 (1956–1957): 71–73.

Westerholm, Stephen. "Jesus, the Pharisees, and the Application of Divine Law." *Église Théologie* 13 (2, 1982): 191–210.

White, R. E. O. *The Biblical Doctrine of Initiation.* Grand Rapids: Wm. B. Eerdmans Publishing Company, 1960.

Wilkinson, John. *Jerusalem as Jesus Knew It.* London: Thames & Hudson, 1978.

Willi, H.-U. "Das Privilegium Paulinum (1 Kor 7,15f)—Pauli eigene Lebenserinnerung? (Rechtshistorische Anmerkungen zu einer neueren Hypothese)." *Biblische Zeitschrift* 22 (1, 1978): 100–8.

Williams, Don. *The Apostle Paul and Women in the Church.* Glendale, Calif.: Regal Books, 1977.

Wilson, R. McL. *Gnosis and the New Testament.* Philadelphia: Fortress Press; Oxford: Basil Blackwell, 1968.

Wilson, Stephen G. *Luke and the Pastoral Epistles.* London: S. P. C. K., 1979.

Witherington, Ben, III. "Matthew 5.32 and 19.9—Exception or Exceptional Situation?" *New Testament Studies* 31 (4, 1985): 571–76.

_____. *Women in the Ministry of Jesus: A Study of Jesus' Attitudes to Women and their Roles as Reflected in His Earthly Life.* Society for New Testament Studies Monograph 51. Cambridge: Cambridge University Press, 1984.

Wolfson, Harry Austryn. *Philo: Foundations of Religious Philosophy in Judaism, Christianity, and Islam.* 2 vols. 4th rev. ed. Cambridge: Harvard University Press, 1968.

Worsfold, T. Cato. *The History of the Vestal Virgins of Rome.* 2d ed. London: Rider & Co., 1934.

Wyschogrod, Michael. "Judaism and Evangelical Christianity." Pp. 34–52 in *Evangelicals and Jews in Conversation on Scripture, Theology, and History.* Edited by Marc H. Tanenbaum, Marvin R. Wilson, and James A. Rudin. Grand Rapids: Baker Book House, 1978.

Yadin, Yigael. "L'attitude essénienne envers la polygamie et le divorce." *Revue Biblique* 79 (1, 1972): 98–99.

_____. *The Scroll of the War of the Sons of Light against the Sons of Darkness.* Translated by Batya and Chaim Rabin. Oxford: Oxford University Press, 1962.

Zateski, J. "Problem 'wyjatku' w 1 Kor 7,15–16 (Le problème de 'l'exception' en 1 Cor 7:15–16)." *Collectanea Theologica* 53 (3, 1983): 43–63. (NTA 28:268)

Ziesler, J. A. "Matthew and the Presence of Jesus (2)." *Epworth Review* 11 (2, 1984): 90–97.

Zimmerman, H. *"Mē epi porneia* (Mt 19,9)—ein literarisches Problem. Zur Komposition von Mt 19,3–12." *Catholica* 16 (4, 1962): 293–99. (NTA 7:311)

Index of Ancient Sources

My procedure in examining the views relating to divorce and remarriage held in the NT world has been to start from as broad a base of data as possible. I do not, of course, accept all the material I have cited to be of equal value. This is true, first of all, because not all of the material cited in the endnotes predates the NT, although I have avoided, insofar as possible, most data suspected to be dependent on the NT (such as most later Gnostic texts). The dating of rabbinic and some of the pseudepigraphic literature (such as Test. 12 Patriarchs) is problematic; even purportedly Tannaitic (earlier) traditions in later rabbinic collections are not always attributed accurately, and the earliest Tannaitic collections themselves (Mishnah, Tosefta, Mekilta, Sifra, Sifré Num. and Deut.) are more than a century later than the bulk of the New Testament. But while I have used later texts to illustrate points, I have attempted to reconstruct the New Testament milieu by comparing the widest possible range of early sources, and throughout I have worked on the principle that some evidence is better than no evidence. Those who will most wish to evaluate my use of sources will also be aware of the usual dating of those sources, and I have assumed this knowledge on their part. Date, however, is not the only complication in employing ancient sources: the early material may be localized in Palestine, as in the case of the Dead Sea Scrolls, 1 Enoch, and Jubilees, or it may reflect a particular author's *Tendenz*, as with Josephus and Philo. But where our various strands of evidence point to the same conclusions, we are, I believe, on firm ground, and my research procedure has been to compare as many diverse sources of data as possible.

8   199
9:5   46, 55, 102, 169
9:13   189
12–14   85
12:13   167
12:28–30   81
12:28   190
12:31   81, 191
14:1   81, 191
15:36   143

2 Corinthians
6:15   54
8:21   198
11:28   173
11:29   189
13:1   148

Galatians
3–4   60
3:1   143
3:14–29   157
3:28   167
5:3   206
5:12   70

Ephesians
2:11–22   167
4:11   85
4:25   22
5:21–6:9   101
6:1   22
6:4   98, 198
6:9   5
6:16   189

Philippians
1:1   190
2:20–21   46
3:6   191

Colossians
2:21   184
3:5   145
3:13   108

1 Thessalonians
4:5   157
4:6   155, 156, 184
4:9   183
4:12   199
5:22   198

1 Timothy
1:6   195
1:20   149
2:1–7   100

2:11–15   85, 92
3:1–13   84
3:1   85, 190
3:2–7   85, 100, 102
3:2–3   86
3:2   xii, 83–103, 86, 188
3:3   96
3:4–5   95
3:4   95
3:6   99
3:7   85, 86, 99
3:10   191
3:12   95
4:1–3   95
4:3   92, 94, 101, 184
4:12   90
4:13   96
4:14   90
5:1–6:19   90–91
5:1–2   90
5:4   91
5:5   90
5:7   91, 100
5:9   84, 89–92, 94
5:10   91
5:11–12   94
5:13–15   92
5:14   92, 94
5:16   91
5:17   90
5:19   148
6:3–10   198
6:4   195
6:14   100

2 Timothy
2:24–26   195
2:24–25   96
3:16   198
4:13   ix

Titus
1:5–9   84
1:6–9   86
1:6   95
1:7   96
1:9   96
1:10–11   101
1:11   95

Hebrews
12:5–11   198
13:2   196
13:4   145

James
2:10   206
2:11   155
2:20   143
3:1   20

1 Peter
3   105, 106
3:1–8   101, 168
3:1–6   57
3:7   175
4:9   196
5:1–2   85
5:5   193

2 Peter
2:14   144

1 John
5:14–16   149

Revelation
14:4   172

Dead Sea Scrolls

1QH
  206

1QM
2.4   86, 191
7.1–3   86
7.1   191
13.7   204

1QS
1.6–7   144
4.10   185
4.13–14   140
5.25–6.1   148
6   198
6.3   149, 150
6.6   150
6.12   190
7.15–17   143
8.16   160

4QpNah
  202

4QTemple
56:18–19   161, 192
61:6–7   148
61:7–11   143
64:8   148